SOFT POWER WITH CHINESE CHARACTERISTICS

This book examines the Chinese Communist Party's attempts to improve China's image around the world, thereby increasing its "soft power." This soft, attractive form of power is crucial if China is to avoid provoking an international backlash against its growing military and economic might.

The volume focuses on the period since Xi Jinping came to power in 2012, and is global in scope, examining the impact of Chinese policies from Hong Kong and Taiwan to Africa and South America. The book explains debates over soft power within China and delves into case studies of important policy areas for China's global image campaign, such as film, news media and the Confucius Institutes. The most comprehensive work of its kind, the volume presents a picture of a Chinese leadership that has access to vast material resources and growing global influence but often struggles to convert these resources into genuine international affection.

Soft Power With Chinese Characteristics will be invaluable to students and scholars of Chinese politics and Chinese media, as well as international relations and world politics more generally.

Kingsley Edney is a lecturer in Politics and International Relations of China at the University of Leeds, UK. He is the author of *The Globalization of Chinese Propaganda: International Power and Domestic Political Cohesion* (2014) and co-author of *Environmental Pollution and the Media: Political Discourses of Risk and Responsibility in Australia, China and Japan* (Routledge, 2017).

Stanley Rosen is Professor of Political Science at USC at the University of Southern California, USA. His publications include *Chinese Politics: State, Society and the Market* (2010, co-edited with Peter Hays Gries) and *Art, Politics and Commerce in Chinese Cinema* (2010, co-edited with Ying Zhu).

Ying Zhu is Professor of Cinema Studies at the City University of New York, USA, and Director of the Center for Film and Moving Image Research at Hong Kong Baptist University. Her recent publications include *Two Billion Eyes: The Story of China Central Television* (2013) and *Television in Post-Reform China: Serial Drama, Confucian Leadership and the Global Television Market* (2008).

"Provides astute analyses of the Chinese government's efforts to employ soft power as a component of national strategy, alongside coercive actions that undermine the efficacy of these efforts."

Professor June Teufel Dreyer, *University of Miami*

"This is the book on the issue of China and soft power that scholars in the field have been waiting for – and one specialists in other areas can benefit from greatly as well. Particularly appealing is how truly global and robustly interdisciplinary it is. The editors did a great job of lining up contributors from four continents and many fields and subfields of the humanities and social sciences, and then shaping the chapters into a nicely coherent set of works that speak to rather than past one another."

Professor Jeffrey Wasserstrom, *co-author of* China in the 21st Century: What Everyone Needs to Know

SOFT POWER WITH CHINESE CHARACTERISTICS

China's Campaign for Hearts and Minds

Edited by Kingsley Edney,
Stanley Rosen and Ying Zhu

Routledge
Taylor & Francis Group

LONDON AND NEW YORK

First published 2020
by Routledge
2 Park Square, Milton Park, Abingdon, Oxon OX14 4RN

and by Routledge
52 Vanderbilt Avenue, New York, NY 10017

Routledge is an imprint of the Taylor & Francis Group, an informa business

British Library Cataloguing-in-Publication Data
A catalogue record for this book is available from the British Library

Library of Congress Cataloging-in-Publication Data
A catalog record for this book has been requested

ISBN: 978-1-138-63165-6 (hbk)
ISBN: 978-1-138-63167-0 (pbk)
ISBN: 978-1-315-20867-1 (ebk)

Typeset in Bembo
by Apex CoVantage, LLC

For Andy, whose wit, wisdom, and gentle caring
I took for granted until it was too late.

—YZ

For XYB.
—SR

For Otis.
—KE

CONTENTS

TABLES AND FIGURES

Tables

Figures

CONTRIBUTORS

Janet Borgerson is Senior Wicklander Fellow, Institute for Business and Professional Ethics, DePaul University. She works at the intersections of philosophy, business and culture. She earned a B.A. (Philosophy) from University of Michigan, Ann Arbor, and M.A. and Ph.D. (Philosophy) from University of Wisconsin, Madison, completing postdoctoral work at Brown University. Her research has appeared in a broad range of journals, such as *European Journal of Marketing*, *Philosophy Today* and *Sociological Review*, and she is co-author of *From Chinese Brand Culture to Global Brands: Insights from Aesthetics, Fashion and History* (2013). She has served as Malmsten Visiting Professor at Gothenburg University, Sweden, Research Fellow at University of Auckland, New Zealand, and Visiting Professor at Walailak University, Thailand, and at the Shanghai Institute of Foreign Trade.

Yun-han Chu is Distinguished Research Fellow of the Institute of Political Science at Academia Sinica and Professor of Political Science at National Taiwan University. He specializes in politics of Greater China, East Asian political economy and democratization. He has been the Coordinator of Asian Barometer Survey, a regional network of surveys on democracy, governance and development covering more than 17 Asian countries. Among his recent English publications are *How East Asians View Democracy* (2008), *Citizens, Elections and Parties in East Asia* (2008), *Dynamics of Local Governance in China During the Reform Era* (2010) and *Democracy in East Asia: A New Century* (2013).

Kingsley Edney is Lecturer in Politics and International Relations of China at the University of Leeds. His research examines the international implications of China's contemporary ideology and propaganda. He is the author of *The Globalization of Chinese Propaganda: International Power and Domestic Political Cohesion*

(2014) and co-author of *Environmental Pollution and the Media: Political Discourses of Risk and Responsibility in Australia, China and Japan* (2017). His work has also been published in *Pacific Review, Journal of Contemporary China* and *Australian Journal of International Affairs*.

R. Evan Ellis is a Research Professor of Latin American Studies at the U.S. Army War College Strategic Studies Institute with a focus on the region's relationships with China and other non–Western Hemisphere actors, as well as transnational organized crime and populism in the region. Dr. Ellis has published over 250 works, including *China in Latin America: The Whats and Wherefores* (2009), *The Strategic Dimension of Chinese Engagement with Latin America* (2013), *China on the Ground in Latin America* (2014) and *Transnational Organized Crime in Latin America and the Caribbean* (2018).

Antonio Fiori is Associate Professor of History and Institutions of Asia at the University of Bologna and Adjunct Professor at Korea University in Seoul. He has been a visiting scholar at the United International College (Zhuhai, PRC), the East-West Center (Honolulu, USA), and Kyujanggak Center for Korean Studies (Seoul National University, Korea). He has published widely in the fields of inter-Korean relations, North Korea's domestic and international affairs and China's foreign policy. His latest co-edited book, titled *The Korean Paradox: Domestic Political Divide and Foreign Policy in South Korea*, was published by Routledge in June 2019.

Falk Hartig was until recently a postdoctoral researcher at Goethe University in Frankfurt. He is the author of *Chinese Public Diplomacy: The Rise of the Confucius Institute* (2016) and has published articles in *Politics, International Studies Review, The Hague Journal of Diplomacy, Journal of Communication Management* and the *Asian Studies Review*, among others. His research focuses on international political communication and China's communicative engagement with the world.

Min-hua Huang is Professor in the Department of Political Science and Director of the Fu Hu Center for East Asia Democratization Studies, College of Social Science, National Taiwan University. Before joining the National Taiwan University, Professor Huang worked at Shanghai Jiaotong University, Texas A&M University and National Chengchi University. He was also a visiting fellow at the Center for East Asia Policy Studies at the Brookings Institution (2014–2015). His recent publications include "The Sway of Geopolitics, Economic Interdependence and Cultural Identity," *Journal of Contemporary China* (2015) and "The Internet, Social Capital, and Civic Engagement in Asia," *Social Indicators Research* (2017).

Dalton Lin is Assistant Professor at the Sam Nunn School of International Affairs, Georgia Institute of Technology, and Executive Editor of the website, Taiwan

Security Research (http://taiwansecurity.org). Before joining Georgia Tech, he was a postdoctoral research fellow at Princeton University with the Princeton-Harvard China and the World Program. His current research interests center around explaining contemporary China's behavior in the international system and regional countries' responses to it. His previous work on Taiwan has been published in *Survival,* the *Diplomat* and other journals.

Jie Lu is Professor of Political Science at Renmin University of China in Beijing. Previously he taught at American University in Washington, DC. He was also a Visiting Research Fellow at the East Asian Institute in Singapore. His research has focused on local governance, institutional change, public opinion and political participation in Greater China and East Asia. His writing includes "Revisiting the Eastonian Framework on Political Support: Assessing Different Measures of Regime Support in Mainland China," *Comparative Politics* (2019); "Revisiting Political Wariness in China's Public Opinion Surveys: Experimental Evidence on Responses to Politically Sensitive Questions" with Xuchuan Lei, *Journal of Contemporary China* (2017); and a book, *Varieties of Governance in China: Migration and Institutional Change in Chinese Villages* (2014).

Daniel C. Lynch is Professor of Asian and International Studies at the City University of Hong Kong and a former Associate Professor of International Relations at the University of Southern California. He is the author of three books published by Stanford University Press, including *China's Futures: PRC Elites Debate Economics, Politics, and Soft Power* (2015). Lynch is also the author of numerous journal articles, including "Is China's Rise Now Stalling?" *The Pacific Review* (2019).

Stanley Rosen is Professor of Political Science at the University of Southern California, specializing in Chinese politics and society. The author or editor of eight books and many articles, his most recent books include *Chinese Politics: State, Society and the Market* (2010) (co-edited with Peter Hays Gries) and *Art, Politics and Commerce in Chinese Cinema* (2010) (co-edited with Ying Zhu). He is the co-editor of *Chinese Education and Society*, a frequent guest editor of other translation journals and an associate editor of *Global Media and China*. Professor Rosen has escorted 13 delegations to China for the National Committee on US–China Relations and has consulted for the World Bank, the Ford Foundation, the United States Information Agency, the Los Angeles Public Defenders Office and a number of private corporations, law firms and US government agencies.

Gilbert Rozman is Editor-in-Chief of The Asan Forum, an online journal on international relations in the Indo-Pacific region, and the Emeritus Musgrave Professor of Sociology at Princeton University. Rozman is a Northeast Asianist, who does research on national identities and bilateral ties in China, Japan, Russia and South Korea. He also edits an annual volume on security, national identity, economic regionalism and North Korea for the Korea Economic Institute.

Jonathan Schroeder is the William A. Kern Professor in the School of Communication at Rochester Institute of Technology in New York. His Ph.D. is from the University of California, Berkeley. He has published widely on branding, communication, consumer research and identity. He has held visiting appointments at London School of Economics; Wesleyan University; Göteborg University; University of Auckland; Bocconi University, Milan; Indian School of Business, Hyderabad; Stockholm University; and Walailak University, Thailand. He is co-author of *From Chinese Brand Culture to Global Brands: Insights from Aesthetics, Fashion and History* (2013).

Wanning Sun is Professor of Media and Communication Studies at the University of Technology Sydney (UTS), Australia. She is best known for her research in a number of areas, including Chinese media and cultural studies, rural-to-urban migration and social change in contemporary China, soft power, public diplomacy and diasporic Chinese media. Wanning is the author of a major report "Chinese-Language Media in Australia: Developments, Challenges and Opportunities" (2016). She is currently leading an Australian Research Council Discovery Project "Chinese-Language Digital/Social Media in Australia: Rethinking Soft Power" (2018–2020). Wanning is the editor of two Routledge volumes on media, communication and Chinese diaspora (2006, 2016).

Zhiyan Wu is Assistant Professor at the School of Management, Shanghai International Business and Economics University. She has a B.A. in English from Beijing Foreign Studies University, an M.Sc. in International Management and a Ph.D. in Management from University of Exeter, UK. She has published in *Advances in Consumer Research, Journal of Brand Management* and *Marketing Theory*. She is co-author of *From Chinese Brand Culture to Global Brands: Insights from Aesthetics, Fashion and History* (2013).

Zhan Zhang is a Postdoctoral Research Fellow of China Media Observatory (CMO), Institute of Media and Journalism (IMeG) at Università della Svizzera italiana (USI), Lugano, Switzerland. She is also the Program Coordinator of Master of Media Management. She publishes in the field of media narrative analysis, strategic communication, media diplomacy and international news, as well as Chinese media studies. She is the co-founder and international director since 2014 of Europe-China Dialogue: Media and Communication Studies Summer School.

Suisheng Zhao is Professor and Director of the Center for China–US Cooperation at Josef Korbel School of International Studies, University of Denver. A Campbell National Fellow at Hoover Institution of Stanford University, Associate Professor of Political Science and International Studies at Washington College in Maryland, Associate Professor of Government and East Asian Politics at Colby College in Maine and Visiting Assistant Professor at the Graduate

School of International Relations and Pacific Studies (IR/PS) at University of California–San Diego, he is the founder and editor of the *Journal of Contemporary China* and the author and editor of more than a dozen books and several dozen articles on Chinese nationalism, Chinese politics/political economy, Chinese foreign policy, US–China relations, Cross-Taiwan Strait relations and East Asian regional issues.

Ying Zhu is Professor of Cinema Studies at the City University of New York and Director of the Center for Film and Moving Image Research at Hong Kong Baptist University. She has published eight books, including *Two Billion Eyes: The Story of China Central Television* (2013), *Television in Post-Reform China: Serial Drama, Confucian Leadership and the Global Television Market* (2008), and *Chinese Cinema during the Era of Reform: The Ingenuity of the System* (2003). Zhu is a recipient of a National Endowment for the Humanities Fellowship (2006), an American Council of Learned Societies Fellowship (2008) and a Fulbright (China) Senior Research Fellowship (2017).

David Zweig is Professor Emeritus, Hong Kong University of Science and Technology. He is also Director of Transnational China Consulting Limited, Vice-President of the Center on China's Globalization (Beijing) and CEO of an NGO called China–California Heart Watch. He lived in the Mainland for four years (1974–1976, 1980–1981, 1986 and 1991–1992) and in Hong Kong since 1996. He was a Postdoctoral Fellow at Harvard and has a Ph.D. from University of Michigan. He is the author or editor of 10 books, including *Internationalizing China: Domestic Interests and Global Linkages* (2002) and *Sino–U.S. Energy Triangles: Resource Diplomacy under Hegemony* (2015).

PREFACE

This has truly been a long-term effort involving multiple editors and a large number of authors all working together in order to produce a single, cohesive volume. It was spring 2014 when Ying first brainstormed with Stan about a possible project on soft power, be it a special journal issue, a co-authored book or an edited book volume. In an email to Stan dated April 16, 2014, Ying wrote, "I'm open to an edited volume so long as it does not take years." Sure enough, the effort has taken more than five years to come to fruition. Along the way we collected expert contributors who brought new ideas. The most valuable asset we "collected" was Kingsley, who came aboard in the second half of 2015, a year into Ying and Stan's on-again, off-again attempt to jump-start the project. A meeting in Beijing between Ying and Kingsley in summer 2016 solidified the joint editorship. Kingsley helped to kick the project into higher gear.

Life interfered, particularly for Ying, who lost her husband and life partner to illness in October 2016. As Ying mourned her personal loss, the project persisted, thanks to Stan and Kingsley who harnessed new contributors as several others moved on, partly as the result of the glacial speed at which the project had been traveling. We are particularly grateful to those contributors who were present at the origin, and kept the faith, keeping whatever private misgivings they might have had to themselves. Our publisher also remained enthusiastic, and we would particularly like to thank Stephanie Rogers at Routledge for her help and encouragement along the way. At times we questioned the continuing relevance of the soft power concept in this rapidly evolving world. As China and the United States wrestle for power and influence around the globe it is reassuring to see Joseph Nye, in his foreword to our book, arguing that soft power, and the ability to shape and disseminate the popular narratives that generate it, are more important than ever. When he was originally asked to contribute a foreword in November 2014, Joseph had the foresight to agree only on the promise from Ying that we would deliver a timely book on China and soft power. Despite the passage of time and the changes in international politics we have witnessed over the last five years, we hope the book lives up to our expectation of contributing something useful to the ongoing scholarly dialogue concerning China's trajectory and influence.

Ying, Stan and Kingsley

FOREWORD

Joseph Nye

Three decades ago, there was a widespread belief that America was in decline, but I disagreed with that analysis. After I assessed American military and economic power resources, I realized that something was still missing. Power is the ability to affect others to get the outcomes one wants and that can be accomplished by attraction as well as coercion or payment. I introduced the concept of soft power to suggest that a nation's power does not rely *solely* on the hard power of economic strength and military force, but also attraction—"the universalism of a country's culture and its ability to establish a set of favorable rules and institutions that govern areas of international activity are critical sources of power [and that] these soft sources of power are becoming more important in world politics today" (Nye, 1990, p. 33).

Five years ago I again took issue with what had become a widespread view that the American century was over (Nye, 2015). Most recently, the cover and six articles in the July/August 2019 issue of the influential journal *Foreign Affairs* went even further, asking "What Happened to the American Century?", with most of the contributors suggesting, as Fareed Zakaria put it, that the death of "American hegemony" was largely self-inflicted, although many noted, as I had in 2015, that the rise of China posed a set of new problems that had not been faced in American competition with the former Soviet Union (Zakaria, 2019). America's role in the world had changed, but as much because of the rise of nativist populism at home as the rise of China abroad. I would argue, in the current competition between China and America, that public diplomacy in the form of soft power is more important than ever. In today's world the most compelling story transmitted and accelerated via cyberspace triumphs as the ability to disseminate the story and shape people's perceptions becomes ever more crucial. But soft power need not be a zero-sum game. If the United States and

China wish to avoid conflict, a rise of Chinese soft power in the United States and American soft power in China is a joint gain. Unfortunately, that is not the current policy direction. The US government has retreated from investing in public diplomacy based on credibility and opted instead for military and economic coercion. Indeed, President Trump's budget director and chief of staff Mick Mulvaney once said that he wanted a hard power budget, not a soft power budget. Polls show that American attractiveness and soft power have declined considerably since 2017.

I was interested in 2007 when President Hu Jintao told the 17th Congress of the Chinese Communist Party that China needed to invest more in soft power. That is a smart strategy. As a country's hard economic and military power grow, it may frighten its neighbors but can soften its image by attraction. China's leaders remain clearly focused on presenting a more "favorable" picture of their country to the outside world. At his first national meeting on propaganda and ideology in August 2013, newly inaugurated president Xi Jinping instructed China's propaganda workers to find new ways to "tell China's story well, and properly disseminate China's voice." In November 2014 at a foreign affairs work conference, Xi emphasized that China "must raise our country's soft power, telling China's story well." In pursuit of this objective, China has committed significant material resources into disseminating its views globally via the expanded presence of state-run media. The international arm of China's state-owned broadcaster, China Global Television Network, now broadcasts in at least 140 countries with 70 bureaus, while state-owned China Radio International broadcasts in 65 languages from more than 70 stations worldwide. China Watch, an English-language supplement offered with monetary incentives by China's state-run newspaper *China Daily*, is currently inserted into about 30 daily newspapers around the world, including *The Wall Street Journal*, *The Washington Post* and *The Daily Telegraph*. The unilateral retreat of America's soft power under President Donald Trump has opened the door for China to step in and advocate a different set of rules, but compromise on an agreed rules-based international order can help both countries to deal with transnational challenges such as financial stability, climate change and pandemics. Both countries need to learn that soft power can help them learn the importance of power with as well as over others. Which version of soft power prevails will determine the world we live in. Instead of images of a new Cold War, the United States and China should see their relationship as a cooperative rivalry, with as much emphasis on the cooperation as on the competition.

While the concept of soft power has been written into official doctrine for more than a decade, the "new era" in China calls for a reappraisal of the soft power framework within the China context as we observe a new phase in China's soft power development, which this book attempts to do. As the only significant challenger to US primacy, China now represents the most important international test case for the practice of soft power. The volume presented here is a timely addition to our understanding of soft power in theory and practice.

References

Nye, Joseph S., Jr. 1990. *Bound to Lead: The Changing Nature of American Power*. New York: Basic Books.

Nye, Joseph S., Jr. 2015. *Is the American Century Over?* Cambridge and Malden, MA: Polity Press.

Zakaria, Fareed. 2019. "The Self-Destruction of American Power," *Foreign Affairs*, July/August, pp. 10–16.

INTRODUCTION

Kingsley Edney, Stanley Rosen and Ying Zhu

[handwritten: Chinese goal of enhancing soft power]

China's rising power is reshaping the global economic and political landscape. This growth in power and status provides China with the opportunity to become more actively involved in various forms of international cooperation but also carries with it a serious risk of rising tension and even full-blown conflict between China and other countries. China's policy makers and strategists are acutely aware of the need to encourage positive perceptions of their country while minimizing negative responses to its growing military power and economic influence. The goal of enhancing China's "soft power" has been at the heart of China's efforts to shape international perceptions so that the world is more welcoming and less fearful of China.

Under Xi Jinping China has entered what the Chinese Communist Party (CCP) calls a "new era of socialism with Chinese characteristics." Xi is consolidating his personal power within the country while at the same time indicating that China will take on a more assertive role in shaping the international order. Some of the country's bilateral relationships have gone through periods of volatility and escalating tensions as China has become more closed at home and assertive abroad. Xi's China nonetheless still allocates significant resources to projects designed to enhance its attractiveness to foreign audiences. While the concept of soft power has been written into official doctrine for more than a decade, now that China is moving into this so-called new era there is a need to reexamine China's global "soft power" campaign for hearts and minds. What is the current state of Chinese soft power strategy and practice under the leadership of Xi Jinping? While China's attempt to generate soft power has attracted international scholarly attention (e.g. Callahan, 2015; Edney, 2012; Rosen, 2012; Nye and Wang, 2009; Cho and Jeong, 2008; Gill and Huang, 2006), and book-length assessments of Chinese power now routinely include sections relating to China's soft power (e.g. Chung, 2015; Shambaugh, 2013; Lampton, 2008), the rise of Xi Jinping provides an opportunity to observe a new phase in China's soft power development. Our book makes the attempt in assessing the state of China's "soft power" under Xi.

Unlike hard power, which manifests through the use of coercion or incentives to generate influence, soft power involves a country attracting and co-opting others to admire and share its core interests. Soft power draws on resources such as culture, values and exemplary foreign policy behavior to create an international environment where others will be more inclined to cooperate and less likely to oppose the state's objectives (Nye, 2004). The effectiveness of soft power resources depends on context; just as the effectiveness of military force cannot be accurately assessed without reference to the physical landscape in which that force will be applied, soft power cannot be understood without reference to the social context in which it operates (Nye, 2004, p. 12). When the concept of soft power first emerged in the 1990s it was primarily used to analyze the foreign relations of the United States, but since then it has been applied to a number of other countries, including Japan (Otmazgin, 2008; Watanabe and McConnell, 2008), India (Wagner, 2010), Canada (Potter, 2009) and, of course, China. China in particular appears to be extending its global influence even as its rivalry with the United States intensifies, presenting us with a crucial opportunity to explore the concept of soft power in greater depth.

The Chinese articulation of soft power

China's leaders have taken the idea of soft power very seriously—perhaps more so than the leaders of any other major state—and soft power has been widely debated by Chinese foreign policy analysts, media and communications experts, and commentators in a number of other fields (Li, 2009). Although the soft power *concept* was introduced into China as early as 1992 with the Chinese translation of Nye's (1990) book *Bound to Lead*, and the first Chinese academic article on soft power appeared in 1993 (Wang, 1993), as Hongying Wang and Yeh-Chung Lu note in their analysis of the China Academic Journals Database, the phrase only began to take off after 2001 (Wang and Lu, 2008, p. 426), the year the Chinese media launched a "going global" project partly as a response to Western media making inroads in China, and in part to allay anxieties over the "threat" from China's rise (Zhao, 2009, p. 248).[1] More specifically, analyzing the same database, Mingjiang Li has noted the increasing usage of the term from 1994, when the database begins, to 2007. From 1994–2000, the term "soft power" appeared in the titles of only 11 journal and periodical articles, increasing in the 2001–2004 period to 58, followed by a large increase to 416 articles from 2005–2007 (Li, 2009, p. 24). Following the 17th Party Congress in 2007, where General Secretary Hu Jintao emphasized the increasing importance of the promotion of Chinese culture, both at home and abroad, the attention to soft power in the Chinese media increased further (Hu, 2007), with a number of Chinese journal articles specifically citing the importance of Hu's speech as a spur to promoting Chinese soft power abroad (Ni, 2008).[2] The number of Chinese articles in social science journals that reference soft power in their title jumped markedly to 826 in 2008 and continued to rise steadily in subsequent years, reaching a peak of 1,134 articles in 2012 before declining to fewer than 500 articles in 2018. This did not indicate that soft power was becoming less important to Chinese leaders, however, but rather that the concept had been incorporated into and become an important component of Xi Jinping's new China Dream discourse (Callahan, 2015). Indeed, beginning with the inaugural issue of June 2016, there is a bimonthly Chinese journal devoted to research on soft power edited by the Institute of Marxism at Wuhan University and managed by the Ministry of Education (*Wenhua ruan shili yanjiu* [*Studies in cultural soft power*]). Many Chinese scholars from a range of academic disciplines have also published books on soft power (e.g. Guo, 2014; Zhang, 2011; Li, 2010; Shu, 2010; Meng, 2009; Yi, 2009; Han, 2008). As noted by the former CCP propaganda chief Li Changchun, "In the modern age, whichever nation's communication methods are most advanced, whichever nation's communication capacity is strongest . . . has the most power to influence the world" (Farah and Mosher, 2010, p. 7).

Not surprisingly, given this recognition, the Chinese leadership has not been satisfied with simply discussing the concept in abstract terms, but has invested significant financial resources in an attempt to enhance China's global soft power. China has spent hundreds of billions of US dollars to expand the international reach of its media outlets, organize major events such as the 2008 Olympic Games and 2010 Shanghai Expo, launch hundreds of Confucius Institutes to teach Chinese language and culture, host summits attended by world leaders and sponsor forums on regional security and prosperity. In 2009 the Hong Kong newspaper *South China Morning Post* reported that China was planning to allocate 45 billion yuan to state media outlets such as CCTV-International, Xinhua News Agency, *China Daily*, and China Radio International to improve their international news coverage and global presence (Wu and Chen, 2009). Fueled by the injection of these funds, the CCP's theoretical journal, *Seeking Truth*, launched an English edition in July 2009 to "make the core values of the party more understandable to Western societies, especially in theoretical and academic circles there" (*Shanghaiist*, 2009). In September 2009, CCTV-International launched a Russian-service channel that targeted 300 million viewers across the former Soviet Union. "There is continuous bias and misunderstanding against China in the rest of the world," Zhang Changming, the then vice president of CCTV complained as he unveiled the Russian channel, citing as evidence "biased and untrue reporting about weather and food quality problems" leading up to the 2008 Beijing Olympics (Zhu, 2012, p. 174). "One of the major goals of the expansion of international channels is to present China objectively to the world," said Zhang, as quoted in Zhu (2012, p. 174). As Zhu discusses in her book (2012), Chinese state media, particularly CCTV's international branches, are tasked with projecting a positive image of China to the world. More recently, David Shambaugh (2015, p. 100) has claimed that China's annual budget for "external propaganda" is approximately $10 billion. The Chinese state has also launched an effort for the country's film and media industry to "tell China's stories."

Promoting China's soft power is a desire shared not only by foreign policy strategists and nationalist citizens. Major financial interests are also at stake, particularly for high-profile Chinese exporters who benefit from positive associations with "brand China" and, conversely, suffer in countries where China's reputation is poor. Chinese state, corporate, elite and popular interests have converged on the common urge to defend and explain China, and as the party line and the bottom line converge to form a united front, the big corporations benefit from state financial and logistical support for their global expansion. Major corporations can emerge as effective tools for nation branding to generate soft power. Just as Sony and Matsushita (Panasonic) have been among the representative faces of Japan, can Alibaba, Baidu or Tencent be the new face of China? The high-tech summit in Seattle in September 2015 was in part an attempt to provide high visibility for Chinese brands, interacting as equals with their American counterparts. Huawei in particular has been at the forefront of the struggle over brand China. The US government has labeled the communication technology company a security threat due to its links to the Chinese state and has pressured the other members of the Five Eyes intelligence network to prevent it from participating in the building of new 5G communication infrastructure, with mixed results.

In China's quest for soft power the stakes are high and the potential consequences are global. Reducing international fear and mistrust helps China achieve goals in the short term by dampening resistance to its foreign policies and is vital for smoothing China's long-term path to a peaceful rise and avoiding becoming trapped in security dilemmas with other states. Soft power also plays an important role in China's domestic politics by improving the internal legitimacy of the CCP and confidence in China's political system amongst its population through increasing China's international status. Appealing to the national pride of Chinese citizens by demonstrating that foreigners admire and are attracted to China is one of the main ways, alongside competent governance and fear of instability, that the CCP attempts to build public support for its rule. Since Xi came to power in late 2012 the domestic political environment has become significantly more closed, with Xi now installed as indisputable leader for the foreseeable future. Chinese foreign policy has become noticeably more assertive, particularly in relation to China's territorial claims in the South China Sea, but also in the economic realm, where China has embarked on an ambitious campaign to expand multilateral and bilateral investment through the Asian Infrastructure Investment Bank and the Belt and Road Initiative. Tensions with the United States have risen, resulting in clashes over trade and maritime security.

The Chinese practice of (soft) power

This slide toward a more strongman personality and ideologically strict style of authoritarianism at home and assertive foreign policy abroad, combined with the ratcheting up of tensions with the United States, might well be viewed as an indication that China is moving away from its previous soft power objectives, or perhaps has even failed in its soft power mission. China appears no closer to solving the fundamental problem of how to cultivate an association with the kinds of political values that resonate positively beyond its borders and overcome the deep-seated suspicions of authoritarian states held by people in liberal democracies. Even in the developing world it remains uncertain whether China's political values will be able to attract local partners in a way that transcends political expediency or economic self-interest and generates a common bond that runs deeper than platitudes about "win-win cooperation" (Suzuki, 2010). China ranked last on a 30-country index of soft power released in July 2015 by a British political consultancy and public relations agency.[3] The index assessed countries on six measures of reputation and influence—government, culture, education, global engagement, enterprise and digital—after polling more than 7,000 people in 20 countries covering each region of the world. China ranked ninth on the culture metric yet was held back in its overall ranking by a political system that curbs free press and information access.[4] The 2018 edition of the index had China three places higher but, as Rosen argues in Chapter 3, the study's methodology makes it impossible for China to score highly due to the inbuilt bias against states that are not liberal democracies.

Yet the reality is more complex than a narrow focus on China's lack of appealing political values might imply. The Global Financial Crisis of 2008 undermined confidence in the Western-led economic order, and illiberal political movements have made significant gains in democracies in recent years. Although mass public support for democracy still appears high in many countries, public attitudes to the other pillar of Western international order—neoliberalism—are more ambivalent (Allan, Vucetic and Hopf, 2018) and younger people in democratic states appear to be increasingly disillusioned with liberal democratic institutions (Foa and Mounk, 2017). The internal divisions within the Western world, exemplified in 2016 by Britain's vote to leave the European Union as well as the election of Donald Trump in the United States, have been accompanied by a resurgence of strongman politics and illiberal populism in places such as Turkey, the Philippines, Brazil, Poland and Hungary. These developments may not in themselves make China appear more attractive, but they at least serve to reduce the coherence and persistence of the liberal critique of China's political system.

As the West appears divided and uncertain, China's leaders have looked to shore up belief in their own policies and political system at home. Xi Jinping has spoken of "four confidences"—in China's path (*daolu*), theory (*lilun*), system (*zhidu*) and culture (*wenhua*)—that are fundamental to the "great rejuvenation of the Chinese nation" (Xinhua, 2018). The CCP also continues to promote its own concept of "socialist core values" to its citizens. Despite what seems to be a persistent soft power weakness in the realm of values, China's leaders appear to have become less accommodating toward Western critics and more outspoken in articulating their own political vision. Yet this push for greater belief in China's political path has not meant that the CCP is comfortable ignoring foreign criticism, particularly when it touches on so-called core interests, such as China's territorial claims. Where does soft power fit in to China's foreign policy now that its ability to employ coercion or inducements to achieve its objectives is greater than it has ever been? Strength and self-confidence have the potential to generate attraction, but is China's ability to persuade and attract others growing alongside its material capabilities, or does the ease with which it can draw on hard power resources undermine the effectiveness of its soft power? As the CCP gains access to greater material resources, then new tools for coercion or inducement also become available to those who aim to reshape China's global image. This can lead to the temptation to employ these harder options as an alternative to soft power approaches, either to shut down unwanted public discourse or to buy influence in foreign debates about China. This use of hard methods to shape international discourse on China has been well documented in recent studies of China's "sharp power" or international influence operations (Brady, 2017; National Endowment for Democracy, 2017). China's growing ability to use hard power in the form of coercion or inducements to achieve its objectives has the potential to undermine its soft power by reinforcing existing fears of those who see China as a threat, even when its use of hard power is intended to shape foreign perceptions of China. However, one argument that comes out in some of the articles in the soft power journal from Wuhan, as Daniel Lynch points out in Chapter 2, is that the rise of an economically strong and politically flourishing China will stimulate a new trend in world development "toward a glorious future of great universal harmony," thereby providing a new model that will replace the outdated pattern established by the Western powers who have created the soft power concept simply to further their own agenda (Zhan, 2016, p. 51).

Close to home the CCP has a particularly wide range of tools for coercion or inducement at its disposal. In Hong Kong, as David Zweig argues in Chapter 13, the Party enjoys a significant structural soft power advantage from its network of United Front organizations embedded in the territory. Yet Zweig claims that increasing soft power is not necessarily an important goal for the CCP in Hong Kong. Despite the clear risks of undermining the Mainland's image in the eyes of Hong Kong residents and further fueling localist politics, the CCP now appears willing to employ coercive tactics to shut down the expression of undesirable political ideas in cases where persuasion or inducements have failed. In the wider world, Chinese responses to perceived insults that paint the country in a negative light or to statements that contradict certain political truths have also employed coercive tactics. In Chapter 3 Stanley Rosen notes that when a thin-skinned lack of self-confidence is exposed by what is perceived to be insulting speech or the behavior of foreigners, then China is only too willing to threaten the use of boycotts and other coercive tools. While these coercive responses might achieve a short-term goal, this can come at the cost of downgrading the bilateral relationship. China's hardline diplomatic performance in Norway, Sweden, Australia and South Korea certainly defies the normative practice of soft power.

In the subtitle of Nye's (2004) book on soft power he refers to it as "the means to success in world politics." Nye's concept has been helpful in highlighting the importance of the element of attraction for assessments of power in international politics, but it is also unwise to consider a country's soft power goals in isolation from its broader power context. To claim that China's leaders take the development of soft power seriously is not to argue that presenting a pleasing and attractive face to the outside world is their sole or even primary consideration when making policy decisions. While increasing soft power has important long-term strategic benefits, at times these may take a back seat to other more immediate considerations such as national sovereignty and political and social stability. Even when public opinion is taken into account when making decisions about foreign policy the target audience often seems to be the domestic population or the Chinese diaspora. China's leaders desire influence over foreign audiences, but soft power is not the only way to achieve this. The cultivation of soft power is a long-term prospect, and we can expect China to be willing to sacrifice some degree of attractiveness in order to enhance its immediate influence over crucial policy outcomes.

The relationship between material incentives and soft power also needs to be examined more closely. China's ambitious approach to international investment has significant potential to add to its attractiveness around the world, but here, too, the picture is mixed. With recent commitments of $50 billion for the Asian Infrastructure Investment Bank, $41 billion for the New Development Bank, $40 billion for the Silk Road Economic Belt and $25 billion for the Maritime Silk Road, the total bill for China's charm offensive on the economics front is substantial.[5] At times, China's economic engagement with developing regions such as Africa has generated tensions and drawn criticism from local actors who fear a repeat of past exploitative colonial practices or are concerned about an increase in corruption or unemployment. The Pew Research Center's 2013 Global Attitudes Project survey showed that China struggled to generate soft power even in Africa and Latin America, where it has made substantial investments in local economies (Shambaugh, 2015, p. 107); however, the spring 2018 Pew survey, which included Kenya, Nigeria and South Africa among its 25 countries canvassed, showed favorable ratings for China as high as 67% in Kenya (17% unfavorable), 61% in Nigeria (17% unfavorable) and 49% in South Africa (38% unfavorable) (Pew, 2018). As Chinese investors have begun to buy up property in cities such as New York and London and purchase iconic Western brands, it has become clear that this mix of admiration and fear generated by China's newfound economic influence is a phenomenon that affects not only poorer countries but the developed world as well. When investment occurs in areas directly related to China's international image, such as media companies, this can also stoke fears. In Chapter 5, for example, Ying Zhu notes the backlash in the United States to the acquisition of US film assets by Chinese media companies, most notably Dalian Wanda. Then there is also the question of the sustainability of China's economic growth model—the hotly contested "Beijing Consensus," which has been compared to the more familiar "Washington Consensus"[6]—particularly with China's stock market meltdown in the summer of 2015, the subsequent depreciation of the RMB and shrinking foreign currency reserves, which affect China's capacity to inject money into developing countries and thus tarnishes China's brand of economic miracle.

Things took yet another turn for China's economy when Donald Trump came to power. While Trump's re-election campaign will drive his trade policy with conflicting impulses, the trade war is slowing down China's economic growth. Back in May 2000, China was on course for membership in the World Trade Organization (WTO), under which member countries are required to extend preferential trading treatment to one another, or what the United States calls permanent normal trade relations (PNTR). That required an act of Congress. Business leaders stood nearly united in their support of the bill, arguing that the vote would serve only to open China's markets to US exports. They were joined in that argument by George W. Bush who by then had locked up his party's presidential nomination. The bill passed the House by a vote of 237 to 197. The Senate approved it 83 to 15 in September. But there is now bipartisan unhappiness about the way bilateral trade with China has turned out for the United States. The opposition has come from all sides. Peter Navarro, a professor of economics and public policy at the University of California–Irvine at the time and now the hawkish Trump China advisor, considered the passage of the China PNTR the most destructive trade event in US history. Senator Bernie Sanders once described PNTR as "not a good deal for American workers" and led a bipartisan effort for China PNTR repeal in 2005. Sen. Sherrod Brown (D-Ohio) predicted in 2016 with Trump clinching the Republican nomination that the fracture that began with the China vote could end up splitting the GOP much like civil rights split Democrats in 1968. The legislation, as argued by some, caused a series of economic and political earthquakes that helped usher in Trump, the most anti-trade Republican candidate in modern history. Others have made similar observations that suggested that PNTR with China "helped create" Trump. In a hyperbolic *Washington Post* op-ed, written on March 21, 2016, Jim Tankersley asserted that the Republican establishment began losing its party to Donald Trump on May 24, 2000, at 5:41 p.m., on the floor of the House of Representatives when three-quarters of House Republicans voted to extend the status of PNTR to China. It is indeed the case that Trump built his insurgent campaign in part on opposition to what he called a bad deal with China, which helped him rally support from conservative voters. As Trump heads more deeply into uncharted waters on his China trade policy, the effect on China's growth potential, an important component of its soft power and international influence, remains uncertain.

While economic development and the subsequent wealth it generates can produce its own attractive power that complements the potential of material resources to shape behavior through the use of direct inducements, it can be difficult to disentangle the mechanisms of economic inducement from the ideational attraction of soft power. Material resources do play an important role in the development of soft power by providing the infrastructure for the transmission of ideas and information to new audiences. China's soft power can be enhanced

China vs. US approach to soft power)

State v. civil society actors (China vs US approach to soft power)

when credible actors such as media organizations or public figures are materially incentivized to reproduce the kind of narratives about China that the CCP would like to promote and to suppress or downplay more critical perspectives.

In addition to the complex relationship between material resources and soft power, we also observe an important, yet underexplored relationship between the agents whose actions contribute to a nation's soft power and the authorities who aim to employ those actors in pursuit of a national soft power strategy. A soft power version of the classic principal–agent problem (Laffont and Martimort, 2002), which involves a misalignment of interests between those who have the authority to issue orders and those who have the responsibility to carry them out, appears to be present even for authoritarian states such as China. In Chapter 3 Rosen notes the sharp contrast between China's approach to soft power, in which the state plays a central and guiding role, and the US approach, in which the state has tended to operate at a distance from the civil society actors that are its most effective resource for the generation of soft power. Yet in Chapter 5 Ying Zhu notes that filmmakers can be unreliable partners for states wishing to promote their desired images abroad. Hollywood studios have been a traditional generator of soft power for the United States but their financial stake in the Chinese market sometimes puts them at odds with some US lawmakers who would like to see a more assertive expression of their political values on film.

CCP would like to use local actors

Ideally, the CCP would like to make use of local actors to relay a positive narrative of China as they will be more credible to their respective audiences than the official voice of the Chinese state. In Chapter 4 Wanning Sun documents this strategy of "borrowing a boat to go to sea" in the context of overseas Chinese media organizations. Gaining influence over the diaspora communities in Australia and New Zealand is certainly an interesting experiment in creating the climate under which Chinese soft power can extend to the wider non-Chinese public. Yet the effort can cause problems for the key players in places where there is a significant ideological tension with China. In Chapter 12 Dalton Lin and Yun-han Chu note that when individuals in Taiwan make positive statements about China they are often labelled as "selling out" the island. This dynamic can also be observed in Australia, where the CCP has attempted to shape public discourse on China by employing inducements in the form of money for academic research and political donations to the major parties. This has led to a divisive debate where those espousing a more positive view of China or warning against overstating a "China threat" are labeled naïve or morally compromised by their critics. In cases where defending China's political system is already considered ideologically suspect and there is an observable connection between the local individual or organization speaking out in favor of China and a CCP-linked counterpart on the Chinese Mainland, the CCP's capacity and desire to provide material inducements to shape its global image undermines the credibility of its message.

own backing

At other times, officials or other agents may become overzealous in defending China's official position or even employ coercive tactics in ways that reinforce an image of China as an authoritarian state that is intolerant of free speech. In 2014 Confucius Institute head Xu Lin oversaw the removal of pages from the brochure of an academic conference in Portugal that her organization was sponsoring because they contained references to a Taiwanese sponsor, producing accusations of Chinese interference in academic freedom (Sudworth, 2014). More recently a UK-based CCTV journalist was ejected from the 2018 Conservative Party Conference and charged with assault after staging an angry intervention in a panel on the effects of Chinese rule on freedoms in Hong Kong (Weaver, 2018). As Falk Hartig points out in his chapter on the Confucius Institutes, Xu initially linked the Institutes to the development of Chinese soft power but later appeared to downplay any connection between the organization and China's international power and influence. Yet despite this apparent sensitivity to how China's cultural or educational initiatives are perceived overseas, Xu's actions in Portugal indicate that the need to be seen to respond strongly to challenges to Chinese sovereignty can at times override concerns about the reputational damage generated by such forceful interventions.

Finally, when analyzing China's soft power it is important to consider the factors that influence China's attractiveness but have little or nothing to do with Chinese policies or values. Global or even local events can shift the narratives that are used to understand China's actions for various audiences around the world. The Global Financial Crisis in 2008 provided an opportunity for China to be seen in a new light by those inclined to be receptive to its economic model and, as Gilbert Rozman points out in Chapter 11, the emergence or decline of particular perceptions of the Asian region in countries such as Japan and South Korea have also shifted views of China held by their publics.

Book structure

This book assesses the current state of China's soft power theory and practice in a new period of Chinese assertiveness. As the contributions to this volume demonstrate, Chinese soft power is complex, contradictory and diverse. China's experience appears to reflect neither a smooth path to "peaceful development" nor an inevitable drift toward conflict with other states. China is large enough and diverse enough to generate not only a powerful attractive pull but also a range of negative responses, such as fear, anger or disdain. The first section of the book takes a thematic approach to analyzing China's soft power. Beginning with an examination of the relationship between soft power and traditional Chinese views of international order, academic debates over soft power within China, and the soft power competition between China and the United States, the section then closely examines four key areas where China's "going out" policies have aligned with its soft power strategy: news media, film, branding and education.

Suisheng Zhao, in "Projection of China's Soft Power in the New Century: Reconstruction of the Traditional Chinese World Order," begins this section with an exploration of the Chinese rediscovery and reconstruction of the traditional

Chinese world order in the 21st century. To calm fears of their neighbors, Chinese leaders have claimed that China's rise will be peaceful because its great power aspirations are different from the imperialism and hegemony of the Western powers. To bolster this argument China's leaders and scholars have looked to the traditional China-centered East Asian order, which they claim was characterized by a form of benevolent governance and benign hierarchy that was not only unique but also more peaceful than its counterparts in other parts of the world. Indeed, when scholars from the Peterson Institute for International Economics, based in Washington, DC, visited China in late May 2019 during the "trade war" with the United States, they were given a "50-minute non-stop lecture . . . about this being a clash of civilizations" by a member of the Chinese Politburo, who noted that the United States was a "Mediterranean culture," based around belligerence and internal division, thus explaining its "oppressive foreign policy" (Magnier, 2019). In this context, although the concept of "harmonious world" has received less emphasis under the current leadership, Xi Jinping has continued to refer to China's traditional order to project a peaceful image. However, Zhao's analysis shows that despite these attempts to present a harmonious world order to China's neighbors, Chinese leaders in fact perceive the world through a social Darwinist lens and behave accordingly in order to maximize China's power and security and expand its influence and control within the Asian region. This gap between the Chinese authorities' professed ideals and the way they actually perceive the world highlights the difficulty for China in identifying and promoting political values that not only resonate internationally but also line up with the behavior of the Chinese state at home and abroad.

In the second chapter, Daniel Lynch provides a detailed assessment of the current state of academic debate over soft power in China. As China's global image has generally worsened over the last ten years, Lynch looks for evidence of critical reflection on the part of soft power scholars in China. Finding that they appear increasingly willing to acknowledge the setbacks suffered by China in its ongoing attempts to improve its soft power, Lynch nevertheless notes that Chinese commentators tend to blame the West for these failures rather than question China's strategy or message. He identifies a resentful or hubristic optimism toward soft power that seems to be based more on a sense of right or grievance rather than evidence of likely success. Lynch links this optimism to Xi Jinping's campaign for greater self-confidence as well as confidence in China's rising material capabilities. However, he also notes that this confidence could end up being misplaced and lead to greater frustrations if the economic growth stalls or, alternatively, if China's rising material wealth and propensity to employ its material power in pursuit of its interests in fact undermines its soft power appeal.

Stanley Rosen, in "Ironies of Soft Power Projection: The United States and China in the Age of Donald Trump and Xi Jinping," highlights the gap between the Chinese government's massive investment in soft power and its poor results, particularly in the United States. Rosen points out that the United States has been relatively successful at cultivating soft power in China and throughout the world despite a lack of government investment, the generally negative views of US foreign policy, and the best efforts of the Chinese government to undermine American soft power. Rosen argues that US soft power has been successful precisely because it is *not* linked to the American government, which makes it easier for the Chinese public and audiences elsewhere to dissociate their negative views of American foreign policy from their feelings of attraction toward American culture and society, whereas the Chinese promotion of soft power hardly exists apart from the efforts of its government. Although favorability ratings for the United States have declined in most of the world, in some cases drastically, under the "America First" policies of President Donald Trump, there is as yet no clear indication that China has benefited from this decline. In part this is owing to an understanding that American culture and values are independent from Trump's initiatives, but also because soft power is not a zero-sum game between China and the United States. Rather than China, the nations that now score higher than the United States on soft power indices are Western European countries, primarily Germany, France and Great Britain.

The news media is a key component of China's strategy for turning its sizeable economic resources into soft power. While most observers focus on the high-profile flagship publications and broadcast networks controlled by the Chinese state, Wanning Sun's chapter instead examines the often-overlooked yet crucially important Chinese-language news outlets run by and for Chinese diaspora communities around the world. The CCP aims to employ these news outlets as part of its soft power strategy to reshape China's international image. Through a variety of links with these diaspora news outlets, ranging from content provision agreements to outright ownership, the Chinese authorities aim to use the expertise, audience and reputation of these outlets for their own purposes. For the CCP, gaining influence over the diaspora communities is an important precursor to extending its desired discourse about China to the wider non-Chinese public, enhancing China's image and attractiveness. Sun delves into the complexities of these arrangements, pointing out that the agency of these diaspora media entrepreneurs in negotiating the political economy of Chinese soft power is often overlooked. At the same time, new media platforms such as WeChat have altered the dynamics of soft power in diaspora communities by providing new methods for the transnational transmission of discourse.

Film is another area where market forces and political values intersect. Ying Zhu's chapter, "The Battle of Images: Cultural Diplomacy and Sino–Hollywood Negotiation," examines how cinema has become a battlefield for competing political and cultural values. At the same time, however, she also analyzes how commercial interests complicate political and ideological posturing on both sides. Zhu compares the context and terms of Hollywood's Republican era triumph to those of its repeat performance in the post-1995 Reform era to reveal historical continuities and changes that do not appear in the standard historical accounts of political and ideological contests, of international economic development and of global expansion of media corporations, American and Chinese. She argues that

power dynamic plays out in film

the history of Sino–Hollywood engagement is a case of political, cultural and economic rivalry and co-optation. It is a grand negotiation between competing cultural and economic values; developmental models, as well as nationalism and exceptionalism; and a shifting global power dynamic playing out in the art and artifice of filmmaking, distribution and exhibition.   *nation branding*

"Branding as Soft Power: Brand Culture, Nation Branding, and the 2008 Beijing Olympics," co-authored by Janet Borgerson, Jonathan Schroeder and Zhiyan Wu, utilizes nation branding as a framework to explore the ways in which brand culture research perceives pathways of Chinese soft power. They look specifically at the case of the 2008 Beijing Olympics Opening Ceremony, which is seen as an expression of China's soft power—a cultural, consumer and strategic branding event that showcases a sophisticated, yet earnest and nostalgic effort to position China as a modern economic, political and cultural power with a long historical and cultural legacy that will continue to influence global cultures. They argue that branding practices involve a process of co-creation, through which brand identities interact with "market myths." Thinking about soft power in this way highlights the importance of considering global cultural myths when analyzing the Chinese authorities' efforts to build an international brand for China that resonates with target audiences around the world.

Confucius institutes

In "A Decade of Wielding Soft Power Through Confucius Institutes: Some Interim Results," Falk Hartig draws on fieldwork he has conducted at Confucius Institutes (CIs) around the world in order to unpack the often intense debate over the function and value of these high-profile examples of Chinese soft power generation. Despite the criticism that has been leveled at CIs by concerned scholars in some Western countries, there is still strong global demand from universities to host CIs. They remain a particularly attractive proposition for universities seeking to internationalize and to gain access to China's higher education market. Nevertheless, Hartig shows that CIs are still significantly limited in what they can achieve, both in terms of their practical operational resources as well as their ability to reach target audiences in their host countries. His research inside these organizations presents a rather less effective tool for soft power generation than is often assumed by critics, with one of the major problems being the lack of suitable teachers. Resourcing issues are such that even a number of CI directors hold the view that there are too many Institutes competing for the available resources. He argues that reducing the overall number of Institutes and providing the remaining ones with better funding and staffing is necessary if their potential is to be fully realized.   *how to make CIs more useful*

To understand China's contemporary pursuit of soft power and its global implications, we have also sought to place Chinese soft power in comparative perspective, examining China's soft power projection in a variety of regional contexts. Investigating a country's soft power in abstract terms may help to identify a general increase or decrease in its global influence, but it is of little use when attempting to analyze the specific foreign policy problems that it faces. Something that is a powerful source of attraction in the context of one social relationship may be irrelevant or even repulsive in another (Nye, 2004, pp. 12–13). For this reason, the second half of this book is dedicated to in-depth case studies of China's soft power relationships with seven different countries and regions around the world. Although it is impossible to address the entirety of China's global soft power efforts in detail, here we present a wide-ranging account of Chinese soft power across a broad spectrum of case studies. These include both the developed and developing world, China's immediate neighborhood in Asia as well as more distant audiences in Latin America and Africa.

Zhang Zhan's chapter, "The Dilemma of China's Soft Power in Europe," examines the impact and limitations of China's soft power since the establishment of a strategic partnership between China and Europe (EU and various European countries) in 2003. As Zhang discusses, the partnership agreement resulted in increased trade and economic cooperation between China and Europe, and thus played a vital role as part of China's soft power strategy in Europe. However, all the efforts undertaken by the Chinese government—including public diplomacy by Chinese ambassadors, the opening of European branches of some Chinese state-owned media outlets, the purchasing of European media businesses such as radio stations and cinemas by Chinese state-owned and private media companies and the opening of large numbers (34% of the global total) of CIs—have failed to significantly improve China's image in Europe. Public opinion polls suggest that European publics continue to have relatively "negative" perceptions of China (in some cases the most "negative" global perception). Zhang analyzes some of the main obstacles that have limited and continue to limit the effectiveness of China's public diplomacy in Europe: concerns regarding the lack of political freedoms, human rights and credibility and transparency within China. The study also points out another key obstacle that contributed to the contradiction between an improving diplomatic relationship and worsening European public perceptions—the problematic communication of Chinese authorities with international (European) journalists working in China, which pushed the journalists into taking sides in negative coverage that eventually impacted the view of overseas audiences.

In "The Evolution of Chinese Soft Power in the Americas," Evan Ellis examines the Latin American response to China's soft power, noting that much of China's attractiveness in the region is linked to a belief that it offers significant economic opportunity. China presents an alternative model for development and a political counterweight to Western-dominated international institutions that is attractive not only to leftist regimes but also to moderate governments that want to widen their range of foreign and economic policy options. China's investment in Latin America goes beyond commercial transactions to also include funding for local elites and other influencers, such as journalists, politicians and students, to visit and develop greater ties with China. Ellis notes that while much of China's attractiveness in the region stems from an expectation of potential material benefits, rather than culture or shared values, this is not only a product of actual economic exchange but is also driven by China's image and local beliefs about its future development trajectory in relation to the United States.

Antonio Fiori and Stanley Rosen, in "The Sino–African Relationship: An Intense and Long Embrace," examine the history of China's interactions with Africa. Here, the interplay between economic and diplomatic objectives seems particularly important, as mutual images are filtered through the lens of economic cooperation and South–South solidarity. Yet Fiori and Rosen also point out the importance of educational ties, the growing presence of Chinese media and telecommunication companies in Africa and cooperation in areas such as peacekeeping and health. While Chinese actors have not always escaped criticism, the dynamic between China and developing states in Africa is rather different than between China and the West. In contrast to the West, Chinese actors in Africa can often simply present themselves as preferable alternatives to other foreign companies or organizations, rather than compete directly with well-established locals. Moreover, as the authors note, the major speech on Africa in December 2018 by former American National Security Advisor John Bolton, where he essentially warned African countries that they needed to make a choice between China and the United States in terms of funding models for development, has greatly raised the stakes for African decision makers.

Gilbert Rozman looks at China's soft power in Northeast Asia through a comparison of South Korea and Japan. This comparison is instructive because the two countries are viewed as opposites in the recent effectiveness of China's soft power. While negative views toward China have become more widespread in Japan in recent years, the opposite has occurred in South Korea. Rozman draws on media accounts, scholarly writing on bilateral relations and polling data in the two countries in order to assess perceptions of China in Japan and South Korea and subsequently build a framework with which to systematically compare Chinese soft power. He looks at how China's soft power fortunes have shifted not only due to changes in China's circumstances and behavior but also because of how China fits into narratives of regional relations that have been dominant in Japan and South Korea at various times. This highlights the importance of considering how China's identity might be framed in terms of the national narratives of countries that are the target of China's soft power efforts, while being aware that these narratives can and do change over time.

Staying in the region, Dalton Lin and Yun-han Chu focus on Taiwan and the question of China's economic soft power. Lin and Chu question why China's offers of stability and prosperity since 2008, oftentimes sweetened by concessions by the mainland, have failed to attract people in Taiwan. Making the important distinction between forced and voluntary economic dependence they argue that economic soft power is present where there is low potential dependence, which is a decreasing function of the number of potential partners of economic integration, combined with high realized economic dependence. They use this innovative theoretical framework along with data from the Asian Barometer Survey to explain shifts in Taiwanese people's attitudes to economic integration with

China. Lin and Chu's analysis highlights how China's soft power approach to Taiwan maintains a coercive element that ultimately weakens its persuasiveness for its Taiwanese audience. They argue that Beijing's approach turns the logic of soft power on its head by setting a hard political precondition—acceptance of the reunification agenda—for the establishment of positive relations, rather than first establishing the soft power resources that would generate sufficient attraction to make this a desirable proposition for the Taiwanese people. At the same time, they note that a wide ideological gap between China and Taiwan makes it more likely that Taiwanese who speak out in ways that are supportive of the Mainland are suspected of attempting to "sell out" the island in pursuit of their own personal interests.

David Zweig's chapter, "Familiarity Breeds Contempt: China's Growing 'Soft Power Deficit' in Hong Kong," examines how the rise of "localism" in Hong Kong, which attempts to highlight divisions between Mainland China and Hong Kong and between Mainlanders and Hong Kong residents, interacts with recent calls to encourage Hong Kong youth to spend more time on the Mainland as tourists or students in order to deepen their understanding of the PRC. Using data from the Hong Kong Transition Project as well as the author's own surveys of Hong Kong students, Hong Kong students studying on the Mainland and Hong Kongers working on the Mainland, Zweig examines the effects of interactions with Mainland China on Hong Kongers' attitudes toward Beijing. Zweig finds that the identity gap between Hong Kong and the Mainland and disaffection toward Beijing has increased since the 2008 Olympics. Although the Mainland enjoys a clear structural advantage in its soft power efforts in Hong Kong due to its use of United Front organizations and tactics, increasing soft power is not necessarily the most important goal for the CCP in Hong Kong.

Finally, Yun-han Chu, Min-hua Huang and Jie Lu's chapter "How East Asians View a Rising China" uses Asian Barometer survey results to examine how China's attempts to promote the economic benefits of its ambitious strategy of "One Belt, One Road," while at the same time taking a more assertive approach to territorial disputes in the South China Sea, have been received in the region. In some countries the attraction of China's economic plans have neutralized negative perceptions generated by territorial clashes. Overall, East Asians have a broadly positive view of China but still express considerable admiration toward the American model. They desire to maintain a strong American presence in the region, but this is combined with the hope that they will not have to choose sides in any future strategic competition between China and the United States, a hope shared by African states as well. Surprisingly, when it comes to acting as an economic model for the region China sits in third place, behind not only the United States but also Japan.

Conclusion

China's continuing emphasis on enhancing its soft power, backed by a commitment of significant material resources, is taking place in a world in transformation.

In an ironic sense, Joseph Nye's concept of soft power has returned to the place where Nye began. In the preface to *Bound to Lead: The Changing Nature of American Power*, where Nye introduced his concept in book-length form for the first time, he begins by acknowledging that there is a widespread belief that America is in decline and should reduce its external commitments. But Nye also notes that whether or not the United States is in decline is the wrong question to ask, instead arguing that the more relevant question is: "How is power changing in modern international politics?" (Nye, 1990, p. ix). He then goes on to note how his thinking was stimulated by Paul Kennedy's best-selling *The Rise and Fall of the Great Powers: Economic Change and Military Conflict from 1500 to 2000*, where Kennedy observes that US decline has been continuous, and argues that "the historical record suggests that there is a very clear connection *in the long run* between an individual Great Power's economic rise and fall and its growth and decline as an important military power (or world empire)" (Kennedy, 1987, p. xxii, italics in original). Kennedy's book makes the basic point that economic resources are necessary to support a large-scale military establishment, and also notes that in the international system, both wealth and power are always *relative* (Kennedy, 1987, p. xxii, emphasis in original). As the book's subtitle suggests, for Kennedy a nation's power, and by extension its rise and fall, depends solely on the hard power of economic strength and military force. Nye introduced the concept of soft power to challenge that argument. Influenced by Robert Cox's work on the peaceful international orders established by Britain in the 19th century and America in the 20th century, Nye (1990, p. 33) argues that "the universalism of a country's culture and its ability to establish a set of favorable rules and institutions that govern areas of international activity are critical sources of power" and that the resources that produce this soft, co-optive form of power are increasingly important in international politics.

It is important to go back 30 years to the origins of the soft power concept because the current international order and the intellectual arguments introduced to explain the changes that have taken place strongly suggest that Kennedy's argument for the primacy of economic and military power has resurfaced, albeit in a somewhat different form. To paraphrase Nye, is power once again changing in international politics? The challenge China poses to the United States and the American response to that challenge, as McClory (2018, p. 12) calls the "growing swell of voices warning about the coming collapse of the current rules-based liberal international order," are at the heart of this question. The rise of China, the use of sharp power by authoritarian nations and the elevation of strong leaders in the United States and elsewhere who are pursuing narrow nationalist agendas are all challenging the continuing relevance of soft power. Yet even where material competition seems to be intensifying, we can see the ongoing importance of images and attractiveness. Reactions of governments around the world to Huawei's bid for 5G leadership are influenced not only by material factors such as national security and economic efficiency, but also by questions relating to the trust and credibility of both China and the United States. Huawei is China's greatest global branding success to date, but the US government is now engaged in a sustained effort to rebrand it as the tool of a dangerous authoritarian power. The significance of Huawei for China, both in terms of its material success in building a new global telecommunications infrastructure and in terms of its intangible brand, seems clear, but for now the company's overall contribution to China's power, whether hard or soft, remains uncertain. Despite this uncertainty, it is crucial to identify where forms of soft and hard power intersect and to continue to explore their interaction in order to understand better the nature of contemporary power in international relations.

Recent commentaries on the potential transformation of the international system highlight the role of China. As Nathan Gardels notes, if China were to succeed in establishing a post-American world order, it would not be multilateral, but would be composed of multiple bilateral relationships linked to the Chinese core. In addition, following China's "one world, many systems" perspective, it would not be based on a convergence of values as the American-led world order has been, but on a convergence of interests (Gardels, 2018). Some commentators in support of such a new world order have urged China to take advantage of the demise of Nye's version of soft power and replace it with a new version, where soft power would be decoupled from its liberal ideological basis. Eric X. Li suggests that China has succeeded precisely because it rejected Western liberal values and that China's success could become a model for a Chinese version of soft power that is in many ways the opposite of Nye's formulation. As Li puts it, "you don't have to want to be like us, you don't have to want what we want; you can participate in a new form of globalization while retaining your own culture, ideology, and institutions" (Li, 2018). Though positing that soft power does not need to involve competition, and diverse cultures, ideologies and institutions can coexist, China does advocate a different set of rules rooted in the concept of *hexie shehui* (harmonious society) seen as a new model of sovereignty in which individual subjectivities are understood in relational, not autonomous, terms. The word *tianxia* (all under heaven) helps justify China's biopolitical power and its ambition to expand it across the globe. Others accept the continuing relevance of soft power, but argue that America's illiberal turn under Trump—in effect a unilateral abandonment of America's soft power advantage—could benefit China if it formulated policies that capitalized on these new opportunities. For example, as skilled workers from around the world look beyond the United States to make a better life for themselves, China could create a path for citizenship for some categories of immigrants. With the United States foregoing participation in the Trans Pacific Partnership, China could strengthen its position as the economic leader of East Asia by bolstering regional trade and expanding its trade agreements in that region (Yan, 2017).

China has been at the forefront as the liberal international order and, by extension, Nye's concept of soft power, have been challenged by recent developments. The chapters in this volume are an attempt to understand not only how

China has tried to use soft power in pursuit of its foreign and domestic policy goals, but also to offer some insights into the role that soft power may play in future Chinese policy decisions with serious global ramifications.

Notes

1 Wang and Lu searched for "soft power" under three possible Chinese expressions: *ruan shili, ruan liliang* and *ruan quanli.*
2 The emphasis on culture appears in Part VII of the speech to the Congress ("Promoting Vigorous Development and Prosperity of Chinese Culture").
3 Source: www.ejinsight.com/20150721-despite-huge-investment-china-ranks-dead-last-soft-power/
4 The United States ranked best for education, culture and digital but was held back by negative perceptions of its foreign policy.
5 It has amounted to US$1.41 trillion, according to Ray Kwong (www.ejinsight.com/20150721-despite-huge-investment-china-ranks-dead-last-soft-power/).
6 Among a substantial literature on this subject, see the discussion entitled "debating the China model of modernization" in *Journal of Contemporary China*, 19(65), June 2010, particularly Scott Kennedy, "The Myth of the Beijing Consensus," pp. 461–477.

References

Allan, Bently B., Srdjan Vucetic and Ted Hopf. 2018. "The Distribution of Identity and the Future of International Order: China's Hegemonic Prospects," *International Organization* 72(4), pp. 839–869.

Brady, Anne-Marie. 2017. "Magic Weapons: China's Political Influence Activities Under Xi Jinping," *Wilson Center*, September 18. www.wilsoncenter.org/article/magic-weapons-chinas-political-influence-activities-under-xi-jinping.

Callahan, William A. 2015. "Identity and Security in China: The Negative Soft Power of the China Dream," *Politics* 35(3–4), pp. 216–229.

Cho, Young Nam and Jong Ho Jeong. 2008. "China's Soft Power: Discussions, Resources, and Prospects," *Asian Survey* 48(3), pp. 453–472.

Chung, Jae Ho (ed.). 2015. *Assessing China's Power.* London: Palgrave Macmillan.

Edney, Kingsley. 2012. "Soft Power and the Chinese Propaganda System," *Journal of Contemporary China* 21(78), pp. 899–914.

Farah, Douglas and Andrew Mosher. 2010. "Winds from the East: How the People's Republic of China Seeks to Influence the Media in Africa, Latin America, and Southeast Asia," *Centre for International Media Assistance*, September 8. www.cima.ned.org/wp-content/uploads/2015/02/CIMA-China-Report_1.pdf.

Foa, Roberto Stefan and Yascha Mounk. 2017. "The Signs of Deconsolidation," *Journal of Democracy* 28(1), pp. 5–15.

Gardels, Nathan. 2018. "China Is Laying the Groundwork for a Post-American World Order," *The Washington Post World Post*, June 18. www.washingtonpost.com/news/theworldpost/wp/2018/07/27/america-china/?utm_term=.d659bdd1f693.

Gill, Bates and Yanzhong Huang. 2006. "Sources and Limits of Chinese 'Soft Power'," *Survival* 48(2), pp. 17–36.

Guo, Jiemin. 2014. *Ruan quanli xin tan: lilun yu shijian [New Exploration of Soft Power: Theory and Practice].* Shanghai: Shanghai shehui kexue yuan chubanshe.

Han, Tieying. 2008. *Ruan quanli de xitong fensi [System Analysis of Soft Power].* Tianjin: Tianjin renmin chubanshe.

Hu, Jintao. 2007. "Hold High the Banner of Socialism with Chinese Characteristics and Strive for New Victories in Building a Moderately Prosperous Society in All Respects," *Xinhua*. http://news.xinhuanet.com/english/2007-10/24/content_6938749.htm.

Kennedy, Paul. 1987. *The Rise and Fall of the Great Powers: Economic Change and Military Conflict from 1500 to 2000*. New York: Random House.

Laffont, Jean-Jacques and David Martimort. 2002. *The Theory of Incentives: The Principal-Agent Model*. Princeton: Princeton University Press.

Lampton, David M. 2008. *The Three Faces of Chinese Power: Might, Money, and Minds*. Berkeley: University of California Press.

Li, Eric X. 2018. "The Rise and Fall of Soft Power," *Foreign Policy*, May 29. https://foreign policy.com/2018/08/20/the-rise-and-fall-of-soft-power.

Li, Mingjiang (ed.). 2009. *Soft Power: China's Emerging Strategy in International Politics*. Lanham, MD: Rowman and Littlefield.

Li, Xiguang. 2010. *Ruan shili yaosu [Soft Power Elements]*. Beijing: Falü chubanshe.

Magnier, Mark. 2019. "Chinese Official Picks Up 'Clash of Civilisations' Theme in Lecture to Visiting US Scholars," *South China Morning Post*, May 29. www.scmp.com/news/china/diplomacy/article/3012208/lecture-visiting-us-scholars-chinese-official-picks-clash.

McClory, Jonathan. 2018. *The Soft Power 30: A Global Ranking of Soft Power*. Portland and USC Center for Public Diplomacy. https://portland-communications.com/publications/a-global-ranking-of-soft-power-2018.

Meng, Liang. 2009. *Daguo ce: tong xiang daguo zhi lu de ruan shili [Great Power Policy: The Soft Power Path to Great Power]*. Beijing: Renmin ribao chubanshe.

National Endowment for Democracy. 2017. *Sharp Power: Rising Authoritarian Influence*, December 5. www.ned.org/sharp-power-rising-authoritarian-influence-forum-report.

Ni, Zhen. 2008. "Ruan shili he Zhongguo dianying" ["Soft power and Chinese film"], *Dangdai dianying [Contemporary Cinema]* 2, pp. 4–10.

Nye, Joseph S., Jr. 1990. *Bound to Lead: The Changing Nature of American Power*. New York: Basic Books.

Nye, Joseph S., Jr. 2004. *Soft Power: The Means to Success in World Politics*. New York: Public Affairs.

Nye, Joseph S., Jr. and Wang Jisi. 2009. "Hard Decisions on Soft Power: Opportunities and Difficulties for Chinese Soft Power," *Harvard International Review*, Summer, pp. 18–22.

Otmazgin, Nissim Kadosh. 2008. "Contesting Soft Power: Japanese Popular Culture in East and Southeast Asia," *International Relations of the Asia-Pacific* 8(1), pp. 73–101.

PEW Research Center Global Attitudes and Trends. 2018. October 1. www.pewresearch.org/global/2018/10/01/international-publics-divided-on-china.

Potter, Evan H. 2009. *Branding Canada: Projecting Canada's Soft Power through Public Diplomacy*. Montreal and Kingston: McGill-Queen's University Press.

Rosen, Stanley. 2012. "Il 'Soft Power' Ancora Americano" ["Soft Power Speaks American Once More"], *Limes Rivista Italiana di Geopolitica [Limes Italian Journal of Geopolitics]* 6, pp. 195–199.

Shambaugh, David. 2013. *China Goes Global: The Partial Power*. Oxford: Oxford University Press.

Shambaugh, David. 2015. "China's Soft Power Push: The Search for Respect," *Foreign Affairs* 94(4), pp. 99–107.

Shanghaiist. 2009. "CCP to Publish Party Ideology Internationally," July 24. http://shanghaiist.com/2009/07/24/just_when_we_thought_that.php.

Shu, Xintian. 2010. *Zhangwo guoji guanxi miyue: wenhua, ruan shili yu Zhongguo dui wai zhanlüe [Mastering the Code of International Relations: Culture, Soft Power and China's Foreign Strategy]*. Shanghai: Shanghai renmin chubanshe.

Sudworth, John. 2014. "Confucius Institute: The Hard Side of China's Soft Power," *BBC News*, December 22. www.bbc.co.uk/news/world-asia-china-30567743.

Suzuki, Shogo. 2010. "The Myth and Reality of China's 'Soft Power'," in Inderjeet Parmar and Michael Cox (eds.), *Soft Power and US Foreign Policy: Theoretical, Historical and Contemporary Perspectives*. London and New York: Routledge, pp. 199–214.

Wagner, Christian. 2010. "India's Soft Power: Prospects and Limitations," *India Quarterly* 66(4), pp. 333–342.

Wang, Hongying and Yeh-Chung Lu. 2008. "The Conception of Soft Power and Its Policy Implications: A Comparative Study of China and Taiwan," *Journal of Contemporary China* 17(56), pp. 425–447.

Wang, Huning. 1993. "Zuowei guojia shili de wenhua: ruan quanli" ["Culture as National Power: Soft Power"], *Fudan xuebao (shehui kexue ban)* [*Fudan Journal (Social Science Edition)*] 3, pp. 91–96, 75.

Watanabe, Yasushi and David L. McConnell (eds.). 2008. *Soft Power Superpowers: Cultural and National Assets of Japan and the United States*. Armonk, NY: M.E. Sharpe.

Weaver, Matthew. 2018. "Chinese Reporter Who Allegedly Slapped Tory Conference Delegate Released by Police," *The Guardian*, October 2. www.theguardian.com/politics/2018/oct/02/chinese-reporter-who-allegedly-slapped-tory-conference-delegate-released.

Wenhuaruan shili yanjiu [*Studies in Cultural Soft Power*], Wuhan: Wuhan University.

Wu, Vivian and Adam Chen. 2009. "Beijing in 45b Yuan Global Media Drive: State Giants to Lead Image Campaign," *South China Morning Post*, January 13.

Xinhua. 2018. "Yi 'si ge zixin' tuijin xin shidai Zhongguo tese shehui zhuyi weida shiye" ["Use 'Four Self-Confidences' to Advance the Great Task of Socialism with Chinese Characteristics for a New Era"], July 9. www.xinhuanet.com/politics/2018-07/09/c_1123096720.htm.

Yan, Xuetong. 2017. "China Can Thrive in the Trump Era," *The New York Times*, January 25. www.nytimes.com/2017/01/25/opinion/china-can-thrive-in-the-trump-era.html.

Yi, Heng. 2009. *Wenhua zhuquan yu guojia wenhua ruan shili* [*Cultural Sovereignty and National Cultural Soft Power*]. Beijing: Shehui kexue wenxian chubanshe.

Zhan, Dexiong. 2016. "Zhongguo huayu yu meiti de zeren" ["China's Discourse and the Responsibilities of the Media"], *Wenhua ruan shili yanjiu* [*Studies in Cultural Soft Power*] 3, pp. 50–53.

Zhang, Guozuo (ed.). 2011. *Zhongguo wenhua ruan shili yanjiu baogao (2010)* [*Chinese Cultural Soft Power Development Report (2010)*]. Beijing: Shehui kexue wenxian chubanshe.

Zhao, Suisheng. 2009. "The Prospect of China's Soft Power: How Sustainable," in Mingjiang Li (ed.), *Soft Power: China's Emerging Strategy in International Politics*. Lanham, MD: Rowman and Littlefield, pp. 247–266.

Zhu, Ying. 2012. *Two Billion Eyes: The Story of China Central Television*. New York: New Press.

PART 1

Debating China's soft power strategy

1

PROJECTION OF CHINA'S SOFT POWER IN THE NEW CENTURY

Reconstruction of the traditional Chinese world order

Suisheng Zhao

Once an ancient empire in East Asia, China began a steady decline in the 19th century and suffered defeats and invasions by imperialist foreign powers. After more than a century of struggle for rejuvenation, China has resurged in the 21st century to regain the glory it enjoyed two centuries ago. China's rise has included building tangible economic-military power and an attempt to raise political-cultural power to enhance its statecraft. As a matter of fact, "The concept of soft-power advocacy has made a strong impression in China" (People's Daily Online, 2006) after Joseph Nye made the conceptual distinction between hard and soft power. The utility of soft power has become one of the most discussed topics in Chinese media and academic circles. In the meantime, the Chinese government has surged in its investments in "soft power" diplomacy.

China has readily embraced the concept of soft power because, as Joseph Nye indicated, "in a global information age, soft sources of power such as culture, political values, and diplomacy are part of what makes a great power. Success depends not only on whose army wins, but also on whose story wins" (Nye, 2005). In particular, the concept offers a tool to ease the anxieties among some countries in East Asia where China had a long history of cultural and political dominance, about what sort of great power China is poised to be. China's military modernization and muscle-flexing has produced mounting suspicions and growing frictions in its relations with some of its neighboring countries embroiled in territorial disputes. To calm fears of their neighbors, Chinese leaders have claimed that China's rise will be peaceful because its great power aspirations are different from the imperialism and hegemony of the Western powers. To support the claims, Chinese leaders and scholars have evoked China's past as a peaceful nation to project a benevolent governance and benign hierarchy of a China-centered East Asian order that is purportedly unique and more peaceful than its Western counterparts. Some Chinese scholars even went so far as to argue that imperial China resisted the temptation of expansion and won the admiration of its neighbors. The collapse of the Chinese world order, therefore, was a result of the clash of civilizations between the benevolent East Asian system and the brutal European-centered nation-state system. China's rise is thus to restore justice in an unjust world and will bring peace and order to the region. A connection between China's imperial past and its contemporary peaceful rise is thus established.

This chapter will start with an exploration of the Chinese rediscovery and reconstruction of the traditional Chinese world order in the 21st century and then place the Chinese reconstruction in the context of scholarly debate about the traditional Chinese world order and particularly its critiques. The third part examines the irony that while Chinese leaders have presented a harmonious world order to its neighbors, they have adopted a social Darwinist worldview and approach to maximize China's power and security and expand its influence and control over its neighborhoods. The conclusion looks at the gap between China's efforts at soft power projection and the results.

Reconstruction of the benevolent Chinese world order

World order is "an aggregate conception of dominant values, norms, and structures as well as of established patterns of actors' behavior that give shape and substance to international society at any given time" (Kim, 1991, p. 4). The modern world order began to acquire its present shape and definition more than three centuries ago with the emergence of a nation-state system in Europe. The principle of state sovereignty has provided the general framework from which evolved specific state practices on war, peace, commerce and political competition. World order meant very different things to the Chinese prior to the coming of the Western powers in the 19th century. John Fairbank and his colleagues coined a concept of Chinese world order known as "a Sinocentric hierarchy" to characterize imperial China's relations with its East Asian neighbors (Zhao, 2015). The concept, which has become a conventional paradigm ever since, portrayed China as an Asian Empire with a self-sufficient agricultural economy and workable bureaucracy, overshadowing other nations in the region, holding a different world outlook from the West and maintaining an ethnically based hierarchical regional order.

This Chinese centrality was based on the belief of "China being internal, large, and high and the barbarians being external, small, and low" (Yang, 1968, p. 20). The concept of legal equality or sovereignty of individual states did not exist. All countries arranged themselves hierarchically around the Chinese emperor known as the Son of Heaven (天子). China's central position was manifested in a highly sophisticated tributary system, a term John K. Fairbank started using in the 1940s, that was, in effect, the only institution for international relations in the region (Fairbank and Teng, 1941, pp. 135–148). Imperial China considered other countries its cultural inferiors, in recognition of which they were expected to appear in the Chinese capital, make obeisance to the emperor and present tribute.

Although the tributary system sometimes embarrassed the tributary states and bore a heavy cost to China, it was described as valuable for both the tributary states and the tribute receiver. For tributary states, the presentation of tributes enabled them to trade with China through the legalization of controlled trade along their frontiers (Ch'en, 1968, p. 161). Politically, the tributary states received validation of their political power from the Chinese emperor in the form of patents of office and investiture. This was a valuable technique for the establishment of legitimacy by local rulers. The Chinese court also benefited from this system as the tribute received from neighboring countries was the ritual that acknowledged the superiority of the Chinese culture, recognized the greatness of the Chinese civilization, and acknowledged the existence of Chinese authority and, consequently, the inviolability of China's frontiers. Economically, China was able to trade with its neighbors for items necessary without admitting China's dependence on these items of trade with the barbarians, thereby preserving "the myth of China's self-sufficiency" (Mancall, 1963, p. 30).

China's centrality was regarded as a function of its civilization and virtue, particularly the virtue of China's rulers. As Lucian Pye suggested, "the Chinese, with their Confucianism, created an elaborate intellectual structure of an ethical order which all enlightened peoples were expected to acknowledge and respect" (Pye, 1985, p. 41). The Chinese world order, therefore, was as much as an ethical as a political phenomenon. Harmony internationally and domestically was the product of the emperor's virtue and the highest goal of a Chinese society. Thus, the Chinese emperor's superior position exhibited through proper conduct, including ceremonies, gave one prestige among others and power over them. In the Chinese world order, hierarchical power relationship, therefore, was by definition more "moral" than in the West (Mancall, 1963, p. 31).

The prospect of China's reemergence as a great power in the wake of the 21st century has led to a rediscovery of the benign Chinese world order by Chinese leaders and scholars. Assuring the world of China's peaceful development, President Hu Jintao in his September 15, 2005, speech at the United Nations General Assembly presented the concept of harmonious world, which was derived from traditional Chinese thinking that "harmony" was at the core of dealing with everything from state affairs to neighborly relations (Liu, 2009, p. 479). After President Hu made the presentation, a *China Daily* story made it clear that the concept was part of China's soft power projection because the ideas of taking the peaceful development road and building a harmonious society and a harmonious world help resolve doubts on China's rapid development (People's Daily Online, 2006). Another article in *China Daily* confirmed that

China hopes to dissolve the misconception of its development as the 'China threat' by making its traditional value systems known to the world. . . . Once they come to know the Chinese people better, they will find out that harmony is an essential part of Chinese tradition and a country that values harmony poses absolutely no threat to the rest of the world.

(China Daily, 2006)

Since coming into office, President Xi Jinping has enthusiastically pushed Chinese officials, journalists and scholars to tell the so-called China story to the world as part of China's soft power offense. President Xi has become obsessed in citing Confucian classics and using Chinese history to explain China's domestic as well as foreign policy positions. He even went so far as to speak in Beijing as he hosted leaders from India and Myanmar that "China does not subscribe to the notion that a country is bound to seek hegemony when it grows in strength. Hegemony or militarism is not in the genes of the Chinese" (Reuters, 2014). President Xi repeated in another occasion that the deepest spiritual desire of a nation has to be found from "the genes' order (基因测序) of inherited national spirit (薪火相传的民族精神)." The pursuit of peace, concord and harmony (和平、和睦、和谐的追求) has been deeply rooted in the spiritual world of the Chinese nation and the blood of the Chinese people. China's unswerving pursuit of peaceful development represents the peace-loving cultural tradition the Chinese nation has inherited and carried forward over the past thousands of years. He cited Confucian wisdoms such as "A warlike state, however big it may be, will eventually perish" (国虽大,好战必亡), "Peace is of paramount importance" (以和为贵), "seek harmony without uniformity" (和而不同), "replace weapons of war with gifts of jade and silk" (化干戈为玉帛), "bring prosperity to the nation and security to the people" (国泰民安), "forming friendships with neighbors" (睦邻友邦), "achieve universal peace" (天下太平) and "Great Harmony of Tianxia" (天下大同) to prove his point. He asserted that "China was long one of the most powerful countries in the world. Yet it never engaged in colonialism or aggression. The pursuit of peaceful development represents the peace-loving cultural tradition of the Chinese nation over the past several thousand years, a tradition that we have inherited and carried forward." He thereby proclaimed that "the Chinese nation is a peace-loving nation" (中华民族是爱好和平的民族) (Xinhua News Agency, 2014).

As part of the rediscovery effort, Chinese scholars have reconstructed the Chinese world order. Portraying the Chinese order as a self-centered tributary system (自我为中心的朝贡体系) and the etiquette system of the heavenly dynasty (天朝礼治体系), one Chinese scholar found that Imperial China produced an open hierarchy as the foundation of the East Asian international system (东亚国际体系的原始形态) (Guo, 2014). A traditional Chinese term, Tianxia (all-under-heaven, 天下), based on Wangdao (the royal ethics, 王道), has emerged as a uniquely "Chinese normative principle of international relations in contrast with the principles of sovereignty and the structure of international anarchy which form the core of the contemporary international system" (Carlson, 2011, p. 89).

In his book, *All-Under-Heaven System* (天下体制) and many articles, Zhao Tingyang, a Chinese philosopher, describes Tianxia as a universal system inherited

Tianxia

from the Zhou dynasty about 3,000 years ago (Zhao, 2005). Designed to create the compatibility of all peoples of all nations, Tianxia presupposes the Oneness of the universe (天下归一) as the political principle of "inclusion of all" in the world. Tianxia commits to the Oneness as the intact wholeness that implies the acceptance of the diversities in the world where nothing is left out and no one is treated as an outsider (Zhao, 2006, pp. 29–41). This is a world order with the emphasis on harmony defined as reciprocal dependence, reciprocal improvement or the perfect fitting for different things. Guanxi (reciprocal relationship) thus became the organizational principle of the Tianxia system (Zhao, 2009, pp. 5–18). The Tianxia system, maintained by cultural attraction and ruling by virtue, is embodied in the Chinese ideal of perpetual peace. Notably different from the aggressive empires that existed in other places, imperial China was more concerned with establishing itself as an everlasting power than with the plight of endless expansion because of the unaggressive and adaptable characteristics of the Chinese culture (Zhao, 2014, p. 128). Qin Yaqing of Beijing Foreign Affairs University also states that

> the core of the notion of Tianxia revolves around the idea of a "Chinese system." . . . Tianxia is where nature and humanity intersect, a space where political authority and social order interact. . . . Order is always intrinsic in the system envisioned by the notion of Tianxia. Within the Tianxia system, structure is hierarchical because only such an arrangement could sustain its stability and harmonious order. Order could only be achieved when there is a clear stratification of classes and there is likewise an orderly relationship between them.
>
> (Qin, 2011, pp. 42–43)

Tianxia is thus presented as a world system in contrast to the anarchic Westphalian system, which is regarded as conducive to discord and war. *Chinese Social Sciences News* (中国社会科学报) published a special session in 2014 to discuss the differences between the Tianxia system and the contemporary international system dominated by Western powers. Zhang Chi-hsiung of Taiwan's Academia Sinica suggests that Tianxia was a harmonious world system expressed by the following equations: all-under-the-heaven = the Chinese world = center + periphery = Chinese + barbarians = we race + they race = kingdom + tributary = China + tributary = suzerainty + tributary states = Chinese world empire = tributary common community = China-centered common community > East Asian common community. The China-centered hierarchical order was a Tianxia common community (天下共同体), in which the center protected the periphery and the periphery subordinated to the center (中心保护周边，周边藩屏中心), forming a pattern of interdependence, co-existence and co-prosperity between China and its four frontiers of neighbors (形成中国与四邻互相依赖、共存共荣的格局). China never interfered in the internal affairs of tributary states. Nationality, autonomy and kingdom self-governance were developed. The traditional East Asian international system, therefore, maintained stability for more than 2,000 years (Chang, 2014).

Royal ethics (王道) is used to explain why the perpetual peace of Tianxia was created and maintained. Yan Xuetong of Tsinghua University led a project on China's pre-Qin political thoughts, which determined that ancient Chinese thinkers advised rulers to rely on ethics (道), benevolence (仁) and morality (德) to win the world (取天下), and to take a defensive posture (非攻) using benevolent government (仁政) to rule the world (治天下) (Yan, Xu, et al., 2009). Citing ancient Chinese philosopher Xunzi, Yan distinguishes three types of ethics in ancient China: royal ethics (王道), hegemonic ethics (霸道) and tyranny (强道). Royal ethics focused on peaceful means to win the hearts and minds of the people at home and abroad. Tyranny—based on military force—inevitably created enemies. Hegemonic ethics lay in between: frequently indifferent to moral concerns, it often involved violence against non-allies but did not cheat the people at home or allies abroad. Royal ethics would win in any competition with hegemony or tyranny (Yan, 2011). Xing Qi, Vice President of the Chinese Cultural Promotion Society (中国文化促进会), claimed that royal ethics played an invaluable role in the stabilization and prosperity of the Chinese cultural ring (中华文化圈) because the starting point of royal ethics was an internal holy process (内圣) rather than an external imposition to reach a harmony between human and nature. The highest level of royal ethics is to achieve the external royalty (外王), in which the emphasis is to avoid hegemony in handling relations and reach harmony among different peoples, nations and civilizations. Harmony, in this case, is not uniformity, but rather seeking common ground while preserving differences (和而不同) (Xin, 2011). Wei Zhijiang of Zhongshan University in Guangzhou even argues that the Chinese world order created an East Asian security system guided by royal ethics and etiquette (礼制), which was widely shared by the vassal states (Wei, 2014).

Many Chinese scholars have portrayed imperial China as a peaceful state, working within the premise of royal ethics. What sustained the political centripetal forces of the surrounding regions was morality, not coercion. The ancient Chinese rulers developed a very prudent and defensive strategic culture and tried hard to arrive at their objectives without using force (不战而屈人之兵). Rulers were very cautious to wage just wars (义战) based on moral rather than material interests. The clear difference between just and unjust wars was the motivation of the war and its effect on civilians. People's support was the most important standard to measure whether or not a war was just. The ultimate goal of just wars was not only to punish the war criminals but also to reestablish the universal moral ethics of "unity and harmony of heaven and human beings" (Liu, 2014, p. 562). Two Chinese military scholars, therefore, generalize the following three paradigm differences between the imperial Chinese and the Western statecrafts: "justice" versus "interests," "human factors" versus "weapon factors" and "stratagem" versus "strength" (Zhang and Yao, 1996, pp. 209–221).

In comparison with Western imperialist countries that used coercive power to build colonies, the Chinese world order was thus more civil because it caused the tributary states to admire China without using force. In the traditional Chinese world, the relations among countries were in harmony based on benevolent governance (仁治). East Asian countries shared the Chinese cultural ideals and values that emphasized peace (和), harmony (合) and a middle way (中庸) (Xiong, 2013). Quoting Tang Emperor Li Shiming who said that "although China has been regarded superior and barbarians inferior since ancient time(s), I love them all the same" (自故皆贵中华，贱夷狄，朕独爱之如一), one Chinese scholar even went so far as to claim that "Emperor Li emphasized equality among all nationalities more than one thousand years ago, showing the open-minded Tang ruler in foreign relations" (Li, 2012). With the emphasis on etiquette and trade, the tributary system "forged the common ground for Imperial China and its surrounding regions, and served as the foundation for exchange and coordination between the two sides." Emphasizing benevolent governance, etiquette, peace and denying the imperialistic nature, imperial China and its relations with surrounding regions were far more advanced than the colonialism of Western countries. Yet some Chinese scholars have argued that the root of all troubles in Chinese diplomacy today is China's lost opportunities for expansion because of being pedantic and caring too much about morality and principles. "The surrounding countries should be grateful for China's benevolent governance, and that the imperial order should be re-established, yet they don't like moderation and self-restraint as part of the imperial tradition" (Yu, 2014, p. 1183).

The scholarly debate on the Chinese world order

This type of reconstruction of the Chinese world order and its disintegration is obviously a narrative that serves China's foreign policy and strategic objectives rather than reflecting on historical facts. In fact, there has been an emerging scholarly debate about whether imperial China was uniquely benevolent. Some Western scholars have accepted the Chinese reconstruction and argue that the benign Chinese world order as more peaceful than the European system and China's reemergence has, therefore, created an opportunity to reshape the Western-centric world order. Martin Jacques published a book in 2009 with a sensational title, *When China Rules the World: The End of the Western World and the Birth of a New Global Order*, which argues that China is a "civilization-state," inheritor of the oldest continuous history in the world, whose underlying cultural unity and self-confidence were without equal. Long before the West, its rulers created the first modern bureaucracy, imbued with a Confucian outlook, controlling domestic subjects more by moral education than force, and organizing adjacent regions into a consensual tributary system. As it rapidly reassumes its traditional place at the center of East Asia, the old tributary system would resurface in a modern form, contemporary ideas of racial hierarchy would be redrawn and China's age-old sense of superiority would reassert itself. China's rise signals the end of global dominance by the West and the emergence of a world which it would come to shape in a host of different ways and which would become increasingly disconcerting and unfamiliar to those who live in the West (Jacques, 2009).

David Kang's (2010) book argues that although China was the unquestioned hegemon in the region, the tributary order entailed military, cultural and economic dimensions that afforded its participants immense latitude. Because the tributary system played a positive role in maintaining stability in East Asia and in fostering diplomatic and commercial exchange, China engaged in only two large-scale conflicts with its principal neighbors, Korea, Vietnam and Japan, from the founding of the Ming dynasty in 1368 to the start of the Opium Wars in 1841. These four states otherwise fostered peaceful and long-lasting relationships with one another (Kang, 2010). In an earlier book, he criticized those scholars who downplayed the role of political cultures and suggested a rising China would be a destabilizing force in the region. He instead argued that China's rise had brought about more peace and stability than at any time since the Opium Wars of 1839–1841. East Asian states had grown closer to China because certain preferences and beliefs were responsible for maintaining stability in the region (Kang, 2007).

On the other side of the debate, William A. Callahan criticizes the Fairbank paradigm as an "idealized version of a hierarchical Sinocentric world order with the Chinese empire at the core and loyal tributary states and barbarians at the periphery" (Callahan, 2011, p. 6). Peter Perdue labels the tributary system a myth, which endured because it reflected the political concern of the time. Many of the scholars writing with Fairbank in the 1960s were émigrés from China and, in opposition to prevailing views that China was merely another totalitarian Communist state during the height of the Cold War, they argued for China's distinctive history as a long civilized society, with the implication that the current Communist direction might be temporary, and that long-term historical trends would prevail. Although the paradigm now serves useful purposes for those who endorse and predict the coming hegemony of China in Asia, Perdue argues that there is a "scholarly consensus" that "there was no tributary system" and "historians who investigate the actual conduct of foreign relations by Chinese dynasties have, by now, nearly uniformly rejected the validity of this concept" (Perdue, 2015). To prove his point, Perdue cites the contribution by Mark Mancall in the Fairbank volume that "the concept of the tribute system is a Western invention for descriptive purposes. . . . The Confucian scholar-bureaucrat did not conceive of a tribute system (there is no Chinese word for it) as an institutional complex complete within itself or distinct from the other institutions of Confucian society" (Mancall, 1968, p. 63).

Indeed, there is not a Chinese term accurately corresponding to the English term. The closest terms in Chinese are 进贡 (pay tribute) and 朝贡 (pay respect and tribute), but neither of them implies an institutionalized relationship. A

Chinese scholar, therefore, distinguishes the tributary (朝贡) system from what he called the patriarchal-vassal (宗藩) system. Tributary relations were not institutional and were often conducted on a case-by-case basis in more or less equal footing between imperial China and the tributary states for the purpose of trade. Only was the patriarchal-vassal system institutionalized and maintained as a part of hierarchical monarch relations (君臣关系). The Chinese emperor treated local rulers not as equals but as vassals, which accepted the canonization (册封) of the Chinese court. The vassal states had to pay tributes regularly, following the rituals defined by the Chinese court. During the Ming and Qing periods, there were three vassal states that had institutionalized tributary relations with China: Korea, Annam (Vietnam) and Ryukyu. Nepal, Laos, Burma and other Southeast Asian states only had irregular tributary relations with China (Wei, 2014).

A Thailand scholar's study of diplomatic documents (letters) exchanged between the Qing court and the Siamese (Thai) court in the 1780s found that although Siam responded to the tributary system, it did not accept the Chinese perception of world order. In Siamese letters to the Chinese emperor, the Siamese court preserved its identity as an independent kingdom equal to the Qing court. When the tributary missions arrived in the Chinese port, Guangzhou, the Chinese officials edited the letters in their translation to comply with the Chinese hierarchical concept before presenting them to the Chinese emperors. The Chinese letters from the Qing court to the Siamese court, written in hierarchical terms, were similarly edited in translation and arrived in the Siamese court as diplomatic documents exchanged between two equal rulers. Examining the Siamese tributary articles and the Chinese imperial gifts, this study found that the major role played by the tributary missions was commercial. Through imperial gifts from China, Siam received certain luxuries and commodities unavailable locally, whereas China acquired goods and medicines. Since trade with China was vital to the Siamese, they were willing to trade through the tributary system, but the Siamese court never accepted the canonization from the Qing Court (Manomaivibool, 2014).

In this case, Perdue's criticism of the tributary system as a myth makes sense because most of the tributary relations were more ritualistic than substantive. But his flat rejection of the existence of the tributary system went too far. Odd Arne Westad presents a more balanced view suggesting that "there was no *overall* 'tributary system'" and that the tributary relationship was one of a variety of ways imperial China conducted foreign relations. He found that the Qing operated in three distinct spheres of foreign affairs in the 19th century: Central Asia, where the theme was expansion; coastal Asia, where the theme was trade tribute; and Russia, where the theme was diplomacy. Recognizing the existence of "a Sino-centric system, in which Chinese culture was central to the self-identification of many elite groups in the surrounding Asian countries," Westad raised the critical question—what if Chinese centrality was maintained mostly by cultural superiority or coercive power? His study revealed that "The dramatic Qing penetration of Central Asia is a story of intense conflict and,

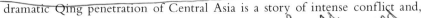

eventually, of genocide." His evidence was the Qianlong emperor's expedition in the 1750s into the Zungharia, a mighty khanate led by Mongols, covering the territory between western Central Asia and the Mongolian heartland, down to the Tibetan borders. After having defeated Zungharia in battle, the Qianlong emperor ordered his army to kill all of the Zunghar elite whom they could lay their hands on. "Then he incorporated most of eastern Zungharia and the minor Khanates to its south into China, creating one region that Qianlong, triumphantly, referred to as China's new frontier (Xinjiang)" (Westad, 2012, pp. 9–10).

Indeed, warfare was a constant in imperial China that was often in disunion or under foreign invasion. Prior to the Qin dynasty, China was divided into many small warring kingdoms fighting wars to balance power. After the establishment of the first Chinese dynasty by the Qin emperor, the geographical scope and military power of the Chinese empire began to expand immensely. China's ruler during the Yuan dynasty, Kublai Khan, expanded the empire by military expedition, stretching across Central Asia, Burma and Vietnam. In 1263, Kublai Khan made Korea his vassal and aspired to the conquest of Japan. His fleets twice reached the shores of Japan in 1274 and 1281 but were shipwrecked by typhoons, which were to become legendary in Japan as the *kamikaze*, or "divine wind" (Buss, 1964, pp. 34–35). The last Chinese dynasty, Qing, expanded to unprecedented size, nearly doubling in land from the previous Ming dynasty mostly through military force.

It is from this perspective that Peter Perdue's study claims that the China of today is a product of the vast conquests of the Manchu rulers, who defeated the Zunghar Mongols, and brought all of modern Xinjiang and Mongolia under their control, while gaining dominant influence in Tibet (Perdue, 2010). Perdue argues that the techniques used by the Ming and Qing dynasties to legitimize their rule over their subjects and to claim superiority over rivals were not radically different from those of other empires. Citing the comparative history studies that pointed to substantial similarities of the Ming and Qing to the Russian, Mughal and Ottoman imperial formations, or even to early modern France, Perdue suggested that the concept of "colonialism" (殖民主义) could be usefully employed to describe certain aspects of Qing practice (Perdue, 2015).

The emerging literature on Chinese strategic culture since the 1980s has also documented that the Chinese empire was maintained as much by military force as by virtue, even though Confucian teachings, of harmonious rule through the civilized power, stated to the contrary. Viewing war as a central feature of interstate relations, imperial China used military force as strategically and constantly as other empires. Alastair Iain Johnston's study of Ming dynasty classics reveals two sets of Chinese strategic culture. One is a symbolic or idealized set and the other is an operational set. The symbolic set is based on Confucianism—that conflict is avoidable through the promotion of good government and the co-opting of external threats. When force is used, it should be applied defensively, minimally, only under unavoidable conditions, and then only in the name of the righteous restoration of a moral-political order. The symbolic set, for the most part, is disconnected from the operational decision rules governing strategy and appears mostly in a discourse designed, in part, to justify behavior in culturally acceptable terms. The operational set assumes that conflict is a constant feature of human affairs, due largely to the threatening nature of the enemy. In this zero-sum context, the application of violence is highly effective for dealing with the enemy. This operation set, in essence, argues that the best way of dealing with security threats is to eliminate them through the use of force (Johnston, 1995). Chinese decision makers have internalized this ideationally based strategic culture that has persisted across vastly different interstate systems, regime types, levels of technology and types of threat (Johnston, 1996).

Imperial China had to use military force to defend and expand the empire because its territorial domain, defined loosely by its cultural principles, was not always accepted by its neighbors. Following the policy of fusion and expansion (融合扩展), whenever imperial China was powerful, it always tried to expand it frontiers and territories (开疆扩土) by claiming suzerainty over its smaller neighbors. The expansion, however, often met with resistance. Although Vietnam, Korea and Burma became the vassals of the Middle Kingdom, they refused to be fused (融合) into the Chinese empire. Mongols, Tibetans and other Central Asian peoples accepted Buddhism and Islamism rather than Confucianism. Never shy about military conquest to sustain the illusion and sometimes the reality of imperial power, the Chinese empire had to deploy various instruments of persuasion and coercion, including the art of statecraft or using one neighbor against another, awarding those who were obedient and chastising those who were defiant. Such practices worked successfully when the empire was unified and strong. When the empire was weak and divided, the neighbors in turn conquered it.

The clash of civilizations and social Darwinism

Although some scholars have criticized the Chinese world order as a myth and an idealized version of imperial China, many Chinese scholars still insist that imperial China was a uniquely benevolent and peaceful empire with war employed only as last resort for defensive purposes. Rejecting the comparability of the Chinese empire with other empires, some Chinese scholars criticize Western historians such as Peter Perdue and Odd Arne Westad as writing a "New Qing History" (新清史) that describes the Qing dynasty as having an expansion tendency similar to other empires at the time (具有与同时代的其他帝国类似的扩张倾向). Their works are not welcome in China because their "findings" violate (有悖于) the Chinese positon that the Kangxi emperor's Western expedition (康熙西征) was aimed at maintaining the unity of the multiple nationalities. Chinese scholars have regarded Perdue and some other Western historians who endorse the China threat theories as having tried to discover the aggressive and imperialist characters of ancient Chinese history to demonstrate the unavoidable connection between today's China and its imperial characters in history (Lu, 2012).

Looking at imperial China as uniquely benign and the Chinese world order as stable and peaceful, some Chinese scholars have come to see the collapse of the Chinese empire as a result of the clash of civilizations that led to the century of humiliation. China was not only forced into the international system dominated by European powers where it lost its tributary states, but was also treated unequally and suffered in the hands of imperialist powers. Accepting the statement by Lowell Dittmer that "The Sino-Western conflict in the nineteenth century was not so much an international conflict as it was a system-to-system conflict, a mismatch between Western nationalism and Chinese culturalism" (Dittmer and Kim, 1994, p. 249), Chang Chi-hisung went further arguing that "the primary course for the collapse of the East Asian order were the clash of the principles of international orders between the East and the West" (东西方国际秩序原理的冲突). He lamented that as the tributary states, managed by the Vassal Affairs Department (礼部藩属), were lost and became colonies of the Western powers, imperial China was downgraded (降为) from the Tianxia royal dynasty (天下皇朝) to a sovereign state (主权国家) and reluctantly to advocate (不得已乃改倡) the sovereign equality (主权平等). Imperialist powers defeated China by force and then repudiated the Chinese benevolent governance. A treaty system (条约体制) was formed through international law and unequal treaties while the Chinese world order principles and the status it knew were completely repudiated and eventually extinguished (Chang, 2014).

Indeed, the process through which China was forcibly drawn into the European-dominated international system was through the demise of the Chinese world order, a process of "China's struggle to resist aggressive European expansion, to adjust itself to the changing international realities, to meet its problems without totally abandoning its imperial tradition, and finally to accept slowly and gradually, though sometimes reluctantly, some of the European standards, institutions, rules and values" (Zhang, 1991, p. 16). This process took several centuries. China's defeat in the 1840 Opium War was a heavy blow to the Chinese sense of superiority and led to the collapse of the Chinese world order. In the 60 years after its humiliating defeat, the Qing government was forced to sign numerous treaties with foreign powers. This began a transition from the old tributary system to a treaty system. The Chinese empire was forced to enter into "the Eurocentric family of nations" (Fairbank, 1968, p. 258). The new treaty system affirmed the principle of diplomatic equality between China and its treaty partners. The first decade of the 20th century was the end of transition from the Chinese world order to a modern nation-state system. China no longer constituted a world unto itself, but was part of the greater world, a unit in the anarchical international system. After the long and sustained resistance, the Chinese world order collapsed, giving way to an international order defined by Western powers.

Ironically, however, while the wars, unequal treaties, and territorial losses suffered by China during the century of humiliation were the painful road that the Middle Kingdom walked into the modern nation-state system, the Chinese quickly embraced the concepts of territorial sovereignty and became a zealous defender of its sovereign rights. Embracing the Western concepts of legal equality and territorial sovereignty, the Chinese political elite moved to vigorously defend Chinese national and territorial sovereignty against foreign invasion. When China began to accept the idea of equality among nation-states and struggled to defend its sovereignty, however, the world had come under the domination of imperialist powers that did not treat weak nations as equals. This was a social Darwinian world in the eyes of many Chinese elites. The status of a nation-state was determined by its economic and military strength. China was stagnant and weak and therefore had to fight for a status equal to other nation-states.

Coming to recognize a social Darwinian world in which the status of a nation-state was determined by its economic and military strength, Chinese intellectuals and political leaders have become die-hard realists who believe that international politics is a struggle for power and have sought to maximize China's security by expanding influence and control over its immediate neighborhoods, and in some cases, far beyond. The world is unjust and unfair only in the sense that China was stagnant and weak and therefore had to suffer and be humiliated in the late 19th and the early 20th centuries. The collapse of the China-centered East Asian order was because China's strength (实力) was not strong enough to defend its existence. China has to follow the iron law (铁则) of the strongest survival (强者生存) and the weakest eliminated (弱者淘汰) to become the strongest again (Chang, 2014).

Emphasis on territorial sovereignty thus characterized much of China's thinking of international relations in the 20th century, and this has continued into the 21st century even as many of the originators of that system have begun to move away from strong views on state sovereignty. China's efforts to establish diplomatic recognition with other countries of the world on a reciprocal basis, and to participate in the United Nations and other world organizations with the condition of non-interference of domestic affairs, speak to an insistence on the absolute nation-state sovereign. China's political leaders have all shared a deep commitment to overcome humiliation, secure redress of past grievances and achieve a position of equality with all other major powers. That is why a persistent theme of Chinese foreign policy has been to win back the territories lost during the country's time of internal disintegration and humiliation by other powers in the 19th and 20th centuries. China's rise in the 21st century has reinforced this social Darwinist thinking of international relations.

Translating its wealth into a stronger military and more assertive regional posture, China has behaved increasingly as a typical muscle-flexing great power—seeking dominance in the Asia-Pacific and expanded interests by advancing its

[margin handwritten notes: "core interests", "expanded core interests", "China's social Darwinism or IR vs. benign Chinese world order"]

territorial claims in the East and South China Seas. Core interest (核心利益), a new term in China's foreign policy vocabulary, has suddenly become fashionable and appears more frequently in Chinese statements. Obviously chosen with intent to signal the resolve in China's sovereignty and territorial claims that it deems important enough to go to war over, core interest is defined as "the bottom-line of national survival" and "essentially nonnegotiable" (Chen, 2011, p. 4). While China's official statements on the sovereignty and territorial integrity used to refer almost exclusively to Taiwan, Tibet and Xinjiang issues (Wu, 2012, p. 393), Chinese leaders have expanded the core interest issues to include territorial claims in the South and East China Seas. Taking an unusually strong position to assert its sovereignty in these disputed waters, Beijing repeatedly attempted to prevent Vietnamese vessels from exploring oil and gas while it sent Chinese oil rigs to disputed waters with Vietnam, deployed ships to blockade the Philippines garrison on a contested shoal and rejected Manila's bid for International Court of Justice arbitration, and scaled up land reclamation of "island-building" on the disputed reefs in the South China Sea. It also sent law enforcement ships and fighter jets to challenge the status quo of the Japanese administration of the disputed Diaoyu/Senkaku Islands following the Japanese government's decision to nationalize some of them, and declared an Air Defense Identification Zone (ADIZ) covering the Diaoyu/Senkaku Islands as well as the greater part of the East China Sea, including the Socotra Rock (also known as Ieodo or Parangdo), which has been effectively controlled by South Korea but claimed by China as the Suyan Rock.

China's social Darwinist view of international relations, in this case, is in contrast to its reconstruction of the benign Chinese world order and has been a liability in its diplomacy. In response to China's rise in the 21st century, a Western scholar raised a controversial question: "Are Westerners ready to adjust to the Chinese civilization's re-emergence as one of the main sources of global order?" (Gosset, 2006). He did not give a definite answer at the time, but one may find some important clues by looking at the evolving Chinese view of the world order after China's entry into the modern international system. It is from this perspective that June Teufel Dreyer wrote that "Supporters of the revival of tianxia as a model for today's world are essentially misrepresenting the past to reconfigure the future, distorting it to advance a political agenda that is at best disingenuous and at worst dangerous." She also points to the contradiction that the Chinese government has accepted these principles yet zealously defends its sovereign prerogatives even as it makes efforts to educate the world on the virtues of a Confucian Great Harmony and its supporters advocate following a somewhat nebulously defined Chinese model (Dreyer, 2015). One Korean scholar also points out that while Choson Korea was China's tributary state with independence in domestic affairs and diplomacy assured in the Chinese world order, the Qing court attempted to legally incorporate it as part of China's territory by international treaty in the 1880s but ended in failure. As a continuation of such expansionist policy, Republican Chinese textbooks and historical geography regarded Choson Korea and other tributary states in East Asia as recently lost Chinese territories. Such an "expansionist territorial imagination" has come back and gained ground in China as it is reemerging as a great power (Yu, 2014).

Conclusion

The reconstruction of the traditional Chinese world order is only one tool in the growing Chinese soft power tool kit. Sometimes known as "public opinion warfare," the projection of China's soft power includes establishment of more than 500 Confucius Institutes on university and secondary school campuses around the world, massive investments in setting up English-speaking China Central Television bureaus around the world, flooding major newspapers with *China Daily* inserts, establishment of a Chinese government scholarship fund for foreign students to enroll in Chinese universities for year-long studies, high-visibility projects such as the Beijing Olympics and the Shanghai Expo, and providing a national development model, the Beijing Consensus, as an alternative to the Washington Consensus.

With all these efforts and investments and extensive branding campaign, China has improved its soft power capacity, especially after President Donald Trump came to office in the United States. The annual Soft Power 30 Index published in July 2017 showed the US score falling nearly 10% from 2016, dropping from the first place to third, while China was up to 25th from 28th. One author of the Index commented that "While 'America First' has translated into less global leadership for the US, China has emerged an unlikely champion for globalization and environmentalism" (Liu, 2017).

While pockets of positive views regarding China can be found around the world, China's image has ranged between mixed and poor among all the major international polls for almost a decade. A May 2017 survey by the ASEAN found that more than 73% of correspondents had little or no confidence that Beijing would do the right thing in contributing to global peace, security and governance (PressReader, 2017). Although US global influence has dropped due to President Trump's "American First" policy, it still holds much more soft power than most countries, including China. A Chinese scholar admitted that China might one day overtake the United States in the size of the economy but may never overtake the United States in influence and leadership in the world (Xue, 2015). Another Chinese scholar found that China faced predicaments in devising an international discursive power, known as missing international discursive power (国际话语权缺失). China had never played a world leadership role in history. The traditional Chinese system (华夏体系) was only an East Asian system, not universal, and cannot automatically transform into modern discursive power (Wang, 2015). Until China develops values that appeal universally, it misses one of the core features of global leadership.

Beijing's overreliance on its economic prowess as the key diplomatic instrument reveals the short of credible normative power. Despite its rising economic

Money cannot buy loyalty [handwritten annotation]

wess and growing military might, China's efforts to use economic ties to influence other states' behavior have only achieved limited success. Money cannot buy loyalty. Influence does not simply derive from a country's coffers. While closer economic ties are important, they are hardly sufficient to build strong political and strategic trust between countries—especially those with conflicting security interests. China's efforts to project soft power often fail to resonate abroad partly because China displays little empathy with the sensitivities of those living beyond its borders (Jonquieres, 2016).

As a result, China's neighbors have hardly been convinced that China's rise is peaceful and China's great power aspiration is necessarily different from the imperialism and hegemony of Western powers. It is difficult to find any of China's neighbors who want to live under China's shadow or are keen to accept a Chinese-dominated regional order. China's rising power itself, in fact, has motivated some of its neighbors to pursue balancing activities, including realignment with the United States and with each other.

As for causes of the gap between China's efforts at soft power and the results, one study lists imbalance of resources, legitimacy concerns of its diplomacy and lack of a coherent agenda as three major factors hindering its efforts to project its soft power effectively (Gill and Huang, 2006, p. 26). Another study points to a blind spot in China's exercise of soft power as "the absence of Chinese non-governmental organizations (NGOs) on the international stage, which deprives China of a crucial soft power tool, hampers its public diplomacy, weakens the credibility of the messages it seeks to send out, and reduces the amount of feedback" (Lu, 2007). Still another study suggests two major factors that have constrained Beijing's ability to project its soft power. One is the gap between an increasingly cosmopolitan and confident foreign policy and a closed and rigid domestic political system. The other is the constant tensions between its multiple foreign policy objectives and the still nascent soft power resources. From this perspective, it claims that "soft power remains Beijing's underbelly and China still has a long way to go to become a true global power" (Huang and Sheng, 2006, p. 41). While all these factors are important, one scholar made a powerful explanation for the particular reason of the failure; that is, China's more assertive behavior toward its neighbors—in the South China and East China Seas and along the Indian–Chinese border—and its continuing military buildup has undercut its "peaceful rise" narrative with countries in the region and with the United States. Combined with the strategic uncertainties that arise from China's system of closed decision-making, Beijing's hard power policies have created a dynamic in which its soft power efforts have been less effective than they might otherwise have been (Schmitt, 2014).

mismatch [handwritten annotation in left margin]

References

Buss, Claude A. 1964. *Asia in the Modern World: A History of China, Japan, South and South-east Asia*. London: Coller-Macmillan Limited.

Callahan, William A. 2011. "Introduction: Tradition, Modernity, and Foreign Policy in China," in William A. Callahan and Elena Barabantseva (eds.), *China Orders the World: Normative Soft Power and Foreign Policy*. Washington, DC: Woodrow Wilson Center Press, pp. 1–17.

Carlson, Allen. 2011. "Moving Beyond Sovereignty? A Brief Consideration of Recent Changes in China's Approach to International Order and the Emergence of the *Tianxia* Concept," *Journal of Contemporary China* 20(68), pp. 89–102.

张启雄 [Chang, Chi-hsiung]. 2014. "近代东亚国际体系的崩解与再生" ["The Collapse and Rebirth of Modern East Asian International System"], 中国社会科学报 [*Chinese Social Science News*] 613, June 27. http://ex.cssn.cn/djch/djch_djchhg/guojishijiaoxiadeguojitixibianqian/201406/t20140627_1230778.shtml.

Ch'en, Ta-tuan. 1968. "Investiture of Liu-ch'iu Kings in the Ch'ing Period," in John K. Fairbank (ed.), *The Chinese World Order: Traditional China's Foreign Relations*. Cambridge, MA: Harvard University Press, pp. 135–164.

陈岳 [Chen, Yue]. 2011. "中国当前外交环境及应对" ["The Current International Environment and the Responses"], 现代国际关系 [*Contemporary International Relations*], November, p. 4.

China Daily. 2006. "'China Threat' Fear Countered by Culture," May 29. http://news.xinhuanet.com/english/2006-05/29/content_4613721.htm.

Dittmer, Lowell and Samuel S. Kim. 1994. "Whither China's Quest for National Identity?," in Lowell Dittmer and Samuel S. Kim (eds.), *China's Quest for National Identity*. Ithaca, NY: Cornell University Press, pp. 237–290.

Dreyer, June Teufel. 2015. "The 'Tianxia Trope': Will China Change the International System?," *Journal of Contemporary China* 24(96), pp. 1015–1031.

Fairbank, John K. 1968. "The Early Treaty System in the Chinese World Order," in John K. Fairbank (ed.), *The Chinese World Order: Traditional China's Foreign Relations*. Cambridge, MA: Harvard University Press, pp. 257–275.

Fairbank, John K. and Shu-yu Teng. 1941. "On the Ch'ing Tributary System," *Harvard Journal of Asiatic Studies* 6(4), pp. 135–148.

Gill, Bates and Yanzhong Huang. 2006. "Sources and Limits of Chinese Soft Power," *Survival* 48(2), pp. 17–36.

Gosset, David. 2006. "A New World with Chinese Characteristics," *Asian Times Online*, April 7.

郭伟华 [Guo, Weihua]. 2014. "甲午战争缘何让'天朝礼治体系'彻底坍塌?" ["How Did the Sino-Japanese War Collapse the Etiquette System of the Heavenly Dynasty?"], 人民网 [*The China News Net*], June 9. www.chinanews.com/mil/2014/06-09/6260301.shtml.

Huang, Yanzhong and Sheng Ding. 2006. "Dragon's Underbelly: An Analysis of China's Soft Power," *East Asia* 23(4), pp. 22–44.

Jacques, Martin. 2009. *When China Rules the World: The End of the Western World and the Birth of a New Global Order*. New York: Penguin Press.

Johnston, Alastair Iain. 1995. *Cultural Realism: Strategic Culture and Grand Strategy in Chinese History*. Princeton, NJ: Princeton University Press.

Johnston, Alastair Iain. 1996. "Cultural Realism and Strategy in Maoist China," in Peter J. Katzenstein (ed.), *The Culture of National Security: Norms and Identity in World Politics*. New York: Columbia University Press, pp. 216–268.

Jonquieres, Guy de. 2016. "Trump's TPP Rejection Does Not Make China the Natural Heir," *Nikkei Asian Review*, November 25. http://asia.nikkei.com/Viewpoints/Viewpoints/Guy-de-Jonquieres-Trump-s-TPP-rejection-does-not-make-China-the-natural-heir?page=1.

Kang, David C. 2007. *China Rising: Peace, Power, and Order in East Asia*. New York: Columbia University Press.

Kang, David C. 2010. *East Asia before the West: Five Centuries of Trade and Tribute*. New York, Columbia University Press.

Kim, Samuel. 1991. "Mainland China and a New World Order," *Issues and Studies* 27(11), pp. 4–9.

李恩柱 [Li, Enzhu]. 2012. "两位皇帝对觐见礼仪的处理" ["The Handling of Meeting Etiquette by Two Emperors"], 华文报摘 [*The Chinese Newspapers Collections*], December 28. www.chinanews.com/hb/2010/12-28/2752435.shtml.

Liu, Coco. 2017. "China Climbs on Soft Power Index While Trump Pulls US Down, But the Gap's Still Huge," *South China Morning Post*, July 18. www.scmp.com/week-asia/article/2103133/china-climbs-soft-power-index-while-trump-pulls-us-down-gaps-still-yuuuuge.

Liu, Jianfei. 2009. "Sino-US Relations and Building a Harmonious World," *Journal of Contemporary China* 18(60), pp. 479–490.

Liu, Tiewa. 2014. "Chinese Strategic Culture and the Use of Force: Moral and Political Perspectives," *Journal of Contemporary China* 23(87), pp. 556–574.

卢汉超 [Lu, Hanchao]. 2012. "中国从来就是一个开放的国家吗—再论西方'唱盛中国'" ["Has China Always Been an Open Country? Think about the 'Praise of China' by the West again"], 清华大学学报: 哲社版 [*Tsinghua University Journal: Philosophy and Social Science Edition*] 3. http://site.douban.com/125457/widget/notes/4971340/note/270982522/.

Lu, Yiyi. 2007. "Blind Spots in China's Soft Power," *The Straits Times*, July 15.

Mancall, Mark. 1963. "The Persistence of Tradition in Chinese Foreign Policy," *The Annals of the American Academy of Political and Social Science* 349, reprinted in King C. Chen (ed.), *The Foreign Policy of China*. South Orange, NJ: Seton Hall University Press, 1972, pp. 30–31.

Mancall, Mark. 1968. "The Ch'ing Tribute System: An Interpretive Essay," in John K. Fairbank (ed.), *The Chinese World Order: Traditional China's Foreign Relations*. Cambridge, MA: Harvard University Press, pp. 63–89.

Manomaivibool, Prapin. 2014. "Viewing Sino-Siamese Tributary Relations via the Two Courts' Letters of the 1780s," paper presented at the 11th Beijing Forum, The Harmony of Civilization and Prosperity for All, November 7–9, Beijing, China.

Nye, Joseph S. 2005. "The Rise of China's Soft Power," *The Wall Street Journal Asia*, December 29.

People's Daily Online. 2006. "The charm of China's Soft Power," March 14. http://english.people.com.cn/200603/10/eng20060310_249577.html.

Perdue, Peter C. 2010. *China Marches West: The Qing Conquest of Central Eurasia*. Cambridge, MA: Harvard University Press.

Perdue, Peter C. 2015. "The Tenacious Tributary System," *Journal of Contemporary China* 24(96), pp. 1002–1014.

PressReader. 2017. "ISEAS Poll Shows Low Trust of China in the Region: More Than 70% of Respondents Have Little to No Confidence That Beijing Will 'Do the Right Thing'," May 5. www.pressreader.com/singapore/today/20170505/281552290765338.

Pye, Lucian W. 1985. *Asian Power and Politics: The Cultural Dimensions of Authority*. Cambridge, MA: Harvard University Press.

Qin, Yaqing. 2011. "The Chinese School of International Relations Theory: Possibility and Necessity," in William A. Callahan and Elena Barabantseva (eds.), *China Orders the World: Normative Soft Power and Foreign Policy*. Washington, DC: Woodrow Wilson Center Press.

Reuters. 2014. "Chinese Leader Xi Says Militarism Not in China's Genes," July 1. www.nationmultimedia.com/aec/Chinese-leader-Xi-says-militarism-not-in-Chinas-ge-30237603.html.

Schmitt, Gary J. 2014. "A Hard Look at Soft Power in East Asia," *American Enterprise Institute*, June 19. www.aei.org/papers/foreign-and-defense-policy/a-hard-look-at-soft-power-in-east-asia?utm_source=new-research&utm_medium=paramount&utm_campaign=Schmitt.

Wang, Yiwei. 2015. "Predicament and Pathway in Devising an International Discursive System," *Aisixiang*, August 4. www.aisixiang.com/data/91024.html.

魏志江 [Wei, Zhijiang]. 2014. "论东亚传统国际安全体系与所谓华夷次序" ["Traditional East Asian International Security System and the So-Called Chinese-Barbarian Order"], paper presented at the 11th Beijing Forum, The Harmony of Civilization and Prosperity for All, November 7–9, Beijing, China.

Westad, Odd Arne. 2012. *Restless Empire: China and the World since 1750*. New York: Basic Books.

Wu, Xinbo. 2012. "Forging Sino-US Partnership in the Twenty-First Century: Opportunities and Challenges," *Journal of Contemporary China* 21(75), pp. 391–407.

辛旗 [Xin, Qi]. 2011. "在弘扬中华文化：探讨王道理念，构建和谐世界——王道思想的当代意义研讨会上的致辞" ["Remarks at the Symposium on Royal Ethics and Construction of Harmonious World: Royal Ethics and Its Contemporary Significance"], 中国新闻网 [*China News Net*], April 22. www.chinanews.com/tw/2011/04-22/2992337.shtml.

Xinhua News Agency. 2014. "习近平在德国科尔伯基金会的演讲" ["Xi Jinping Speech at the Korber Foundation, Germany"], March 28. www.gov.cn/xinwen/2014-03/29/content_2649512.htm

熊光清 [Xiong, Guangqing]. 2013. "东亚国家未反省战争 崇尚武力风习阴魂不散" ["East Asian Countries Have Not Reflected Wars: Militancy Ethos Lingers"], *Global Times*, April 1. www.chinanews.com/mil/2013/04-01/4692110.shtml.

Xue, Li. 2015. "Indicator of China's Rise: National Strength or Influence?," *Xinhuanet*, July 27. www.gd.xinhuanet.com/newscenter/2015-07/27/c_1116050936.htm.

Yan, Xuetong. 2011. "How China Can Defeat America," *New York Times*, November 20. www.nytimes.com/2011/11/21/opinion/how-china-can-defeat-america.html?pagewanted=all&_r=0.

阎学通, 徐进, 等著 [Yan, Xuetong, Xu, Jing, et al.]. 2009. 王霸天下思想及启迪 [*The Thoughts of World Leadership and Implications*]. Beijing: Shijie Zhishi Chubanshe.

Yang, Lien-sheng. 1968. "Historical Notes on the Chinese World Order," in John K. Fairbank (ed.), *The Chinese World Order: Traditional China's Foreign Relations*. Cambridge, MA: Harvard University Press, pp. 20–33.

Yu, Haiyang. 2014. "Glorious Memories of Imperial China and the Rise of Chinese Populist Nationalism," *Journal of Contemporary China* 23(90), pp. 1174–1187.

柳镛泰 [Yu, Yongtae]. 2014. "以四夷藩属为中华领土：明国时期东亚认识的另一面" ["Territorial Imagination and Perception of East Asia in the Republic China"], paper presented at the 11th Beijing Forum, The Harmony of Civilization and Prosperity for All, November 7–9, Beijing, China.

Zhang, Junbo and Yao Yunzhu. 1996. "Differences between Traditional Chinese and Western Military Thinking and Their Philosophical Roots," *Journal of Contemporary China* 5(12), pp. 209–221.

Zhang, Yongjin. 1991. *China in the International System, 1918–20, the Middle Kingdom at the Periphery*. New York: St. Martin's Press.

Zhao, Suisheng. 2015. "Rethinking the Chinese World Order: The Imperial Cycle and the Rise of China," *Journal of Contemporary China* 24(96), pp. 961–982.

赵汀阳 [Zhao, Tingyang]. 2005. 天下体制: 世界制度哲学导论 [*The All-under-Heaven System: A Philosophy for the World System*]. Jiangsu Education Press, Nanjing China.

Zhao, Tingyang. 2006. "Rethinking Empire from a Chinese Concept 'All-under-Heaven'," *Social Identities* 12(1), pp. 29–41.

Zhao, Tingyang. 2009. "A Political World Philosophy in terms of All-under-Heaven (Tian-xia)," *Diogenes* 56, pp. 5–18.

Zhao, Tingyang. 2014. "The 'China Dream' in Question," *Economic and Political Studies* 2(1), pp. 127–142.

2

THE END OF CHINA'S RISE

Consequences for PRC debates on soft power

Daniel C. Lynch

In the years following Xi Jinping's assumption of power in 2012, the vaunted Chinese powerhouse economy finally began to sputter and skid. Most immediately relevant for the PRC's soft power, imports from foreign partner countries plummeted by 13.3% from 2013 through 2016, while export growth during the period remained flat (National Bureau of Statistics, 2017). Both exports and imports recovered briefly during 2017–2018 as a consequence of unsustainable debt-driven stimulus (National Bureau of Statistics, 2018), but then export growth leveled off again and imports tanked from mid-2018 through mid-2019 as the PRC's traditional levers for stimulating the economy faltered just as China got hit by US President Donald Trump's tariff war.

Simultaneously, the Chinese labor force was rapidly shrinking. This debilitating process began in 2013 and would continue indefinitely for decades into the future, with 23% of the labor force projected to be lost by 2050 ("China's Working-Age Population," 2016). In other countries in which the working-age population declined inexorably (after 1960), the average annual GDP growth rate was only 1.5% (Sharma, 2016). To continue rising in relative power terms, China would have to maintain a GDP growth rate significantly higher than that of the United States, which hovered around 2% from the early 1990s until the mid-2010s, but then increased to nearly 3% during the first two years of the Trump administration. In other words, China would have to perform much, much better than the countries in Sharma's post-1960 database that it resembled demographically. By the mid-2010s, China's rise was in crisis—even if most outside observers remained largely unaware of the significance of this dramatic turn of events (Lynch, 2019).

Inside China, the inescapability of this slowly gathering storm—the mounting threat to the PRC's continued economic rise—was already well understood by most Chinese economists as early as 2008. They openly discussed the threats to the country's economic dynamism and the failures of the CCP leadership to address them in publication after publication, using sharp and occasionally even mocking language (Lynch, 2015, pp. 20–67). This raises an important question: Did gradually increasing recognition of these inescapable economic realities induce a mellowing in the Chinese discourse on soft power—a reduction in the hubris often seen in Chinese discussions of soft (and hard) power during the years of the "new assertiveness" after 2008? Were Chinese commenters on the soft power dimensions of international contestation adjusting the tone and content of their analyses to bring them into line with—and adapt to—the inescapable new material realities discussed frankly by Chinese economists?

The answer is: "not exactly." On the one hand, Chinese writers did become increasingly willing to acknowledge that China was not competing successfully with the West, and especially the United States, specifically for relative soft power in the narrow sense of the term—a concession, perhaps, to the scarcely deniable reality (as reflected in public opinion polls) of a worsening in the PRC's image in most parts of the world after 2008. On the other hand, many Chinese writers soon began arguing confidently that they had discovered the *reason* for China's poor soft-power performance, and this critical factor was something that it was within China's capacity to change. The critical factor was simply that the "US-led West," through its media, telecommunications, Internet, and computer empires, exerted hegemonic control over the world's flow of discourse, and twisted the content of that discourse against China. But fortunately, because of China's growing relative material might, the PRC *could*, many writers argued, begin to use its material agency to wrest control of discourse power from the West and then use that discourse power to reshape information flows to convey the "truth" about China, thereby automatically increasing its soft power. For these and similar reasons, most Chinese writers continued to express a high degree of ultimate confidence in the sustainability of China's relative rise, whether in hard or soft power, and they showed little to no concern that there might be something fundamentally unattractive or fatally flawed about the Chinese system that limits its soft power potential.

There is one caveat in asserting this interpretation. While the writing in recent years—including the articles discussed below—appears superficially to be positive and confident, it cannot be said with certainty that the analysts truly hold such thoughts or else instead are simply *following orders* to express optimism. At various points during 2012–2017, and then especially after the official promulgation of "Xi Jinping Thought on Socialism with Chinese Characteristics for a New Era" at the 19th Party Congress (October 2017), General Secretary Xi demanded that the Party and the nation "consolidate self-confidence in taking the road of socialism with Chinese characteristics;

in our theory and institutions; and in our culture. Cultural self-confidence is the most basic, the deepest, and the most enduring force" (quoted in Xiao Bo, 2016, p. 112). Because of the inescapable linkages between culture and soft power, and because of the intense repressiveness of Xi's "New Era," Chinese soft power specialists must certainly worry that expressing pessimism about the PRC's soft power potential would leave them open to the charge of lacking self-confidence or even being dangerously, perniciously nihilistic. Consequently, it cannot be said with certainty that when Chinese soft power specialists express ultimate optimism they genuinely believe it. On the other hand, they do typically offer elaborate explanations for why they think optimism is warranted, even if sometimes their explanations lack logical consistency or fall short on details. The Chinese assessments are worth examining to gain insight into PRC elite thinking about the linkages between material and ideational power in the international relations of the 21st century.

Discourse power

An analyst named Bian Qin—an evidently influential social-media figure identified simply as "a female writer traveling in France"—provides the most comprehensive explanation of the discourse power dynamic in an article published in *World Socialism Research*, a journal of the Chinese Academy of Social Sciences (CASS). Arguing that "the world's flow of discourse vitally affects the prospects for survival of our nation and civilization," Bian contends that China "must meticulously plot and strategize [to increase power over the flow], knowing ourselves and knowing the enemy" (Bian, 2016, p. 78). She finds that the age of colonialism has left a world in which the West still controls most significant discourse—through the mass media, but also, evidently, less public networks—and uses its power to exalt Western civilization while demeaning others, especially China. To extricate China from this subaltern position, Chinese people must (1) recognize that the struggle will be long and arduous, because the West's control over discourse (through which it disseminates perniciously anti-Chinese values) is intricate, comprehensive and tight; and (2) recover their civilizational self-confidence—the Xi Jinping goal—which also will not be easy because the West circulates values that belittle and marginalize Chinese civilization. "The power to manipulate [global] public opinion lies not only in making oneself look good, but also in maligning and smearing the other . . . , from beginning to end, a war" (Bian, 2016, p. 79).

Bian is concerned that Chinese people will assume blithely that rising material power will lead *automatically* to rising discourse (and, consequently, soft) power. This is not the case; and indeed, there is a real threat that China could develop economically only to melt and disappear into the Western world system, having no voice and taking a subservient role—much like Japan became rich after World War II but remains a second-class world citizen when it comes to discourse and the articulation of values. This is not an acceptable ultimate outcome for the rise of China. The PRC must actively use its material power to seize control over the flow of the world's discourse (Bian, 2016).

Bian initially struggles to explain who, exactly, it is in the West manipulating the flow of discourse, or whether the manipulation occurs as a not-necessarily intended consequence of structural factors. But eventually she hits upon an anthropomorphized power source: "the invisible hand." One reason the power to control discourse is so critically important is that the state or civilization that controls it can also control the world economy, insofar as "the flow of discourse not only determines how much a shirt, for example, will be valued, but also how much a piece of art will be valued, or even how much an individual human being will be valued." In this we can see how the West stacks the deck against China: "The fact that 'made in China' products are valued less highly than products of comparable quality made by foreign countries is a function of the operations of the 'invisible hand' that controls the world's flow of discourse." Bian finds that the invisible hand "can, over many years, use the exchange of information (including false information) to turn a country's products into utterly valueless items—a kind of invisible plundering that even the gods don't know about and the ghosts cannot detect" (Bian, 2016, p. 79). She gives as an example women's handbags. China produces handbags of exactly the same quality as the famous French handbags that so many people pay large sums of money to buy, she says. And yet consumers will not pay equally high prices for Chinese-made handbags because they are "brainwashed" to esteem Western products while sneering at those produced by China (Bian, 2016, p. 80).

Bian is arguing against a so-called free flow of information and individualist-rationalist notions of a global marketplace for exchanging ideas, images and information. She is, in effect, mocking the invisible hand metaphor to suggest that there really *is* a hand: a source of agential power "out there," controlled by the West (perhaps its "elite stratum," a term she uses at various points in the essay) and wielded actively to structure the arenas in which ideas, images and information are exchanged to pursue the interests of Western states and Western civilization, invariably at the expense of China, but also other countries and civilizations. She is rejecting the idea that individuals and groups in a denationalized world society might freely and autonomously and validly decide that "products" ranging from Chinese handbags to Chinese political practices are relatively undesirable. Bian is in effect suggesting that the only way such a decision would be possible is if the assessor is brainwashed, and that they would reach a very different conclusion if only they could liberate themselves from the vice-grip of Western (especially US) discourse power.

Renmin University's Wang Yiwei, a professor in the School of International Studies, agrees that (1) "soft power is regarded as one of China's highest-level strategic concerns," and yet that (2) soft power as a concept is problematic because it intrinsically privileges the United States—after all, the concept was invented in the United States by an American (Joseph Nye), who was using the concept to reassure Americans that their international importance and relative power were not declining after the Cold War when in fact they were (Wang, 2016, p. 12). Writing in the second issue of a new journal devoted to the subject, *Studies in Cultural Soft Power*, Wang argues that the soft power concept is "deeply steeped in American exceptionalism and the notion of manifest destiny . . . , [claiming that] America is eternally right, America stands at the foot of God, America stands on the right side of history, and America is the world's unique and special exception" (Wang, 2016, p. 11). By definition, therefore, China cannot compete with America for soft power, because the concept itself is US-centric. Trying to compete with the United States for soft power would only "damage our Three Self-Confidences": confidence in the road of socialism with Chinese characteristics, Chinese theory and institutions, and Chinese culture, as called for by Xi Jinping.[1]

To Wang Yiwei, the significance of China's rise is that it blows the comparatively shallow and loaded (because it is US-centric) soft power concept out of the water. "China's rise is a civilizational renaissance that subverts the West-centric world view. The consequence of the rise of China will be that the [claimed] universal will become the local; the sacred will become the vacuous; and the self will become the other" (Wang, 2016, p. 14). Not just any rising country would be able to "decenter" the West so profoundly in world history and international relations. In effect, only China could do it: "In today's world or even the history of humanity, not many countries have had the qualifications to pronounce themselves as special [*cheng ziji wei tese*]. China's specialness surpasses the unique characteristics of other countries, [and] to emphasize China's specialness is to realize China's self-confidence, self-awareness, and particular burdens" to history (Wang, 2016, p. 14).

The burdens are big indeed. Wang argues that just as China absorbed and transformed Buddhism and Marxism in the past, so today—or in the near future—the rising PRC will absorb "Western universal values" and repackage them for inclusion in a new and less parochial category he calls "the common values of the human race" (*renlei gongtong jiazhi*) (Wang, 2016, p. 15). The common values of the human race will include—in addition to "Western universal values"—Chinese Confucian values, insofar as the success of China's rise will also mean "the realization of the Chinese national spirit," but not in a narrowly nationalistic sense because "the specialness of China originates in China but belongs to the world" (Wang, 2016, p. 15). Consequently, the success of China's rise will equate to great successes for the human race as a whole, because the rise will bring about "the realization of perpetual development for all of humanity, in which all civilizations and all development models can complement each other insofar as each is beautiful in its own way; and the realization of a perpetually-peaceful, collectively-prosperous world of harmony" (Wang, 2016, p. 15). Wang ties the argument together with a final bow to Xi Jinping by asserting that the "China Dream," an early Xi Jinping concept, "brings opportunity, happiness,

and hope to the world—and it can be an inexhaustible source of Chinese soft power in the future" (Wang, 2016, p. 15). But not at the present, because the West still exercises control over the world's flow of discourse.

Curiously, then, Wang belittles and mocks the concept of soft power when examining the international relations of today, but considers that the concept will become valid and important after China's soft power levels exceed those of the United States. His reasoning seems to be that *everything* in a world in which China is not at the top and in the central position is of dubious legitimacy. But once China's recentering in world history and international relations is complete, concepts such as soft power take on a new meaning as the universalism formerly claimed by the West becomes local; the sacred as asserted by the West is exposed as vacuous; and the West generally evolves into a civilizational other to the world center which is China.

Going on the offensive

Studies on Cultural Soft Power, the journal in which Wang Yiwei published his almost chiliastic article, is edited at Wuhan University, the site of a "summit forum" on soft power bringing together "several dozen first-line specialists" to launch the journal on June 6, 2016 (Xiao, 2016). Wuhan University is also the home institution of Professor Liu Ying, who teaches at the university's Institute of Marxism. Funded by a grant from the PRC Ministry of Education in the special category of "Research into Building an Academic Discourse System with Chinese Characteristics," Liu published an article in 2017 consistent with the discourse-power-as-fundamental theme, but she presented the West-dominated world as more challenging to China—the struggle as more cutthroat. She argued that the time has come for China to go on the offensive.

Liu states straightforwardly that "we don't want simply to keep a low profile" (*tao guang yang hui*)—thus rejecting the Deng Xiaoping injunction to behave cautiously in international affairs (although Liu did not use Deng's name). "We don't want simply to concentrate on material construction. We want to "have something to say" that manifests the real China. We don't want simply to have an economic national rise. We also want to have a national rise in discourse" for the purpose of "controlling and directing the course of China's rise" (Liu, 2017, pp. 162–163).

The reason Liu regards this as necessary is that the rise of China has reached the stage in which the world's competing civilizational power centers will battle to determine the rise's *meaning*. The civilization that controls the world's flow of discourse will define what the risen China is and implies. "If China doesn't speak [that is, take control of the processes of defining China's rise], others will speak for it. If China doesn't manufacture its own national image, others will manufacture one for it" (Liu, 2017, p. 163). Moreover, the image that the (Western) others will manufacture will be negative and false. This is clear from the current "main global melody" concerning China's rise as manufactured by the West. The main global melody includes the following themes: China will collapse; China is an energy, economic, environmental, soft-power, ideological, military, and/or food threat; China is a bully; China is arrogant; China is not democratic; China does not respect human rights; Chinese people do not have freedom; China is an irresponsible power; and more—almost any combination of which can be trotted out (by the Western forces, or people, that control discourse power) at any time to twist and distort the world's understanding of China, causing the image of China to depart from Chinese reality. This harshly dissonant main melody is, moreover, intentionally composed and performed to inflict pain on China and to vanquish it in the great struggles of international relations. "Using Western standards to cut China down to size, using Western interests to judge and evaluate China, using Western 'authority' to articulate China—this is discourse hegemony operating according to the logic of thuggish domination, and discourse competition according to 'the law of the jungle'" (Liu, 2017, p. 164). Under the circumstances, China has no choice but to fight back—nothing less than the meaning of its national rise is at stake, and this is of critical importance to all of humanity.

The image of China that must replace the Western caricatures and stereotypes can be found in the real China, the China as reflected accurately in the Chinese "self-perception." The key elements of this real China, as perceived correctly by the Chinese people, include that: China is a civilized great power with 5,000 years of a brilliant history; China is a robust power that has been tested in multiple wars and crises but never collapses, always re-emerging as a pillar of the world in the East; China is a "great power that fulfils its responsibilities"; China is a country in which all the nationalities are united; China is a country possessing a pluralistic culture whose elements all integrate harmoniously; China has a clean and un-corrupt political system; and China is economically dynamic and culturally vibrant, increasingly easy to get along with internationally, and bursting with hope and liveliness (Liu, 2017, pp. 161–162).

Liu will probably appear to most foreign readers as a constructivist—and even a disingenuous constructivist calling for the propagation of "alternative facts" and outright fabrications. But she does not present the contest (or "war") as a struggle over who will define reality cynically. She presents it instead as a struggle between those ("the Chinese people") who articulate objective truth versus hegemonistic Westerners who propagate malicious fabrications. "Inside the arena of international discourse competition, the discourse itself has long since been polluted by state power. Factual reality is no longer important . . . Western countries monopolize discourse power [and] block international audiences from directly perceiving the real China" (Liu, 2017, p. 163). Liu underscores her own fact-based reasonableness by acknowledging that even despite its enormous accomplishments, China has problems. The problems, however, are not fundamental—*and they are the problems identified by the Chinese people*, not by the West. These problems are conceived and assessed within the Chinese ideational universe, and so they are contained:

> We must realize that China's problems are not so numerous or serious that they can drown out China's successes. Elevating discourse self-confidence is not to ignore China's problems. Rather, it is to affirm China's successes while directly confronting the problems and simultaneously rejecting the West's discursive tarnishing of China's reputation.
>
> *(Liu, 2017, p. 166)*

Liu additionally perceives that the image of a rising China that China has the right and responsibility to construct must be an image that is "understandable and recognizable for international [especially Western] audiences" (Liu, 2017, p. 165). The image must resonate with international audiences because China's rise is an event not only in Chinese history, but also in world history. Or even more: China's rise is relational and communicational, because it cannot have meaning even to Chinese people unless it also has meaning (a positive meaning, as shaped by the CCP) to foreign audiences. This means, practically, that "it would be useless to try to claim that everything is good in China," because all countries have problems. "Formulations such as 'Tibet has been an integral part of China since ancient times' and 'hurt the feelings of the Chinese people' are treated as empty slogans by international audiences." China must summon the self-confidence and the intelligence to exert power over the world's flow of discourse, but not bludgeon it in an ultimately self-defeating way. A useful slogan might be to "take what the self fabricates as the core, and what the other fabricates as the ancillary" (*yi zisu wei zhu, tasu wei fu*) (Liu, 2017, pp. 165–167). Evidently, China will become the chief subject or actor in the world's future history—particularly insofar as defining China is concerned—but the West can still play—even must still play—an important supporting role as a kind of subaltern "other" to dominant China.

The "China solution"

The West will also, it would appear, play minor roles in the search for solutions to developing countries' problems and global problems as China moves into the central world position. In his speech marking the 95th anniversary of the CCP's founding on July 1, 2016, Xi Jinping offered "the China Solution" (this is the official English-language translation of "Zhongguo Fang'an") for consideration "as the world searches for a better social system" in the aftermath of the 2008–2009 Global Financial Crisis (GFC), a massive failure of Western "solutions." Han Qingxiang and Huang Xianghuai, two scholars with the Central Party School's Theory of Socialism with Chinese Characteristics Research Centre, set about explaining the China Solution in a January 1, 2017, article in *Seeking Truth* (*Qiushi*) (Han and Huang, 2017). They spend three full pages explicating, but in the end, the China Solution boils down to a negative; that is, a rejection of the "Western model" as universally valid. In contrast, "the China Solution is a solution that stresses China's distinctive characteristics and respects the world's diversity"—a solution that stresses not imposing one country's values on other countries, but that could nevertheless serve as a new developmental standard and model in an age in which the West has so obviously failed (Han and Huang, 2017, p. 20). "China's success in reality expresses the success of a set of values [and] a spiritual inheritance different from the package of values associated with Protestantism and the spirit of capitalism" (Han and Huang, 2017, p. 20). Foreign countries can be expected to find the China Solution inspiring and then chart their own developmental courses in a non-Western, non-universal direction, but somehow—albeit vaguely—consistent or aligned with China's.

Note that in such articles—addressed primarily (it would appear) to audiences of social scientists, journalists and Party propaganda cadres—there is little to no attention given to the practical/logistical challenges associated with promoting the "China Solution" or more broadly China's discourse power. There is instead an embedded, unexamined materialist assumption that the economic rise will eventually lead almost automatically to what might be called an "ideational rise" (encompassing both discourse and soft power). Ideational power is obviously considered critical, and yet is often treated implicitly as derived from material power. CCP leaders must still exert agency to realize it, but rarely are the difficulties associated with deriving ideational from material power examined—other than perfunctorily.

In a colorfully worded article published in the third issue of the new journal *Studies in Cultural Soft Power*, Zhan Dexiong sounds conceptually similar to Han and Huang (above) as he presents Western discourse power as caging Chinese (and foreign) minds. "It can be said that everything we think and do, the opinions that we express, have all—consciously or unconsciously—been influenced by the West, to the point that we normally use Western standards to judge right and wrong" (Zhan, 2016, p. 50). Just as the initial successes of reform and opening in the 1980s and 1990s *might* have allowed China to start claiming some discourse power, America tried to rope the PRC into the so-called world mainstream, which was actually a stream directed by, and serving, the United States. "To achieve this objective, the West wrapped its values in the cloak of 'universal values'. . . . But if we had admired and worshipped the West, we would have become the West's spiritual slaves" (Zhan, 2016, p. 51). As with Han and Huang of the Central Party School, Zhan finds the GFC to be a critical turning point in world history paving the way for the China Solution (although Zhan uses the term "model") to take center stage. "We can say with certainty that an economically-developed, politically-flourishing China that treats humanity with concern and speaks with reason will lead the trend of world development, breaking off from the West's well-worn old path to proceed toward a glorious future of great universal harmony. The road will be long and uneven, *but the future belongs to us*" (Zhan, 2016, p. 52; emphasis added).

Although here Zhan presents China as already launched on a developmental course that will result in an inevitable vanquishing of the West with its universalist claims, leading to a China-centric world harmony, his main thrust—as a practicing journalist—is to argue that success will not come automatically and that the CCP-controlled media must begin to tell the "China story" more effectively. Journalists and other media professionals have a responsibility to educate themselves in the "principles" that distinguish China from the West—and then to communicate those principles in their reporting and programming. Zhan offers four such distinctions (ironically, in the light of distinction 2, binary distinctions) for consideration:

1   Whereas the West emphasizes individuals selfishly seeking profits, China emphasizes acting for the community and the common global good, with the result that China can help lead the world out of the "vicious cycle of pursuing profits above all else," which produced the disaster of the GFC (Zhan, 2016, p. 52).

2   "In terms of thinking methodologies, Westerners easily slide into 'if it's not black, it's white' absolute binaries—viewing themselves as civilized, others as barbaric, themselves as democratic, others as authoritarian, . . . and play zero-sum games . . . [But] China, since ancient times, has always understood the principle of harmony and the unity of opposites. Consequently, we [Chinese] seek both-sides-win and the-community-wins solutions" (Zhan, 2016, p. 52).

3   Whereas the United States seeks hegemony and a Pax Americana, "China promotes the notion of everyone under Heaven belonging to one big family and forming a community of common destiny" (Zhan, 2016, p. 52).

4   On the question of domestic political systems—critical models for possible emulation—"Western-style democracy" centers on "money politics, corrosive party struggles, and pathologies of decision-making that impede the government's smooth functioning." In contrast, "China promotes a democratic centralism that takes the people as the foundation and that skillfully balances the relationship between freedom and discipline—not a perfect system, but one that clearly manifests a potent vitality" (Zhan, 2016, p. 53).

So transparently could these critiques of the West be applied to China that at first glance it might seem as though Zhan is offering an elliptical criticism of the contemporary PRC. But the overall triumphalist tone of his essay—including his proclamation that "the future belongs to us"—suggests instead that either he believes in his assertions fervently and/or he wants his readers to believe in them. The possibility of a personage in the propaganda *xitong* offering even an elliptical criticism of China's system in the era of Xi Jinping, and in a new soft power journal, is remote.

A message to Party members

Zhan's use of a bombastic tone and his somewhat careless argumentation possibly reflects the more popular nature of his broader audience of media professionals. Adopting a more sober tone—but delivering essentially the same message—is Fudan University professor Su Changhe (of the School of International Relations and Public Affairs), writing in the journal *Party Construction*, and thus aiming his message at CCP cadres.

Su posits the chief problem to be China's need to fight for a degree of discourse power commensurate with its rising level of material power so that it can offer the world fresh ideas about governance and a compelling new model of development. As ever, China's chief obstacle is said to be the United States, which is using its "power to guide and influence the operation of international organizations, the authoring of international rules of the game, and the maintenance of international norms and order-maintaining institutions"—what Su calls "the invisible superstructure of international relations"—to contain China and block its rise (Su, 2016, pp. 28–29). Su makes three recommendations to Party members for increasing China's discourse power under such hostile circumstances.

First, reject the two deleterious tendencies of mindlessly pursuing integration into the international realm and wholeheartedly embracing the so-called international rules of the game to push through domestic reforms. Passively "fusing into the systems that other people lead" may produce short-term benefits but only at the cost of becoming dependent on those others (i.e., the US-led Western countries) in the long run. In a worst-case scenario, fusing into the systems that other people lead "could even produce the effect of China 'becoming socialized'" into international norms, a prospect which Su considers to be anathema (Su, 2016, p. 29). "The ultimate objective in great power competition is to see which power can incorporate the others into its international system, and thereby 'socialize' those other powers" (Su, 2016, p. 29). Because China is a responsible and law-abiding country, Su does not propose trying to destroy existing norms and institutions. Some international regimes it can accept:

> However, as to those arrangements that are obviously unreasonable in their treatment of the majority of countries, and those that fail to reflect the international power structure [now that China has risen in material power terms], plus those still-in-the-making to address new global challenges such as the Internet, the environment, the deep seabed, the polar regions, outer space, and artificial intelligence, China must step forward to play a far more active role, reflecting its own perspectives.
>
> *(Su, 2016, p. 29)*

Second, change the Chinese default mode from "passively accepting" the influence of international norms to "moving actively to shape" the norms to make them consistent with PRC interests. By norms, Su means a deeper construct than international regimes. He means discourse power. He gives as an example the culture of the scientific research world, which he believes devalues the accomplishments of Chinese scientists. Su contends that the CCP should work actively to change the culture of the scientific research world to the point that, for example, Chinese academic journals will become more respected than Western journals—as a reflection of Chinese scientists' tremendous real-world accomplishments (Su, 2016, p. 30). However, Su does not explain exactly how this ambitious goal might be achieved. Su also contends that the world's discursive realm—the realm where values are created and propagated—must be made, in the course of China's material rise, consistent with the reality of China's complex greatness. Using discourse power, the CCP *must make international relations legitimate to the Chinese people* (not the other way around), and the only way to achieve this objective is to change international relations to the point that the Chinese people can clearly see that the international realm recognizes and exalts China's myriad accomplishments.

Third, and more concretely, increase discourse power to reshape (although not hegemonically) international norms and institutions to better serve Chinese businesses and other actors who have already "gone out" to places like Africa and Latin America. At present, when Chinese entities need services abroad, they sometimes lobby the Chinese government to provide them, but they also lobby foreign governments. This is embarrassing and can cause negative consequences for Chinese nationals. The CCP must take the initiative to remake the playing field so that the services Chinese entities demand while abroad can be provided more easily or even automatically (Su, 2016, p. 30). The outside world must be made safer and more convenient for Chinese entities and individuals—and this will ultimately be in the interests of the outside world itself.

Evidence of the current weakness of Chinese discourse power

Three articles from 2014 published by the *neibu* (internal-circulation-only) journal *Leadership Reference*—directed (as with *Party Construction*) at CCP elites—illuminate how the limitations of Chinese discourse power can have real-world consequences in the everyday politics of CCP efforts to inspire awe.

The first article laments the lackluster consequences of a CCP initiative to use Confucian Classrooms to teach Mandarin to primary and secondary school students in Thailand, a key target country in the CCP's quest to increase PRC influence over Southeast Asia. Zhou Fangye, a researcher at the Chinese Academy of Social Sciences National Institute of International Strategy (the organization's official English-language name), complains of "the problems existing in the promotion of the Chinese language in Thai elementary and middle schools" (Zhou, 2014, p. 45). The problems stem not from active Thai resistance to the Chinese initiative; instead, they result from the Thai side not being impressed enough to implement the instructions of the Chinese "Confucius Institute Headquarters" (*Han Ban*) other than perfunctorily. Zhou complains that the Thai side exercises too much control over the language programs and will not follow through even on its own initiatives. Rather than implement serious language training programs, Thai teachers and administrators content themselves with offering an occasional special program or some simple conversation classes once or so a week. Zhou argues that unless the Confucius Institute Headquarters steps up and starts asserting greater control over the direction of the Confucian Classrooms, Thai schoolchildren will simply not be learning Mandarin.

Yet Zhou acknowledges that Thai schoolchildren have very little incentive to learn Mandarin, because—as he reports—Thai people are not finding that studying Chinese for a few years is increasing their competitiveness (or their children's competitiveness) in the job market. Unless and until that happens, goading the Thai teachers and administrators into taking Chinese language study more seriously is not likely to make much of a difference (Zhou, 2014, p. 47). Thai people—including the parents of the schoolchildren—seem to consider Chinese-language study to be amusing but not essential, in contrast to English, which they regard as critically important for their children to succeed.

A second example comes from Hong Kong—not "international," but still, for many purposes, a part of the "outside world." "Interior" (*neidi*) Chinese people must constantly battle the problem of having a negative image in Hong Kong because of the bad behavior of a few—despite the PRC's economic rise, which has benefited the Hong Kong economy (Mainlanders believe) enormously. Jiang Shenghong, of the Tianjin Academy of Social Sciences School of Public Opinion Research, addresses this problem in a 2014 *Leadership Reference* article, analyzing "the network public opinion spawned by Mainland children urinating on Hong Kong streets" (Jiang, 2014). Consistent with the many other articles in effect blaming outsiders for having a negative impression of China—a problem that could be rectified by increasing the PRC's discourse power—Jiang argues in his *neibu* article that the sharp criticism in Hong Kong only reflects the jealousy of Hong Kong people aroused by the contrast of dynamic Mainland economic growth with Hong Kong stagnation. In their insecurity, Hong Kong people allow emotion to overcome rationality, insofar as "people from any part of the world might possibly face situations in which they must let children urinate in the street" (Jiang, 2014, p. 34). Instead of recognizing the normality of this situation, Hong Kong people—especially "the media" and "Internet opinion leaders"—choose to distort and sensationalize it, whereas instead they should explain it carefully to their compatriots so that Hong Kong people will feel warm, friendly and welcoming toward Mainlanders even as their children relieve themselves in the street (Jiang, 2014, p. 34).

Sometimes Hong Kong media and Internet opinion leaders even go so far as to report an incident of public urination as a far more serious incident of public defecation, thereby "causing society to become disharmonious" (Jiang, 2014, pp. 35–36). The significance of this issue for soft and discourse power is that if the CCP (or "China") could control the flow of discourse—as called for by other authors—the "normal" acts of public urination could be defined and defended as such and no one would look seriously askance.

While the public urination problem as exacerbated by the media and Internet opinion leaders may seem to be trivial, a Chinese Academy of Social Sciences World History Task Force warned in a third *Leadership Reference* article that the long-term consequence of allowing negative images of China to circulate in the world's communication networks could be serious threats to PRC sovereignty. The task force (whose individual members are not identified) calls for the CCP actively to guard against the maligning of China's reputation in (particularly) the Western media, or else the PRC could eventually lose elements of its sovereignty—just as the Qing lost sovereignty over China's 19th-century judicial system as a result of slanderous Western rumor-mongering about Chinese jurisprudence. The distorted impressions that resulted from the rumor-mongering were used to strengthen Western imperialist calls for establishing extraterritoriality in China (Chinese Academy, 2014, p. 29). To avoid a similar calamity in the 21st century, the CCP should mobilize people of Chinese ancestry in foreign countries to publish op-ed pieces and make media appearances in which they refute negative assertions being made about China in the global communication networks (Chinese Academy, 2014, pp. 30–32). The task force members seem to think that ethnic Chinese people in foreign countries will be quick to take umbrage when their ancestral land is vilified but more effective in rebutting the negative imagery than citizens of the PRC itself.

One slightly dissenting voice

Overwhelmingly, the Chinese writing on soft power is realist, in IR theory terms, imagining a world of fierce contestation between China and the West, particularly the United States. But one writer who, to a degree, rejects a realist ontology is Wang Lili, an associate professor at the Renmin University of China's National Development and Strategy Research Institute. Writing in the aftermath of Brexit and of Donald Trump's election as US president, Wang contends that China's rise is now threatened by anti-globalization forces in the West. Within this context, the CCP must mobilize Chinese energies to play a critical role in working with like-minded foreigners to wage a new and unanticipated struggle to save globalization from the atavistic forces trying to destroy it (Wang Lili, 2017). Instead of scheming to take advantage of US and Western political disarray to advance China's relative position, the CCP should, in Wang's view, "urgently make use of public diplomacy to strengthen mutual understanding, dialogue, and cooperation" with those Americans who understand globalization's importance "so that a foundation can be built for mutual trust" (Wang Lili, 2017,

p. 45). Wang finds this effort to be "a time-critical practical responsibility"—and she offers some earlier statements of Xi Jinping made in different contexts to buttress her case.

Wang seems to be arguing against the many Chinese analysts who berate and malign the West and portray China as locked in a mortal struggle for civilizational survival with particularly the United States. But what is especially significant about her article is that she presents China as already possessing the power and the agency to play a primary role in saving globalization. She shares with her more cynically realist counterparts an evident confidence in the robustness of China's rise. Western anti-globalization movements may threaten the rise, but China need not be a passive victim. China has the power—soft and otherwise—to turn back the tide, or at least to contribute critically to an international effort to turn back the tide. Working with pro-globalization groups in the West, China can do more than save itself; it can help save the world from what Wang regards as some of its own worst tendencies (Wang Lili, 2017, pp. 46–47).

The outlook: look out?

All of the Chinese writers surveyed for this chapter assert a potency for the PRC—a capacity to transform the international system—that the economic, demographic and environmental data strongly suggest may not be warranted. The data also suggest that the disconnect between the Chinese analysts' expressed self-confidence (in addition to the "mass" self-confidence encouraged by Xi's China Dream campaign) and material reality can only be suppressed from conscious awareness for so long: how long is not clear, but the capital flight of 2014–2017 (eventually contained by use of capital controls) suggests that many PRC citizens already understand the situation for what it is. Possibly the analysts, too, understand the situation, and express self-confidence only because the Party Centre has effectively ordered them to do so. But either way, encouraging excessively high expectations about how glorious China's future can be or how profound China's international influence can become risks encouraging popular and elite expectations to depart from realistic possibilities. This is important, because only rarely in other times and places has the frustration of rising and/or excessive expectations ended well.

These emerging contradictions point to the precise significance of the sort of articles analyzed in this chapter. The question posed at the beginning was whether the Chinese economic slowdown of the mid-2010s and beyond (which looks likely to dissolve into substantially slower long-term economic growth) has affected the optimistic hubris of CCP discourse concerning China's rise that characterized the period of the new foreign policy assertiveness after 2008. This is not the same question as whether the slowdown has affected popular thinking on China's rise. The question, rather, concerns the expressed self-confidence of the CCP leadership, as reflected in the discourses its propaganda apparatus articulates directly and through the intellectuals and journalists the Party pressures (even more so, it would appear, under Xi Jinping than under his immediate predecessors) into shaping their research and writing to comport with CCP objectives. The answer seems clearly that the Party and those working under its guidance are continuing despite the economic slowdown and likely end of China's relative rise to express an optimism bordering on hubris regarding the soft power dimension of China's imagined comprehensive ascent. This optimism is in a sense an angry or resentful optimism to the extent that writers complain China should *already* have a higher level of soft power than it actually does have relative to the United States and the broader West. What keeps China down, they complain, is behind-the-scenes, illegitimate Western manipulation of the levers of discourse power, which shadowy Western actors use to malign China's reputation.

The weakness in most of this Chinese writing is that the academic and journalistic figures supplying the analyses and thereby conveying the official Xi-ist optimism do not explain how, exactly, China will eventually surpass the US-led West in soft power. They suggest by implication that China's continually increasing relative material power will somehow—automatically, in effect—transform first into discourse power and then into soft power. But there is no evidence this has been happening so far—indeed, there may be a negative relationship between rising Chinese material power and the PRC's levels of soft power (partly because more Chinese material wealth may make the country seem more fearsome to outsiders). Why should this tendency now change? Even more pointedly, the economy has now slowed to the point that it seems quite clear China's rise relative to the United States has stalled. The CCP-guided analysts' failure to confront this material fact is the chief weakness in their assessments. If they implicitly assume the economic rise will eventually solve the soft power deficit automatically, their optimism will prove profoundly misplaced if, in fact, the economic rise in relative terms is over. The Chinese analysts—and those members of the general public they do manage to influence—would suffer from the frustration of rising expectations being nurtured under the "China Dream" rubric. The CCP would then have to contend with a whole new set of vexing challenges in governance, domestic and international.

Note

1 Xi's Three Self Confidences became Four Self Confidences in July 2016 (Gan, 2017).

References

Bian Qin. 2016. "Huayu liuxiang shiguan guojia yu wenming de sicunwang" ["The Vital Significance of the Direction of Discourse Flow to the Survival of the Nation and Civilization"—title translation provided by journal], *Shijie Shehuizhuyi Yanjiu* [*World Socialism Research*] 2, pp. 78–80.

"China's Working-Age Population to Shrink 23% by 2050." 2016. *Global Times*. www. globaltimes.cn /content/995952.shtml.

Chinese Academy of Social Sciences Institute of World History Task Force on Social Change and Stability. 2014. "Yi shi wei jian, jianli wo guo zhendui Xifang yulun de jiandu he ganyu jizhi" ["Learn the Lessons of History and Set Up a Mechanism for Monitoring and Interfering with Western Public Opinion"], *Lingdao Cankao* [*Leadership Reference*] 674(June 15), pp. 29–32. Neibu faxing.

Gan, Nectar. 2017. "Xi Jinping Thought: The Communist Party's Tighter Grip in 16 Chinese Characters," *South China Morning Post*, October 25.

Han Qingxiang and Huang Xianghuai. 2017. "Wei renlei dui geng hao shehui zhidu de tansuo tigong Zhongguo fang'an" ["Proposing 'the China Solution' for Consideration as the World Searches for a Better Social System"], *Qiu Shi* [*Seeking Truth*] 686(January 1), pp. 19–21.

Jiang Shenghong. 2014. "Neidi xiao hai Xiang Gang jietou xiao bian yinfa de wangluo yulun fenxi" ["Analyzing the Network Public Opinion Spawned by Mainland Children Urinating on Hong Kong Streets"], *Lingdao Cankao* [*Leadership Reference*] 674(June 15), pp. 33–36. Neibu faxing.

Liu Tao. 2017. "Xin gainian, xin fanchou, xin biaoshu: dui wai huayu tixi chuangxin de xiucixue guannian yu lujing" ["New Concepts, New Categories, and New Forms of Expression: Perspectives from the Study of Rhetoric on Remaking the External Discourse Apparatus"], *Xinwen yu Chuanbo Yanjiu* [*Journalism and Mass Communication Research*] 138, pp. 6–17.

Liu Ying. 2017. "Huayu, guojia xingxiang, yu Zhongguo jueqi" ["Discourse, the National Image, and China's Rise"], *Lilun Yuekan* [*Theoretical Monthly*] 1, pp. 161–167.

Lynch, Daniel. 2015. *China's Futures: PRC Elites Debate Economics, Politics, and Foreign Policy*. Stanford, CA: Stanford University Press.

Lynch, Daniel. 2019. "Is China's Rise Now Stalling?," *The Pacific Review* 32(3), pp. 446–475.

National Bureau of Statistics of China. 2017. "Statistical Communique of the People's Republic of China on the 2016 National Economic and Social Development." www. stats.gov.cn/english/pressrelease/201702/t20170228_1467503.html.

National Bureau of Statistics of China. 2019. "Statistical Communique of the People's Republic of China on the 2018 National Economic and Social Development." www. stats.gov.cn/english/PressRelease/201902/t20190228_1651335.html

Sharma, Ruchir. 2016. "The Demographics of Stagnation: Why People Matter for Economic Growth," *Foreign Affairs*, March/April. www.foreignaffairs.com/articles/ world/2016-02-15/demographics -stagnation.

Su Changhe. 2016. "Tansuo tigao wo guo zhiduxing huayuquan de youxiao lujing" ["Exploring Effective Ways for Our Country to Elevate Its Systemic Discourse Power"], *Dangjian* [*Party Construction*] 4, pp. 28–30.

Wang Lili. 2017. "Dangdai Zhongguo dui Mei gonggong waijiao: yulun taishi yu renzhi kongjian" ["Contemporary Chinese Public Diplomacy toward the United States: Trends in Public Opinion and Cognition Space"], *Xiandai Guoji Guanxi* [*Contemporary International Relations*] 1, pp. 45–51.

Wang Yiwei. 2016. "Lun ruan shili beilun ji qi Zhongguo chaoyue" ["On the Paradox of Soft Power and How China Can Transcend It"], *Wenhua Ruan Shili Yanjiu* [*Studies in Cultural Soft Power*] 1(2), pp. 9–17.

Xiao Bo. 2016. "Yi kexue jingshen tansuo wenhua ruan shili fazhan de Zhongguo daolu" ["Use the Spirit of Science to Explore for a Chinese Road to Cultural Soft Power"], *Wenhua Ruan Shili Yanjiu* [*Studies in Cultural Soft Power*] 1(2), pp. 111–116.

Zhan Dexiong. 2016. "Zhongguo huayu yu meiti de zeren" ["China's Discourse and the Responsibilities of the Media"], *Wenhua Ruan Shili Yanjiu* [*Studies in Cultural Soft Power*] 3, pp. 50–53.

Zhou Fangye. 2014. "Taiguo zhongxiaoxue Hanyu tuiguang gongzuo cunzai de wenti yu jianyi" ["The Problems Existing in the Promotion of the Chinese Language in Thai Elementary and Middle Schools and Some Suggestions for Solving Them"], *Lingdao Cankao* [*Leadership Reference*] 662(February 15), pp. 45–48. Neibu faxing.

3

IRONIES OF SOFT POWER PROJECTION

The United States and China in the age of Donald Trump and Xi Jinping

Stanley Rosen

Ten years ago, in an article examining China's soft power deficit compared to Western nations, the Deputy Director of the General Administration of Press and Publications noted pessimistically that the United States held 43% of the soft power in the world, while the European Union accounted for another 34%. Excluding Japan and Australia, China and the rest of Asia was limited to less than 4% (Jiang, 2010). While the methodology that produced these striking conclusions can be questioned since soft power is notoriously difficult to measure, the Chinese concern with their own lack of success was clear. A decade later and several years into the presidency of Donald Trump, the evidence of the decline of the American image internationally is overwhelming. Writings by scholars, journalists and political pundits appear uniformly to agree that the actions of President Trump have severely damaged America's strong advantage in soft power—getting what you want through attraction and persuasion rather than coercion and payment—particularly in relation to its competition with a rising China, which has been investing heavily in promoting its own brand as an alternative to the United States. The results from the spring 2017 Pew Research Center Global Attitudes Survey are especially striking. When respondents in 37 countries were asked about their confidence in the American president to do the right thing in world affairs, comparing the results Obama received at the end of his presidency with Trump's results, only two countries—Russia and Israel—had more confidence in Trump. The gap was particularly large in Western European countries, Japan and South Korea, Canada and Australia (Pew Research Center, 2017).

Given these results, the two questions of most current interest are: (1) What are the longer-term implications of the damage inflicted on American soft power by the Trump presidency? (2) Has China has been able to reap the rewards from the American decline and, if so, are China's gains sustainable?

China has, to be sure, made efforts to fill the vacuum created by Trump's "America First" policy, with President Xi Jinping's January 2017 speech at the Davos World Economic Forum promoting China's belief in globalization and win–win strategies a clear response. Even with Trump attending the 2018 Davos Forum to reassure investors that "America first doesn't mean America alone," and in the absence of Xi, the subsequent reporting suggested that "the geopolitical momentum [still] lay with Beijing, not Washington" (Bradsher, 2018). Moreover, as some leading Chinese international relations theorists had suggested, China has moved to expand a "green card" program to provide permanent residency to "high end" foreigners (Ives, 2017; Yan, 2017), precisely when the United States has moved to restrict its H-1B visa processing lottery for skilled foreign workers (Yu, 2017). The Pew survey provides compelling evidence that China is indeed catching up. The number of nations in which the United States holds a competitive advantage in favorability over China has halved over the last few years, from 25 to 12; whereas the United States once had a 12-point lead over China in terms of a global median, by 2017 that lead had shrunk to 2 points. Regionally, China is particularly well liked in Latin America and the Middle East, while the United States scores higher in Europe and the Asia-Pacific region.

Other surveys, however, suggest that while the United States has indeed fallen, China's rise has been rather less dramatic. For example, the annual Portland Soft Power 30, which uses a more complex methodology, shows that while the United States fell to number 4 by 2018, after a 2016 ranking as number 1, and is now surpassed by the United Kingdom, France and Germany, China came in at number 27, down two places from 2017, and well behind leading democracies in Western Europe, North America and East Asia (Portland Soft Power 30, 2018). In addition, the annual Gallup poll of 134 countries, taken one year into the Trump presidency, shows how closely the American decline is tied to its president. The median global approval rating of the job performance of US leadership stands at a new low of 30%, down nearly 20 points from the 48% approval rating in the last year of President Obama's administration, and four points lower than the previous low of 34% in the last year of President George W. Bush's administration. However, it is useful to note that the approval rating for China's leadership was only 31%, the same figure as in 2010, and there has been little variation in recent years; indeed, the high for China was 37% in 2008, the year of the Beijing Olympics. By contrast, German leadership, at 41%, scores far higher than the United States or China (Gallup, 2018).

As I will suggest, using additional data and evidence to be discussed below, the current decline of the American image under President Trump notwithstanding, there are compelling factors that will make it difficult for China to surpass the United States in the generation of soft power. However, as I will also note, despite a good deal of rhetoric and a great deal of expense, China may in fact be less interested in soft power than is commonly suggested, and has shown, even in the absence of soft power, an ability to influence other nations, if not to do what China desires, at least to *not do* what they abhor.

First, it has been well documented that American soft power has been successful in China and elsewhere despite the indifference of the US government, while a massive Chinese governmental effort at a cost of over $10 billion a year in support of its "go abroad" (*zouchuqu*) strategy, while certainly enjoying some success, has been less effective in the United States and most countries outside the Third World. What is striking, however, is that American soft power has been notably successful in China—and throughout the world—despite the lack of soft power promotion by the American government, a strong aversion to American foreign policy and the belief that such foreign policy is designed to keep China weak and maintain American hegemony, and Chinese government efforts to impede the American success. American government neglect of soft power promotion is due, in part, to the nature of the American political and electoral systems, and in part to the belief that America is strong enough to do as it pleases with or without approbation from outside its borders. When the bipartisan Bowles-Simpson Commission came up with proposals to stem the burgeoning federal budget deficit, the cuts were concentrated in areas the American public already questions, for example the State Department and America's foreign operations, not entitlements, military expenditures or changing the tax system, where the real money is located. As one Congressman told Joseph Nye, the academic who coined the term soft power in 1990, "You are right about the importance of combining soft power with hard power, but I cannot talk about soft power and hope to get re-elected" (Nye, 2002, 2004, 2011). The cuts in funding to the Voice of America China programs—what one critic called "unilateral disarmament"—have been widely reported and lamented (Bosco, 2012). WikiLeaks has released cables from the American Consulate in Shanghai pleading for government support for the American pavilion at the Shanghai Expo, warning that "the US business community . . . is not enthusiastic about a 'national' pavilion that must be 100% funded by the private sector." On the verge of informing the Shanghai authorities that the Expo would have to go forward without US participation, American diplomats warned Washington that in addition to the inevitable damage to US–China relations, "the damage to the US public image will be global" (WikiLeaks, 2008). In the end, the $61 million funding was provided by around 60 multinational corporations, resulting in a pavilion whose most visible attribute was a series of product placements leading, according to a recent documentary film, to a serious loss of face for America among Chinese and foreign visitors (Chow, 2018). Seen in this context, the Trump administration's announcement that the State Department's budget would be cut by 31%, while dramatic and eye-catching, was in a sense an extension of the long-standing emphasis on hard power over soft power (Harris, 2017). What Trump has done is to move from the American government's benign neglect to active sabotage of soft power.

If it seems ironic that American soft power has been successful in China and elsewhere despite the indifference of the US government, it is equally ironic that the massive Chinese governmental effort has made only limited inroads in the United States and most countries outside the Third World. However, there is an explanation for this seemingly surprising outcome. American soft power,

[handwritten margin note: ✻ US soft power successful because it is not linked to gov]

it could be argued, has been successful precisely because it is *not* linked to the American government, whereas the Chinese promotion of soft power hardly exists apart from the efforts of its government. Chen Shengluo, a Chinese academic who does surveys on university student attitudes toward the United States and other countries, noted the existence of "two Americas" in the minds of Chinese students, a "hegemonist" America on the international stage and an America in which a high level of development has been achieved at home because of its values and social system (Chen, 2003). American culture could succeed in China (and elsewhere) only because the students (and foreign publics) could accept this separation. Indeed, when the NATO-led US bombed the Chinese Embassy in Belgrade, Yugoslavia in May 1999 during the war in Kosovo, the Chinese media tried to link the hegemonist United States with the cultural United States, asserting that everything from American blockbuster films to the promotion of human rights and globalization, not to mention "Western civilization" more generally, was part of a deliberate conspiracy by America to control the world. This approach was highlighted in an award-winning series in *Beijing Youth Daily* (*Beijing qingnian bao*) (Rosen, 2003).[1] Surveys done in China soon after the bombing strongly suggested, however, that such governmental efforts were unsuccessful, that popular disillusionment toward US culture was short-lived (Zhao, 2002).

Several months after Trump's inauguration the 2017 Pew survey in effect acknowledged this separation between government and popular and political culture, with the results suggesting continuing support for Americans, American culture and civil liberties. For example, while showing widespread disapproval of Trump's major policy proposals and his personal characteristics, 65% of respondents in the 37 countries "liked" American music, movies and television (29% did not); 58% held a favorable view of Americans (26% did not); and 54% said the US government respected the personal freedoms of its people (39% dissented) (Pew, 2017). The clear unpopularity of Trump among most Americans was a likely contributing factor in the willingness to isolate him from overall views of the United States. Joseph Nye noted that he doubted the decline in the American image is likely to persist over the long term, unless Trump gets the United States into a major war, or if he gets elected to a second term and damages the American system of checks and balances and America's reputation as a democratic society (Osnos, 2018). Indeed, there are early warning signs of the latter. The Pew survey showed that slightly more people disliked American ideas about democracy than liked them (46% to 43%), with a larger percentage suggesting opposition to American ideas and customs spreading to their own countries (54% opposed, 38% in favor).

[handwritten margin note, left side: China's highest priority remains domestic]

Second, and equally important, despite the large investment China has made in getting its message to the outside world, China's highest priority remains domestic, the maintenance of political and social stability *within* China. They have repeatedly demonstrated, with the arrests of human rights lawyers and activists, harsh policies affecting Uyghurs and Tibetans and their retaliation against

China uses soft power to promote domestic legitimacy (negative soft power) [handwritten margin note]

countries such as Norway, the Philippines, France, South Korea and Canada, that a bad press outside China, or even a reputation as a "bully," is an acceptable price in their hierarchy of values. William Callahan, in arguing that China uses soft power more for domestic policy—to promote legitimacy—than for foreign affairs, has called this "negative soft power" (Callahan, 2015).

Further evidence that soft power, which takes a considerable time to generate, is not China's primary goal can be seen in behavior that the National Endowment for Democracy, in assessing the overseas activities of Russia and China, has characterized as "sharp power," where the attraction of culture and values associated with soft power is replaced by attempts to coerce and manipulate opinion abroad, particularly in democratic societies (National Endowment for Democracy, 2017; Nye, 2018). However, while the term is recent, China's use of sharp power is not new, albeit the most recent methods to manipulate public opinion, as the revelations and pushback from Australia suggest, are more covert. After a series of media reports on China's efforts to interfere in Australian politics, in part through the funding of local politicians by Chinese-born political donors, Australia's prime minister Malcolm Turnbull introduced a series of proposed laws to curb foreign influence. The Chinese Embassy reacted by railing against the "typical anti-China hysteria in media accounts," noting that the criticism of China has "unscrupulously vilified the Chinese students as well as the Chinese community in Australia with racial prejudice, which in turn has tarnished Australia's reputation as a multicultural society," in effect taking a criticism of Chinese Communist Party covert activities and conflating it into an attack on all Chinese (Cave, 2017). Within China, the media made it clear that Australia, which relies heavily on Chinese trade and investment, as well as the tuition students pay at Australian universities, was only harming itself in terms of Chinese public opinion. This view was advanced in the results of an online poll where Chinese netizens were asked to choose the "least friendly country to China in 2017." As China's *Global Times* noted, Australia won "in a landslide," followed by India, the United States, Japan and South Korea (Global Times, 2017). Done at different times, of course, the poll would have found a different rank order, and other countries equally high on this list. Although no such survey was done at the end of 2018, it is likely that the primary enemy would then have been Canada, as a result of the detention of Meng Wanzhou, the daughter of the founder of Huawei, and its chief financial officer, and for 2019 it presumably would have been the United States, as a result of the Sino–American "trade war." It is precisely this sensitivity within China to the image of the country that is portrayed overseas, and the retaliation, or threat of retaliation, against those countries that are deemed to have offended China, that shows a continuing lack of self-confidence and which remains a major obstacle to its soft power ambitions.

This apparent contradiction—the commitment of extensive resources to promote China's soft power, while prioritizing other goals such as political and social stability, along with the willingness to sacrifice short-term soft power in order to defend China's honor—becomes more understandable in Chinese official and academic writings on soft power. Most authors exude strong self-confidence in the inevitability of the increase in China's soft power as the country's economic and international status continue to rise, suggesting that were it not for the continuation of the long history of American and Western policies to deny China its rightful place in the world, using their control of global media, China would have already succeeded. As with the United States, the argument goes, Chinese soft power will flow from the recognition of China's hard power (Shen, 2017), a point that is also emphasized in Daniel Lynch's chapter in this volume.

Indeed, China is correct about the importance of global media not under their control but, as noted above, their own target audience is primarily domestic and their intention is to avoid negative reporting, particularly on sensitive subjects. Thus, a *Wall Street Journal* reporter was the latest journalist to be expelled from China for reporting on an Australian investigation of the activities of a cousin of Xi Jinping, leading to strong condemnation by the Foreign Correspondents' Club of China (Wee, 2019). This also explains their reporting on the unrest in Hong Kong, where they have compared protestors to Nazis and cockroaches, and tools of foreign forces, while inflaming nationalist sentiment by the selective airing of videos showing images of violence from protestors. Facebook and Twitter have removed hundreds of accounts they determined were "state-backed," and Twitter has now forbidden state-run media outlets from paying to get their tweets promoted so they appear prominently in users' timelines. At home this strategy appears to be highly successful, but outside China, where diverse sources of information are available, their efforts appear to have backfired (Yuan, 2019).

That said, the competition between China and America is not a zero-sum game where China automatically gains when the United States loses nor, as we have seen under President Trump, does soft power directly follow from hard power. As then Defense Secretary James Mattis noted, in decrying the loss in American soft power while giving an impromptu speech to American troops in Jordan in August 2017, despite America's widely acknowledged "power of intimidation," the United States has lost the "power of inspiration" (Betley, 2017). In a similar manner, the economic and military rise of China, and the increasing use of China's sharp power, has been intimidating but at least in the democracies of the world, it has not been inspiring.

China's constraints in its soft power competition with the United States and other actors

The most familiar and visible area of American success of course is cultural, although cultural soft power is only one dimension, with some surveys measuring soft power along economic, human capital, political and diplomatic dimensions, in addition to culture (Bouton and Holyk, 2011). Then Secretary General Hu Jintao, in an internal speech in October 2011 at a Central Committee plenum, focused on the cultural as he railed against the penetration of Western culture into China, noting that the West and China were engaged in an "escalating war" in which China must respond to the "strategic plot" to Westernize and divide the country, with the ideological and cultural fields seen as the "focal areas of [the West's] long-term infiltration." As he concluded, in contrast to the strong culture of the West, the international influence of Chinese culture "is not commensurate with China's international status" (Wong, 2012). However, it is important to understand that the problem suggested by General Secretary Hu goes well beyond the success of Hollywood films at the Chinese box office, or the popularity of Lady Gaga and Beyoncé in China or, as one Chinese book title put it, "We don't have Avatar" (Han, 2011).[2] As it seeks to compete with American, European, Japanese and South Korean soft power throughout the world, particularly beyond the other authoritarian systems, the constraints China faces reflect, most fundamentally, the nature of the Chinese political system, Chinese government policies, and the continuing influence of traditional Chinese culture.

Robert Cain, in analyzing why South Korea, despite its smaller size and more limited state investment, has a far greater global cultural impact than China, pointed to five reasons (Cain, 2012). First, China has invested in hard assets such as production and post-production facilities, but not in the kind of training that would nurture creative talent. Second, the political regime has remained deeply antagonistic toward true artistic expression. Third, Chinese storytelling emphasizes the collective over the individual, while American blockbusters succeed by emphasizing heroes or even anti-heroes who succeed by ignoring the rules. Fourth, censorship tends to be unpredictable, with government suspicion and interference possible at every stage, stifling creative and innovative ideas. Fifth, the educational system emphasizes obedience to authority and discourages idiosyncratic expression (Cain, 2012). Other analysts have noted that Chinese soft power "lacks credibility," that the projection of soft power needs to be matched by deeds (D'Hooghe, 2011). Massive state funding cannot compensate for the fact that China lags far behind in those areas Joseph Nye has identified as most important for soft power projection: a dominant culture and ideology close to prevailing norms, credibility enhanced by domestic and international performance and access to multiple channels of communication, which enables the framing of issues. While China is addressing some of this deficit, particularly with regard to expanding its communication channels, the state's self-imposed limits on what can be communicated remain a serious obstacle.

A good example of South Korean success in an area where China should be well placed to succeed was the soap opera *My Love from Another Star* (*lai zi xing-xing de ni*), which reportedly garnered over three billion views online despite the fact that it was never broadcast over any of China's major television networks. It led to soul-searching by Chinese officials, becoming a hot topic for discussion at the National People's Congress and Chinese People's Political Consultative Conference (CPPCC) meetings in Beijing. One CPPCC delegate suggested that "it is more than just a Korean soap opera. It hurts our national dignity" (Wan, 2014a). When another South Korean drama, this time with a military theme, *Descendants of the Sun (taiyang de houyi)* again dominated the ratings and trending topics on Weibo, China's version of Twitter, the response from Chinese officialdom was more forceful and direct. The Ministry of Public Security warned via their Weibo account that "watching Korean dramas could be dangerous, and may even lead to legal troubles," citing some real-life cases of domestic violence, divorce and plastic surgery, all of which it related to an obsession with Korean dramas and accompanied with photos of similar incidents from various Korean television series (Tan, 2016). Politburo Standing Committee member Wang Qishan, also a big fan of *House of Cards*, had noted in reference to earlier dramas, that "Korean drama is ahead of us," while also pointing out that "the core and soul of the Korean [soap] opera is a distillation of traditional Chinese culture; it just propagates traditional Chinese culture in the form of a TV drama," ironically suggesting that South Korea is better at presenting Chinese culture than China itself (Wan, 2014a). Wang's comments suggest that this (and similar) Korean family dramas may be indirectly enhancing China's soft power. This is reminiscent of an earlier debate over the DreamWorks blockbuster *Kung Fu Panda* films, where some in China sought to vilify and boycott the first film because it had co-opted for its own profit two important symbols of Chinese culture, pandas and martial arts, while others felt that it was respectful to those symbols and even helped promote Chinese culture to a global audience. Indeed, as I have argued elsewhere, examining the dialogue and the reception within China of *Kung Fu Panda, 2012*, and other films, Hollywood quite consciously does a better job of promoting Chinese soft power than China's own film industry (Rosen, 2011).

Nevertheless, there remains a concern, even a fear, of foreign cultural imports which are *too* successful in China, as the Ministry of Public Security's warnings about *Descendants of the Sun* indicated. More importantly, following the line of reasoning suggested above, culture and soft power more generally are subordinate to other, more important values, particularly politics. Thus, when South Korea agreed to deploy the American THAAD (Terminal High Altitude Area Defense) missile system against the threat from North Korea, despite strong Chinese objections over the impact on China's own missile deterrent system, Song Joong Ki, the star of *Descendants*, was one of many Korean celebrities and K-pop groups prohibited from appearing on Chinese television, giving concerts or attending public events, with many netizens quoted in the Chinese media in support of the Chinese government's position (Chheda, 2016).

Arguably, another example of this phenomenon may be the American television series *House of Cards*, which had great success since the first season began to be streamed by Sohu, roughly a Chinese equivalent of Netflix, in March 2013. The first season had 24.5 million Chinese views, with the largest proportion coming from government employees and Beijing residents. The release of season two in February 2014 received more than nine million views in its first weekend, ranking number one among American shows streamed by Sohu, beating out

The Big Bang Theory. As the official Xinhua News Agency acknowledged, "A large number of our country's senior leaders in government and enterprises and opinion leaders also highly recommend this show" (Wan, 2014b). Perhaps it is not surprising that China's leaders would find this show appealing. Wang Qishan, who seems to spend a fair amount of time watching foreign TV programming, was reported to "attach great importance" to protagonist Kevin Spacey (Frank Underwood in the show) as majority whip in the House of Representatives, since his role is to "maintain party unity" (Wertime, 2013). China's ambassador to the United States, Cui Tiankai, in noting that he had watched two seasons of the show, suggested that it exposes the disadvantages of American bipartisan politics and "embodies some of the characteristics and corruption that is present in American politics," where "many things can never be accomplished because the interests of each party are of the greatest importance" (China Envoy, 2014).

While China was merely a peripheral part of season one, mentioned only when a billionaire with close personal ties to the president is speaking Chinese on his cellphone in the pursuit of his business interests, season two had a politically well-connected and corrupt Chinese businessman as a major player. In addition to increasing the show's popularity in China, it also led to an interesting debate, as with Hollywood films, over whether the show represents a "victory" for Chinese soft power (Zhu, 2014). Those who argue in favor of such a conclusion point to a telling and smirking aside to the audience from Underwood, after his political machinations have landed him the vice presidency, that he is now only a heartbeat away from the top without getting a single vote, adding for emphasis that "democracy is so overrated," a line that could have been written in Zhongnanhai. Season two also showed the arrival of China on the world stage, with the power of a Chinese protagonist to influence American politics at the highest level.

However, although *House of Cards*—a favorite of then President Obama as well—clearly reveals a political system that is highly corrupt and often dysfunctional, it is not self-evident that the show enhances Chinese soft power. Indeed, one possible reason for the show's popularity is that the (fictional) Washington portrayed is much closer to Chinese politics than it is to American politics. The line about not getting a single vote—after all, Frank Underwood was elected multiple times to Congress in his district in South Carolina—applies much more to politicians in China than to politicians in the United States. The corrupt Chinese businessman is closely connected to his political patrons at the top of the political system, very reminiscent of Bo Xilai and his financial backers. Several Chinese viewers, no doubt tongue in cheek, suggested in Weibo postings, "How could the American Ministry of Propaganda have allowed this show to be broadcast?" (China Digital Times, 2014). The program also reveals the complicated nature of the American political system, with its checks and balances between the executive and the legislature, the critical role of the press as a watchdog on government corruption and malfeasance, and the interaction between the representative and his or her constituency, represented most forcefully by the tragic character of Peter Russo and his working-class constituents in

Philadelphia. As will be noted below, surveys in China have shown that among elite university students, the American political system is seen as far better than the Chinese political system in combatting corruption, in part because there is surprising admiration for the separation of powers; by contrast, there appears to be skepticism that a one-party authoritarian system with no institutional checks on its power can police itself. It would be interesting to do a similar survey on the reception of *House of Cards* in China to see whether this positive assessment of the American political system has been reinforced or negated by the show's revelations.

Ironically, the freedom to create shows of this nature, or even films such as *Kung Fu Panda*, which features this iconic symbol of China as fat and lazy when he is first introduced to the audience, is particularly frustrating to China's own filmmakers. At a meeting of delegates from the culture and entertainment industry at the CPPCC, Chinese censorship was cited as one of the key reasons why a program such as *House of Cards* could never be produced within China. Film director Feng Xiaogang noted that while he waits for a film to go through the "examination and approval system," his "heart trembles," while another entertainer said that "my wings and imagination are all broken" as a result of the vetting process (Wan, 2014b). One recent example of this phenomenon which attracted worldwide attention was the withdrawal—for "technical reasons"—of the latest film from Zhang Yimou, China's most prominent filmmaker, at the last minute from the 69th Berlin International Film Festival in 2019. This led to the entire jury appearing onstage to make the announcement and express their great disappointment over this decision, and to media throughout the world openly speculating on the possible reasons for this decision, ranging from the subject matter—the Cultural Revolution—to the new role of the Communist Party's Propaganda Department in the entertainment sector. From a soft power perspective, this familiar lack of transparency is counterproductive to the enhancement of China's global image (Qin, 2019).

The continued success of American cultural products in China is likely to be tested by the deteriorating relationship over trade and other issues that has marked the regimes of Presidents Trump and Xi, as anti-US sentiment has soared in Chinese official media and online discussions. However, such sentiment did not dampen the enthusiasm for viewing the final episode of HBO's *Game of Thrones*. After Chinese authorities blocked HBO in 2018 over an episode in which John Oliver mocked Xi Jinping on his comedy show *Last Week Tonight*, the only official channel showing *Game of Thrones* was Tencent Video, which postponed showing the finale because of a "technical issue." After the "postponement," which in effect was a cancellation, "online Chinese fans were in uproar" (Zhang, 2019). Many viewers turned to pirated versions of the final episode, noting that Tencent edited the content for violence and "lewd content" anyway, and demonstrating once again how Chinese youth could compartmentalize the "bad America" (foreign policy) and separate it from the attractions of American culture, albeit both aspects are included in Nye's definition of soft power.

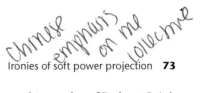

House of Cards and *Game of Thrones* are also good examples of Robert Cain's point, noted above, that American blockbusters often feature heroic or anti-heroic individuals fighting against the system while in China the emphasis is placed on the collective over the individual. His point was strikingly evident in the response within China to Chinese writer Mo Yan's success in winning the 2012 Nobel Prize for Literature. As the first "mainstream" Chinese writer to be accorded such an honor, which has also eluded scientists who are citizens of the PRC, it was not surprising that Mo Yan's victory was front-page news. However, while Mo noted that it was an individual prize and suggested that it was unlikely to have a lasting impact on Chinese literature or even the popularity of his own works, local officials in his hometown of Gaomi in eastern Shandong province emphasized the value of the prize for the larger community (Tam, 2012). Within a week they announced plans to spend 670 million RMB ($107 million) to transform Mo Yan's home village into a "Red Sorghum Culture and Experience Zone," and have local residents cultivate the red sorghum that had already been proven to be unprofitable. As a local official noted to Mo's 90-year-old father, "Your son is no longer your son, and the house is no longer your house" since your son is now the pride of China. "It does not really matter if you agree or not" (Xin Jing Bao, 2012; Moore, 2012; Link, 2012). An official from the local tourism bureau explained that provincial authorities ordered Gaomi to execute the tourism program regardless of how Mo Yan and his family felt about it (Li, 2012).

A rather similar situation applied in the case of tennis star Li Na, winner of the French Open in 2011 and the Australian Open in 2014, after which she retired. Her victory in France was celebrated with a picture of Li kissing the trophy at the top of the front page of *People's Daily* (Renmin ribao, 2011). Her victory at the Australian Open received much more international publicity, in part because it was her last event before retiring, and in part because of her widely acclaimed speech—in English—which demonstrated not only her linguistic ability, but her sharp sense of humor. She thanked her agent, who "makes me rich," and her husband: "You're a nice guy; also, you are so lucky to find me" (YouTube, 2014). Indeed, after winning the French Open she secured endorsements worth US$40 million, making her the third-best-paid female athlete in the world. Given all the people she thanked, it was striking that she didn't refer to her time in China, prompting Xinhua to note that her success "would not have been possible without her time on the national team" (Economist, 2014). What Xinhua did not report was her escape from the national team in 2002, returning to the university and leaving tennis. She agreed to return only when she was allowed to choose her own coach and retain 90% of her earnings, instead of giving over 50% to the state. It was also striking to contrast the visual image of a smiling Li opening a champagne bottle in Australia (Getty Images, 2014) to the unsmiling picture of her, back home in China, receiving a reward of 800,000 yuan ($132,000) from a local official. Her 22 million followers on Sina Weibo ensured that the latter picture went viral (Economist, 2014).

Such independent thought from Chinese athletes surfaced again during the 2016 Olympics when swimmer Fu Yuanhui went off-script during an interview with a Chinese reporter to explain why her team came in fourth in the 4 × 100 medley relay. The reporter, noticing her bent over, hands on her midsection, asked whether she was experiencing stomach pain. Li's unexpected response was that her "period started last night . . . so I'm feeling pretty weak and really tired. But this isn't an excuse . . . I just didn't swim very well" (Hollywood Reporter, 2016). It was not just Chinese netizens on social media who praised such candor; the comments section following *The Hollywood Reporter* article was filled with praise from Westerners who noted that Fu had become their favorite Olympian, just as the comments on Li's YouTube speech offered glowing praise for "their favorite tennis player." The spontaneity and individualism of Li and Fu vividly demonstrate one of the major problems of Chinese soft power projection, the inability to allow the individual to succeed and behave as an *individual*, apart from the state apparatus that, in the official discourse, has created that success.

Given the rise of the middle class and a consumer society in recent years it is perhaps not surprising to find individualism and other values associated with the United States and the West gaining prominence in China. However, even in the sensitive area of politics, China has faced a soft power deficit. For example, an extensive survey done by Chen Shengluo found, to his great surprise, that elite university students in Beijing had a decided preference for the American political system over the Chinese system. In particular, as suggested above, they admired the separation of powers. In his sample of 505 students at Beijing's best universities, 31.7% liked the separation of powers a great deal and 43% liked it somewhat. When those who chose "so-so" (*yiban*) are added, the total comes to 95.8%, with only 4.2% choosing "somewhat dislike it" and not a single student choosing "entirely dislike it."[3] Chen interpreted these results as an indication that the students felt the Party's monopoly of power would never be able to solve the problem of official corruption—the number one grievance in Chinese society according to many surveys—and that the American system did a better job in this regard (Chen, 2011). His findings are congruent with an earlier internal government survey done among Chinese university students that found well over 80% agreeing that Western visual culture products propagate Western political concepts and lifestyles, but only 17% noting they "don't identify with them" (Rosen, 2010; *Lingdao canyue*, 2007).

The 2012 American presidential election and the political transition in China, occurring at virtually the same time (November 6 and November 8), also offers some valuable lessons on why American political soft power has been more successful than its Chinese counterpart, which can be seen from the reaction of the Chinese media and Chinese citizens to the operation of the two political systems. While there was a virtual blackout in the Chinese media on the Chinese transition, and the focus on the American election included some discussion of the familiar "China-bashing" that has been a feature of many American presidential elections, the general public appeared to be less interested in the actual issues and more excited by the process through which the candidates sought to attract votes (Liu, 2012). In a rather similar manner, the 2016 American election was widely discussed in China, with one Chinese observer who studied the election and the Chinese reaction noting that her friends "are fascinated by the unprecedented fierce competition among the candidates and by the fact that the so-called anti-establishment candidates have gained so much popularity" (Zhang, 2016).

By contrast, despite public interest, politics in China remains off limits as a topic of discussion and debate. It is instructive to examine the reporting on the abolition of presidential term limits in China in 2018, with Western reporters treating the story as a turning point in the West's understanding of China, noting that "decades of optimism about China's rise have now been discarded" (Economist, 2018). China's state-run media was extremely low-key, suggesting that the repeal was one of a number of constitutional changes, an "adjustment," or "a perfecting of the term system for president." By contrast, it was a major topic on Chinese social media, with censors hard at work to remove the many critical comments that appeared online (Rosen, 2018).

Conclusion

More than 25 years ago, following the demise of Communism in the Soviet Union and the Eastern bloc, Francis Fukuyama famously declared victory for liberal democratic governments (Fukuyama, 1992). The rise of China, however, has presented a very different challenge to liberal democracies. As David Runciman argues in a recent book, the rival and bitterly opposed worldviews that marked the central political contests of the 20th century have been replaced by competing versions of the same basic goals: economic results and widespread prosperity (Runciman, 2018a, 2018b). As did Fukuyama, Runciman also sees human dignity joining material satisfaction as an essential component for political legitimacy, with the less ideological, more pragmatic Chinese Communist Party far more successful in delivering dignity to the Chinese people than the Russians had been.

That said, the disadvantage China faces in competing with American soft power, I would argue, is closely related to the differences between the Chinese and American dreams. As I have noted elsewhere, unlike the American dream, which offers an individual success without reference to the nation or any collective force beyond his or her own efforts, the Chinese dream is more about the nation than the individual, where individual dreams are expected to fit within the larger narrative of a collective dream for China, and where self-sacrifice may be necessary (Rosen, 2014, 2017). In Runciman's terms, the Chinese approach to human dignity assumes a collective national dignity, which comes in the form of demanding greater respect for China itself (Runciman, 2018a). Even individual achievements, as the Mo Yan and Li Na cases suggested, cannot be *just* individual achievements, but *must* become part of this larger collective narrative of a rising China, fully worthy of world respect. In a similar manner, when other

explains chinese soft power disadvantage

countries disrespect or offend China, they must be confronted and punished. The primary audience for these messages is domestic, to show the Chinese public the overriding value of the state in supporting their achievements and defending their interests. While this conflation of the individual with the state is unlikely to be appealing in developed democratic societies, the "Chinese model," marked by economic success and a rising middle class, resonates much better in countries yet to make this transition, a conclusion that is supported by the high favorability ratings China has received in many Third World countries.

Notes

1 The articles in this series included: "A Renewed Understanding of Human Rights" (May 15); "A Renewed Understanding of Freedom of the Press" (May 16); "A Renewed Understanding of National Strength" (May 17); "A Renewed Understanding of Globalization" (May 18); "A Renewed Understanding of American Blockbuster Films" (May 19); and "A Renewed Understanding of Western Civilization" (May 20). More generally, a separate article was entitled "The Chinese Take Another Look at the United States" (May 19).
2 Han addresses the different definitions and uses of soft power, including its role as a foreign policy and a cultural instrument (e.g., pp. 193–201).
3 Chen's work of course cannot be published openly in China, but it has been internally circulated among Chinese officials.

References

Beijing Youth Daily [*Beijing qingnian bao*]. 1999. May 15–20.
Betley, Alexander M. 2017. "The Decline of American Soft Power: Will It Persist after Trump? *MinnPost*, October 6. www.minnpost.com/community-voices/2017/10/decline-american-soft-power-will-it-persist-after-trump.
Bosco, Joseph A. 2012. "Why Voice of America Is Losing to Voice of Communist China: At Home and Abroad," *The Christian Science Monitor*, April 27. www.csmonitor.com/Commentary/Opinion/2012/0427/Why-Voice-of-America-is-losing-to-voice-of-communist-China-at-home-and-abroad.
Bouton, Marshall M. and Gregory G. Holyk. 2011. "Asian Perceptions of American Soft Power," in Sook Jong Lee and Jan Melissen (eds.), *Public Diplomacy and Soft Power in East Asia*. New York: Palgrave Macmillan, pp. 191–222.
Bradsher, Keith. 2018. "At Davos, the Real Star May Have Been China, Not Trump," *The New York Times*, January 28. www.nytimes.com/2018/01/28/business/davos-trump-china.html.
Cain, Robert. 2012. "The Korean Conundrum: Why South Korea Has Greater Global Cultural Impact than China, Part 1 and Part 2," *chinafilmbiz*, October 11 and 17. https://chinafilmbiz.com/2012/10/10/the-korea-conundrum-why-south-korea-has-greater-global-cultural-impact-than-china-part-1/ and https://chinafilmbiz.com/2012/10/17/the-korea-conundrum-why-south-korea-has-greater-global-cultural-impact-than-china-part-2/.
Callahan, William A. 2015. "Identity and Security in China: The Negative Soft Power of the China Dream," *Politics* 35(3–4), pp. 216–229.
Cave, Damien. 2017. "China Scolds Australia over Its Fears of Foreign Influence," *The New York Times*, December 7, p. A10.

Chen, Shengluo. 2003. "Two Americas: How Chinese College Students View the United States," translated in Stanley Rosen (ed.), *Chinese Education and Society* 36(6), pp. 7–31.

Chen, Shengluo. 2011. "Chinese University Students' Perceptions of the Political Systems of China and the United States," in Stanley Rosen and Chen Shengluo (eds.), *Chinese Education and Society* 44(2–3), pp. 13–57.

Chheda, Manthan. 2016. "'Descendants of the Sun' Actor Song Joong Ki Banned from All Chinese Projects Including Vivo," *China Topix*, August 13. www.chinatopix.com/articles/98145/20160813/descendants-of-the-sun-actor-song-joong-ki-banned-from-all-chinese-projects-including-vivo.htm

China Digital Times. 2014. "China in *House of Cards*, and *House of Cards* in China," February 2014. https://chinadigitaltimes.net/2014/02/china-house-cards-house-cards-china/.

China Envoy. 2014. "U.S. Dirty Politics Shown in House of Cards," *Al Arabia News*, March 14. https://english.alarabiya.net/en/variety/2014/03/14/China-envoy-House-of-Cards-shows-U-S-dirty-politics.html.

Chow, Mina. 2018. *"Face of a Nation: What Happened to the World's Fair?"* Mina Chow, director and writer; Mina Chow, Mitchell Block and Alessandra Pasquino, producers.

D'Hooghe, Ingrid. 2011. "The Limits of China's Soft Power in Europe: Beijing's Public Diplomacy Puzzle," in Sook Jong Lee and Jan Melissen (eds.), *Public Diplomacy and Soft Power in East Asia*. New York: Palgrave Macmillan, pp. 163–190.

Economist, The. 2014. "Free Spirit: Not Thanking the Motherland," February 1. www.economist.com/news/china/21595486-tennis-star-gives-officials-cold-shoulder-free-spirit.

Economist, The. 2018. "What the West Got Wrong," March 3, pp. 9–10.

Fukuyama, Francis. 1992. *The End of History and the Last Man*. New York: Free Press.

Gallup. 2018. "Rating World Leaders: 2018: The U.S., vs. Germany, China and Russia." news.gallup.com/reports/225587/rating-world-leaders-2018.aspx#aspnetForm.

Getty Images. 2014. www.gettyimages.co.uk/detail/news-photo/li-na-of-china-poses-with-champagne-following-her-victory-news-photo/465063097#/li-na-of-china-poses-with-champagne-following-her-victory-over-of-picture-id465063097.

Global Times. 2017. "Australia Least Friendly Country in 2017: Poll," December 27. www.globaltimes.cn/content/1082374.shtml.

Han, Heyuan. 2011. *Women meiyou afanda: zhongguo ruan shili weiji* [*We Don't Have Avatar: The Crisis of Chinese Soft Power*]. Beijing: China Development Press.

Harris, Gardiner. 2017. "A Shift from 'Soft Power' Diplomacy," *The New York Times*, March 17, p. A19.

Hollywood Reporter. 2016. "Chinese Swimmer Fu Yuanhui Cites Being 'Really Tired' from Her Period after Team Finishes Fourth at Rio Olympics," August 16. www.hollywoodreporter.com/news/fu-yuanhui-period-olympics-chinese-swimmer-919858.

Ives, Mike. 2017. "China Wants to Attract More Foreigners (of a Certain Kind)," *The New York Times*, February 24, p. A8.

Jiang, Jianguo. 2010. "Tuijin wenhua tizhi gaige, tigao guojia wenhua ruan shili" ["Carry Out Cultural System Reform, Enhance the State's Cultural Soft Power"], *Renmin ribao*, November 22. http://politics.people.com.cn/GB/30178/13279140.html.

Li, Raymond. 2012. "Mo Yan's Hometown Is Looking to Cash In," *South China Morning Post*, October 19, p. 7.

Lingdao canyue [Reference Reading for Leaders]. 2007. "Dui woguo qingnian xuesheng zai xinyang deng 21 ge zhongda wentishang de wenjuan diaocha ji jianyao fenxi" ["A Brief Analysis of Responses to a Survey Questionnaire on Belief Systems and 21 Other Important Questions Given by Young Chinese Students"] 19, July 5, pp. 24–28.

Link, Perry. 2012. "Does This Writer Deserve the Prize?," *The New York Review of Books*, December 6. www.nybooks.com/articles/2012/12/06/mo-yan-nobel-prize/.

Liu, Nicole. 2012. "Chinese Media: Quiet on Communist Party Congress, Gaga for U.S. Election," *Los Angeles Times*, October 22 (online blog, no longer available).

Moore, Malcolm. 2012. "China to Spend 70 Million Pounds Sprucing Up Nobel Prize Winner's Hometown," *The Telegraph*, October 18. www.telegraph.co.uk/news/worldnews/asia/china/9617803/China-to-spend-70-million-sprucing-up-Nobel-Prize-winners-hometown.html.

National Endowment for Democracy. 2017. *Sharp Power: Rising Authoritarian Influence*, December. www.ned.org/sharp-power-rising-authoritarian-influence-forum-report/.

Nye, Joseph S. Jr. 2002. *The Paradox of American Power: Why the World's Only Superpower Can't Go It Alone.* New York: Oxford University Press.

Nye, Joseph S., Jr. 2004. "The Decline of America's Soft Power," *Foreign Affairs*, May–June. www.foreignaffairs.com/articles/2004-05-01/decline-americas-soft-power.

Nye, Joseph S. Jr. 2011. "The War on Soft Power," *foreignpolicy.com*, April 12. http://foreignpolicy.com/2011/04/12/the-war-on-soft-power/.

Nye, Joseph S. 2018. "How Sharp Power Threatens Soft Power," *Foreign Affairs*, January 24. www.foreignaffairs.com/articles/china/2018-01-24/how-sharp-power-threatens-soft-power.

Osnos, Evan. 2018. "Making China Great Again: As Donald Trump Surrenders America's Global Commitments, Xi Jinping Is Learning to Pick Up the Pieces," *The New Yorker*, January 8. www.newyorker.com/magazine/2018/01/08/making-china-great-again.

Pew Research Center Global Attitudes and Trends. 2017. "U.S. Image Suffers as Publics around World Question Trump's Leadership," June 26. www.pewglobal.org/2017/06/26/u-s-image-suffers-as-publics-around-world-question-trumps-leadership/.

Portland Soft Power 30: A Global Ranking of Soft Power. 2018. "Portland and USC Center on Public Diplomacy." https://portland-communications.com/publications/a-global-ranking-of-soft-power-2018/.

Qin, Amy. 2019. "Chinese Director's Film Is Pulled From Festival," *The New York Times*, February 13, p. A11.

Renmin ribao [People's Daily]. 2011. "Li Na dengding da manguan" ["Li Na reaches the pinnacle in a Grand Slam event"], June 5, p. 1.

Rosen, Stanley. 2003. "Chinese Media and Youth: Attitudes toward Nationalism and Internationalism," in Chin-Chuan Lee (ed.), *Chinese Media, Global Contexts.* London and New York: RoutledgeCurzon, pp. 97–118.

Rosen, Stanley. 2010. "Chinese Youth and State-Society Relations," in Peter Hays Gries and Stanley Rosen (eds.), *Chinese Politics: State, Society and the Market.* New York: Routledge, pp. 160–178.

Rosen, Stanley. 2011. "The Use of Film for Public Diplomacy: Why Hollywood Makes a Stronger Case for China," *PDiN Monitor* 2(5). http://uscpublicdiplomacy.org/pdin_monitor_article/use-film-public-diplomacy-why-hollywood-makes-stronger-case-china

Rosen, Stanley. 2014. "Comparing Exceptionalisms and Dreams: The Relevance of the Chinese and American 'Models' for Post-80's and Post-90's Chinese Youth," paper presented at the conference on "Chinese Exceptionalism: Imagined or Historically Grounded?" at the University of Nottingham. Rosen.Chinese.Exceptionalism.Nottingham.PAPER.7.19.2014.Academia.Upload.docx.

Rosen, Stanley. 2017. "The Chinese Dream in Popular Culture: China as Producer of Films at Home and Abroad," in Jacques deLisle and Avery Goldstein (eds.), *China's Global Engagement: Cooperation, Competition, and Influence in the 21st Century.* Washington, DC: Brookings Institution Press, pp. 359–388.

Rosen, Stanley. 2018. "Xi's Indefinite Grasp on Power Has Finally Captured the West's Attention: Now What?," *The Conversation*, March 16. https://theconversation.com/xis-indefinite-grasp-on-power-has-finally-captured-the-wests-attention-now-what-92721.

Runciman, David. 2018a. "China's Challenge to Democracy," *The Wall Street Journal*, April 26. www.wsj.com/articles/chinas-challenge-to-democracy-1524756755.

Runciman, David. 2018b. *How Democracy Ends*. New York: Basic Books.

Shen, Zhuanghai. 2017. "Wenhua qiangguo jianshede zhongguo luoji" ["The Chinese Logic of the Construction of Cultural Power"], *Wenhua ruan shili yanjiu* [*Studies on Cultural Soft Power*] 2, pp. 5–13.

Tam, Fiona. 2012. "It Is Hard to Be Happy Even in Joy, Mo Yan Says," *South China Morning Post*, October 16, pp. 7.

Tan, Huileng. 2016. "Descendants of the Sun Smash Hit Prompts Beijing to Warn on South Korean Dramas," *CNBC*, March 18. www.cnbc.com/2016/03/16/descendants-of-the-sun-smash-hit-prompts-beijing-to-warn-on-south-korean-dramas.html.

Wan, William. 2014a. "Chinese Officials Debate Why China Can't Make a Soap Opera as Good as South Korea's," *The Washington Post*, March 7. www.washingtonpost.com/world/asia_pacific/chinese-officials-debate-why-china-cant-make-a-soap-opera-as-good-as-south-koreas/2014/03/07/94b86678-a5f3-11e3–84d4-e59b1709222c_story.html.

Wan, William. 2014b. "'House of Cards' Finds Avid Audience in China," *The Washington Post*, February 18. www.washingtonpost.com/world/house-of-cards-finds-avid-audience-in-china/2014/02/18/158c5eee-9884-11e3-8461-8a24c7bf0653_story.html?utm_term=.1759ac53d3ff.

Wee, Sui-Lee. 2019. "China Expels Journalist after Article on Xi's Cousin," *The New York Times*, August 30, p. B1.

Wertime, David. 2013. "China's Frank Underwood? Wang Qishan May Be Taking the Wrong Lessons from '*House of Cards*'," *Tealeafnation.com*, December 12. http://foreignpolicy.com/2013/12/13/chinas-frank-underwood/.

WikiLeaks. 2008. "Grim Outlook for Expo Participation," *Cable 08SHANGHAI430*, *SBU*. http://wikileaks.org/cable/2008/09/08SHANGHAI430.html.

Wikipedia. n.d. https://en.wikipedia.org/wiki/Meng_Wanzhou.

Wong, Edward. 2012. "China's President Lashes Out at Western Culture," *The New York Times*, January 4. www.nytimes.com/2012/01/04/world/asia/chinas-president-pushes-back-against-western-culture.html.

Xin Jing Bao [New Beijing News]. 2012. "Mo Yan jiaxiang yi tou 6.7yi hengyang hong gaoliang wenhua; guanmin jun kangfen" ["Mo Yan's Home Village Will Rely on an Investment of 6.7 Million RMB to Promote Red Sorghum Culture: Officials Are All Very Excited"], October 18. https://boxun.com/news/gb/china/2012/10/201210180935.shtml.

Yan, Xuetong. 2017. "China Can Thrive in the Trump Era," *The New York Times*, January 25, p. A25.

YouTube. 2014. "Li Na's Brilliant Winner's Speech: Australian Open 2014," January 25. www.youtube.com/watch?v=M-uVsj2pJDo.

Yu, Frida. 2017. "Is Anyone Good Enough for an H-1B Visa," *The New York Times*, November 24, p. A27.

Yuan, Li. 2019. "China Spins Hong Kong, But World Isn't Buying," *The New York Times*, August 20, p. B1.

Zhang, Fan. 2016. "The U.S. Presidential Election: The View from China," *Center for American Progress*, June 22. www.americanprogress.org/issues/security/reports/2016/06/22/140119/the-u-s-presidential-election-the-view-from-china/.

Zhang, Phoebe. 2019. "Chinese Fans Cry 'Shame' for Game of Thrones End But Still Love US Shows," *South China Morning Post*, May 25. www.scmp.com/news/china/society/article/3011699/chinese-fans-cry-shame-game-thrones-end-still-love-us-shows.

Zhao, Dingxin. 2002. "An Angle on Nationalism in China Today: Attitudes among Beijing University Students after Belgrade 1999," *The China Quarterly* 172, pp. 885–905.

Zhu, Ying. 2014. "Why Frank Underwood Is Great for China's Soft Power," *ChinaFile*, February 27. www.chinafile.com/Frank-Underwood-Great-Chinas-Soft-Power.

4

VESSELS OF SOFT POWER GOING OUT TO SEA

Chinese diasporic media and the politics of allegiance

Wanning Sun

The experience of Chinese migrants across the globe is now redefined by a few important developments, including China's ascent as a global economic powerhouse, China's global media expansion and the newly articulated role for the diaspora in China's soft power project. Yet, despite this crucial role, the response of the Chinese diasporic communities, not to mention the impact of these developments on the diasporic Chinese-language media, is little understood. Existing work on soft power and Chinese media tends to focus on the actions of the Chinese state, contributing to a general view that much of what China has produced is in fact "propaganda offshore" under the guise of soft power initiatives (Brady, 2008; Wang, 2011; Edney, 2014; Shambaugh, 2013, 2015). But we still do not know if and to what extent China's "media going global" strategy has been effective. More specifically, how do China's expansion and globalization of Chinese media interact with specific diasporic Chinese media institutions and their publics to produce new cultural practices among the Chinese diaspora? And do these interactions produce a particular form of political allegiance, which translates into both concerted support for the CCP's policies on core political issues (such as the status of Taiwan) and voluntary participation in promoting China's foreign policy and international relations agenda (e.g., in relation to the South China Sea)? This chapter seeks to answer these questions. It first analyzes how the Chinese government justifies the reconfiguration of the diasporic Chinese communities and their media in moral discourses and policy statements. It then maps the patterns and strategies of the Chinese-language media in various global destinations in response to China's rise and its overtures of partnership. The final section discusses how myriad political, economic, and cultural forces intersect to shape the contour of Chinese-language media in Australia, and in doing so, situating these global developments in a specific empirical context.

Reconfiguring the diaspora Chinese media

There is a general perception among Western media commentators—and, to a lesser extent, Western scholars—that China's going global initiative is motivated by an ambition to conquer the world. This is in contrast to the discourse internal to China, which is not one of power and influence, but of grievance. In other words, rather than aiming to become an imperialistic power, China sees itself as engaged in a necessary struggle for discursive decolonization. In pushing for this agenda, Chinese political and intellectual elites are drawing moral and intellectual strength from a number of sources, ranging from the collective memory of the humiliation and subjugation China suffered at the hands of Western powers in the 19th and 20th centuries, to the anti-Western populist sentiment entertained by "nativists"—a cohort of writers who are "populists, nationalists, and Marxists"—the twin of the "new left" (Shambaugh, 2013, p. 27).

In the opinion of these writers, China has been robbed of its rightful *huayu quan* 话语权("discursive sovereignty") and has no voice in a world dominated by the imperialistic media power of the West. One phrase that often appears in many scholarly and official statements is *xi qiang wo ruo* 西强我弱 ("the West is strong and we are weak"). Another frequently used phrase in justifying China's going global initiative is *beidong aida* 被动挨打("being in the passive position and often beaten up"). These phrases are so often used that they have taken on the appearance of a self-evident truth. They capture a deep-seated sense of injustice, which in turn provide important moral justification for China to contest Western *huayu baquan* 话语霸权 ("discursive hegemony"). China's soft power initiative, of which expansion into the global media landscape is a part, aims to increase China's media presence globally, with the main purpose being to reduce or even eradicate the "bias" and "prejudices" against China that are seen as pervasive in Western media. The overriding conviction that fuels this drive is that China has been robbed of its rightful voice in a world dominated by the imperialistic media power of the West, and China now must "overcome humiliation, secure redress of past grievances, and achieve a position of equality with all other major powers" (Zhao, 2009, p. 255).

In their search for strategies and pathways to address this discursive imbalance, Chinese scholars appear to have identified four vehicles that could carry the content of China's international communication. The first two vehicles are what Chinese scholars call vehicles of "direct communication" (*zhijie chuanbo* 直接传播). The first is the international arm of China's state media organizations which are explicitly charged with the task of "external propaganda." These include the *People's Daily*, *China Daily*, China Central Television (CCTV), China Radio International (CRI), Xinhua News Agency, China News and the Foreign Language Press, and more recently China Global Television Network (CGTN). The second vehicle refers to Chinese media that lie outside the purview of the state media's external propaganda agenda. Given the de-territorial nature of communication technology and its diverse pathways of communication, these media may nevertheless be crucial in shaping the world's perception of China. This category includes the Chinese Internet, social media and the commercial sector of the Chinese media. Together with tourists, students and business individuals, this media sector contributes to the "expanded domain of external propaganda" (*da wai xuan* 大外宣, literally "bigger circle of external propaganda"). The third vehicle is foreign correspondents in China who produce their own reporting on China based on their interviews and investigations in China, whereas the fourth vehicle is the international media per se. The third and fourth are vehicles of "indirect communication" (*jianjie chuanbo* 间接传播). In other words, they are potential carriers of media content about China based on information they gather from the Chinese media (Chen, 2011), but in reality they seldom do.

So far, one important strategy of expansion involves some key state media players signing formal content deals with the state or commercial media of foreign countries, mainly in Asia, Africa and, to a lesser extent, South America. These tend to be countries that are non-Western, non-liberal democratic states, and that have a strong state media presence under an authoritarian, in some cases former Communist, regime. Usually lacking correspondents to report on China, these countries rely on international news services for coverage of China (Cook, 2013). These countries appreciate the assistance China gives to their national state media in the form of technical and infrastructural support, professional training and exchange of journalists and media content (Gagliardone, Repnikova and/Stremlau, 2010). Although too early to tell, preliminary research in Africa is pointing tentatively toward the emergence of a Chinese "news-gathering paradigm that stands in stark contrast to the West's traditional view of the media" (Farah and Mosher, 2010). There are also signs of more positive coverage of China globally as a result of its closer engagement in Africa (Kurlantzick, 2007; Wasserman, 2011). Indeed, in many respects this kind of partnership with overseas organizations is a much more direct and effective way of reaching audiences abroad.

However, if China has relatively greater success in embedding its media content in the mainstream media in some countries, there is widespread skepticism—even distrust—regarding the credibility of Chinese state propaganda among the publics in Western nations. To make it more difficult, these countries do not allow Chinese satellites to broadcast directly into their territories. To tackle this problem, China needs the assistance of a third party that has the appearance of autonomy from the Chinese government. Acutely aware of the myriad difficulty of reaching the West as well as the importance of securing of the diasporic Chinese communities, the Chinese government deems it logical to utilize ethnic Chinese communities and their media enterprises as platforms to access overseas Chinese audiences and, through them, mainstream Western society. No longer considered by the CCP as somewhat disloyal, unpatriotic, and thus less "Chinese," migrants of Chinese descent are now reconfigured as both the target and vehicles of China's soft power agenda. Policy thinkers are clearly recognizing the fact that diasporic Chinese could be a crucial intermediary and a key node in global communication serving to relay China's external propaganda content. Chinese-literate migrants outside China constitute the largest demographic component of the international audience for Chinese media content. Additionally, in comparison with Western media, Chinese-language media in the diaspora have been found to be much more willing and compliant partner in China's going global project (Jin, 2009; Sun, 2014). A metaphor, *Jie chuan chu hai* (借船出海), which can be translated literally as "to borrow someone's vessel to go out to sea," is used frequently by Chinese policy makers. Diasporic Chinese are now viewed as vessels that can carry China's message to enter the symbolic space of the mainstream West in a "roundabout" way.

There has been a concerted effort on the part of the Chinese government to mobilize diasporic Chinese support. Since 2001, operating under the auspices of the State Council of China's Overseas Chinese Affairs Office (OCAO), the China News Service (CNS), China's official news agency for external communication, has hosted a biennial International Forum of Chinese-Language Media. In 2013, the new director of the OCAO, Qiu Yuanping, used the seventh forum to explain Chinese President Xi Jinping's concept of the "China dream." The concept, Qiu said, was created to encourage not only the citizens of China but also all overseas Chinese. "The same ancestry and affection shared by the Chinese media worldwide are the foundations of their solidarity, influence, credibility, and right to free speech." She also hoped that the Chinese media abroad would publish objective reports on China and become "storytellers of real Chinese stories" (China News Service, 2013).

Media, migration and the Chinese diaspora: a global view

As one of the most established "ethnic" identities in relation to mainstream society, diasporic Chinese communities in the West have for a long time been well equipped with their own Chinese business organizations, Chinese language schools and Chinese-language media—often dubbed as the three pillars of any sizeable Chinese migrant community. The social and cultural roles of these global diasporic Chinese-language media were clearly identified and well acknowledged. First, Chinese-language press bridges the Chinese migrant communities and their host societies, communicating crucial economic, legal and educational information—the policies, rules and regulations of the host country—to Chinese-speaking citizens and residents. Second, it gives voice to community leaders, who advocate to the government and mainstream public on behalf of the political, economic, social and cultural interests of Chinese communities in their host societies through the actions of community leaders. Third, the Chinese-language press is a vital means of maintaining migrants' command of the mother tongue—in most cases Cantonese in earlier decades—through regular exposure to Chinese-language cultural products, and in doing so, they facilitate the identity formation of ethnic subjects in multicultural societies (Sun, 2006; Sun and Sinclair, 2016). Fourth, since most Chinese-language newspapers were owned by and catered to Cantonese-speaking migrants from outside the People's Republic of China (PRC), they were mostly critical of the Chinese government and its communist ideology. In other words, the production and the consumption of this press was a means of marking a different Chinese identity, one which distanced the diasporic Chinese community from its mainland counterpart. Despite internal differences, it is safe to say that traditionally these Chinese-language media outlets have maintained a guarded—if not hostile—distance from Communist China.

The Chinese-language migrant media, like other ethnic media in the host society, had for many decades existed in the marginal space that is often described in the English-speaking world as the "ethnic media." It was discrete from the Chinese-language media in the Chinese societies on the one hand, and mainstream media of the host society on the other. There also seemed to be a clear boundary—geographic, cultural and political—between the Chinese media that is mostly confined to media landscape of the PRC and the diasporic Chinese-language media outside China.

Early formations of the diasporic Chinese media

There is a long and well-documented history of the Chinese-language press in the Chinese-speaking migrant communities outside Chinese societies of Hong Kong, Taiwan and the People's Republic of China. One such key media institution which embodied the global diasporic Chinese media network prior to the rise of China is the *Singtao Daily*. With its headquarters in Hong Kong, and boasting a long history and a global circulation. *Singtao* has been considered a key icon of the "global Chinese media network" which predates the arrival of the PRC migrants in many countries and which maintains independence from the political influence of the PRC. *Singtao* was established in 1938 by the famous Aw family in China's Fujian Province, who migrated to Rangoon, Burma, in the second half of the 19th century. The Aw family prospered largely thanks to its production of the Tiger Balm, but the entrepreneurship of the Aw family did not stop at producing a household medicine. In 1938, Aw Boon Haw launched Hong Kong's first Chinese daily, the *Singtao Daily* (*Singtao* means "new island" in Cantonese), thus launching the long and tortuous career of the global Chinese newspaper with the longest history.

Mr. Aw finally passed on the business of running the *Singtao Daily* to his daughter, Sally Aw Sian, also known widely as the "tiger girl." During her tours in the United States, Sally Aw discovered a deep cultural need among Chinese migrants in English-speaking cities for Chinese-language news and information. No less entrepreneurial than her father, she decided to expand her father's newspaper business by publishing overseas editions, starting with New York in 1965 and gradually extending to many cities globally, including San Francisco, Los Angeles, Toronto, Vancouver, London, Sydney and Auckland—and major cities of the PRC. The Singtao Group now has more than 20 offices across the globe, publishes 16 daily editions that are distributed in more than 100 cities worldwide and employs in excess of 2,100 staff. It has also recently set up a new international center in New York that coordinates all the overseas offices in international reporting (Ko, 2013).

While *Singtao Daily* is a media conglomerate extending its influence from Hong Kong outwards, there is also *World Journal*, which represents the Taiwan-based United Daily News Group's overseas expansion into North America that began in the mid-1970s. The North American diasporic Chinese media were thus segmented by place of origin: migrants from Taiwan read the *World Journal*, while those from Hong Kong read *Singtao*. They were also internally stratified along socioeconomic lines. For instance, although both *Singtao Daily* and *Ming Pao* were based in Hong Kong and both were available in North America, the latter was considered to be close to an elitist newspaper catering to middle-class businesspeople, many of whom were young, educated professionals and executives with a higher income (So and Lee, 1995). This old diasporic mediasphere was not just limited to print media. Television Broadcasts Limited (TVB), a Hong Kong–based provider of Chinese television, has been a major broadcaster, producer and international distributor of television in the Chinese-speaking world since the 1970s (Curtin, 2007; Wong, 2009).

However, despite the well-documented entrepreneurial spirit of the Singtao Group and its vital role in developing a global Chinese-language media network in the major cities of the world (Sun, 2005), it clearly did not think it would be profitable to extend its business to many far-flung corners of the world, which were also host to Chinese migrants such as Africa and South America. Apart from geographical isolation and lack of local communication infrastructure, the most obvious reason for global Chinese media networks' lack of interest in developing their presence in these locations has been the size of the Chinese community there: it was simply too small to warrant their business expansion. In fact, Chinese migrant communities in many locations which were not covered by this global network—Europe (Gong, 2016; Dai, 2016; Chong, 2016), Southeast Asia (Hoon, 2006; Chua, 2006; Lim and Luan, 2006; Nyíri, 2016), Africa (Sun, 2016b), South America (Stenberg, 2016) and the Caribbean (Sinanan, 2016)—had created their own indigenous Chinese language press, which served the needs of the Chinese communities in a particular host country.

China's rise, para-diaspora and new developments

Since the 1990s, and gathering pace within the first decade of the new millennium, a few developments have conspired to fundamentally and irreversibly transformed the functions and nature of the diasporic Chinese media landscape. The first is the exponential growth in numbers of the Chinese-speaking outbound migrants. Also growing is the population of Chinese sojourners—temporary migrants who plan to return home rather than settle permanently in their host countries—outside China, due to the growing presence of the People's Republic of China in business, resources, property investments, education and international tourism. This growth following China's rise has fundamentally changed the demographic composition of overseas Chinese communities. The second development is a full-scale push for the globalization of Chinese media and culture in recent years, especially since the 2008 Beijing Olympics (Hu and Ji, 2012; Zhao, 2013; Sun, 2014). In response to the overtures for collaboration from the Chinese state media, diasporic Chinese media organizations have developed myriad location-specific strategies as a means of ensuring financial viability. The myriad forms of collaboration between Talentvision of Fairchild Media Group and CCTV, China's official national TV, is an example of how diasporic Cantonese television negotiates China's rise, changing migrant demographics and migrants' changing allegiances in its content production and programming (Kong, 2016).

The third development is the growth of a new Mandarin-language media sector—including print, radio and television—which is owned by, and caters to, Mandarin-speaking migrants, some of whom still have significant business interests in China. While some came to Australia around the Tiananmen Incident in 1989, others migrated to Australia only a few years ago. It is for this reason that "para-diaspora" (Sun, 2002) may be a more accurate term to describe this first-generation migrant cohort. This sector now exists alongside the traditional Cantonese-language mediascape. For instance, the rapid growth and conglomeration of the Mandarin-language radio in many capital cities in Australia is largely due to the entrepreneurship of former PRC migrant Tommy Jiang, who maintains close political ties with China (Gao, 2006). His conglomerate CAMG, which now has a global presence in and beyond Australia, not only seriously threatens the viability of existing Cantonese radio, but also significantly reshapes the global Chinese media landscape which previously was dominated by Cantonese-speaking and Hong Kong–based companies (Sun, 2014).

Parallel to and simultaneously impacting on these developments is the proliferation of technological platforms and modes of content distribution in the past decade or so—particularly the growing use of digital and social media such as WeChat (the Chinese equivalent of WhatsApp or Facebook). Rapid changes in the ways in which news and information is produced, distributed and circulated have significant implications for the diasporic Chinese landscape. On the one hand, legacy media forms—radio, television, newspapers—can be equipped with an extensive and interactive online presence, thus enabling those dispersed Chinese readers who live outside metropolitan areas to access their news content, as well as be exposed to the advertising of services and businesses that is part and parcel of the content provided by these media (Sun et al., 2011a). On the other hand, and this is more crucial, is the proliferation of the online-only news and media outlets run by mostly Chinese students studying abroad and young migrant entrepreneurs from the PRC and catering mostly to Mandarin-speaking migrants of the host country. Publishing in Chinese and circulated via WeChat, this online news sector caters to the location-specific content needs of the Chinese community in the host country, be it Australia, the United States or the United Kingdom.

The consequences of these developments are profound and wide-ranging. The diasporic Chinese mediasphere has become complex and intricate. The collective diasporic Chinese identity is becoming further deterritorialized and refashioned in multiple and contradictory ways, and this is being played out in a wide range of global and local contexts. On the one hand, the distinction between the Chinese state media and diasporic media is increasingly blurred. On the other hand, what had existed as parallel universes between various diasporic nodes have been linked by the ubiquitous use of social media, in particular WeChat, as a platform of distribution and circulation. These developments constitute the complex context in which we address the question regarding the efficacy and impact of China's soft-power-through-diaspora initiatives.

Chinese-language media in Australia: challenges ahead

The size and demographic composition of the Chinese migrant community in Australia has changed dramatically over the past two decades, making the PRC the most common overseas birthplace for Australians after the United Kingdom and New Zealand. China has surpassed Japan to become Australia's biggest trade partner, in terms of both imports and exports. This means that China is one of only two countries, along with the United Kingdom, that not only have seen large numbers of migrants settling in Australia but also have proven to be crucial to Australia's economic survival.

Australia's economic dependence on China on the one hand, and its perceived incompatibility with China in terms of political, ideological and cultural values, on the other hand, is the root of a prevailing feeling of fear and anxiety that many Australians have about China. This is most vividly demonstrated by the press conference in May 2017, given by Dennis Richardson, Australia's outgoing Defence Secretary, the most senior public servant in the Australia's Ministry of Defence. In his last address to the Australian media, Richardson said that China is spying on Australia, and that the Chinese media in Australia is controlled by China, and that thereby China, while crucially important to Australia, is not to be trusted. Richardson also made it clear that Australia's allegiance should continue to be with the United States, although it needs to be on friendly terms with China. He succinctly summarized Australia's position vis-à-vis China and the United States as "friends with both, allies with one" (Riordan, 2017). Australia's current prime minister, Scott Morrison, also once described the United States as a "friend" and China as a "customer" (Zhao, Fang and Robertson, 2019). In December 2018, the Australian government passed the Foreign Influence Transparency Scheme, legislation which was believed to target Chinese-Australians (Walsh and Fang, 2019). Increasingly, the difference between

China and the United States/Australia is framed in terms of a civilizational and ideological clash. In the words of Jocelyn Chey, a veteran China scholar, Australia is in danger of falling "into the Huntington trap" (2019). Against this complex and fraught geopolitical backdrop, the Chinese-language media in Australia presents itself as an apposite case study to explore China's soft power initiatives, Australia's "Sinophobia" (Evans, 2019) and their impact on various diasporic Chinese communities.

History of Chinese migration to Australia and changes in the Chinese-language media sector

Migration from China to Australia started from the earliest years of British occupation of the continent, until the early 1950s, when migration from China all but ceased. These links were halted for a generation or more before formal diplomatic relations were established between Canberra and Beijing in 1972. Over this interval, the historical pattern of migration to Australia by people of Chinese descent shifted from China to Hong Kong, Singapore, Malaya/Malaysia, Taiwan and elsewhere as Canberra progressively eliminated racial categories of immigration exclusion. At this time, citizens of China were excluded from the expanded immigration intake not on grounds of race but because they lacked formal channels for migration and mobility between Australia and China.

In the late 1980s and early 1990s, migration from the Chinese mainland resumed and grew in significant numbers, largely as a result of the start of economic reforms in China in the late 1970s and the implementation of its open-door policy in relation to study abroad. After issuing a series of temporary visas to Chinese students in Australia following the Tiananmen incident on June 4, 1989, the Australian government finally decided in 1993 to allow 45,000 Chinese nationals in Australia who had arrived prior to or soon after the Tiananmen incident to settle in Australia permanently. This decision signaled the beginning of the demographic shift from *Huaren* (华人) to *Zhongguoren* (中国人) in Australia's Chinese migrant community. The former refers to pan-Chinese identity of people from various diasporic places outside China, whereas the latter refers to migrants from the PRC.

After the Tiananmen incident, China resumed its course of economic reforms and its commitment to an open-door policy on trade, investment and outbound migration. The tide of going abroad, having started in the early 1980s, gained further momentum. Like a number of Western countries, such as Canada, Germany, Japan and New Zealand, Australia quickly identified language education as a new market segment. Since the Global Financial Crisis of 2008, China has remained a leading source of migrants to Australia in the Skill category (DIBP, 2015). Moreover, there has been a steady shift away from Hong Kong/Macau and toward mainland China as the major source of skilled migrants from the China/Taiwan/Hong Kong/Macau region. As a direct result of Australia's greatly expanded intake of mainland Chinese migrants since the early 1990s,

Australia has seen a rapid and considerable increase in the size of its Chinese-speaking population. The estimated number of ethnic Chinese living in Australia in 1996 was 343,523; however, this number has increased significantly in the past ten or so years. According to the 2011 census there were about 866,200 Australian residents claiming Chinese origin, and as many as 74% of them were the first generation of their family to move to Australia (Sun, Fitzgerald and Gao, 2017).

Chinese media expansion and Australian responses

In recent years, China's state media have made significant inroads into Australia's media landscape via a number of pathways, including: (1) increasing the number of offshore correspondents for major state media organizations such as Xinhua, Economic Daily, CCTV, and *People's Daily*; (2) securing business deals with mainstream English-language media organizations such as Fairfax to carry Chinese state media content, or entering partnership agreements with mainstream media such as the ABC's AustraliaPlus.cn partnerships with *China Daily*, Beijing TV, CNTV and the Shanghai Media Group; and (3) expanding partnerships and content sharing with existing Chinese migrant media. While the first two pathways are relatively straightforward and small in scale, the third pathway is more extensive. Partnership with PRC media manifests itself in myriad forms and channels, many of which are more demonstrative of diasporic Chinese community and individuals' entrepreneurship than their allegiance to the PRC.

One form of partnership is embodied by Kingold, a company which is owned by billionaire property developer and investor Chau Chak Wing. Kingold, in partnership with the Guangzhou-based Yangcheng Evening News Group, owns the *Australian New Express Daily* (*Xin Kuai Bao* 新快报), one of the four nationally circulated Chinese-language dailies in Australia. Kingold Media also publishes *Fortune Weekly* (*Cai Fu Yi Zhou* 财富一周) and *Lifestyle Monthly* (*Shenghuo Yuekan* 生活月刊). Xin Kuai Bao therefore is an example whereby an Australian Chinese language media outlet is in fact a "sister paper" of a daily Chinese paper of the same name in Guangzhou.

Another form of partnership is exemplified by the story of the Austar Media Group (CAMG). Owned by Australian citizen and former PRC national Tommy Jiang, CAMG was previously known as Austar International Media Group (AIMG). For 17 years after its first incarnation as Chinese-language radio station 3CW in Melbourne, AIMG grew to be a media conglomerate consisting of Chinese-language radio stations in several major Australian cities (but not including Sydney); several Chinese-language periodicals, weeklies, and newspapers; and a range of businesses and services in the field of cultural exchange and other areas. Riding on China's going out initiative and soft power push through international media expansion, CAMG, now a global media having presence in South America, Southeast Asia as well as Australia, is instrumental in bringing the state-owned international broadcaster China Radio International (CRI) to Australia as well as other countries, thereby enabling the content of China's state media to enter the mediasphere of a foreign country in a more roundabout kind of way. In doing so, CAMG exemplifies another form of partnership: a diasporic Chinese media entity owned by a former PRC migrant lends itself as the vehicle of China's media going global initiative.

The third form of partnership may involve a diasporic media institution which takes sponsorship from a PRC-based media organization. For instance, Nan Hai Media Group in Australia, which, established in 2011, specializes in publishing Chinese-language media and hosting artistic and cultural performance troupes from the PRC. Nan Hai also signed a partnership deal with Tencent, WeChat's parent company in China, and became WeChat's official representative in the Oceania region. The company claims to have partnerships with the China News Agency, Bank of China and Air China.

The most invisible yet most insidious kind of partnership between diasporic Chinese-language media and the PRC media is in the form of content reproduction. This strategy is particularly attractive to those formerly Cantonese media organizations which are cash-strapped and keen to capitalize on the demographic change in the Chinese community and exploit the Chinese media's going global initiatives for purposes of expanding readership. The Chinese Newspaper Group (Aozhou Zhongwen Baoye Jituan 澳洲中文报业集团) is one of them. Established in 1986, it claims to be the only privately owned company in Australia that specializes in publishing in Chinese. Its portfolio consists of nine publications in some of Australia's major cities, as well as websites, tablet and social media offerings, including the online news website www.1688.com.au and property website www.ozhouse.com.au. Its mastheads include the *Daily Chinese Herald* (*Aozhou Ribao* 澳洲日报).

China's global media expansion is indeed motivated by China's own political ambition. However, as these examples suggest, this process has at the same time also provided business opportunities for Chinese migrant entrepreneurs. Following these partnership initiatives, the landscape of Chinese-language media in Australia is much more dynamic and competitive. There are now four paid daily Chinese newspapers in Sydney, namely, *Singtao Daily*, *Australian Chinese Daily*, *Daily Chinese Herald*, and *New Express Daily*. The latter three papers are locally produced and distributed, unlike *Singtao Daily*, and have a much shorter history. In addition to these three dailies, *Singtao Daily* also jostles with around 20 free and paid weekly and monthly newspapers and magazines, not to mention myriad local radio and television stations. All of these legacy media now have extensive online presence.

What has further complicated the media landscape is the emergence of a vibrant online-only Chinese language news sector in Australia. These online publications have a subscription account with WeChat, which enables their content to be delivered to mobile devices such as the smartphone and iPad. These are mostly comprehensive websites with a news and current affairs component. Some—such as SydneyToday.com—are owned by locally based Australian Chinese media companies; others are subsidiaries of China-based companies. Such websites are usually owned, operated and staffed by young, mostly student migrants from the PRC with Australian university degrees in IT, business or media. Mostly financed through advertising revenue, these online media provide news and current affairs in Australia, in addition to a wide range of information across all aspects of everyday life. The news and current affairs component features stories—both serious and flippant—about mainstream Australian society and Australia's Chinese community.

These media outlets mostly do not generate news content from their own in-house journalists, but instead translate news and current affairs from a wide range of media outlets, while providing links to the original stories. Their sources of news range from Chinese state media on the one hand, and Australia's English-language mainstream media on the other. They usually do not feature serious op-ed pages, but the editors do pay close attention to hot-button issues that concern the Chinese community. News from China tends to be light and soft nature, usually eschewing serious and politically sensitive topics. While these young media practitioners are not interested in simply being mouthpieces for China's propaganda, they are nevertheless staunchly nationalistic in favor of China. This means that while their websites usually avoid politically sensitive news about China, they may effectively give voice to the opinion of the Chinese community on certain controversial issues where China may be in conflict with Australia. They may also be effective tools for mobilizing the Chinese community over controversial issues that threaten to strain Australia–China relations (Sun, 2016a).

Most of the print media outlets are struggling to survive in an environment of dwindling audience, lack of cash and resources and threat of irrelevance in the age of the Internet. Generally speaking, these outlets have little discursive influence in the mainstream host society. But the new online digital/social media sector may have a different prospect. Unlike the traditional ethnic print media, the Chinese digital/social media sector has become a fluid and dynamic space where information and opinions routinely interface with mainstream English-language media, PRC media and user-generated content from individual social media users. While individual WeChat subscribers can repost links to stories from these online media, the latter organizations—as well as mainstream English media—themselves rely on user-generated material as a source for news stories. The involvement of Chinese digital and social media in the organization of protests in Melbourne and the mainstream English language media's coverage of the protests—discussed below—is a good example. As a result, the audience for this content could be mainland Chinese, mainstream Australians, diasporic Chinese in Australia or transnational Chinese in other parts of the world. This sector indeed brings actual and potential opportunities for China's state media to reach Western audiences, but it remains to be seen if and how this sector plays the expected role of the "vessel."

Evidence of shifting allegiance

The Chinese-language media institution that stands to benefit most from China's media expansion and Australia's changing Chinese demographics is the *Singtao Daily*. Following its success in the North America, the launch of the Australia edition in 1982 coincides with the first phase of Sino–British negotiations over the future of Hong Kong. *Singtao*'s stance toward China was critical, and this is evidenced not only in its coverage of the future of Hong Kong, but also the future of China per se. The newspaper's critical coverage of the Tiananmen incident of June 4, 1989, is also a telling example of its anti-CCP position. The Singtao Group changed ownership in 2001, and due to the new owner Charles Ho's close connection with the Chinese government, there have been widespread predictions of a shift of political allegiances. This view was put to the test in *Singtao*'s response to another key issue that affected the future of Hong Kong: the July protests in 2003 about the controversy surrounding the proposed introduction of an anti-subversion amendment to the Hong Kong Basic Law. In contrast to its editorial stance during Thatcher's first visit in 1982 and in the week of the Tiananmen incident in 1989, *Singtao* published three editorials on this matter during the massive anti-government protests in early July 2003, and these editorials are often cited now by Hong Kong's media watchers as some of the earliest indications of *Singtao*'s shift toward a pro-government position. The ultimate proof of *Singtao*'s editorial stance so far has been its coverage of the 2014 Umbrella Movement—a pro-democracy student- and scholar-led movement in Hong Kong. The largest and the most sustained pro-democracy movement in Hong Kong to date, this protest took place between late September and December 2014, when university students and some academics occupied Central Hong Kong to protest against the Chinese government's refusal to let Hong Kong residents nominate their own candidates to run for the position of chief executive. Throughout this period of more than two months, *Singtao* was mostly critical of the pro-democracy students and championed for stability and social order, which was the official position of central government in Beijing (Sun, 2019).

Singtao Australia has traditionally positioned itself as a middle-class newspaper, targeting middle-aged and older readers who have a sizeable disposable income. In recent years, it has experimented with various initiatives in order to attract younger, Mandarin-speaking readers. For example, it has shifted its printing style from vertical (top-to-bottom, right-to-left) to horizontal (left-to-right) to make it more reader-friendly to PRC readers. It also ensures that any uniquely Cantonese words and expressions are translated into Mandarin for the Australian edition. In addition, *Singtao* has formed several partnerships with PRC media. For instance, starting in 2002, the Australian edition of *Singtao Daily* has been carrying one page of content from *Wenhui Daily*, a popular and long-standing newspaper based in Shanghai.

Both scholarly research and media commentaries have pointed to a discernible shift in Chinese language migrant media from a mostly critical to a mostly supportive stance in their coverage of China, the Chinese government and issues and topics that are considered to be politically sensitive in China. More important, sensitive news stories involving issues such as Tibet and Falun Gong are commonly dealt with through omission. For instance, Australia's Chinese-language media were mostly silent on the 25th anniversary of the Tiananmen Square incident (Sun 2016a). In contrast, official visits to Australia and the PRC embassy by China's leaders, and the various initiatives and Chinese community activities of China's consuls general in Australia receive premium and welcoming coverage in the Chinese-language papers (Sun et al., 2011a, 2011b). Also, through their transmission of radio content from CRI, Australia's Chinese-language radio stations report positively on key political events in China such as the National Congress of the Chinese Communist Party (Sun, 2014).

While it is important to distinguish between toeing Beijing's Party line and expressing pro-China nationalistic sentiment on the part of the diasporic Chinese individuals, it is equally important to note that Chinese-language media, especially online and social media, are playing an increasingly crucial role in aligning diasporic sentiment with China's foreign policy and international relations agenda. This is especially the case when the mainstream media of the host society is expressing and pandering to anti-Chinese, and even racist views of China. On occasions where tensions run high between the Australian and Chinese government, media and publics over controversial issues such as Tibet, Taiwan and China's territorial disputes with its neighbors, WeChat and online Chinese media were also instrumental in mobilizing and coordinating pro-China public opinions. For instance, China's state media criticize the United States and Australia for meddling in the South China Sea dispute, whereas the mainstream Australian media criticize China for its aggressive behavior in asserting sovereignty rights in the region. A high-profile rally in Melbourne on July 23, 2016, to protest against The Hague's verdict on the South China Sea, is a case in point. Widely reported in both state Chinese media and Chinese media in Australia, the rally involved 169 Chinese community organizations, 15 Chinese-language media organizations and some 3,000 participants. The event was also covered live on yeeyi. com, a very popular online Chinese news service in Australia, and relayed by some other similar news websites. According to the organizer, Li Hai, and a few participants, the main purpose of the rally was to raise awareness among the Australian public of the "fact" that the Americans were behind The Hague verdict, and to urge Australians not to toe the American line. They were also concerned that the Australian public should not be manipulated by "misinformation" about the South China Sea issue and The Hague verdict. The rally was planned, organized, coordinated and promoted mostly online and via social media. Mainstream English-language media not only covered the protests but noted the role of the

Chinese media in the organization of the event. Situations such as these may allow mainstream Australian audiences to hear the points of view of the Chinese community. At the same time, it can also heighten Australia's awareness of the China's growing influence in Australia, further fueling, rather than addressing, a general sense of anxiety and fear about China.

Conclusion

In view of China's rise and its soft power initiatives, the inevitable question is whether emerging diasporic Chinese positions are able to maintain their ideological and political distance from the PRC. Or, to put it in another way, whether these media outlets have become platforms whereby PRC migrants' ideological, political and cultural allegiance to China is expressed and maintained. This discussion, particularly in the Australian context, seems to point to the latter. It is fair to say that the Chinese-language media now not only functions to reflect their own cultural and economic interests as member of a migrant community in a host society, but more important, it also plays a part in advocating China's political and economic interests. That said, it is also safe to say that, despite the demonstrated potential of the new digital Chinese media sector to play the expected role of the vessel, so far, the diasporic Chinese media and its audiences exist more as targets and less as vessels of China's going global agenda.

However, as this discussion also shows, the reasons for this shift are manifold and more complex than usually imagined. A general view that much of this sector has now been bought off, taken over, owned or directly controlled by China's propaganda authorities is simplistic, and insufficient alone to account for these complexities. Closer to the truth is the fact that the going global expansionist initiatives of the Chinese state media have dovetailed with the business acumen of elite Chinese migrants in these locations. Across the board, the Chinese-language media in diaspora have had to shift their business strategies in order to cater to this Mandarin-speaking cohort, thereby sustaining the viability of their businesses. The arrival of Chinese-speaking migrants from the PRC has not only injected a much needed boost to their dwindling audiences, but it has also become a source of resources and skills that are desperately needed to revive a declining media environment. Seen in this light, an increasingly pro-China stance is as much about the need to adopt new business strategies as it is about a change of heart in political terms. In one way or another, diasporic Chinese are practitioners of "flexible citizenship," defined as the cultural logics of capitalist accumulation, travel, and displacement that induce subjects to respond "fluidly and opportunistically to changing political-economic conditions" (Ong, 1999, p. 6). Their partnership with China is motivated as much by a desire to take advantage of the opportunities that come with China's economic power as it is by a willingness to identify with the CCP's policies and positions.

It is also important to realize that the diasporic Chinese community, existing in the margins of the host society, often have to make choices in terms of their allegiance. As the Australian case indicates, too often, individuals in this community are confronted with conflicting and competing perspectives on Australia and China, or other relevant global affairs. The tensions and dilemmas facing individuals from the Chinese migrant community become a source of cultural anxiety, frustration and alienation. Their current experience of being politically and racially singled out for their PRC background and association by the mainstream media of the host society may, ironically, further foster pro-China nationalism. While this discussion testifies to China's success in harnessing diasporic Chinese communities, it also makes it clear that this success has aroused a high level of fear and anxiety among the publics in the countries that host them, thereby pointing to the Chinese government's lack of success to reach the other—and more elusive—target audience: the mainstream public in the global West. This paradoxical outcome begs the question as to whether China's going global strategy has been in fact "cost-effective" in both political and economic senses.

References

Brady, Anne-Marie. 2008. *Marketing Dictatorship: Propaganda and Thought Work in Contemporary China.* Lanham, MD: Rowman and Littlefield.

Chen, Manli. 2011. *Duiwai chuanbo jiqi xiaoguo yanjiu [A Study of External Communication and Its Effects].* Beijing: Peking University Press.

Chey, Jocelyn. 2019. "Civilisations Should Not Clash," *Pearls and Irritations*, May 31. www.johnmenadue.com/jocelyn-chey-civilisations-should-not-clash/.

China News Service. 2013. "Qiu Yuanping xi wang Huawen mei ti ji ji chuan di 'Zhongguo hao sheng yin'" ["Qiu Yuanping Hopes That the Chinese-Language Media Abroad Represent 'the Voice of China'"], September 7. www.gqb.gov.cn/news/2013/0907/31004.shtml.

Chong, Cindy Cheung-Kwan. 2016. "Politics of Homeland: Hegemonic Discourses of the Intervening Homeland in Chinese Diasporic Newspapers in the Netherlands," in Wanning Sun and John Sinclair (eds.), *Media and Communication in the Chinese Diaspora: Rethinking Transnationalism.* London: Routledge, pp. 109–129.

Chua, Beng Huat. 2006. "Gossip about Stars: Newspapers and Pop Culture China," in Wanning Sun (ed.), *Media and the Chinese Diaspora: Community, Communications and Commerce.* London, Routledge, pp. 75–90.

Cook, Sarah. 2013. "The Long Shadow of Chinese Censorship: How the Communist Party's Media Restrictions Affect News Outlets around the World," *Center for International Media Assistance*, October 22. www.cima.ned.org/wp-content/uploads/2015/02/CIMA-China_Sarah%20Cook.pdf.

Curtin, Michael. 2007. *Playing to the World's Biggest Audience: The Globalization of Chinese Film and TV.* Berkeley, CA: University of California Press.

Dai, Nan. 2016. "Unique Past and Common Future: Chinese Immigrants and Chinese-Language Media in France," in Wanning Sun and John Sinclair (eds.), *Media and Communication in the Chinese Diaspora: Rethinking Transnationalism.* London: Routledge, pp. 87–108.

DIBP (Department of Immigration and Border Protection). 2015. *Historical Migration Statistics*, March. www.border.gov.au/about/reports-publications/research-statistics/statistics/live-in-australia/historical-migration-statistics.

Edney, Kingsley. 2014. *The Globalization of Chinese Propaganda: International Power and Domestic Political Cohesion*. New York: Palgrave Macmillan.

Evans, Gareth. 2019. "Breaking the 'Bamboo Ceiling'," *Sir Edward "Weary" Dunlop Asia Lecture in Sydney, Asialink*, March 13. https://asialink.unimelb.edu.au/stories/asian-australians-breaking-the-bamboo-ceiling.

Farah, Douglas and Andrew Mosher. 2010. "Winds from the East: How the People's Republic of China Seeks to Influence the Media in Africa, Latin America, and Southeast Asia," *Centre for International Media Assistance*, September 8. www.cima.ned.org/wp-content/uploads/2015/02/CIMA-China-Report_1.pdf.

Gagliardone, Iginio, Maria Repnikova and Nicole Stremlau. 2010. *China in Africa: A New Approach to Media Development?* Oxford, UK: University of Oxford Programme in Comparative Media Law and Policy (PCMLP). www.hirondelle.org/wp-content/uploads/2011/03/ChinainAfricanewapproachtomedia.pdf.

Gao, Jia. 2006. "Organized International Asylum Seeker Networks: Formation and Utilization by Chinese Students," *International Migration Review* 40(2), pp. 294–317.

Gong, Tian. 2016. "Bridge or Barrier: Migration, Media, and the Sojourner Mentality in Chinese Communities in Italy and Spain," in Wanning Sun and John Sinclair (eds.), *Media and Communication in the Chinese Diaspora: Rethinking Transnationalism*. London: Routledge, pp. 69–86.

Hoon, Chang-Yau. 2006. "'A Hundred Flowers Bloom': The Re-emergence of the Chinese Press in Post-Suharto Indonesia," in Wanning Sun (ed.), *Media and the Chinese Diaspora: Community, Communications and Commerce*. London: Routledge, pp. 91–118.

Hu, Zhengrong and Deqiang Ji. 2012. "Ambiguities in Communicating with the World: The 'Going-Out' Policy of China's Media and Its Multilayered Contexts," *Chinese Journal of Communication* 5(1), pp. 32–37.

Jin, Kaiping. 2009. "Zhongguo de qiangguo zhilu yu huawen meiti de guoji hua" ["China's Size and the Globalization of Chinese-Language Migrant Media"], *Di wujie shijian huawen luntan lunwen ji* [Conference Proceedings from the 5th Global Conference on the Chinese-Language Media]. Hong Kong Chinese News Publishing Company, Hong Kong.

Ko, Simon. 2013. "Presentation at the UTS Multicultural and Indigenous Media Forum," NSW Parliament House, February 25. www.youtube.com/watch?v=urFdo-5yXXY.

Kong, Shuyu. 2016. "Geo-Ethnic Storytelling: Chinese-Language Television in Canada," in Wanning Sun and John Sinclair (eds.), *Media and Communication in the Chinese Diaspora: Rethinking Transnationalism*. London: Routledge, pp. 147–164.

Kurlantzick, Joshua. 2007. *Charm Offensive: How China's Soft Power Is Transforming the World*. New Haven, CT: Yale University Press.

Lim, Khor Yoke, and Ng Miew Luan. 2006. "Chinese Newspapers, Ethnic Identity and the State: The Case of Malaysia," in Wanning Sun (ed.), *Media and the Chinese Diaspora: Community, Communications and Commerce*. London: Routledge, pp. 137–149.

Nyíri, Pal. 2016. "'New Migrants' from the PRC and the Transformation of Chinese Media: The Case of Cambodia," in Wanning Sun and John Sinclair (eds.), *Media and Communication in the Chinese Diaspora: Rethinking Transnationalism*. London: Routledge, pp. 15–31.

Ong, Aihwa. 1999. *Flexible Citizenship: The Cultural Logics of Transnationality*. Durham, NC: Duke University Press.

Riordan, Primrose. 2017. "China Has Been 'Spying in Australia'," *The Australian*, May 12. www.theaustralian.com.au/national-affairs/defence/china-spying-in-australia-dennis-richardson-says/news-story/84b92773d886d02c42636db75981c38f.

Shambaugh, David. 2013. *China Goes Global: The Partial Power*. New York: Oxford University Press.

Shambaugh, David. 2015. "China's Soft-Power Push: The Search for Respect," *Foreign Affairs* 94(4), pp. 99–107.

Sinanan, Jolynna. 2016. "*Xin Yimin*: 'New' Chinese Migration and New Media in a Trinidadian Town," in Wanning Sun and John Sinclair (eds.), *Media and Communication in the Chinese Diaspora: Rethinking Transnationalism*. London: Routledge, pp. 203–219.

So, Clement Y.K. and Alice Y.L. Lee. 1995. "Tapping 'Yacht Immigrants': Overseas Editions of Hong Kong Newspapers as Econo-Cultural Spin-Off," *Asian Journal of Communication* 5(2), pp. 122–141.

Stenberg, Josh. 2016. "An Overseas Orthodoxy? Shifting toward Pro-PRC Media in Chinese-Speaking Brazil," in Wanning Sun and John Sinclair (eds.), *Media and Communication in the Chinese Diaspora: Rethinking Transnationalism*. London: Routledge, pp. 48–68.

Sun, Wanning. 2002. *Leaving China: Media, Migration and Transnational Imagination*. Lanham, MA: Rowman and Littlefield.

Sun, Wanning. 2005. "Media and the Chinese Diaspora: Community, Consumption and Transnational Imagination," *Journal of Chinese Overseas* 1(1), pp. 65–86.

Sun, Wanning. 2006. "Introduction: Transnationalism and a Global Diasporic Chinese Mediasphere," in Wanning Sun (ed.), *Media and the Chinese Diaspora: Community, Communications and Commerce*. London: Routledge, pp. 1–25.

Sun, Wanning. 2014. "Foreign or Chinese? Reconfiguring the Symbolic Space of Chinese Media," *International Journal of Communication* 8, pp. 1894–1911.

Sun, Wanning. 2016a. *Chinese-Language Media in Australia: Developments, Challenges and Opportunities*. Australia-China Relations Institute (ACRI) Report. http://bit.ly/2kABPaE.

Sun, Wanning. 2016b. "The Conundrum of the 'Honorary Whites': Media and Being Chinese in South Africa," in Wanning Sun and John Sinclair (eds.), *Media and Communication in the Chinese Diaspora: Rethinking Transnationalism*. London: Routledge, pp. 32–47.

Sun, Wanning. 2019. "China's Vessel on the Voyage of Globalisation: The Soft Power Agenda and Diasporic Media Responses," in Jessica Rettis and Roza Tsagarousianou (eds.), *The Handbook of Diasporas, Media, and Culture*. Hoboken, NJ: Wiley Blackwell, pp. 165–178.

Sun, Wanning and John Sinclair (eds.). 2016. *Media and Communication in the Chinese Diaspora: Rethinking Transnationalism*. London: Routledge.

Sun, Wanning, John Fitzgerald and Jia Gao. 2017. "From Multicultural Ethnic Migrants to the New Players of China's Public Diplomacy: The Chinese in Australia," in Bernard P. Wong and Tan Chee-Beng (eds.), *China's Rise and the Chinese Overseas*. London: Routledge.

Sun, Wanning, Jia Gao, Audrey Yue and John Sinclair. 2011a. "The Chinese-Language Press in Australia: A Preliminary Scoping Study," *Media International Australia* 138, pp. 137–148.

Sun, Wanning, Audrey Yue, John Sinclair and Jia Gao. 2011b. "Diasporic Chinese Media in Australia: A Post-2008 Overview," *Continuum* 25(4), pp. 515–527.

Walsh, Michael and Jason Fang. 2019. "Why Do Some Chinese-Australians Feel Targeted by the Government's New Foreign Influence Laws?," *ABC*, March 29. www.abc.net.au/news/2019-03-29/chinese-australians-confused-over-foreign-influence-laws/10936524.

Wang, Jian (ed.). 2011. *Soft Power in China: Public Diplomacy through Communication*. New York: Palgrave Macmillan.

Wasserman, Herman. 2011. "China in Africa: The Media's Response to a Developing Relationship," paper presented at China in a Global Context workshop, May, University of Nottingham, Ningbo, China.

Wong, Cindy H.-Y. 2009. "Globalizing Television: Chinese Satellite Television Outside Greater China," in Ying Zhu and Chris Berry (eds.), *TV China*. Bloomington: Indiana University Press, pp. 201–220.

Zhao, Iris, Jason Fang and Holly Robertson. 2019. "Australian-Chinese Community Outraged over Scott Morrison Referring to Beijing as a 'Customer'," *ABC*, May 14. www.abc.net.au/news/2019-05-14/chinese-community-in-australia-reacts-scott-morrison-customers/11111186.

Zhao, Suisheng. 2009. "The Prospect of China's Soft Power: How Sustainable?," in Mingjiang Li (ed.), *Soft Power: China's Emerging Strategy in International Politics*. Lanham, MD: Lexington Books, pp. 247–266.

Zhao, Yuezhi. 2013. "China's Quest for 'Soft Power': Imperatives, Impediments and Irreconcilable Tensions," *Javnost: The Public* 20(4), pp. 17–30.

5

THE BATTLE OF IMAGES

Cultural diplomacy and Sino–Hollywood negotiation

Ying Zhu

Hollywood dominated China's film market during the Republican era (1912–1949), taking up to an 80% share. The Communist victory in 1949 and the outbreak of the Korean War in 1950 led to an official ban on Hollywood films in 1950. The ban lasted until 1994 when, amidst declining domestic film output and theater attendance, Chinese policy makers reopened the market to an annual quota of ten imported films. Predictably, Hollywood blockbusters predominated. The imports generated huge revenue, instantly restoring Chinese audiences' theatergoing habit and subsequently revitalizing China's domestic film production (Zhu, 2003). Hollywood has been a regular fixture in China ever since, spurring simultaneous rejection, repulsion, admiration, emulation, competition and coercion. Rejection and repulsion for perceived offenses against China's image, admiration and emulation for the sheer allure and market prowess of Hollywood pictures, competition and coercion for Hollywood's global dominance and, lately, a new determination to draft Hollywood into the service of promoting China's global image.

Under President Xi Jinping's leadership, China is desperately seeking soft power—"soft power" being the *au courant* term (the term that Xi himself uses) for an older idea about using cultural sex appeal to win friends and influence people. Cinema was routinely employed as a form of culture-driven persuasion in Soviet Russia, and numerous European countries have actively cultivated their national image in film. In the United States, of course, soft power is more or less synonymous with Hollywood, including film, television and popular music. Indeed, Mike Medavoy, the Shanghai born veteran Hollywood producer, co-authored a book with political strategist Nathan Gardels in 2009 (*American Idol After Iraq: Competing for Hearts and Minds in the Global Media Age*) arguing that the United States should let its entertainment industry instead of its military forces pursue America's goals in the Middle East.

Hollywood, with its vast market penetration, has indeed done an exceptional job in spreading American culture and values around the globe, triggering cultural and economic anxieties in its export destinations, leading to national film policies intended to protect cultural image and limit domestic market erosion. China has a long history in molding culture and art in the service of national interest. When it comes to Hollywood imports, Chinese government policies and censorship during both the Republican and the PRC era have exercised image controls, monitoring and shaping what could and should be said about China. This chapter compares the context and terms of Hollywood's Republican era China triumph to those of its repeat performance in the post-1994 era, and the subsequent expansion of a powerful Chinese film market, to suggest historical contingencies, and the continuities and changes in an ongoing Sino–Hollywood dynamic with competing political, cultural and economic interests on and off screen.

Banning of "character-assassination" films

In 2014, the controversy surrounding James Franco-Seth Rogen's *The Interview*, a rowdy comedy about the assassination of the North Korea's supreme leader, triggered a diplomatic crisis. In June 2014, the North Korean government threatened action against the United States if the film were to be released. North Korea's UN ambassador declared that the movie was an act of war against North Korea: "To allow the production and distribution of such a film on the assassination of an incumbent head of a sovereign state should be regarded as the most undisguised sponsoring of terrorism as well as an act of war" (Reuters, 2014). In other statements, North Korea threatened a "resolute and merciless" response if the United States didn't ban the film. Columbia delayed the film's release from October to December and reportedly re-edited the film to make it more acceptable to North Korea. In November, the computer systems of the studio's parent company Sony Pictures Entertainment were hacked by the Guardians of Peace, a group with ties to North Korea, as per FBI claims. The group also threatened terrorist attacks against cinemas that dared to show the film. Major cinema chains opted not to release the film, leading Sony to release it for online rental and purchase on Christmas Eve, followed by a limited release at select cinemas the next day. In a press conference, President Barack Obama said that he thought Sony had made a mistake: "We cannot have a society in which some dictator in some place can start imposing censorship in the United States. I wish they'd spoken to me first. I would have told them: do not get into the pattern in which you are intimidated" (Stacey, 2015). On December 27, the North Korean National Defense Commission released a statement accusing President Obama of forcing Sony to distribute the film. The film was released on iTunes on December 28.

The *Interview* debacle was viewed by some career international relations experts and film historians with whom I consulted in private as the US government's failure in exercising due diligence over Hollywood and Sony's failure in reining in a reckless and tasteless exercise in farce. In the past, the US government actively provided guidance to Hollywood on matters concerning national interest. For example, in the 1930s, the failure of the United States to join the League of Nations after World War I, and the "Neutrality Acts" and general isolationist climate of the interwar period, led to America's isolationist policy toward East Asian conflicts. Moreover, Hollywood's interest in gaining a foothold in both the Chinese and Japanese markets meant that no direct reference or allusion to Japanese military aggression against China could be shown in pre–Pearl Harbor Hollywood films (Chung, 2006). After the Pearl Harbor attack and the subsequent entrance of the United States into World War II, Hollywood became openly anti-Japanese and pro-Chinese. The Bureau of Motion Pictures of the Office of War Information (OWI) regulated the political content of wartime Hollywood films, directly influencing the representations of Asian allies as well as enemies (Chung, 2006). Fast forward to 2014, given the hostile nature of the US–North Korea relationship, and the fact that Hollywood has no market stake in North Korea, even though an assassination tale does not immediately threaten America's national interest it still defies international norms. North Korea's demand to cancel all screenings, burn all the prints, formally apologize and promise not to do it again is not necessarily unusual. Many countries have made the same demand in protesting Hollywood's perceived insensitivity to their domestic situations. China in particular has been vocal in calling out Hollywood for its "China-humiliating" films.

Although most Hollywood films sailed through China with few challenges during Hollywood's golden age, its China-themed films by contrast ran into repeated roadblocks since the mid-1920s, a time when China's nationalist and anti-imperialist sentiment ran high amidst Western military aggression, leading to complaints about Hollywood's representation of China and Chinese on screen that kept on recycling time-honored stereotypes in the likes of Fu Manchu, the bandit, the warlord, the houseboy and the laundry-man. Public sentiment echoed the elite's view concerning Hollywood's China stereotyping, and a number of popular protests erupted in the 1930s and 1940s against Hollywood films such as *Welcome Danger* (Clyde Bruckman & Malcolm St. Clair, 1929), *East Is West* (Monta Bell, 1930), *Shanghai Express* (Josef von Sternberg, 1932), *The Bitter Tea of General Yen* (Frank Capra, 1933) and *The General Died at Dawn* (Lewis Milestone, 1936). *Welcome Danger*, Harold Lloyd's first talkie set in San Francisco featuring stock Chinese characters stealing, robbing and kidnapping their way around Chinatown, triggered a strong reaction in China and among the Chinese American community in the United States. Upon learning the film's setting of Chinatown, the Chinese Consulate in San Francisco immediately contacted Paramount, requesting that the Consulate be consulted during the production. When the film premiered in the United States on November 22, 1929, the Chinese Consulate received complaints from the local Chinese Chamber of Commerce expressing concerns that the negative depiction of Chinese would harm the relationship between white and Chinese people. Deputy Consul-General Li Zhaosong (李照松) promptly dispatched a letter to the San Francisco mayor on November 26, urging the mayor to have the film banned. The mayor's intervention led to the cutting of a scene at a Chinese household where opium was discovered. Paramount Studios further promised not to make films that would be detrimental to China and Chinese Americans.

As recounted in Wang Yiman (2014), just as the Chinese Consulate in the United States considered the matter successfully resolved, the film caused a stir when it debuted in China. During a February 22, 1930 screening at Shanghai's Grand Theater, US-trained dramatist Hong Shen was so offended by the film that he interrupted the screening to plead for the audiences to walk out and demand their money back. Hong was detained by a Shanghai foreign policeman, who told him that the film was a farce and shouldn't be taken literally. Hong was not amused and saw no humor in Chinese being made fun of (Wang, 2014, p. 191). Hong's detention led to a public protest that quickly snowballed into a campaign against "China-humiliating films." The local Shanghai Censorship Committee reacted swiftly, issuing an order for the Grand Theater to immediately halt all screening of the film. The Committee took out a public announcement in a Shanghai newspaper the next day, urging Chinese audiences to boycott the film. On February 24, the Committee ordered newspapers to cease running ads for the film and demanded that the two theaters screening the film "apologize to the public, discontinue and burn the film prints" (Wang, 2014, p. 192). Theaters were requested to submit all Paramount films for censorship approval and to stop showing films featuring Lloyd, who was then enormously popular in China. The KMT government contacted the Chinese consulate in San Francisco on March 22, seeking an apology from Lloyd. Lloyd initially demurred, explaining that "Why, all countries have bad men, but that doesn't mean a whole race is bad" (Wang, 2014, p. 192) and that "If we start apologizing, who'll we have left to poke fun at?" (Wang, 2014, p. 192). Lloyd's response led to a nationwide ban on the film on March 31, essentially pushing the film out of circulation except at a few theaters in foreign concessions. Lloyd eventually backed down as the financial stakes turned high. On May 29, he telegraphed the Chinese consul-general in San Francisco to offer "sincere apologies" and to reassure the "Chinese authorities of his admiration for the Chinese people, civilization and culture" (Wang, 2004, p. 193). The Shanghai Film Censorship Committee responded by resuming reviewing his films for approval and eventually lifting the ban on his films by the end of September. The *Welcome Danger* incident led to a joint manifesto of Chinese theater and cinema professionals denouncing Western imperialism and its smear campaign demonizing China and Chinese. The ban on *Welcome Danger* in 1930 led to the KMT government to bar all films with negative Chinese and China images from being released in China. Universal's *East Is West* (Bell, 1930), Paramount's *Shanghai Express* (von Sternberg, 1932) and *The General Died at Dawn* (Milestone, 1936), Columbia's *The Bitter Tea of General Yen* (Capra, 1933) and MGM's *China Seas* (Garnett, 1935) all became casualties of the KMT censors.

The Good Earth and the KMT's Ban on Hollywood's "China-humiliating" films

Dorothy B. Jones, who served as chief of the film reviewing and analysis section of the US Office of War Information (OWI) during World War II, observed that the Chinese government did not begin to take active measures at the policy level to safeguard its national image until the 1930s. As she notes, prior to the 1930s,

> the Chinese as a people had not yet developed any appreciable degree of nationalism and were more concerned with family affairs than with matters having to do with the Chinese people as a nation. . . . By the early 1930s, however, when China began to take her place in the community of nations and to build up a functioning foreign service which could put her more closely in touch with other countries of the world, the Chinese government began to express itself with the manner in which China and Chinese customs and people were being portrayed in American motion pictures.
>
> *(Jones, 1955, p. 5)*

Yet nationalism in China emerged as early as the late 19th century, a time when Western military powers and modern ideas shook the foundation of ancient Chinese civilization. China's defeat in the Opium Wars (1839–1860) and later by the Japanese in 1895 led to early nationalist efforts to save the country from disintegration and humiliation at the hands of Western powers. Chinese cultural elites lobbied for tough film censorship against "China-humiliating" films starting in the 1920s. But years of civil war in China made it impossible for a centralized effort at regulating film content. A film censorship apparatus at the national level was able to emerge only after the KMT consolidated its political control in China. Upon taking control of China in March 1927, the KMT established its central government in Nanjing on April 18. On May 15, 1928, the party convened a meeting of China's higher education, during which the susceptibility of youth to the influence of cinema, particularly foreign films, was addressed. On August 18, 1928, the Party's Shanghai Municipal Propaganda Department established a Drama and Cinema Review Committee to issue an order that requested all films be submitted for review and approval before being released for public screening in Shanghai. The committee was renamed Shanghai Film Censorship Committee on September 12, 1929, to regulate film contents, including rooting out American films that "insulted China." The Committee became the first censorship body with legitimate political authority to regulate cinema. The Committee successfully handled the case of *Welcome Danger*, Harold Lloyd's first talkie set in San Francisco that featured stock lowlife Chinese characters stealing, robbing and kidnapping their way around Chinatown. In January 1931, the KMT formally established the National Film Censorship Committee, for the first time putting the control of film regulation in the hands of the central government. The National Film Censorship Committee was to ensure that the Chinese film industry would serve to advance the party's national reconstruction project, and as such, film contents that deviated from this core mandate would be eliminated.

It is worth noting that the KMT's active political intervention in the nation's cultural affairs shared similar tenets and pedigree with its archenemy, the CCP; both were trained by the Soviets. In the early 1920s, when the Western powers continued to consider the Beiyang Government as China's official government, thus refusing to recognize the KMT's newly established Guangzhou government, the KMT turned to the Soviet Union for support. Soviet advisers including Mikhail Borodin, a prominent agent of the Comintern, arrived in China in 1923 to help reorganize and consolidate the KMT along the lines of the Communist Party of the Soviet Union, thus establishing a Leninist party structure that lasted well after the KMT's retreat to Taiwan. The Soviets advised the KMT on mass mobilization techniques and Chiang Kai-shek was sent by the Party to Moscow for military and political training in 1923. In 1924, at its first Party Congress in Guangzhou, the KMT adopted Dr. Sun's "Three Principles of the People" political theory: nationalism, democracy and people's livelihood. The KMT's governing structure was highly centralized under one-party rule, which aimed to facilitate the Party's total control of China's political, economic, military and cultural affairs. Chiang remarked that "Unity of Thinking is the most important thing" and that "it will be difficult to build up China if there is not a unified thinking" (Chiang, 1928). Unity of thinking refers to the adherence to the Three Principles of the People, of which nationalism was the most salient and seen as the galvanizing force behind the popular support for the KMT. The KMT's cultural policy encouraged arts and literature that elevated China's global standing. As in the Soviet Union and indeed in the United States where cinema was seen as a tool for cultural propagation, the KMT paid close attention to cinema as a vehicle for agitprop for the Party's Three Principles of the People.

The government restructured the National Film Censorship Committee in March 1934 and renamed it the Central Film Censorship Committee (CFCC). In addition to inspecting imported films, the CFCC strengthened its oversight on films shot in China by foreign studios. It promulgated "Regulations and Procedures for Foreigners Making Films in China," which stipulated that foreigners attempting to make films in China must first submit scripts to the Film Script Inspection Committee for review. Once the script was approved, they then had to apply for a production license. A commissioner from the CFCC needed to be on site for supervision if necessary. Finally, the studio had to obtain an export permit from the CFCC before screening the film overseas. The convoluted approval process of *The Good Earth* (Sidney Franklin, 1937), an adaptation of Pearl Buck's novel of the same name about the tribulations of a Chinese family in a rural village in early 20th century China, offers a glimpse of how Chinese censors interacted with Hollywood studios.

When the book came out in 1931, elements of its story capturing religious fundamentalism, racial prejudice, and gender and sexual oppression made the Chinese cultural gatekeepers and KMT officials uneasy. The book was black-listed in China but went on to win the Pulitzer Prize in 1932 and was quickly adapted for a Broadway play back in the United States. The Broadway play intrigued MGM production's head, the wonder boy Irving Thalberg who paid $50,000, a record-breaking amount at the time, to secure the book's screen rights. The Chinese Consulate in Los Angeles was alarmed upon learning the news and quickly dispatched Vice Consul Kiang Yiseng to MGM to obtain assurance that the screenplay would steer clear of any objectionable elements including opium, banditry, squalor, foot-binding and superstitions. When the production started, Thalberg wanted to send his film crew to northern China for location shooting. Chinese regulators rejected the idea. The studio turned to Willys Peck, the US Counselor of Legation at Nanjing for help. After several failed attempts at persuading Chinese censors, Peck resorted to name-dropping, hinting that the project had the attention of President Franklin D. Roosevelt. MGM also solicited the US State Department to lobby for Chiang Kai-shek's support. Chiang reportedly sent a telegram to the KMT Film Censorship Committee encouraging a green light (Chung, 2006). Perhaps the Chinese censors realized that MGM would make the film with or without their approval, that images of a real China would be better than what Hollywood might come up with in its backlot in the San Fernando Valley, and that some control over the filming process would be better than none, so the Ministry of Foreign Affairs in Nanjing granted permission in December 1933 for the MGM crew to enter China. The KMT's Publicity Department nonetheless demanded various modifications to the script including changing the title to disassociate the film from the controversial novel and adding a prologue stating that the film did not follow exactly the text of *The Good Earth*. The studio rejected the title change but reaffirmed its willingness to accommodate reasonable modifications to the original story. The movie script was more sympathetic to China than the novel had been. The Chinese government further demanded that representatives from the NFCC be present during production in China and in the United States. The United States strongly opposed hosting a Chinese censor in Hollywood for fear that it might encourage similar demands from other nations. It also feared that the censor could pass Hollywood trade secrets on to China's own film industry and that such an arrangement would make MGM more susceptible to the KMT's propaganda effort. The concern about trade secrets speaks volumes about the competitive nature of national film industries. At the time a minor studio relying on low-risk products appealing to independent and overseas distributors, MGM had to make sure that the final product would be completed to everybody's satisfaction, and thus consulted the Chinese every step of the way to ensure the cooperation of the Chinese government and secure a China release.

China's unusual demand of an in-house censor sent a chill to Hollywood, prompting studios to voluntarily consult with the Chinese consulate on all future

China-related projects. The Chinese consulate was able to monitor Hollywood production and frequently alerted Nanjing for preemptive measures against "anti-Chinese" films even before prints were made available for review. So much so that Frederick Herron, the foreign manager of the MPPDA, complained frequently about the Chinese consul's meddling, calling the Chinese diplomat a "little whippersnapper" (Chung, 2006, p. 95; Herron, 1936). Throughout the MGM–China negotiation, Peck mediated between Chinese government censors and MGM representatives and regularly forwarded documents to the secretary of state in Washington to report progress and solicit instructions. MGM eventually settled on a compromised approach allowing the Chinese to send in a traveling instead of resident censor at the expense of the studio. MGM further agreed to exclude contents deemed insulting and to insert a "foreword" to distance itself from the original novel. It also agreed to submit for the Chinese approval footage taken in China before shipping it back to America. On their part, the Chinese showed their good faith by lending their army for the filming of war scenes and by eventually allowing footage to be sent back to the United Sates without local inspections. In return, MGM "reduced the viciousness of the Chinese characters including the uncle and cousin, and toned down the sexual dimension of the Lotus character," a Chinese temptress who seduced the main character and ruined his family (Xiao, 2002, p. 281). Thalberg's initial pledge for an all-Chinese cast was quickly dropped as MGM needed its star Paul Muni to carry the film so needed to cast him in the leading role as the Chinese patriarch. The anti-miscegenation rules in Hays Code prevented non-white performers being casted as partners in a marriage to white performers so the idea of casting the Chinese American actress Anna May Wong as the wife to Paul Muni's character was also dropped. Thalberg died before the production was completed. The film opened in the United States to sensational response and was posthumously named Thalberg's "last great achievement." *The Good Earth* passed the Chinese censors in January 1937 and was released in China with only deletions of a few scenes depicting poverty and violence. Ironically, although the film successfully passed both the US and Chinese censors in 1937, when MGM submitted it for broader overseas release in 1943 the hyper-cautious US Office of War Information (OWI) objected to the film's references to slavery and concubinage, which it deemed offensive to Chinese sensibilities. To secure China's support in the US military campaign against the Japanese, OWI encouraged Hollywood to emphasize the nobility of the Chinese people and to not portray them as "backwards illiterates." US national interests dovetailed with Chinese national interest during the Pacific war, albeit at the expense of *The Good Earth*.

Transformers and film censorship during the CCP era

The dynamic between Hollywood and China has changed significantly since Hollywood returned to China in the mid-1990s. The Chinese film market has expanded rapidly in recent years, with predictions that it will overtake North

America as the world's largest film market in 2020. China can break or make a film. In 2016, the Hollywood film *Warcraft* (Duncan Jones), with a price tag of $160 million, was a critical and financial flop in the United States. Yet it racked up $156 million in its first five days in China. Now, a sequel to *Warcraft* could conceivably be made solely for the Chinese market. What does that have to do with China's image building? The Hong Kong martial arts film star turned Chinese cultural ambassador Jackie Chan made the connection when he remarked that "*Warcraft* made 600 million yuan (£64 million) in two days. This has scared the Americans. If we can make a film that earns 10bn yuan (£1bn), then people from all over the world who want to study film will learn Chinese, instead of us having to learn English" (Lee, 2016). The great leap forward from the power of the Chinese box office to the propagation of the Chinese language suggests that economic power can confer cultural power. The expansion of the Chinese film market has Hollywood fawning to Chinese regulators and audiences with sanitized film images of China and Chinese. While Sino–Hollywood cooperation during the Republican era was perceived as friendly and harmless, and was facilitated by the US government, Hollywood's new compromises are viewed through a harsher lens. Hollywood is being called out for promoting the Chinese government's interest at the expense of Western cultural principles, a trend that has alarmed broader US media interests and the government.

In the summer of 2014, *Transformers 4: Age of Extinction* (Michael Bay) set a Chinese box office record, selling over $300 million worth of tickets against a $244 million US take. With its numerous Chinese product placements, generously featured Chinese landmarks and cameos by Chinese pop stars, *Transformers 4* serves as an interesting example on what localizing can deliver at little to no cost to the studios. The Chinese paid to have their products and landmarks shown and Chinese stars eagerly appeared in minor and incoherent roles in the film. *Transformer 4*'s Chinese collaborators provided efficient production assistance and a brilliant marketing campaign in China for Paramount. But jubilation over the film's earnings was dampened by jeers from major news outlets in the West that the film was yet another example of Hollywood pandering to China, joining other recent instances: *The Martian* (2015) made sure that the China National Space Administration played a prominent role in a life-saving rescuing mission; *Iron Man 3* (2013) inserted a scene of doctors played by major Chinese movie stars discussing surgery on the superhero and thus showcased China as a savior of the world civilization; *Mission: Impossible III* (2006) expunged a scene of Shanghai featuring underwear hanging from a clothesline that the Chinese regulator deemed primitive and portrayed China as "a developing country;" the remake of *Red Dawn* (2012) originally featured Chinese soldiers invading an American town but digitally changed the invaders to North Koreans during post-production as a precaution to fend off anticipated China grievances.

From *Welcome Danger* and *The Good Earth* to these more recent films, the power of screen images to shape perceptions and values has been on both the Chinese and US governments' radar. While the concern for the Chinese during China's

Republican era had to do with image building and protection, the new goal is to draft Hollywood into the service of promoting Chinese soft power. How is Hollywood faring under this pressure? The picture is not entirely clear. Let's return to *Transformers 4* as an example. Critics of *Transformers 4* were dismayed over its perceived pro-Chinese-government message. The film takes familiar jabs at the CIA and depicts a timid White House beholden to both the military–industrial complex and vapid high-tech evangelicals. Juxtaposed against this we see a Chinese state led by an upright-looking Chinese defense minister determined to save Hong Kong from an alien robot attack. Many Western commentators worried that the Chinese Communist Party comes across as the good guy. *The Guardian* (Child, 2014) called the movie "sinister," as it showcased an autocratic political system as more functional and humane than Western democracy. *The Financial Times* (Shone, 2014) lamented that the Chinese military appears more efficient and disciplined. It is indeed the case that Michael Bay included the Chinese military under pressure from his Chinese partners. Yet the Chinese defense minister gets only a few perfunctory shots as he vows to scramble China's fighter jets to defend Hong Kong. No Chinese fighter jets ever appear and no Chinese government action is shown. Instead, it is left to a few renegade Americans from Texas to drop into the Far East and save the human race. As Zhu noted (2014), the film perpetuates the myth of triumphant American individualism and exceptionalism. Positive or not, the Chinese on the screen, including the upright defense minister, are reduced to sidekicks and bystanders. *Variety* gets it wrong when it declares that "*Transformers* is a very patriotic film" but that "it's just Chinese patriotism on the screen, not American" (Cohen, 2014). By portraying a Texan who comes to the rescue of China and the world, *Transformers 4* displayed American supremacy at its most potent. Critically, the film was panned by most major film reviewers in the United States and United Kingdom—*The Telegraph* called it "spectacular junk" (Collin, 2014). But the record number of Chinese captivated by this "spectacular junk" constituted another victory for US popular culture, or soft power.

One counter-strategy for the Chinese is to absorb Hollywood talent to make a China story instead of a Hollywood story with token Chinese elements, and this has led to a new co-production model matching Chinese investment and talent with major Hollywood stars, unlike the old co-production model with Hollywood investment and cheap Chinese labor. These films can bypass quota restrictions for imports, guarantee China releases and improve the percentage of box office receipts US companies can collect to about 40%. That became the strategy in a 2016 Sino–Hollywood co-production, the epic fantasy adventure film *The Great Wall* (Zhang Yimou), about a group of European mercenaries who come to China in search of black powder but wind up joining the Chinese imperial army in defense of the Great Wall against a horde of monstrous creatures. Shot on location in China with a budget of $150 million and featuring a China-centric story with an English screenplay developed by seasoned Hollywood screenwriters, the film was at the time the biggest Sino–Hollywood co-production. Directed by China's most recognized filmmaker, Zhang Yimou, it stars Matt Damon, Korean boy band megastar Lu Han, Hong Kong veteran Andy Lau and well-known Chinese actors and actresses. Despite much anticipation in both Hollywood and China, the film came out to overwhelmingly negative reviews in China, though the official media insisted on being positive and went so far as to crack down on negative reviews. The response in the West was hardly more encouraging, particularly when it became embroiled in Hollywood's "whitewashing" controversy. To criticism that the film features a white hero in an essentially China story, Zhang Yimou explained, "If we didn't have Matt Damon, if we didn't speak English in the film, then it would just be a purely Chinese film" (Qin, 2017). Matt Damon was mocked by Jimmy Kimmel in his 2017 Oscar opening monologue for giving up an Oscar-nominated role in *Manchester by the Sea* (dir. Kenneth Lonergan, 2017) for a mercenary character in a Chinese propaganda film, what Kimmel termed "a Chinese ponytail movie." "Spectacularly made with the director's trademark of scale, order, color, light, and rhythm," the film suffers from anemic character and story development (Zhu, 2017).

As Zhu commented in her ChinaFile/Foreign Policy conversation with Coonan and Rosen (2017), the film is a Sino–Hollywood co-production run amok. Burdened with a Chinese nationalist fantasy that displays Chinese military might and pageantry at its most excessive, the film leaves little room for sophisticated characters and human drama. Dwarfed by the gigantic Great Wall, the gunpowder-crazed European mercenaries appear dumbfounded by the enormity of China and Chinese culture. They are, in time, taught a moral lesson, chiefly by the righteous Chinese female commander, on fighting for trust and honor instead of gunpowder. The clichéd narrative fits the myth of Western barbarians being tamed and enlightened by Chinese civilization on the benefits of patriotism and bilateral action. It is as if the entire Western canon of medieval adventures did not exist. In their eagerness, Hollywood and its Chinese partners concocted a colorfully synchronized mass devoid of real feelings and imagination. The film is a reminder that a big budget, star actors and excessive visual effects do not magically translate into compelling stories, Hollywood or Chinese. The film did little for Chinese soft power, but it did make money for some Chinese investors, grossing $334 million worldwide against its $150 million production budget, but it was reportedly a $75 million loss for Universal and led to a complete overhaul of the leadership at Legendary Pictures, with the exit of Peter Loehr and Tom Tull (McClintock and Galloway, 2017).

But there is also counter-measure two—the Chinese film industry is determined to manufacture its own globally aimed blockbusters that speak Chinese and feature China's own action hero. A year after the lukewarm reception of *The Great Wall*, *Wolf Warrior II* (dir. Wang Jing, 2017), a Chinese version of *Rambo: First Blood* featuring a muscular Chinese action hero fighting rebels and Western mercenaries in a nameless African country where China is seen building hospitals and providing humanitarian aid, grossed a whopping $854 million. It generated a media buzz in Hollywood. Notably, when *Rambo: First Blood* was screened in

China in 1985, the film's raw action shocked Chinese audiences who had been isolated from the vibrant global film scene during the Mao era. While many in the West objected to *Rambo*'s fascist undertone, Chinese officials readily endorsed the film's plot of a wronged Vietnam veteran resisting the arbitrary brutality of oppressive capitalist authorities represented by US army troops and officers, state police and a sheriff wearing a US-flag shoulder patch. Chinese audiences were in awe of the action sequences involving "helicopters, four-wheel-drive vehicles, and big guns, the likes of which most Chinese viewers have never seen" (Baum, 1985). *Rambo* made Sylvester Stallone an instant household name in China. It took 32 years for China to come up with its own version of *Rambo*, which featured a Chinese rebel not against his own government, but against evil Western forces. The martial arts star turned director and lead actor Wu Jing hired Joe and Anthony Russo as consultants, Sam Hargrave as the stunt director and Joseph Trapanese as the composer, who brought along a largely foreign sound unit. American actor Frank Grillo starred alongside Wu as an antagonist. The mixture of action, comic relief, some English dialogue and the participation of veteran Hollywood talent as antagonistic forces worked wonders, and Chinese audiences responded favorably to the film's patriotism and to the relentless action provided by Wu. *Wolf Warrior II* is not a co-production, but a Chinese production employing US talent to showcase China's largess in Africa and its newly amassed international power. China no longer collaborates with Hollywood but simply purchases its expertise, technology and talent to construct and sell China's own story. As Bayles observed (2018, p. 94), the film marked a shift from soft power of attraction and persuasion to what Christopher Walker and Jessica Ludwig (2017) called "sharp power" that "pierces, penetrates, or perforates the political and information environments in the targeted countries."

But the ultra-violent Chinese film did not quite match *Rambo* for wider global appeal. The jingoism cloaked as Chinese patriotism and the racist depiction of the nameless and witless Africans are out of step with contemporary sensibilities. The world is not thrilled to replace American saviors with Chinese saviors. China's answer to American jingoism failed to capture hearts and minds outside China. *Wolf Warrior II* only grossed $2.3 million in the North America market while its China box office accounted for 98.1% of the total gross. China needs to consider what kind of power it wishes to project to the rest of the world via its cinematic images now that it is capable of generating such images on its own terms. Domestically, the film beat Hollywood imports at the box office, providing a boost to the Chinese film industry and a reminder that the domestic market is lucrative enough on its own, never mind the global culture mission.

The turn to sharp power: from image building to asset building

Recent years witnessed the acquisition of US entertainment assets by Chinese companies, most notably Dalian Wanda, the Chinese media conglomerate led by the real estate tycoon Wang Jianlin, whose Wanda Group acquired in rapid succession big-league US film assets including AMC Theatres, the largest American chain, in May 2012 for $2.6 billion; Legendary Entertainment, one of Hollywood's biggest production companies, in January 2016, for $3.5 billion; and Carmike Cinema, the fourth largest movie theater chain in the United States, in November 2016, for $1.2 billion. Cash-strapped Hollywood welcomed the infusion of Chinese investment. It is business as usual in the age of global mergers and acquisitions, but Chinese firms are playing an increasingly prominent role, replacing the Japanese in the late 1980s and the South Koreans in the late 1990s. US lawmakers have responded with alarm. To them, China's expansion into the United States is not a simple matter of a new East Asian power replacing old ones—China poses an existential threat to Western liberal democratic principles and norms. In 2016, members of Congress wrote to various agency chiefs to express their concerns over Chinese firms' encroachment on US media assets, specifically citing Dalian Wanda. In a letter to the Government Accounting Office the lawmakers asked, "Should the definition of national security be broadened to address concerns about propaganda and control of the media and 'soft power' institutions?" (Shaheen, 2016). The letter stated "growing concerns about China's efforts to censor topics and exert propaganda controls on American media" and called for greater oversight of Chinese corporate purchases, including movie theaters and studios (Tartaglione, 2016). Representative Christopher H. Smith, Republican of New Jersey, stated that "Beijing is increasingly confident that its version of state authoritarianism can be exported, though the Communist Party's efforts at 'soft power' outreach have little credibility or impact at this point" (Wong, 2016). "Would any movies favorably portraying the Dalai Lama, Liu Xiaobo or Chen Guangcheng be greenlighted if they risked the loss of Chinese investment—I don't think so," he added, naming three prominent political adversaries of the CCP (Wong, 2016). Wanda's proposed $1 billion takeover of the Dick Clark Production Company, the venerable producer of Golden Globe awards, subsequently collapsed in March 2017.

By then the Chinese government and public sentiment had also soured on Chinese firms' outbound deals, which many see as part of the massive capital flight scheme. Chinese companies have in recent years aggressively invested in foreign companies as a way of moving money out of China amidst China's tightening anti-corruption campaign that has brought down ranking politicians and big name business owners and frozen their assets. In July 2017, Chinese regulators ordered Chinese banks to stop lending money to Wanda to finance the conglomerate's foreign acquisitions—six deals in particular, including Wanda's $3.5-billion purchase of Legendary Entertainment (Frater, 2017). But AMC, with Carmike under its belt, was able to complete the pre-arranged acquisition of Starplex Cinemas, Odeon & UCI and Nordic Cinema Group by July 2017, making the Wanda-owned theater chain the largest in the United States and the world, although the theater chain claimed that the funding for these acquisitions did not come from Wanda. Concern about whether Hollywood is beholden to China's interests is at the core of the current relationship between Hollywood and the Chinese film industry. With *Wolf Warrior II*, the Chinese film industry has demonstrated that it can now bypass Hollywood by poaching its talent and technologies and replicating its formulas for its own purposes.

From *The Good Earth* to *Wolf Warrior II*, China's image has witnessed a dramatic remake. China's economic prosperity bought China unprecedented negotiating power in dictating what kind of image can be constructed about China. The use of the market as leverage for image building and protection existed long before the current round of Sino–Hollywood negotiation. If the Chinese have been insistent, Hollywood is equally *consistent*. When Japan threatened to reduce the intake of US movies late in the 1930s, US negotiators warned the Japanese if that happened they might become the villains in American pictures (Segrave, 1997). Meanwhile, Hollywood pledged its willingness to work with the State Department to spread the American gospel abroad. In a speech delivered in London in October 1923 that outlined the international aims of the US motion picture industry, Will Hays, the head of the Motion Picture Producers and Distributors of America (MPPDA), proclaimed that the "Members of our Association have taken . . . definite steps to make certain that every film that goes from America abroad, wherever it shall be sent, shall correctly portray to the world the purposes, the ideals, the accomplishments, the opportunities, and the life of America" (Trumpbour, 2002, p. 17). But the US State Department was frequently unsure about the profit-driven Hollywood's reliability in the battle of ideas and thus exercised due oversight. For example, *Gone with the Wind* was blocked from being screened in Germany by the US occupation authority because of the film's portrayal of slavery and racism.

When it comes to dealing with China, the interests of Hollywood and the interests of US lawmakers do not always collude. Evidence of Hollywood pandering to China such as changing a film setting from the old glory of Paris to the new glory of Shanghai in *Looper*, or portraying Beijing as the land of promise in *The Karate Kid*, are relatively insignificant in comparison to Congressman Smith's charge of Hollywood's change of heart in steering clear of any politically charged movies such as a hypothetical Dalai Lama picture. Hollywood is nothing but consistent in how it assesses the global viability of any film projects. Despite earlier films such as *Kundun* and *Seven Years in Tibet*, which were critical of China's Tibet policy, Hollywood was not out to smear China then and is certainly not on a mission to rehabilitate China now. The Tibet-related pictures came out in the 1990s when the newly opened Chinese market was relatively insignificant to Hollywood. The market has changed and a few pandering plot or location twists to penetrate China's lucrative new market is nothing more than "localizing strategy," the playbook of an industry that has been acutely attuned, from its inception, to what is permissible and indeed preferred in its vast export destinations. The trend has only intensified in the last decade, with the majority of moviegoers now living abroad, which accounts for up to 80% of Hollywood's box office income. As Zhu notes (2013), to maximize overseas distribution, films must be rendered free from international offense. The more expensive the movie, the more scrupulous the studios must be to ensure the avoidance of any potential overseas hazards. To stay out of (financial) trouble, Hollywood has long modified, obfuscated and even eliminated content that is deemed inappropriate in an effort to appease audiences of different cultural, religious and political persuasions. During the Republican era, a significant proportion of the correspondence in the 1920s, 1930s and early 1940s between the Hays Office and China reflected American studio executives' concerns about Chinese sensitivities, both cultural and political. The depiction of China was sanitized to appease the Chinese state and public, both hyper-sensitive to the country's humiliations at the hands of Western powers.

China's Republican and PRC eras are vastly different, with the contours of the world and the international balance of power radically altered between them as China's rapid economic growth in recent decades nurtured its ambition to spread its cultural influence. The evolution of the Sino–Hollywood relationship reflects the shifting power dynamic between China and the United States, with China emerging from an eager apprentice to a formidable competitor and partner who wants market share as well as cultural influence. The Chinese film industry might indeed fancy a day when it can overtake Hollywood as the global alpha dog in box office and influence. But the Chinese film industry has yet to climb the cinematic food chain in terms of prestige, aside from a few independent films playing in overseas art houses, despite the red-hot market and even hotter investment rush. The business of filmmaking is indeed booming in China, but not necessarily the global appeal of Chinese cinema, or the officially sanctioned China stories, whether narrated by Hollywood or by the Chinese film industry. Chinese blockbuster films have yet to overtake Hollywood productions in quantity, quality and recognition. The world has yet to embrace Chinese cinema, judging by the limited appeal of Chinese films globally and Hollywood's continued status at the top of the cinematic totem pole, at least box office–wise. At the core of the problem is the clash of cultural values and divergent political systems and economic structures. The gulf persists between the aim of substantial expansion of China's soft power by various means, creative and strategic/industrial and what actually comes across in the films, which continues to overwhelmingly favor Western values and norms represented by Hollywood in many places around the world. The proposition that a few patriotic films utilizing Hollywood's know-how will dramatically rehabilitate China's international image remains a remote fancy.

References

Baum, Julian. 1985. "Rambo Busts through China's 'Open Door'," *The Christian Science Monitor*, October 15. www.csmonitor.com/1985/1015/oram.html.

Bayles, Martha. 2018. "Dream Factory, or Propaganda Machine?," *Claremont Review of Books*, February 6, pp. 94–97.

Chiang, Kai-shek. 1928. "The Path to China Building" [中国建设之途径; July 18日] in Xiaoyi Qing (ed.), *Thoughts and Remarks of Former President Chiang* [先总统蒋公思想言论总集]. Taipei: Volume 10 of the1984 Edition of the Party History Committee of the KMT Central Committee [中国国民党中央委员会党史委员会], p. 323.

Child, Ben. 2014. "Transformers: Age of Extinction Becomes Highest-Grossing Film of All Time in China," *The Guardian*, July 8. www.theguardian.com/film/2014/jul/08/transformers-age-extinction-highest-grossing-china.

Chung, Hye Seung. 2006. *Hollywood Asian: Philip Ahn and the Politics of Cross-Ethnic Performance*. Philadelphia, PA: Temple University Press.

Cohen, David S. 2014. "'Transformers': A Splendidly Patriotic Film, If You Happen to Be Chinese: Bay, Spielberg and Paramount Kowtow for Cash," *Variety*, July 3. http://variety.com/2014/film/columns/transformers-age-of-extinction-patriotic-for-china-1201257030/.

Collin, Robbie. 2014. "Transformers: Age of Extinction, Review: 'Spectacular Junk'," *The Telegraph*, July 3. www.telegraph.co.uk/culture/film/filmreviews/10931656/Transformers-Age-of-Extinction-review-spectacular-junk.html

Coonan, Clifford, Ying Zhu, Stanley Rosen and Jonathan Landreth. 2017. "Is the Search for a China-Hollywood Blockbuster Doomed? The Flailing 'Great Wall' Aspires to Be a Bicultural Extravaganza: The Result Is a Mess," *Foreign Policy*, February 24. http://foreignpolicy.com/2017/02/24/is-the-search-for-a-china-hollywood-blockbuster-doomed-great-wall-fail/.

Frater, Patrick. 2017. "AMC Theatres Denies Wanda Funding, Says All Acquisitions Completed," *Variety*, July 18. http://variety.com/2017/biz/news/amc-theaters-deny-wanda-deal-financing-says-all-acquisitions-completed-1202498490/.

Herron, Frederick L. 1936. "Letter to Willys Peck," November 9. State Department files on China, 893.4061 Motion Pictures, NARA.

Jones, Dorothy B. 1955. *American Films, the Portrayal of China and India on the American Screen, 1896–1955: The Evolution of Chinese and Indian Themes, Locales, and Characters as Portrayed on the American Screen*. Cambridge, MA: MIT Press.

Lee, Benjamin. 2016. "Jackie Chan: Warcraft's Success in China Scares Americans," *The Guardian*, June 13. www.theguardian.com/film/2016/jun/13/jackie-chan-warcraft-success-china-scares-americans-chinese-box-office-blockbuster.

McClintoc, Pamela and Stephen Galloway. 2017. "Matt Damon's 'The Great Wall' to Lose $75 Million; Future U.S.-China Productions in Doubt," *The Hollywood Reporter*, March 2. https://www.hollywoodreporter.com/news/what-great-walls-box-office-flop-will-cost-studios-981602.

Qin, Amy. 2017. "Pander or Diversify? Hollywood Courts China with 'The Great Wall'," *The New York Times*, January 19. www.nytimes.com/2017/01/19/movies/the-great-wall-matt-damon-chinese-box-office.html.

Reuters Staff. 2014. "North Korea Complains to U.N. about Film Starring Rogen, Franco," *Reuters Online*, July 9. www.reuters.com/article/us-northkorea-un-film-idUSKBN0FE21D20140709.

Segrave, Kerry. 1997. *American Films Abroad: Hollywood's Domination of the World's Movie Screens from the 1890s to the Present*. Jefferson, NC: McFarland Publishing.

Shaheen, Therese. 2016. "American Movies Should Not Have to Be Approved by Bureaucrats in Beijing," *National Review*, December 6. www.nationalreview.com/2016/12/china-united-states-filmmaking-industry-hollywood-self-censorship-soft-power/.

Shone, Tom. 2014. "Hollywood Transformed: How China Is Changing the DNA of America's Blockbuster Movies," *Financial Times*, July 24. www.ft.com/content/60338b6c-1263-11e4-93a5-00144feabdc0#axzz3B2M2GLGE

Stacey, Tim. 2015. "The (Thoroughly Unnecessary) Interview," *The Brock Press*, January 8. www.brockpress.com/2015/01/the-thoroughly-unnecessary-interview/.

Tartaglione, Nancy. 2016. "Hollywood & China: U.S. Gov't Agency Agrees to Review Foreign Investment Panel," *Deadline Hollywood*, October 4. http://deadline.com/2016/10/china-hollywood-congress-wanda-foreign-ownership-gao-1201830426/.

Trumpbour, John. 2002. *Selling Hollywood to the World: US and European Struggles for Mastery of the Global Film Industry, 1920–1950*. Cambridge, UK: Cambridge University Press.

Walker, Christopher and Jessica Ludwig. 2017. "The Meaning of Sharp Power: How Authoritarian States Project Influence," *Foreign Affairs*, November 16. https://www.foreignaffairs.com/articles/china/2017-11-16/meaning-sharp-power.

Wang, Yiman. 2014. "The Crisscrossed State: Propaganda and Protest in China's Not So Silent Era," in Jennifer M. Bean, Anupama P. Kapse and Laura Evelyn Horak (eds.), *Silent Cinema and the Politics of Space*. Bloomington, IN: Indiana University Press, pp. 186–209.

Wang, Zhaoguang. 2004. "Censorship, Control, and Direction: Research on Shanghai Film Censorship Committee," *Modern History Research* 6, pp. 87–121.

Wong, Edward. 2016. "Chinese Purchases of U.S. Companies Have Some in Congress Raising Eyebrows," *The New York Times*, September 30. www.nytimes.com/2016/10/01/world/asia/china-us-foreign-acquisition-dalian-wanda.html.

Xiao, Zhiwei. 2002. "Nationalism, Orientalism, and an Unequal Treatise of Ethnography: The Making of the Good Earth," in Susie Lan Cassel (ed.), *The Chinese in America: A History from Gold Mountain to the New Millennium*. Lanham, MD: AltaMira Press, pp. 274–292.

Zhu, Ying. 2003. *Chinese Cinema during the Era of Reform: The Ingenuity of the System*. Westport, CT: Praeger.

Zhu, Ying. 2013. "Hollywood Powerhouses Meet a Sleeping Giant Perspective: China's Massive Movie Market Is Influencing U.S. Studios: But Mainland Filmmakers also Need American Expertise and Talent," *The Los Angeles Times*, November 9. http://articles.latimes.com/2013/nov/09/entertainment/la-et-mn-ca-china-essay-20131110.

Zhu, Ying. 2014. "How U.S. Soft Power Won the Chinese Box Office: Chinese Have Noticed How 'Transformers 4' Took Their Money: Then Depicted Texans Saving the Human Race Anyway," *Foreign Policy*, September 6. http://foreignpolicy.com/2014/09/06/how-u-s-soft-power-won-the-chinese-box-office/.

Zhu, Ying, Clifford Coonan, Stanley Rosen and Jonathan Landreth. 2017. "Is the Search for a China-Hollywood Blockbuster Doomed?" *Foreign Policy*, February 24. https://foreignpolicy.com/2017/02/24/is-the-search-for-a-china-hollywood-blockbuster-doomed-great-wall-fail/.

6

BRANDING AS SOFT POWER

Brand culture, nation branding and the 2008 Beijing Olympics

Janet Borgerson, Jonathan Schroeder and Zhiyan Wu

A brand culture approach opens up the concept of soft power by emphasizing connections between branding and the promotion of existing cultural accomplishments and cultural heritage. Brand culture also offers insights into the ways in which brands create new culture, including new practices, new rituals, new notions, new objects and new imagery. We argue that in the context of the Beijing 2008 Olympics, Chinese soft power branding models emerge, targeting market myths through historical and mythical Chinese culture paired with modern technology; composing identity myths; and extending these to global identity myths, thus, creating new forms and paths for soft power. We reimagine soft power in relation to engagement with brands and branding. These engagements influence the way people behave, perceive and interact with each other, and these new configurations participate in the workings of soft power. The discussion of soft power and its relationship to branding provides distinctive insight into China's recent efforts to build global brands.

To clarify, in our understanding, the term brand does not refer only to a firm, an organization or a simple logo, but primarily to material and symbolic forms of communication. For example, brands, as communicative objects, embody values or features of products, places and interactions in consumption contexts. Brands, in this sense, foster imaginative engagement between brand actors, which serves to create the differences between brand identity—what a corporate or organizational entity hopes to communicate—and brand image—the meanings and understandings that emerge out in the lived world.

Brands and related branding processes that include advertising, promotion, event marketing and nation branding circulate at multiple intersections of media, political and interpersonal discourses. We argue that brands co-create cultures, including aspects of cultures that have an impact on the attitudes and the values of consumers and of citizens, as well as on the ways in which nations appear to the rest of the world. In other words, mediatized political discourse and the "political effects" of media (Chouliaraki, 2005) come together in brands and branding processes. From this perspective, China itself was the most evident and notable brand of the 2008 Beijing Summer Olympics.

Despite the fact that sport remained a focus, the spectacular staging of the XXIX Olympiad attracted the eyes of many who hoped for a glimpse of contemporary China, often obscured behind a veil of the past. The Beijing Olympics, featuring the spectacular "Bird's Nest" Olympic National Stadium built for the Games, and record-breaking athletic performances—such as U.S. swimmer Michael Phelps's unprecedented eight gold medals—as well as controversies surrounding the development of the Olympic sites, crises within China over contaminated consumer products, concerns about media access and simmering political tensions, drew the attention of the world.

In this way, China effectively and efficiently employed the Olympics to enhance the country's "visibility and the salience of its marketplace on the world stage" (Greyser, 2008, p. 1), in accordance not only with elite sport, modern facilities, and advanced technologies, but also with cultural diplomacy and soft power. The Beijing Olympics can be viewed as

> important occasions to project China's soft power—to influence the hearts and minds of people in other nations through "attraction." Following its introduction into China in the early 2000s, Joseph Nye's concept of "soft power" gained immediate currency and prominence in China's official, academic and popular discourse, largely because it arrived at a time when China tried to project a peaceful international image amidst perceptions of a "Chinese threat."
>
> *(Cao, 2011, p. 8)*

The Olympics, and the spectacle of the Opening Ceremonies, has helped brand many host nations; for example, the 1964 Tokyo Olympics, the 1988 Seoul Olympics and the 2000 Sydney Olympics. In the case of the Beijing Games, branding researcher Stephen Greyser wrote that "China's 'coming out party' reflects and signals its significance in sports, its magnitude as an economy, and its power in global politics" (Greyser, 2008). As one article put it: "the 2008 Beijing Olympic Games can be considered a tool in the soft power and international communication strategy that China has been pioneering in recent years" (Chen, Colapinto and Luo, 2012, p. 188; see also Edney, 2008; Gold and Gold, 2008; Liang, 2011; Zhang, 2010; Zhao, 2014). For example, media scholar Ying Zhu argues that China Central Television (CCTV), which broadcast the Olympics to its home market, functions as a tool of global soft power (Zhu, 2012). Some researchers have downplayed the complex workings of soft power in this context (Manzenreiter, 2010); however, we take a brand culture approach to soft power, highlighting the ongoing co-creation and circulation of brands and cultures (Wu, Borgerson and Schroeder, 2013).

Of course, the Olympics itself is an iconic brand that gains much from top-level athletes' involvement and the infrequency, and thus anticipation, of the event. Furthermore, Olympic sponsorship offers a host of branding opportunities for private companies (e.g., Madrigal, Bee and LaBarge, 2005). Olympic events are held once every two years, and provide vehicles to express world union and national pride, including appeals to the hearts and minds of viewers through the tears, smiles and personal challenges of athletes and coaches. The Beijing Olympics were popular: American television network NBC paid nearly $900 million for broadcast rights for the 2008 Olympic Games and attracted an average broadcast television audience of 30 million viewers each night. Millions more watched on the NBC cable channels. Thirty million unique users visited the NBC Olympics website and 6.3 million shared videos from the streaming coverage (Carter and Sandomir, 2008).

We have argued elsewhere that brand culture approaches represent key opportunities for the development of Chinese global brands (Schroeder, Borgerson and Wu, 2015). In this chapter, we explore the ways in which brand culture research perceives pathways of Chinese cultural diplomacy, and how the Beijing 2008 Olympics Opening Ceremony facilitated a compelling example of Chinese soft power. Soft power is often seen as the prerogative of governments and nations. Branding, even nation branding, is generally understood as the arena of marketing firms and development authorities. But this distinction has evolved. As all manner of organizations, including corporations, universities and sports teams, as well as individuals using social media, participate in branding, the way we understand the ability to influence and engage in so-called cultural diplomacy shifts. The brand culture perspective suggests a re-examination of the ways in which the Opening Ceremony's themes targeted myth markets by rejuvenating Chinese history and myth, and presenting historical stories with advanced technologies. As a branding event that launched a new brand China, the Beijing Olympics Opening Ceremony generates new insights into China's soft power.

A brand culture approach to soft power

Brand culture relates to diverse scenarios of cultural forms, not least of which are new co-creations between branding and cultural forms. A brand culture approach reveals that branding practices perform as, and engage with, other cultural forms, such as, music, movies, sports, fashion and historical narratives. Thus, brand culture sheds light on the diverse ways in which aspects of culture inform and interact with global brands and global branding, such as how the Marlboro cigarette brand strongly links itself to people's impressions of what constitutes the American West, but also bringing insight to Japanese global brands that in fact do little to express "Japanese lifestyle" (Iwabuchi, 2006). From these perspectives, branding no longer merely represents manipulative and hegemonic corporate intentions or mandates for persuasion and consumer passivity: this is 'soft' branding, on a horizon of media and political discourses where brands effortlessly ply the waters of soft power.

Research in brand culture focuses upon the co-creation and circulation of brands and cultures, attending to the ways in which branding processes and practices move beyond subsidiary roles to co-create culture. Brands share stories, build community and solve problems. Brands understood as cultural forms reflect, engage with, and alter, people's ideologies, their lifestyles and their cultural values. A brand culture approach directs our attention to a relational metaphysics, wherein shifts and changes occur through repeated interactions between various actors, including brands and consumers, across time and space. From this perspective, an analysis of brand development draws attention to emerging new knowledge around the co-creation and circulation of brands and cultures. Schroeder and Salzer-Mörling discuss the roles that history and culture play in branding, expanding recognition of research that taps into what they call brand culture, a third realm of branding research in addition to brand image and brand identity (Schroeder and Salzer-Mörling, 2006). In this sense, brand culture involves "the cultural codes of brands—history, images, myths, art, and theatre—that influence brand meaning and value in the marketplace" (Schroeder, 2009, p. 124).

In brand management contexts, it is widely agreed that culture and cultural meanings can be perceived as resources upon which branding processes and practices can draw; and that cultural resources may suggest potentially productive paths for brand development (Schroeder and Salzer-Mörling, 2006). For example, Burberry draws upon cultural notions of British fashion, such as Saville Row bespoke tailoring and punk style (e.g., Peng and Chen, 2012). A classic Chevrolet campaign linked the automobile brand to American cultural icons: hot dogs and apple pie.

However, a brand culture approach posits that the interaction of brands and culture goes much deeper. Research on brand culture reveals that brands do not only draw upon meaning resources from particular cultures and histories, but that new cultural meanings and practices emerge and develop in relationship to brands (e.g., Schroeder, Borgerson and Wu, 2015). Often, studies in international marketing and consumer research overlook the ways in which brand development adapts to market conditions and, importantly, contributes to public discourse. Although contexts and situations may be acknowledged to influence, shift, if not determine, brand meanings, commonly lacking is a focus on the co-creative power of multiple brand actors, including the brands themselves.

Following the brand culture approach, we understand the importance of social, cultural and historical resources in undertaking branding, marketing and consumer research. For example, the presentation of historical culture, or the past, in marketing has been said to include two key understandings: (1) the prevalence of retroactivities is motivated by the consumers' nostalgic and authentic desires (e.g., Stern, 1992; Holbrook and Schindler, 2003), and (2) marketing the past is a way of secularizing sacred historical, cultural and religious elements and beliefs to enhance marketing activities (e.g., Belk, Wallendorf and Sherry 1989; Eckhardt and Bengtsson, 2010; O'Guinn and Belk, 1989). Indeed, numerous researchers indicate that meaningful insights into marketing contexts can be acquired when they are treated as cultural texts, and the apparatus of literary theory has been brought to bear on branding, advertising and marketing (e.g., Belk, 1986; Hirschman and Holbrook, 1982).

A brand culture approach to branding in the global marketplace depends on different attempts to develop an informed historical and cultural analysis of brands. Branding practices are grounded in various cultural perspectives, even "myths," including the archaeological, the political as well as other language-based meaning. Further, global myths are targeted to build international brands. Put simply, global brands call up a global myth. Aspects of a national mythic landscape move into the global brand landscape, and this global myth entails employing variously branded "products," which could include distinctive antiquities and tourist locations, but also recognizable symbols, values and aesthetics, to produce identity discourses. Brand theorist Douglas Holt (2004) notes that part of the work of branding is composing identity myths and extending or reinventing these identity myths. In short, branding may engage knowledge of the country's main existing and emerging myth markets, and demonstrate the cultural and political authority to address these market myths. At the same time, consumer researchers Giana Eckhardt and Julien Cayla (2008) describe the modernity of Asian branding, suggesting that in the Chinese case, it may be valuable to engage the past as a strategic brand-signifying practice.

Cultural, ideological and political environments influence the process of building brands, brand meanings and values. Many successful iconic American brands, suffused with culturally charged myths, attempt to provide facile resolution to social and cultural contradictions (Holt, 2004). More recently, Chinese brand success in Eastern Europe has been explained as satisfying the need for safety and authenticity in these regions (e.g., Strizhakova, Coulter and Price, 2008; Manning and Uplisashvili, 2007). In other words, an analysis of brand meaning derives not only from networks of users, producers and other brand actors, but also from local and global events, such as definitive moments in a nation's history, consumer boycotts and anti-globalization movements. Furthermore, as can be seen in Western brands' impact on global culture, global branding practices influence local culture (Dong and Tian, 2009). Brands, brand meanings and brand values can be understood as cultural, political and ideological forms with the agency to alter the world.

Nostalgia, "authenticity" and branding

Global brand mythologies depend on targeting global cultural myths (Cayla and Arnould, 2008). The Beijing Olympics Opening Ceremony drew upon ancient cultural history and deeply ingrained Chinese myths, and was profoundly dependent on the masterly production of an apparent authenticity through modern technology (Wu, Borgerson and Schroeder, 2013). Sociologist Peter Berger proposed that authenticity refers to identifying what is real in our lives (1973). Branding research has shown that referring to aspects of historical culture in branding campaigns can evoke authentic and nostalgic emotions (e.g., Holbrook and Schindler, 2003; Stern, 1992).

Drawing these relationships out further, nostalgia has been described as an authentic aesthetic response to the evocation of the past (Jameson, 1991). Accordingly, one could argue that brand authenticity refers to the search for the "real" in brands. Thus, "the investment of historical culture into branding campaigns can invoke nostalgia and feelings of being reconnected with an authentic past [although] notions such as 'authentic' are contested—their apparent meanings subject to rethinking and contextualizing—the ways in which brands aim to achieve such goals remain significant" (Wu, Borgerson and Schroeder, 2013, p. 29).

In theory, nostalgia resides in every brand and aids marketing in every product—for example, the fashion for old films, vintage clothes, parents' music and long forgotten recipes; the dominance of traditions and revivals in architecture and the arts; schoolchildren delving into local history and grandparent's recollections; and historical romances and tales of the "good old days" (Lowenthal, 1985; Brunk, Giesler and Hartmann, 2018). Nostalgia transcends yearnings for particular lost childhoods and scenes of early life, and embraces imagined pasts never experienced by specific consumers, citizens or perhaps by anyone (Holbrook and Schindler, 2003). In this way, fictional returns to previous times may attract massive audiences.

Global brand mythologies develop when the global brand landscape absorbs the mythic landscape. Within this landscape, branded products represent identity myths in ways that seemingly unite global consumers ranging across diverse contexts (e.g., Cayla and Eckhardt, 2008). Coca-Cola, for instance, enjoys a mythic status both within the United States and beyond, which is to say for all its mythic associations elsewhere in the world, it is no less, and perhaps even all the more, mythic in the United States. In this way, Coca-Cola represents unity, cultural strength and refreshing taste everywhere. A global myth thus reveals differing relations to cultural anchors. Its myth status applies to cultures both within and outside its origins.

The Beijing Olympics Opening Ceremony targeted historical Chinese culture, an important myth market, in evoking audiences' nostalgia and feelings of authenticity: the darkened stadium with glowing red drumsticks, the intense beaten reverberations of the "Fou" drum, the uniform movement enmeshed the audience in the power of Chinese aesthetics and historical accomplishment. Concepts of authenticity in the consumption context include indexical authenticity and iconic authenticity (Grayson and Martinec, 2004). *Indexical authenticity* refers to an object that has a factual and spatiotemporal link to history, whereas *iconic authenticity* points out an object that is similar to original physicality through the reproduction or recreation of the original objects. "Fou" is an ancient percussion instrument of China with a 3,000-year history, similar to the

Chinese drum described in the Lian Po and Lin Xiangru section of the *Records of the Grand Historian* by Sima Qian in the Han dynasty.

The Beijing Olympics Opening Ceremony presented iconic authenticity through modern advanced technology. Reproduction or re-creation of the past is, indeed, an artificial presentation in the present, no matter how truthfully and precisely we preserve, authentically and properly restore, and deeply and attentively immerse ourselves in past times; yet, iconic authenticity contributes to understanding the past and creating fantasy modes of consuming national identities.

Nation branding and soft power

One of the most direct links between branding and soft power occurs in so-called nation branding, where nations construct strategic campaigns to brand themselves as tourist destinations, cultural icons or sites of economic development. Further, even the most non-strategic–seeming communication about a place can be used and incorporated into soft power missions, the humblest rural practices harnessed attractively for promotional purposes. In other words, an archaeological ruin or unique folk art is also a resource for soft power; and, whereas tourist campaigns and promotion of historical accomplishments may seem innocuous, straightforward communications, quite apart from soft power, we maintain that these often are indiscernible.

A national culture may draw upon and promote historical accomplishments in art, music, architecture, rituals, technology and so on to build national unity, but also for foreign tourism, and in an effort to indicate authentic sights for development, including economic development and exploitation. These communicative efforts form a foundation for articulating resources available for soft power processes. In other words, branding practices and insights are used in soft power processes; brands engage to create new cultural visions that themselves become crucial in the pathways of soft power.

Historically, we can see the outcomes of promotional communications in many nations, particularly around archaeological sites, like the Acropolis in Athens or the pyramids in Egypt, or more general cultural accomplishments, for example the paintings of Renaissance Italy or the distinctive tea rituals of Japan or Great Britain. Further, superiority uperiority in innovation, expertise or even possession of natural wonders form a base for promoting a vision of countries and continents to others around the globe (see Morgan, Pritchard and Pride, 2004; Volcic and Andrejevic, 2011). Diverse European nations such as Ireland, Kosovo and austerity-plagued Greece have had recent nation-branding attempts. In sum, China is not alone in attempting to form its image in an international arena.

Nation branding resembles many aspects of soft power. For example, Kosovo was branded as a new nation that recently came into being, hiring international marketing firm BBR Saatchi & Saatchi to promote the tale of a young country joining the rest of the world. Promotional materials emphasized Kosovo's connections to Europe, its youthful and well-educated population and economic opportunities for investment. Kosovo's "launch" video featured romantic landscapes, children looking to the sky in wonder and a literal "launch" of the nation, as yellow puzzle pieces are fitted together by enthusiastic youth, creating an outline of the nation that is then connected to cloud-shaped helium balloons that lift the "nation" into the bright blue sky—reminiscent of countless destination branding campaigns (Prishtina WB, 2009).

As communications scholar Nadia Kaneva writes, "in its most expansive articulations, nation branding refers to much more than slogans, logos, and colorful advertisements. Rather, it seeks to reconstitute nationhood at the levels of both ideology and praxis, whereby the meaning and experiential reality of national belonging and national governance are transformed in unprecedented ways" (Kaneva, 2012, p. 4). In 2010, Saatchi & Saatchi's Kosovo "Young Europeans" campaign won an M&M award—a global marketing award presented yearly in London to "celebrate the creation and effectiveness of marketing strategies coordinated and implemented across international borders"—for the Best Nation and Place Branding category (Prishtina WB, 2009). The project leader for Saatchi & Saatchi reported: "The Kosovo assignment has been a wonderful challenge for Saatchi & Saatchi because we are literally branding a new nation" (Saatchi and Saatchi Global, 2010). In other words, these are not obscure, under-the-radar practices; the combinatory practices of branding and soft power are much more common than might be expected.

Thus, nation branding often intersects with cultural diplomacy. For example, the Cold War of the mid-20th century dominated international relations. A key tenet of Soviet Cold War propaganda maintained that the United States lacked a distinctive or historically developed culture of its own. America was characterized as obsessed with mindless, uncultured entertainments, trivial consumer goods, and ephemeral distractions. To counter such assertions, the United States deployed key cultural forces of modern design, abstract art and jazz—holding up each as a symbol of consumer sovereignty, freedom, affluence and individual expression (e.g., Barnhisel, 2015; Belamonte, 2008; Castillo, 2010; Fosler-Lussier, 2016). In the United States, individuals were understood to have the freedom to make their own lives, in part thanks to their access to a wealth of available resources, including affordable consumer goods and services. The "sovereign," or self-determining, choices they made among these available options marked a key distinction within US–Soviet propaganda battles. In this way, consumer culture occupied a central role on both sides of the Cold War cultural diplomacy battles, and might be understood via the lens of soft power (Borgerson and Schroeder, 2017).

Whereas political theorist William A. Callahan argues that China uses soft power more in domestic policy than in foreign policy (Callahan, 2015), we propose that a brand culture approach to Chinese soft power sheds light on the complex modes where brands and soft power intersect in the international sphere, as well as in China itself. Callahan understands recent incidences of Chinese soft power as negative, in the sense that China has used soft power opportunities to say negative things (Callahan, 2015, p. 217). As many have noted, soft power typically works thorough positive associations and responses to a country's culture, political values and foreign policies (Nye, 2004; Callahan, 2015). In the sense that soft power has been considered a "weapon of mass attraction" rather than an offensive of coercion or bombs, this strikes him as worth investigating.

We appreciate the dualities and distinctions that Callahan focuses on here, however, we are less interested in parsing the details of Nye's representation of soft power than we are in revealing how soft power can be understood through a branding lens. In short, we attend to the less noticeable, yet powerful, ways in which culture, values and norms are co-created with brands and branding practices and processes. As Chinese brands and branding events become more amorphous and ubiquitous, whether for luxury brands, such as Shang Xia and Shanghai Tang, that emphasize culture and heritage, or in global-scale promotions such as the Beijing Olympics Opening Ceremony, recognizing these for the soft power they wield is important. As Callahan remarks, "the 2008 Olympics is taken as a key success for China's soft power strategy because it presented the PRC to the world as a country that is physically strong, technologically advanced and deeply civilized" (Callahan, 2015, p. 218). We believe that the Beijing Olympics and the Opening Ceremony accomplished a much more nuanced set of outcomes than Callahan's list suggests.

The Beijing Olympics Opening Ceremony

The 2008 Beijing Olympics facilitated the growth of China's historical culture as a resource for global branding by offering the elaborate, theatrical and phenomenally costly Beijing Olympics Opening Ceremony. For China, "hosting the Olympic games was imagined primarily as a symbol of the revival of China's historical greatness and a confirmation of China's emerging status as a major power on the contemporary world stage" (Zhu, 2012, p. 240). We frame the Opening Ceremony as an expression of China's soft power—a cultural, consumer and strategic branding event that showcases a sophisticated and attractive, yet earnest and nostalgic effort to position China as a modern economic, political and cultural power with a long historical and cultural legacy that will continue to influence global cultures.

The 2008 Beijing Olympics are generally considered to have been the most expensive in history, at an estimated cost of over $42 billion, playing a key role in branding China to the world (Fowler and Meichtry, 2008). A cultural theme was intentionally—and strategically—built in to staging the Games. For the Beijing 2008 Olympics, a key policy recommendation from the People's University concluded,

> On this basis, we cautiously propose that in the construction of China's national image, we should hold the line on "cultural China," and the

concept of "cultural China" should not only be the core theme in the dialogue between China and the international community in Olympic discourse, but also it should be added into the long term strategic plan for the national image afterwards.

(Brownell, 2009, p. 1)

The identity myths of a country are important cultural fabrications where myths smooth over people's identity anxieties and create their desired identity (Holt, 2004). China, in the current era, desires to construct its identity in the international arena. The Opening Ceremony, directed by Zhang Yimou, helped China communicate an apparently authentic "Chineseness" (Wang, 2013; Wu, Borgerson and Schroeder, 2013), connected with an attractive lineage of historical innovation, such as the four great innovations of ancient China (paper-making, printing, gunpowder and the compass) and the old Silk Road trade route. The performance also evoked China's diverse cultures and subcultures, helping to lay claim to all of these as part of a unified China. The presence of the Chinese past in the Beijing Olympics Opening Ceremony facilitated building China's brand.

Further, the Opening Ceremony addressed Chinese identity anxieties around authenticity and at the same time served to promote Chinese cultural soft power. Interviews conducted during the Games revealed that the Ceremony stimulated nostalgia for both Chinese and non-Chinese audience members through the presentation of historical culture (Wu, Borgerson and Schroeder, 2013). Audience members spoke of pride in China, especially around the performance of the old Silk Road and the accomplishments of Chinese opera.

Not only was modern advanced high-tech knowledge explored in the performances of "magnificent civilization," seen in the sparkling Fou, the huge movable scroll, the "athletic footsteps painting," the movable printing and the splendid Silk Road map, but the Opening Ceremony also brought the historical Chinese culture into modern life, expressed in the "Glorious Time" section. In the performances of "Magnificent Civilization," the intense drumming gave way to the whimsical, as dozens of ancient "Flying Apsaras" (mythical Buddhist goddesses) soared across the stadium and made an illuminated replica of the Olympic rings raised above the arena. "Flying Apsaras" are often depicted in murals found in Chinese temples and grottos (e.g., the art of flying apsaras in Yuangang, Longmen and Dunhung Grottos in China), and refer to mythical female spirits. Historically, Chinese Buddhist scripture defines "Flying Apsaras" as the gods of heaven, song or music or as fragrant goddesses with sweet voices. Mostly they are young girls with slim figures, plump faces, elegant manners and gentle moods. The scriptures further suggest that generally they appear as a group of girls flying and dancing in the sky with ribbon fluttering elegantly and beautifully in hand. The modern Chinese "Flying Apsaras," modeled on the ancient Chinese "Flying Apsaras," refers to the exploration of outer space. The space-suited figures soaring in space and Li Ning's "walking in outer space" with the lighting of flaming cauldrons were the most notable performances to connect the modern "Flying Apsaras," and by extension Chinese historical culture, to modern life, aspiration and achievement.

Indeed, the Opening Ceremony did not merely present China's historical culture, but also Chinese modernity, wherein China is able to employ advanced technology to reveal historical Chinese culture, in short, Chinese people living a modern life alongside long-standing traditions. For example, Wang Ning, the executive deputy director of the Opening and Closing Ceremonies of the Beijing Olympics told China Radio International that,

> the technology and equipment used in this opening ceremony is very complicated. More than 2,000 tons of equipment were used in the opening ceremony, including [a] large amount of light-emitting diodes. An LED screen 147 meters long and 22 meters wide at the center of the stadium transported the audience into a Chinese dreamland. At the beginning of the show, 29 colossal, footprint-shaped fireworks exploded along the central axis of Beijing to symbolize the pace of the summer games. Sparkles from the final footprint fell into the center of the stadium and "lit up" the floor, bringing out the shining Olympic "Dream Rings" on a huge LED screen and proclaiming the arrival of the Olympiad. Beijing used a smokeless powder to reduce pollution from the 40,000 explosions.
>
> *(Yun, 2008)*

Investing the Opening Ceremony with historical culture was a skillful use of the imagination: imagining the past in branding tends to produce emotional engagement. The performance demonstrated a Chinese identity of sincerity, hospitality, friendliness and innovation, for instance, in the moment when the Fou beaters started a thunderous welcoming ceremony and chanted a Confucian saying: "How happy we are, to meet friends from afar!" (Wu, Borgerson and Schroeder, 2013). In the section that showcased Chinese movable-type printing, 3,000 people, dressed as the 3,000 disciples of Confucius, each held an ancient Chinese book (called *Jian* in Chinese and made by baboons) and chanted renowned epic poems from the *Analects of Confucius* ("All those within the four seas can be considered his brothers"). These myths embrace romance, perhaps a Chinese desire for a simple, peaceful life and harmonious relationships, and the Chinese spirit of exploring and conquering nature. As media scholar Qing Cao states:

> Soft power provides the Chinese elites with a useful conceptual frame to develop a strategic approach to enhance China's international standing, dispel suspicions of the country's wider roles and activities, and articulate a Chinese vision of a world order inspired by Confucian values. Domestically, soft power discourse creates a multiplicity of spaces whereby the Chinese Communist Party (CCP) constructs fresh political identities underpinned partially by traditional values, and envisages the revival of a

cultural China that the nation has long aspired to, since European colonial encroachments centuries ago.

(Cao, 2011, p. 8)

In this way, historical Chinese culture functions not only for the Chinese, but for Westerners as well, and the investment of historical Chinese culture in the Opening Ceremony enables China to target a global myth.

Resistance to Chinese soft power: lessons from brand culture

These soft power branding efforts of the Beijing Opening Ceremony helped create a vision for a new China. As Cao writes, "The most significant aspect of soft power discourse in China lies in a broad consensus by the political and intellectual elites that China's traditional values provide a much needed ontological and epistemological underpinning for the country's future development" (Cao, 2011, p. 20; see also Edney, 2012).

Of course, the global marketplace is not without response or resistance. One aspect of this may be seen regarding China's manufacturing practices, which include the copying, and the producing at a lower price, of products associated with the authentic, local, craft and fine art traditions of other countries and cultures in the world, such as glass in Southern Sweden, woolen cloth and Native American souvenirs in the United States or beautiful paper goods from Italy. From a brand culture perspective, there may be arenas in which China's global ambitions tread on the nation branding and authentic historical culture claims of other nations. Ignoring these concerns may create greater foreign consumer citizen dissatisfaction with Chinese soft power contentions of historically rooted and authentic innovation and expertise—particularly in the face of local job loss, as well as the dissolution of traditional craftsmanship with cultural ties. In other words, in addition to global consumers holding the perception that Chinese goods are cheap, or not made up to the standard of Western goods, a sense that China has stolen aspects of other cultures' pride and heritage may create a damaging image for China even in the face of soft power efforts.

However, if people understand the origins of an object, or arena of goods and expertise, as authentically linked to China—as communicated in the Beijing Opening Ceremony, such as, early production of paper, or ink drawing and painting, and facility with precision technology—this may ameliorate the feeling that China has stolen these from elsewhere. In short, Chinese soft power may invoke the resentment of the developed world for taking over production of goods that had a local and national history of their own. In this sense, then, China's battle does not involve only convincing people that this technologically advanced and historically rich country can produce quality. Indeed, no matter how well China answers questions of quality, there will continue to be resentment, as well as an emotional response to China as a whole (e.g., Ramo, 2007). China may continue to prove that their craftsmanship and skills are as fine as anywhere else and that Chinese history harbors the innovation and brilliance on display in the Beijing Olympics Opening Ceremony. However, if China continues to depend upon making things that have their apparent origins elsewhere, China may be seen as stealing in the face of other countries' attempts to nation brand and honor their own culture histories and heritage. As long as the things that China produces do not have their origins (of object use, skill in creating and producing, as well as historical cultural meaning and design related to this) in China, this resentment may simmer. Of course, these emotional responses may not matter. Low price may win out regardless of how people feel about the dissipating of national historic cultural practices and achievements, and this may provide some reflections on the limits of soft power on both sides.

It could be argued, however, that authenticity indeed will play a part in bringing China and Chinese goods to global consumers in a more satisfying way, and this is the provenance of soft power and brand culture: "projecting soft power is not only strategically imperative in fending off China's negative external portrayal, but morally preferable in extending China's soft influence commensurable to its growing international roles" (Cao, 2011, p. 20). If China focuses upon authentically linked design, objects and themes, that is, those rooted in Chinese aesthetics and history, China may be able to bypass this resentment and communicate China's own attractions in soft power. Chinese historical culture can brand in such a way as to appeal to global consumers. In this, we believe that consumers can feel a part of a different cultural experience, feel connected in new ways and express their difference from typical Western ideals, styles and designs (Wu, Borgerson and Schroeder, 2013). As such, we see the co-creation of brands and culture intersecting with soft power wherein China could build positive associations and appease resentment.

Conclusion

A brand culture approach, which draws upon an interdisciplinary base to understand brands and their role in culture, provides a distinctive and insightful perspective for understanding Chinese soft power. The Beijing Olympic Opening Ceremony employed historical Chinese culture in conjunction with modern technology to target the myth market, evoking consumer nostalgia and enabling feelings of Chinese authenticity. Historical Chinese culture, displayed in the Opening Ceremony, harnessed cultural codes of strength, equality and peace, and offered both Chinese and non-Chinese viewers sacred elements and feelings of wonder, themes constituting hopes and dreams for many in the midst of difficulty, conflict and war around the world. Furthermore, this Ceremony did not merely present China's past, but also envisioned contemporary Chinese life infused with long-standing traditions.

The Beijing Olympics Opening Ceremony created a myth market not merely for the Chinese, but for non-Chinese people as well, in part by tapping into long-held mythologies about China. As myth markets are derived from the gap between what people hope and reality, the Opening Ceremony revealed themes of world harmony—for humans and nature. Thus, the Beijing Olympics Opening Ceremony contributed to the global myth market, the building of Chinese global brands and the facilitating of soft power. As such, the Ceremony represents a large-scale soft power effort that signaled how China's own conception of its history plays in to its global economic and political ambition.

Soft power assumes many forms. Branding—often associated with commercial ventures—intersects with soft power in several ways. Nation branding, in particular, shares aspects with soft power, and provides a conceptual link between governmental originated efforts and private initiatives. China's staging of the 2008 Beijing Olympics offers a cogent example of how the co-creative powers of branding and culture intersect with an aim to promote a positive and attractive vision of China outward to the world, as well as inward to the Chinese people.

References

Barnhisel, Greg. 2015. *Cold War Modernists: Art, Literature, and American Cultural Diplomacy.* New York: Columbia University Press.

Belamonte, Laura A. 2008. *Selling the American Way: U.S. Propaganda and the Cold War.* Philadelphia: University of Pennsylvania Press.

Belk, Russell W. 1986. "Art versus Science as Ways of Generating Knowledge about Materialism," in David Brinberg and Richard Lutz (eds.), *Perspectives on Methodology in Consumer Research.* New York: Springer-Verlag, pp. 3–36.

Belk, Russell W., Melanie Wallendorf and John F. Sherry, Jr. 1989. "The Sacred and the Profane in Consumer Behavior: Theodicy on the Odyssey," *Journal of Consumer Research* 16(1), pp. 1–38.

Berger, Peter L. 1973. "'Sincerity' and 'Authenticity' in Modern Society," *The Public Interest* 31, pp. 81–90.

Borgerson, Janet and Jonathan Schroeder. 2017. *Designed for Hi-Fi Living: The Vinyl LP in Midcentury America.* Cambridge, MA: MIT Press.

Brownell, Susan. 2009. "The Beijing Olympics as a Turning Point? China's First Olympics in East Asian Perspective," *The Asia-Pacific Journal.* www.japanfocus.org/-susan-brownell/3166.

Brunk, Katja H., Markus Giesler and Benjamin J. Hartmann. 2018. "Creating a Consumable Past: How Memory Making Shapes Marketization," *Journal of Consumer Research* 44(6), pp. 1325–1342.

Callahan, William A. 2015. "Identity and Security in China: The Negative Soft Power of the China Dream," *Politics* 35(3–4), pp. 216–229.

Cao, Qing. 2011. "The Language of Soft Power: Mediating Socio-Political Meanings in the Chinese Media," *Critical Arts: South-North Cultural and Media Studies,* 25(1), pp. 7–24.

Carter, Bill and Richard Sandomir. 2008. "A Surprise Winner at the Olympic Games in Beijing: NBC," *The New York Times,* August 17, pp. 1–2.

Castillo, Greg. 2010. *Cold War on the Home Front: The Soft Power of Midcentury Design.* Minneapolis: University of Minnesota Press.

Cayla, Julien and Eric Arnould. 2008. "A Cultural Approach to Branding in the Global Marketplace," *Journal of International Marketing* 16(4), pp. 88–114.

Cayla, Julien and Giana M. Eckhardt. 2008. "Asian Brands and the Shaping of a Transnational Imagined Community," *Journal of Consumer Research* 35, pp. 216–230.

Chen, Chwen C., Cinzia Colapinto and Qing Luo. 2012. "The 2008 Beijing Olympics Opening Ceremony: Visual Insights into China's Soft Power," *Visual Studies* 27(2), pp. 188–195.

Chouliaraki, Lilie. 2005. "Introduction: The Soft Power of War-Legitimacy and Community in Iraq War Discourses," *Journal of Language and Politics* 4(1), pp. 1–10.

Dong, Lily and Kelly Tian. 2009. "The Use of Western Brands in Asserting Chinese National Identity," *Journal of Consumer Research* 36(3), pp. 504–523.

Eckhardt, Giana M. and Anders Bengtsson. 2010. "A Brief History of Branding in China," *Journal of Macromarketing* 30(3), pp. 210–221.

Edney, Kingsley. 2008. "The 2008 Beijing Olympic Torch Relay: Chinese and Western Narratives," *China Aktuell: Journal of Current Chinese Affairs* 2, pp. 111–125.

Edney, Kingsley. 2012. "Soft Power and the Chinese Propaganda System," *Journal of Contemporary China* 21(78), pp. 899–914.

Fosler-Lussier, Danielle. 2016. *Music in America's Cold War Diplomacy*. Berkeley: University of California Press.

Fowler, Geoffrey A. and Stacy Meichtry. 2008. "China Counts the Cost of Hosting the Olympics: Social Programs Are Weighed Beside Image Building," *Wall Street Journal*, 16 July. http://online.wsj.com/article/SB121614671139755287.html.

Gold, John R. and Margaret M. Gold. 2008. "Olympic Cities: Regeneration, City Rebranding and Changing Urban Agendas," *Geography Compass* 2(1), pp. 300–318.

Grayson, Kent and Radan Martinec. 2004. "Consumer Perceptions of Iconicity and Indexicality and Their Influence on Assessments of Authentic Market Offerings," *Journal of Consumer Research* 31(2), pp. 296–312.

Greyser, Stephen A. 2008. "The Three Levels of Branding at Beijing," *Harvard Business Review*, August 6, pp. 1–2.

Hirschman, Elizabeth C. and Morris B. Holbrook. 1982. "Hedonic Consumption: Emerging Concepts, Methods and Propositions," *Journal of Marketing* 46(3), pp. 92–101.

Holbrook, Morris and Robert Schindler. 2003. "Nostalgic Bonding: Exploring the Role of Nostalgia in the Consumption Experience," *Journal of Consumer Behaviour* 3(2), pp. 107–127.

Holt, Douglas B. 2004. *How Brands Become Icons: The Principles of Cultural Branding*. Cambridge, MA: Harvard Business School Press.

Iwabuchi, Koichi. 2006. *Recentering Globalization: Popular Culture and Japanese Transnationalism*. Durham, NC: Duke University Press.

Jameson, Frederic. 1991. *Postmodernism, or, the Cultural Logic of Late Capitalism*. Durham, NC: Duke University Press.

Kaneva, Nadia. 2012. "Nation Branding in Post-Communist Europe: Identities, Markets, and Democracy," in Nadia Kaneva (ed.), *Branding Post-Communist Nations: Marketing National Identities in the New Europe*. London: Routledge, pp. 3–22.

Liang, Limin. 2011. "Framing China and the World through the Olympic Opening Ceremonies, 1984–2008," in D.P. Martinez (ed.), *Documenting the Beijing Olympics*. New York: Routledge, pp. 75–88.

Lowenthal, David. 1985. *The Past Is a Foreign Country*. Cambridge: Cambridge University Press.

Madrigal, Robert, Colleen C. Bee and Monica C. LaBarge. 2005. "Using the Olympics and FIFA World Cup to Enhance Global Brand Equity: A Case Study of Two Companies in the Payment Services Category," in John Amis and T. Bettina Cornwell (eds.), *Global Sport Sponsorship*. Oxford: Berg, pp. 179–190.

Manning, Paul and Ann Uplisashvili. 2007. "'Our Beer': Ethnographic Brands in Post Socialist Georgia," *American Anthropologist* 109(4), pp. 626–641.

Manzenreiter, Wolfram. 2010. "The Beijing Games in the Western Imagination of China: The Weak Power of Soft Power," *Journal of Sport and Social Issues* 34(1), pp. 29–48.

Morgan, Nigel, Annette Pritchard and Roger Pride. 2004. *Destination Branding: Creating the Unique Destination Proposition*. Oxford: Butterworth Heinemann.

Nye, Joseph S., Jr. 2004. *Soft Power: The Means to Success in World Politics*. New York: Public Affairs.

O'Guinn, Thomas C. and Russell W. Belk. 1989. "Heaven on Earth: Consumption at Heritage Village, USA," *Journal of Consumer Research* 16(2), pp. 227–238.

Peng, Norman and Annie Huiling Chen. 2012. "Consumer Perspectives of Cultural Branding: The Case of Burberry in Taiwan," *Journal of Brand Management* 19(4), pp. 318–330.

Prishtina WB. 2009. Kosovo: The Young Europeans [video]. www.youtube.com/watch?v=dQRGHAdQjR0.

Ramo, Joshua Cooper. 2007. *Brand China*. London: The Foreign Policy Centre.

Saatchi & Saatchi Global. 2010. "M&M Award Success for Kosovo 'Young Europeans' Campaign." http://saatchi.com/enus/news/mm_award_success_for_kosovo_young_europeans_campaign.

Schroeder, Jonathan E. 2009. "The Cultural Codes of Branding," *Marketing Theory* 9(1), pp. 123–126.

Schroeder, Jonathan E., Janet L. Borgerson, and Zhiyan Wu. 2015. "A Brand Culture Approach to Chinese Cultural Heritage Brands," *Journal of Brand Management* 22(3), pp. 261–279.

Schroeder, Jonathan E. and Miriam Salzer-Mörling (eds.). 2006. *Brand Culture*. London: Routledge.

Stern, Barbara B. 1992. "Historical and Personal Nostalgia in Advertising Text: The Fin de Siècle Effect," *Journal of Advertising* 21(4), pp. 11–32.

Strizhakova, Yuliya, Robin Coulter and Linda Price. 2008. "Branded Products as a Passport to Global Citizenship: Perspectives from Developed and Developing Countries," *Journal of International Marketing* 16(4), pp. 59–87.

Volcic, Zala and Mark Andrejevic. 2011. "Nation Branding in the Era of Commercial Nationalism," *International Journal of Communication* 5, pp. 598–618.

Wang, Gungwu. 2013. "Chineseness: The Dilemmas of Place and Practice," in Shu-mei Shih, Chien-hsin Tsai and Brian Bernards (eds.), *Sinophone Studies: A Critical Reader*. New York: Columbia University Press, pp. 131–144.

Wu, Zhiyan, Janet Borgerson and Jonathan Schroeder. 2013. *From Chinese Brand Culture to Global Brands: Insights from Aesthetics, Fashion and History*. Basingstoke: Palgrave Macmillan.

Yun, Tu. 2008. "Beijing Opening Ceremony Demonstrates High-tech Olympics," *Chinese Radio International* [CRIEnglish.com], August 13. http://english.cri.cn/6066/2008/08/13/1881s393312.htm.

Zhang, Li. 2010. "The Rise of China: Media Perception and Implications for International Politics," *Journal of Contemporary China* 19(64), pp. 233–254.

Zhao, Yanjun. 2014. "Toward International Harmony: The Role of Confucius Institutes in China's Soft Power Efforts," *China Media Research* 10(1), pp. 22–28.

Zhu, Ying. 2012. *Two Billion Eyes: The Story of China's Central Television*. New York: The New Press.

7

A DECADE OF WIELDING SOFT POWER THROUGH CONFUCIUS INSTITUTES

Some interim results

Falk Hartig

Since 2004, Confucius Institutes (CIs) and their attendant Confucius Classrooms are almost everywhere on the global stage. The non-profit CIs partner with China's Office of Chinese Language Council International (known as Hanban), a Chinese and a foreign entity, normally universities. Their main function is teaching Chinese language and culture. By the end of 2018 a total of 548 CIs and 1,193 smaller Confucius Classrooms (mainly established at high schools and associated to a Confucius Institute) have been established in 154 countries.

In the words of Chinese President Xi Jinping, CIs play "an important role in promoting mutual learning between and among various civilizations in the world and strengthening mutual understanding and friendship between Chinese people and peoples of other countries" (Xi, 2014). CIs address a mainstream public audience that does not normally have specialist knowledge about China. The programs consist mainly of language courses at various levels and a wide range of cultural events such as exhibitions, film screenings and various talks.

Drawing on fieldwork at CIs in different parts of the world and critical engagement with the growing literature dealing with them, this chapter aims to unpack the often intense debate over the function and value of these high-profile examples of Chinese soft power generation. Despite the criticism that has been leveled at CIs by concerned scholars in some Western countries, there is still strong global demand from universities to host CIs. They remain a particularly attractive proposition for universities seeking to internationalize and to gain access to China's higher education market. Nevertheless, this chapter argues that CIs are still significantly limited in what they can achieve, both in terms of their practical operational resources as well as their ability to reach target audiences in their host countries. The chapter furthermore points to a number of contested issues surrounding the CIs and finishes with some thoughts about possible future scenarios for these institutes. Overall, I am of the opinion that in order to use the limited potential CIs have, the number of CIs has to be reduced so that a smaller number of CIs with proper funding and staffing can act as a facilitator of China's soft power.

Confucius Institutes—on everyone's lips

Confucius Institutes frequently cause a stir in public and published opinion, and have come to the increasing notice of academia in recent years both inside and outside China. In the early years, only a few studies comprehensively engaged with CIs (Paradise, 2009; Gil, 2009; Yang, 2010). Normally the institutes were only briefly mentioned in China related international relations literature (Lampton, 2008; Lanteigne, 2009; Friedberg, 2011). However, in most of these works CIs are only mentioned in a few sentences and sometimes not even referred to by the correct name (see, for example, Chan, 2008, p. 178, who refers to "Confucian Institutes").

In recent years, however, in parallel to the ever-growing number of CIs, we see increasing academic interest in CIs: a considerable part of the relevant English literature provides an overview, and discusses critical issues and the connection of CIs to China's soft power (Ding and Saunders, 2006; Gil, 2009; Ding, 2008; Starr, 2009; Paradise, 2009; Zhe, 2010; Siow, 2011; Louie, 2011; You, 2012; Ngamsang and Walsh, 2013; Pan, 2013; Yang, 2010; Zhou and Luk, 2016). Another stream of research presents case studies of CIs in regions or individual countries (Hartig, 2016; Hubbert, 2014; Park, 2013; Stambach, 2014; Starr, 2009; Wheeler, 2014; Lahtinen, 2015) or studies dealing with questions of identity formation in CIs (Fallon, 2015; Schmidt, 2013). Another group of authors approaches CIs from a higher education and language teaching perspective (Gil, 2009; Starr, 2009; King, 2013; Zhao and Huang, 2010; Yang, 2010), yet others approach the topic from a business perspective (Lien et al., 2014) or look at Western media reports about CIs (Lueck, Pipps and Lin, 2014; Metzgar and Su, 2016).

Chinese publications discuss the relationship between soft power, image, Chinese language fever (*hanyure*) and CIs (Xu, 2006; Duan, 2008; Guan, 2012), or focus on cultural components of CIs (Nie, 2012). Others describe CIs and Chinese language teaching for international students as a platform of China's public diplomacy (Han, 2011) and as a means to internationalize Chinese education (Liu, 2007) or present case studies of CIs in individual countries or continents (Shen, 2007; Chen, 2008). More recently Chinese scholars are interested in how CIs are perceived in foreign countries (Peng and Yu, 2016; Lin and Zhang, 2016; Zhou, 2015; Zhao, 2015).

The conceptual puzzle: Confucius Institutes and soft power, public diplomacy and propaganda

What is puzzling though is the ambiguity regarding the conceptualization of Confucius Institutes. Broadly speaking, CIs are described in three different ways: first, they can be understood as an instrument of China's soft power (Gil,

2009; Paradise, 2009; Park, 2013; Schmidt, 2013; Yang, 2010); second, CIs can be understood as an instrument of China's public and/or cultural diplomacy (d'Hooghe, 2015; Hartig, 2016; Pan, 2013; Rawnsley, 2009; Wheeler, 2014); and third, there is a line of scholarship that sees CIs as a "propaganda project" of the Chinese leadership (Brady, 2008, p. 172; Sahlins, 2015). I understand CIs as one instrument of China's public diplomacy which is used to communicate with foreign publics in order to communicate certain narratives about the country, to shape its image and to, eventually, activate its soft power resources. As this volume deals with China's soft power, I will not replicate the debates here, but want to highlight two aspects worth considering with regards to CIs that resurfaced when reading most recent publications linking CIs to China's soft power efforts. One such study discusses the establishment of CIs as "a striking example of how the government promotes soft power through cultural means" (Zhou and Luk, 2016, p. 628). It aims to show that CIs fail to increase the soft power of China because many countries regard them as a propaganda tool and a threat to academic freedom and the local community. Zhou and Luk further aim to show that China's soft power is not so attractive in the eyes of receivers. Another study similarly argues that "the capacity of CIs to spread China's soft power on a global scale is uncertain and systematically limited" (Yuan, Guo and Zhu, 2016, p. 344), while Xiao (2017, p. 46) comes to the conclusion that CIs have been "successfully serving as a platform to promote China's soft power" around the world.

The first point that struck me during my fieldwork is that even though the literature closely links CIs to soft power, it would, however, appear that people in charge of CIs and the Hanban have a certain unease with the very term "soft power." As outlined in the introduction to this volume, the most senior leadership in China did enthusiastically take up the concept during the Hu-Wen era. In 2006, two years after the first CIs were established, Xu Lin, the director-general of the Confucius Institute Headquarters, described CIs as the "brightest trademark of China's soft power" (Xinhua, 2006). In the following years, however, there was a change in perception and attitude. Yang (2010, p. 238) reports that "the Hanban officially denies its intention of soft power projection" and an official from the Chinese embassy in Germany told me in 2012 that Xu Lin "does not like the term soft power." Xu herself later emphasized that CIs "are not projecting soft power, nor aim to impose Chinese values or Chinese culture on other countries" (quoted in Yang, 2010, p. 238). China, Xu continues, "just hopes to be truly understood by the rest of the world. CIs are designed to be an important platform to promote Chinese culture and teach Chinese language."

According to two Chinese scholars I talked with, the reason is possibly that although the discussion is about soft power, it still is a form of power which may sound alarming to Western ears. Paradise (2009, p. 658) quotes a program director at Hanban who makes a very similar point: "I don't like soft power. I think power is aggressive. We just do something all people like." This perception seemingly has not changed too much in recent years. While Xiao (2017) reports occasional statements in which people in charge of CIs would clearly point out that they do promote China's soft power, a typical reaction would be that people in charge "don't view [themselves] as promoting soft power" (Xiao, 2017, p. 33).

This is a fascinating observation which is clearly related to the issue of how China is perceived in the world and how China wants to be seen. Certain voices within China were and are very much aware of potential reactions and potential unease in foreign countries, especially in the Western world. These voices are aware that a China that appears too boastful and self-confident may only fuel negative animosity toward China. They therefore argue the case for keeping a low profile in rhetorical terms, and distance CIs not only from the notion of soft power but also from broader strategic and foreign policy–related intentions (Hartig, 2016).

The empirical puzzle: how to measure success?

The second aspect, the question of success, needs even more attention. It is common sense that soft power is "a contested concept" (Rawnsley, 2016, p. 30) and the question of how to measure soft power, or the *success* of any communicative activity to wield soft power, is one of the most contested debates surrounding this contested concept (McCloy and Harvey, 2016; Ji, 2017). The issue at stake here is that soft power "depends more than hard power upon the existence of willing interpreters and receivers" (Nye, 2004, p. 16) and its effects "depend heavily on acceptance by the receiving audience" (Nye, 2004, p. 99). One of the most fundamental limitations of soft power studies is the lack of "the whole process involving not only the actor exercising soft power and the instruments used but also the receiving agents in their socio-political, economic, and cultural contexts" (Zhang, 2016, p. 6). This is very much the same with regards to scholarship dealing with CIs: we still know much too little about the achievements of CIs. We know about their aims and goals, we know about the practical issues, and we clearly know enough about their credibility problems as they normally do not touch upon sensitive issues such as the status of Tibet and Taiwan or what happened at Tiananmen Square in 1989. But we know too little about the audience and how those people are affected or influenced by CIs. This point brings us to the issue of measuring outputs in contrast to measuring outcomes (see Rawnsley, 2017, on this).

How to measure success: outputs vs. outcomes

With regards to aims and goals we have to acknowledge distinctions between the official Chinese discourse explaining the existence of CIs and the (Western) journalistic and academic interpretation of their existence. The official explanation is reflected in the mission statement put forward by the Confucius Institutes Headquarters (n.d.) which notes:

As China's economy and exchanges with the world have seen rapid growth, there has also been a sharp increase in the world's demands for Chinese learning. Benefiting from the UK, France, Germany and Spain's experience in promoting their national languages, China began its own exploration through establishing non-profit public institutions which aim to promote Chinese language and culture in foreign countries in 2004: these were given the name the Confucius Institute.

The Chinese explanation highlights the reactive approach in the sense that China was, and still is, just meeting, or trying to meet, foreign demand with regards to support for Chinese language teaching. It further points to the fundamental but simple task of promoting Chinese language and culture via CIs. If we take these aims as a benchmark to judge "success," CIs are increasingly successful in introducing knowledge about Chinese language and culture to the world, as the ever growing number of institutes and students indicates (Siow, 2011; Hartig, 2016). As Lo and Pan (2014, p. 12) observe, if "outcomes are measured solely in terms of quantitative leaps . . . the achievements of the CI project are very remarkable." According to Hanban, it is because of the "Confucius Institutes' advocacy and influence [that] the number of those who learn Chinese all over the world exceeds 100 million" compared with about 30 million learners ten years ago (Liu, 2014). Although one should treat those figures with caution, there can be no doubt that there is increasing global interest in and demand for Chinese language and culture, and CIs play an important role in satisfying this demand.

On the ground, however, it can be quite a challenge to actually satisfy this still enormous demand abroad. The most pressing issue in this regard concerns teachers at CIs, especially those dispatched from China. There is a growing demand for teachers to fill the ever-increasing number of institutes, and there is a shortage of teachers who are proficient in local languages. A related issue concerns the teaching quality of teachers and inadequate teaching methods and models which often do not meet the local needs and requirements. While those issues can be found in developed countries (Hartig, 2016), they are even more pressing in developing countries, as research from different parts of Africa illustrates. From my conversations with dispatched Chinese staff it is clear that even South Africa—notably different from other countries on the continent in terms of its standard of living—has a rather negative image in China, which makes it difficult for South African CIs to find teachers (Hartig, 2014). On the one hand, teachers there mentioned harsh living conditions which include loneliness, poor-quality food, and security concerns. On the other hand, they noted that when they arrived they found South Africa better than expected: the clean air was one positive aspect several Chinese teachers mentioned (Hartig, 2014).

Another practical problem concerns the question of teaching materials for CIs in different parts of the world. Lo and Pan (2014, p. 522) note that a number of materials sent from Hanban are considered "too boring to arouse readers' interest." Others echo this understanding and point out that textbooks used by

CIs are considered "problematic mainly for their intellectual simplicity vis-à-vis language simplicity" (Procopio, 2015, p. 117).

While it is relatively easy to affirm the official version that in quantitative means more and more people get in to contact with Chinese language and culture simply because the number of CIs is still growing, it gets much more complicated when we return to the question what impact those CIs can actually have. As pointed out before, one may identify two broad approaches to analyze CIs: the more relaxed approach understands CIs as an instrument of cultural/ public diplomacy with the assumed aim of activating or wielding China's (cultural) soft power and shaping China's image. This avenue of engagement, which might be labeled by critics as the "panda hugger" approach, does not necessarily take issue with the desire of the country to present its nice and friendly face to the world while ignoring the negative aspects. The more concerned approach focuses precisely on these negative aspects and the resulting consequences for the functioning of CIs. This understanding, which opponents may describe as the "dragon-slayer" approach, emphasizes the potential of spreading communist ideology and undermining academic freedom and integrity of host organizations, and thus sees CIs as a propaganda device or as "academic malware" (Sahlins, 2015).

What these opposing approaches have in common is that they, other than official Chinese statements, attribute more to CIs than the seemingly simple dissemination of Chinese language and culture as they assume that CIs, in one way or the other, are intended to shape people's perception of what China is and what it stands for. Eventually, then, CIs are understood as having the potential to influence people and to engage in the often quoted battle for hearts and minds (Nye, 2008). The fundamental problem, however, is that so far we know only very little about the people who go there. We know, to a certain degree, why people go to CIs and a number of reasons seem to be similar in different parts of the world. The former Chinese director of a German Confucius Institute listed three general reasons why people go to CIs. First, people go for work-related reasons (*gongzuo xuyao*), as they either already do or they want to do business with China; secondly, because of cultural curiosity and interest (*wenhua xuyao*). The third reason, strongly informed by the location of the Institute in an East German city, is what the former director described as "special feelings" (*teshu ganqing*) (CNPolitics, 2012). She noted that a lot of elderly people who lived in the former German Democratic Republic come to the CI out of a certain attachment with China due to the, at least assumed, ideological proximity to their former country of origin. Having been at several lectures and discussions at this CI, I can confirm this (Hartig, 2016), even though this assumption ignores the political reality that Chinese–East German relations were not as harmonious as some CI visitors would assume (Slobodian, 2015).

While there might be a general interest in Chinese language and culture (Wheeler, 2014; Hartig, 2016) or a desire to be intellectually challenged (Wheeler, 2014), one obvious reason to engage with the Chinese language is clearly China's economic development and the desire to benefit economically by speaking Chinese (Hartig, 2016; Yang, 2010). This is clearly one major reason for students in Africa attending classes at CIs all over the continent (Wheeler, 2014; Procopio, 2015; King, 2013; Stambach and Kwayu, 2017).

What we do *not* know properly so far, however, is how the receiving audience interprets the messages CIs, intentionally or unintentionally, are communicating about China. There is some anecdotal evidence that students and visitors of CIs decode the messages, or are aware of the awkward handling of so called "sensitive" issues, as the ethnographic work by Hubbert (2014) and Stambach (2014) vividly illustrates. But much more of such research is necessary to better judge CIs. Doing this, however, would mean that scholars working on CIs would have to actually talk to and spend time with those students, participants and visitors, because as John le Carré has noted: "A desk is a dangerous place from which to view the world."

The problem, however, then would be twofold. First of all, in order to find out what effect a CI actually can have on the perception of China it would be necessary, in an ideal but artificial setting, to talk to people before they visit a CI or before they even think about going. This would enable a comparison between pre and post visits and would provide indications if and how CIs may contribute to a certain perception of China. A related issue, and this is not limited to CIs, but any instrument of public diplomacy in my understanding, is the simple but crucial fact that those instruments potentially are only mainly preaching to the already converted. Based on anecdotal evidence from CIs in Australia, Europe and South Africa, I have the impression that people go to a CI if they already have a certain positive interest in China or are at least open-minded enough to go there. Someone who—for whatever reason—perceives China as the evil empire will normally not visit a CI and change his or her mind.

The future of Confucius Institutes: possible scenarios, challenges and perspectives

One of the most fascinating aspects of the CIs is the astonishing number and the tricky issue of consolidation versus growth. In my understanding, this is one of the most fundamental aspects, if not the single most important aspect, if we think about possible future scenarios for Confucius Institutes, and I will discuss this issue in some length in the remainder of this chapter.

For quite some time, international partners have called for Hanban to change its attitude from a focus on quantity, reflected in the growing number of CIs, to a focus on quality. This seems crucial for sustainable development. In 2012 a local Australian director told me that Hanban reassured the existing CIs that it would start consolidating and no longer focus so much on numbers, "but apparently they still keep producing them which is a contradiction to what they say at these conferences." This was clearly the case at the time and is still a valid observation today, even though the growth has slowed down a bit recently.

During an interview in 2011, Xu Lin explained to me the rather awkward position Hanban was in at that time: "Right now there are almost 300 applications from universities in 60 countries on my table, numerous applications even have been submitted multiple times and I can't tell who can get an institute and who not." Xu also admitted that when Hanban decides which applicant can have a CI, "the question is not whether foreign partners meet the selection criteria, but it is much more the case that we struggle to meet them in terms of resources and teachers" (Hartig, 2016, p. 189). While this observation makes perfect sense, the *Development Plan of Confucius Institutes 2012–2020* nevertheless clearly states as one major objective: "Develop Confucius Institutes steadily and Confucius Classrooms vigorously. By 2015, establish 150 news Confucius Institutes, so that the total number reaches 500" (Hanban, 2012, p. 8). This goal had been reached, and overall there seems to be a certain slowdown in the growth rate, but nevertheless new CIs still appear. It is against this background that a number of international CI directors, some more direct and outspoken and others more indirect and subtle, for quite some time already hold the view that there are too many CIs and probably not all of the existing CIs will survive (Hartig, 2016).

Looking at the existing issues and problems many CIs are facing, one possible scenario might be that Hanban, while not activity expediting the closing of CIs, may look for ways to partially back down from its responsibilities in terms of human resources and funding. While admittedly none of the following thoughts have been articulated by Hanban officials, it seems worthwhile to think about a possible "exit strategy" for the Chinese side. Based on impressions and information gathered during three so-called Confucius Institute Conferences[1] and numerous interviews and conversations with people in charge of CIs in different parts of the world, I would cautiously argue that the idea of so-called Model Confucius Institutes (*Shifan Kongzi Xueyuan*) could pave the way for such a partial withdrawal.

In late 2011, the Council of the CI Headquarters agreed on establishing "a large number of model Confucius Institutes and Classrooms [and to] give [those Institutes] pivotal support in areas such as the allocation of personnel and provision of equipment" (N/A 2012, p. 13).[2] During the 2011 CI Conference, the plan was announced "to build 10 Model Confucius Institutes across the five continents in 2012" (Xu, 2012, p. 21). It seems, however, that this plan did not work out because at the 2012 CI Conference the plan to create those Model Institutes was again discussed. It was noted that Model CIs "shall aim to play [a] model role, represent a wide range of areas, and have multiple types" (N/A, 2013, p. 63), and the CI Headquarters was called upon to "establish a taskforce and conduct special researches [sic] to decide on the number of model Confucius Institutes and specify how to support model Confucius Institutes" (N/A, 2013, p. 63).

The topic gained much more importance within the CI universe during the 2013 CI Conference as Xu Lin in her closing remarks made explicit reference to this idea. To achieve the goal of "realizing sustainable development in the next ten years," Xu Lin told representatives from CIs around the world, "we should select some good Confucius Institutes as examples, as models" (Xu, 2014, p. 65). Xu noted two principle requirements for potential Model CIs: first, they should have an independent teaching building of at least 2,000 square meters in floor space. She pointed out that there should be financial support from the Chinese side, but she also made clear that Hanban "cannot promise that the Chinese government will fund an independent building for each of the CIs within the next ten years. If you want to build a Model CI, you have to show that you are being serious by at least procuring a plot of land for that purpose" (Xu, 2014, p. 65). The second principle requirement would be that Model CIs should focus on one of the following core themes: (1) education, with an emphasis on teacher training, education and examinations; (2) research;[3] (3) special aspects like tourism, Chinese traditional medicine or business; (4) vocational and technical training (Xu, 2014). Model Confucius Institutes, according to Xu, "should be about 20% of the total number of institutes" (Xu, 2014, p. 65).

The most comprehensive information regarding the Model CI idea can be found in an internal Hanban document entitled "Methods of Evaluating a Model Confucius Institute in Europe (Draft)/Ou Zhou Shifan Kongzi Xueyuan Pingshen banfa (Cao'an)," probably distributed during the 2014 CI Conference.[4] In order "to run the Confucius Institute in a more scientific and better way in its second ten-year development, one of the most important plans is to select a certain proportion of outstanding Confucius Institutes as 'Model Confucius Institutes'" (CI Headquarters, n.d., p. 1).

The draft lists a number of prerequisites that CIs would have to fulfill in order to be awarded the status of Model CI. Amongst other things, the CI should have run for at least five years and it should have been awarded the title "Confucius Institute of the Year" at least once (CI Headquarters, n.d., p. 1). It should have established "at least 3 Confucius Classrooms and 5 Chinese language teaching sites" and should have kept "long-term cooperative relations with at least 5 local government institutions, enterprises and/or non-governmental organizations" (CI Headquarters, n.d., p. 2). A prospective Model CI should have "at least 10 Chinese language teachers and volunteers dispatched by the Headquarters" and the host institution should "have offered at least 5 full-time or part-time members of staff" (CI Headquarters, n.d., p. 2). The "benefits and privileges" when being awarded include amongst other more technical aspects the following: when a Model CI applies for programs with the Headquarters, it "enjoys priority" compared to other CIs and it may apply for different extra funds and special budgets (CI Headquarters, n.d., p. 6).

During that 2014 CI Conference, the selection criteria for Model CIs were discussed and it was noted that selection criteria "must be transparent and there should be different criteria for different continents" (N/A, 2015, p. 59). It was furthermore suggested that each Model CI should be evaluated every year to determine "whether its standard of teaching and the level of its service to the community have improved, whether it has gained support from the local government and surrounding communities, and whether its courses are meeting local needs" (N/A, 2015, p. 59). The directors of Model CIs "should be very experienced, and its volunteers and teachers should be passionate and committed. A Model Confucius Institute should excel in at least one area, be able to maintain sustainable development and at the same time be able to bring in earnings" (ibid.). Similar ideas were discussed one year later (N/A, 2016).

The problem with all these statements, however, is that they are statements of intent, and it remains somewhat unclear what the reality of Model CIs looks like. This begins with the simple but telling fact that it is not entirely clear how many CIs actually are Model CIs. During the 2015 CI Conference, 15 CIs from around the world were selected as Model CIs, although there was a certain confusion regarding this number. At least two of the awarded CIs noted that they were chosen "as one of the 10 model Confucius Institutes out of 500 from 134 countries and regions" (Feehily, 2016; Hagewood, 2016). A US-based CI reported 20 Model Confucius Institutes (Hale, 2015), a Spanish CI correctly pointed out that 15 CIs around the world were given the award (Universitat de València, 2015) while another European CI referred to 14 award-winning CIs (Sofia University, 2015). According to the official website of the 2016 CI Conference, another 25 CIs were selected as Model Institutes last year.[5] While the selection process remains somewhat dubious, it is clear that being a Model CI presents selected CIs the chance to obtain support from Hanban for new programs and compete for increased additional funding (Hale, 2015; Hagewood, 2016). The CI at the University of Hawaii, which was designated a Model CI in 2015, noted that this "recognition comes with a one-time allocation of $1 million" (Lau, 2015).

While it is thus obvious why CIs would compete for the status of Model CI, this award—which is one of a number of honors which can be awarded to CIs and their representatives—may be seen in a more strategic light as well. In my understanding there is no way around reducing the number of existing CIs, and how many CIs will eventually survive in the long run is unforeseeable. However, to single out a number of Model CIs could perhaps be a first step to get rid of the burden of supporting several hundred entities around the world financially and logistically. Based on Xu Lin's statement that roughly 20% of CIs should become Model CIs, roughly 100 Model CIs would exist in the future. This figure, in turn, would then roughly conform to the 100 CIs which Hanban had in mind when the whole project started in 2004 (Hartig, 2016; Raine, 2009). It would be much easier to find qualified teachers, manage logistics and fund these 100 CIs rather than 500 CIs. Of course, this may not mean that the other 400 CIs would be closed down by Hanban, but if personnel and funding are mainly provided to the 100 Model CIs, the number of "normal" CIs not running very smoothly could increase over the long term, and some might cancel their contracts with Hanban.[6] This, by the way, would also be a face-saving way to react to growing criticism at home, where people do not understand why China has to co-finance language courses for university students, especially at world-leading universities, while schools in rural China still suffer from insufficient funding.

In conclusion it can be said that CIs are probably the most high-profile example of Chinese soft power generation. Despite the criticism and concern in some Western countries, there is still strong global demand from universities to host CIs. They remain a particularly attractive proposition for universities seeking to internationalize and to gain access to China's higher education market. Nevertheless, CIs are still limited in what they can achieve, both in terms of their practical operational resources as well as their ability to reach target audiences in their host countries. Those limitations are also clearly related to the credibility issue that CIs, like other Chinese instruments of soft power generation, are facing. The question thus remains: how can they be successful in wielding China's soft power? One answer to this question is that Hanban should provide CIs with more leeway to engage in more controversial topics; at the same time it will have to find a way to stabilize financial support for the CIs which, in my understanding, would mean reducing their numbers below the current level.

Notes

1 I attended the 6th and 8th Confucius Institute Conferences in Beijing in December 2011 and 2013 as well as the 9th conference in Xiamen in December 2014. These conferences are internal gatherings where teachers and directors of CIs, presidents of host universities from around the world, as well as representatives of Chinese partner universities or institutions, the education departments of related Chinese provinces, and Chinese enterprises involved in the construction of CIs come together to recall the past year and to discuss future developments of CIs. Recent conferences were attended by about 2,000 CI-affiliated participants.
2 According to one European CI director, the idea was first circulated in 2011.
3 It remained—and still remains—unclear what research Xu Lin had in mind.
4 Those internal Hanban documents do not have any dates, and as I attended both conferences in 2013 and 2014, I cannot reconstruct in which year this document was circulated.
5 http://conference.hanban.org/confucius/advanced-en.html
6 Seen purely from this point of view and ignoring the negative publicity, the cynic might suggest that the closure of some of the CIs in the Western world may not present such a dramatic headache to Hanban.

References

Brady, Anne-Marie. 2008. *Marketing Dictatorship: Propaganda and Thought Work in Contemporary China*. Lanham, MD: Rowman and Littlefield.

Chan, Gerald. 2008. "China Joins Global Governance: The 10 Conundrums," in Wang Gungwu and Zheng Yongnian (eds.), *China and the New International Order*. London and New York: Routledge, pp. 168–184.

Chen, Renxia. 2008. "Guanyu zai deguo jianshe kongzi xueyuan de shijian yu sikao" ["Practice and Thoughts about the Establishment of Confucius Institutes in Germany"], *Shijie jiaoyu xinxi* 6, pp. 84–85.

CNPolitics. 2012. "Kongzi xueyuan shi ruhe yunzuo de: yi Deguo Laibixi weili" ["How do Confucius Institutes work: the example of the Confucius Institute in Leipzig, Germany"], in: *Zhengjian CNPolitics*. online at: http://cnpolitics.org/2012/07/konfuzius-institut-leipzig/.

Confucius Institute Headquarters. n.d. "About Confucius Institutes," *Hanban Online*. http://english.hanban.org/node_7716.htm.

d'Hooghe, Ingrid. 2015. *China's Public Diplomacy*. Leiden: Brill.

Ding, Sheng. 2008. *The Dragon's Hidden Wings: How China Rises with Its Soft Power*. Lanham, MD: Lexington Books.

Ding, Sheng and Robert A. Saunders. 2006. "Talking Up China: An Analysis of China's Rising Cultural Power and Global Promotion of the Chinese Language," *East Asia* 23(2), pp. 3–33.

Duan, Yi. 2008. "Ying shili-ruan shili lilun kuang jia xia de yuyan-wenhua guoji tuiguang yu kongzi xueyuan" ["Language-Culture International Promotion and Confucius Institute under the Theoretical Framework of Hard Power and Soft Power"], *Fudan Jiaoyu Luntan* 6(2), pp. 48–51.

Fallon, Tracy. 2015. *Nationalism, National Identity and Politics in the Teaching of Chinese as a Foreign Language*, PhD thesis, Nottingham: University of Nottingham.

Feehily, Jason. 2016. "'Model' Confucius Institute Status," *University of Nottingham Online*, January 6. http://blogs.nottingham.ac.uk/asiabusinesscentre/2016/01/06/model-confucius-institute-status/.

Friedberg, Aaron. 2011. *A Contest for Supremacy: China, America, and the Struggle for Mastery in Asia*. New York: W.W. Norton and Company.

Gil, Jeffery. 2009. "China's Confucius Institute Project: Language and Soft Power in World Politics," *The Global Studies Journal* 2(1), pp. 59–72.

Guan, Bing. 2012. "Guojia ruanshili, hanyure he kongzi xueyuan" ["National Soft Power, Chinese Fever and Confucius Institutes"], *Wuhan Daxue Xuebao (Zhexue shehuikexue ban)* 65(3), pp. 22–28.

Hagewood, Sean. 2016. "UNL Confucius Institute Recognized as Model Institute," *UNL News Room*, January 4. http://newsroom.unl.edu/releases/2016/01/04/UNL+Confucius+Institute+recognized+as+model+institute.

Hale, Whitney. 2015. "UK Receives Funding for Model Confucius Institute," *University of Kentucky Online*, December 15. www.uky.edu/international/node/1559.

Hanban. (2012). *Development Plan of Confucius Institute 2012–2020*. Beijing, Confucius Institutes Headquarters.

Han Zhaoying. 2011. "The Confucius Institute and China's Public Diplomacy" ["Kongzi xueyuan yu zhongguo gonggong waijiao"], *Gonggong Waijiao Jikan* 7(3), pp. 17–20.

Hartig, Falk. 2014. "The Globalization of Chinese Soft Power: Confucius Institutes in South Africa," in Jian Wang (ed.), *Confucius Institutes and the Globalization of China's Soft Power*. Los Angeles: Figueroa Press, pp. 47–66.

Hartig, Falk. 2016. *Chinese Public Diplomacy: The Rise of the Confucius Institute*. New York and London: Routledge.

Hubbert, Jennifer. 2014. "Ambiguous States: Confucius Institutes and Chinese Soft Power in the U.S. Classroom," *PoLAR: Political and Legal Anthropology Review* 37(2), pp. 329–349.

Ji, Li. 2017. "Measuring Soft Power," in Naren Chitty, Li Ji, Gary Rawnsley and Craig Hayden (eds.), *The Routledge Handbook of Soft Power*. London and New York: Routledge, pp. 75–92.

King, Kenneth. 2013. *China's Aid and Soft Power in Africa: The Case of Education and Training*. Woodbridge: James Currey.

Lahtinen, Anja. 2015. "China's Soft Power: Challenges of Confucianism and Confucius Institutes," *Journal of Comparative Asian Development* 14(2), pp. 200–226.

Lampton, David. 2008. *The Three Faces of Chinese Power: Might, Money, and Minds*. Berkeley: University of California Press.

Lanteigne, Marc. 2009. *Chinese Foreign Policy: An Introduction*. London and New York: Routledge.

Lau, Frederick. 2015. "$1 Million Awarded to Center for Chinese Studies' Confucius Institute," *University of Hawaii News*, March 16. www.hawaii.edu/news/article.php?aId=7091.

Lien, Donald, Sucharita Ghosh and Steven Yamarik. 2014. "Does the Confucius Institute Impact International Travel to China? A Panel Data Analysis," *Applied Economics* 46(17), pp. 1985–1995.

Lin, Jie and Zhang Man. 2016. "Dui xifang shaoshu xuezhe zhiyi kongzi xueyuan 'xueshu ziyou' de bo lun" ["Criticism of a Few Western Scholars' Doubt of the 'Academic Freedom' of Confucius Institutes"], *International and Comparative Education* 314(3), pp. 1–7.

Liu, Wenya. 2007. "Kongzi xueyuan: hanyu he zhongguo jiaoyu guojihua de xin jucuo" ["New Measures for the Internationalization of Chinese Language and Chinese Education"], *Jiaoyu Yanjiu* 8, pp. 50–52.

Liu, Y. 2014. "Remarks at the First Global Confucius Institute Day," *Hanban Online*, September 27. www.hanban.org/article/2014-09/27/content_554285.htm.

Lo, Joe Tin-yau and Suyan Pan. 2014. "Confucius Institutes and China's Soft Power: Practices and Paradoxes," *Compare: A Journal of Comparative and International Education* 46(4), pp. 512–532.

Louie, Kam. 2011. "Confucius the Chameleon: Dubious Envoy for 'Brand China'," *Boundary 2* 38(1), pp. 77–100.

Lueck, Therese L., Val S. Pipps and Yang Lin. 2014. "China's Soft Power: A New York Times Introduction of the Confucius Institute," *Howard Journal of Communications* 25(3), pp. 324–349.

McCloy, Jonathan and Olivia Harvey. 2016. "The Soft Power 30: Getting to Grips with the Measurement Challenge," *Global Affairs* 2(3), pp. 309–319.

Metzgar, Emily and Jing Su. 2016. "Friends from Afar? American Media Coverage of China's Confucius Institutes," *Journalism Practise* 11(8), pp. 1000–1025.

N/A. 2012. "Summary of the 2011 Meeting of the Council of the Confucius Institute Headquarters," *Kongzi Xueyuan/Confucius Institute* 18(1), pp. 12–13.

N/A. 2013. "Quality Assessment of Confucius Institutes and Model Confucius Institutes Buildup," *Kongzi Xueyuan/Confucius Institute* 24(1), p. 63.

N/A. 2015. "Xiaozhang luntan—Presidents' Forums," *Kongzi Xueyuan/Confucius Institute* 36(1), pp. 54–59.

N/A. 2016. "Shifan Kongzi Xueyuan jingyan jiaoliu—Best Practices of Model Confucius Institutes," *Kongzi Xueyuan/Confucius Institute* 42(1), pp. 54–55.

Ngamsang, Sirirat and John Walsh. 2013. "Confucius Institutes as Instruments of Soft Power: Comparison with International Rivals," *Journal of Education and Vocational Research* 4(10), pp. 302–310.

Nie, Ying. 2012. "Kongzi xueyuan de zhongguo wenhua jiazhi chutan" ["Chinese Culture Value of Confucius Institute"], *Shandong sheng nongye guanli ganbu xueyuan xuebao*, 29(1), pp. 127–138.

Nye, Joseph S., Jr. 2004. *Soft Power: The Means to Success in World Politics*. New York: Public Affairs.

Nye, Joseph S., Jr. 2008. "Public Diplomacy and Soft Power," *The Annals of the American Academy of Political and Social Science* 6161(1), pp. 94–109.

Pan, Su-Yan. 2013. "Confucius Institute Project: China's Cultural Diplomacy and Soft Power Projection," *Asian Education and Development Studies* 2(1), pp. 22–33.

Paradise, James. 2009. "China and International Harmony: The Role of Confucius Institutes in Bolstering Beijing's Soft Power," *Asian Survey* 49(4), pp. 647–669.

Park, Jae. 2013. "Cultural Artefact, Ideology Export or Soft Power? Confucius Institute in Peru," *International Studies in Sociology of Education* 23(1), pp. 1–16.

Peng, Fei and Yu Xiao 2016. "Yingguo zhuliu meiti baodao zhong de kongzi xueyuan xingxiang yu huayu tixi" ["The Image and Discourse System of Confucius Institute in the Reporting by the British Mainstream Media"], *Academic Exploration* 11, pp. 112–119.

Procopio, Maddalena. 2015. "The Effectiveness of Confucius Institutes as a Tool of China's Soft Power in South Africa," *African East-Asian Affairs* 2, pp. 98–125.

Raine, Sarah. 2009. *China's African Challenges*. London: The International Institute for Strategic Studies.

Rawnsley, Gary. 2009. "China Talks Back: Public Diplomacy and Soft Power for the Chinese Century," in Nancy Snow and Phillip M. Taylor (eds.), *Routledge Handbook of Public Diplomacy*. New York: Routledge, pp. 282–291.

Rawnsley, Gary. 2016. "Reflections of a Soft Power Agnostic," in Xiaoling Zhang, Herman Wasserman and Winston Mano (eds.), *China's Media and Soft Power in Africa: Promotion and Perceptions*. Basingstoke and New York: Palgrave, pp. 19–31.

Rawnsley, Gary. 2017. "China's Soft Power: A Mid-Term Assessment," in Jia Gao, Catherine Ingram and Pookong Kee (eds.), *Global Media and Public Diplomacy in Sino-Western Relations*. London and New York: Routledge, pp. 14–30.

Sahlins, Marshall. 2015. *Confucius Institutes: Academic Malware*. Chicago: Prickly Paradigm Press.

Schmidt, Heather. 2013. "China's Confucius Institutes and the 'Necessary White Body'," *Canadian Journal of Sociology* 38(4), pp. 647–668.

Shen, Lin. 2007. "Riben kongzi xueyuan de xianzhuang ji zhanwang" ["Current Situation and Outlook of Confucius Institutes in Japan"], *Guangdong waiyu waimao daxue xuebao* 18(5), pp. 26–29.

Siow, Maria Wey-Shen. 2011. "China's Confucius Institutes: Crossing the River by Feeling the Stones," *Asia Pacific Bulletin* 91, January. Washington, DC: East-West Center.

Slobodian, Quinn. 2015. "The Maoist Enemy: China's Challenge in 1960s East Germany," *Journal of Contemporary History* 51(3), pp. 635–659.

Sofia University. 2015. "Official Opening of the New Center Confucius Model Institute at Sofia University St. Kliment Ohridski," *Sofia University Online*, September 7. www.uni-sofia.bg/index.php/eng/news/news_and_events/official_opening_of_the_new_center_confucius_model_institute_at_sofia_university_st_kliment_ohridski.

Stambach, Amy. 2014. *Confucius and Crisis in American Universities: Culture, Capital and Diplomacy in U.S. Public Higher Education*. New York and London: Routledge.

Stambach, Amy and Aikande Kwayu. 2017. "Confucius Institutes in Africa, or How the Educational Spirit in Africa Is Re-Rationalised Towards the East," *Journal of Southern African Studies* 43(2), pp. 411–424.

Starr, Don. 2009. "Chinese Language Education in Europe: The Confucius Institutes," *European Journal of Education* 44(1), pp. 65–82.

Universitat de València. 2015. "The Confucius Institute of the Universitat de València Receives the Title of 'Model Confucius Institute'," *Universitat de València Online*, December 17. www.uv.es/uvweb/college/en/news-release/confucius-institute-universitat-de-valencia-receives-title-model-confucius-institute-1285846070123/Noticia.html?id=1285953693823.

Wheeler, Anita. 2014. "Cultural Diplomacy, Language Planning and the Case of the University of Nairobi Confucius Institute," *Journal of Asian and African Studies* 49(1), pp. 49–63.

Xi, Jinping. 2014. "Congratulatory Letter," *Hanban News*, October 16. http://english.hanban.org/article/2014-10/16/content_557308.htm.

Xiao, Yun. 2017. "Confucius Institutes in the US: Platform of Promoting China's Soft Power," *Global China* 3(1), pp. 25–48.

Xinhua. 2006. "2006: Kongzi Xueyuan chengwei Zhongguo 'ruanshili' de zui liang pingpai" ["2006: Confucius Institutes Become the Brightest Trademark of China's 'Soft Power'," *Xinhua Online*, January 1. http://news.xinhuanet.com/overseas/2007-01/01/content_5556842.htm.

Xu, Dan. 2006. "'Kongzi xueyuan' relang xiandong hanyu rechao" ["The Enormous Popularity of 'Confucius Institutes' Enhances the Enthusiasm of Chinese Language Learning"], *Gaojiao guancha* 11, pp. 44–45.

Xu, Lin. 2012. "Report on the 2011 Work and 2012 Plan of the Confucius Institute Headquarters," *Kongzi Xueyuan/Confucius Institute* 18(1), pp. 18–21.

Xu, Lin. 2014. "Conclusion Speech on the 8th Confucius Institute Conference," *Kongzi Xueyuan/Confucius Institute* 30(1), pp. 64–65.

Yang, Rui. 2010. "Soft Power and Higher Education: An Examination of China's Confucius Institutes," *Globalization, Societies, and Education* 8(1), pp. 235–245.

Yuan, Zhenjie, Junwanguo Guo and Hong Zhu. 2016. "Confucius Institutes and the Limitations of China's Global Cultural Network," *China Information* 30(3), pp. 334–356.

You, Zeshun. 2012. "'Confucius Institutes': A Tension between the Construction of Their Cultural Educational Identity and the Colonization of the Marketized Discourse," *Journal of Asian Pacific Communication* 22(1), pp. 22–40.

Zhang, Xiaoling. 2016. "A World of Shared Influence," in Xiaoling Zhang, Herman Wasserman and Winston Mano (eds.), *China's Media and Soft Power in Africa: Promotion and Perceptions.* Basingstoke and New York: Palgrave, pp. 3–16.

Zhao, Hongqin and Jianbin Huang. 2010. "China's Policy of Chinese as a Foreign Language and the Use of Overseas Confucius Institutes," *Educational Research for Policy and Practice* 9(2), pp. 127–142.

Zhao, Mingyu. 2015. "Piping huayu fenxi shijiao xia guanyu kongzi xueyuan xinwen baodao de yanjiu" ["Study of News Reports Concerning Confucius Institute from the Perspective of Critical Discourse Analysis"], *Journal of Bengbu University* 4(5), pp. 39–44.

Zhe, Ren. 2010. *Confucius Institutes: China's Soft Power?* Policy Commentary Sigur Center for Asian Studies. Washington, D.C.: The George Washington University.

Zhou, Luming. 2015. "Kongzi xueyuan shi nian fazhan tongji, chengguo fenxi yu zhanlüe jianyi" ["10 Years of Confucius Institute: Statistics of Development, Analysis of Achievements and Strategic Suggestions"], *Journal of Southwest Jiaotong University (Social Sciences)* 16(1), pp. 38–44.

Zhou, Ying and Sabrina Luk. 2016. "Establishing Confucius Institutes: A Tool for Promoting China's Soft Power?," *Journal of Contemporary China* 25(100), pp. 628–642.

PART 2

China's global soft power under Xi Jinping

8

THE DILEMMA OF CHINA'S SOFT POWER IN EUROPE

Zhan Zhang[1]

Since the establishment of the "comprehensive strategic partnership" between China and Europe (the European Union and several member states) in 2003, the development of Sino–European cooperation has substantially contributed to the change in the world economy and politics. The new economic ties increased China's trade with Europe and also helped several European countries hasten their recovery in the aftermath of the Eurozone debt crisis. After the "17 + 1" framework (formerly called "16 + 1" before Greece entered in 2019), created in 2012 to improve cooperation with Central and Eastern European countries, a more strategic framework—the Belt and Road (formerly called One Belt One Road) Initiative—was introduced by Beijing in 2013 under Xi Jinping's global ambition to reconnect China with Europe as well as Central and West Asia. However, such intensified economic benefits, together with other political and cultural efforts in the past decade, did not result in a significant improvement of China's image in Europe. Ironically, European public opinion of China has been the most negative in the world (Shambaugh, 2013), and according to the Pew Research Center's survey on global attitudes, favorability of China from the main Western European countries even declined between 2006 and 2016 (see Figure 8.1).

In order to understand the apparent contradiction between the growing China–Europe cooperative interactions and the persistent European skepticism of China, this chapter explores the differing perspectives of China and Europe with regard to soft power. First, it elaborates Nye's original concept of soft power (1990) to identify the gaps between the Chinese and the European framing of this enterprise. Second, it discusses the basic variance with regard to political-moral values and the internal-to-external inflexibility that limits China's soft power campaign in European societies. Third, it traces the main lines of the rollout of Chinese soft power in Europe from both Chinese and European perspectives.

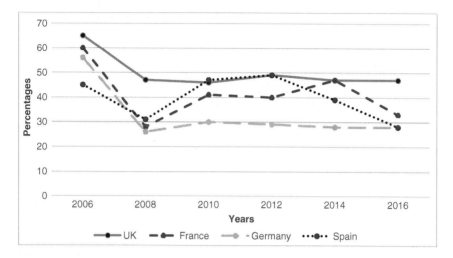

FIGURE 8.1 European favorability toward China, 2006–2016

Finally, it offers critical insights and discussion of the main obstacles that have limited China's ability to attract European hearts and minds.

The chapter concludes by outlining future directions for understanding soft power in both a Sino–European and a global context. The growing interdependence between China and Europe carries a good deal of weight on national, regional and international issues, and it allows the two sides to merge their interests in the process of re-balancing and re-stabilizing dynamic global governance. Such stability in motion becomes even more crucial in the face of today's crises, and especially in the face of the escalated trade war between China and the United States. Popular initiatives calling for greater protectionism and anti-globalization movements are on the rise, placing the existing power structures of the global economy and the established political order at risk. Thus, a well-defined soft power projection between China and Europe is indispensable for a growing European confidence in China's contributions to global economic development and to the new multipolar power balance currently in formation.

The discursive gap of the soft power concept between China and Europe

Joseph Nye introduced the notion of "soft power" in 1990 as "the ability of a country to structure a situation so that other countries develop preferences or define their interests in ways consistent with its own" (Nye, 1990: 168). He identified the three resources a country's soft power rests on, namely, its culture, political values and foreign policies (Nye, 2006), and the types of countries that would best succeed in projecting soft power: "countries whose dominant culture and ideas are closer to prevailing norms; whose credibility is enhanced by their domestic and international performance; and those with the most access to multiple channels to communication and thus more influence over how issues are framed" (Nye, 2002: 69). Based on these identifications, China had, and still has, difficulties exerting significant soft power (Nye, 2005, 2015).

China's focus on enhancing its "soft power" grew significantly after the issue was first documented in Chinese official discourse in 2007. During the 17th National Congress of the Communist Party that year, Hu Jintao, the leader of the fourth generation of Chinese leadership, made a keynote speech mentioning "soft power" ("Hu Jintao's report," 2007):

> We must keep to the orientation of advanced socialist culture, bring about a new upsurge in socialist cultural development, stimulate the cultural creativity of the whole nation, and enhance culture as part of the soft power of our country to better guarantee the people's basic cultural rights and interests, enrich the cultural life in Chinese society and inspire the enthusiasm of the people for progress.

Without specifying the other sources of soft power, Hu focused on the "internal" benefits that cultural soft power (by the Chinese government) brings to the Chinese people and Chinese society. Following the 2008 Beijing Olympics, which offered China a remarkable occasion to boost its national pride and image to the world, the soft power notion was soon reframed with the goal of achieving additional "external" benefits. With the goal of improving China's international image, Beijing began to invest enormously in its cultural industries and to push Chinese state media going abroad (e.g., an investment of 45 billion yuan was made in 2009) in order to strengthen China's soft power ("Xi: China to promote culture soft power," 2014):

> The country needs to build its capacity in international communication, construct a communication system, better use the new media and increase the creativity, appeal and credibility of China's publicity. . . . The stories of China should be well told [i.e., by Chinese media in contrast to the stories offered by "Western" media], voices of China well spread [i.e., through China's own message channels], and characteristics of China well explained [i.e., in line with the image that the Chinese government wishes to share with the world].

Chinese soft power then shifted into a discursive interplay between internal and external goals, which have been discussed in many scholarly works as entailing important differences from Nye's original notion of soft power as a sole focus on international relations (Li, 2008; Barr, 2011; Edney, 2012). Michalski (2012) responded to China's pursuit of its national interest and compared it with the European perspective of soft power that serves to "reinforce the EU's values, norms and principles on the global scene." Although an internal focus can

TABLE 8.1 Comparison of the soft power concept[2]

	Nye's Soft Power	Chinese Soft Power	European Soft Power
Origin of the concept	How the United States should (smartly) lead the world	(Using "morality" to) govern own state, bring justice and virtue to the world (以德--治国, 平天下).	"Normative power Europe"
Objectives	To shape the preferences of other countries through appeal and attraction To foster America's leading role in world politics	To strengthen China's cultural identity To improve China's international image (by offering China's voice) To promote China's culture and the Chinese model To be part of the (multipolar) global governance	To strengthen European countries' cultural prosperity and integrity To promote European history, culture and lifestyle To promote the EU's regional integration model for (multipolar) global governance
Resources of the concept	Culture (pop culture especially) Political values (freedom, democracy, human rights . . .) Foreign policy	Culture (language, heritage, history, nationalism) China's moral values (socialist core values) Foreign policy (bonded with trade agreements/ economic cooperation)	Culture (language, tradition, history) Political values (liberal democracy, rule of law, human rights . . .) Good governance

be found both in the Chinese and European soft power efforts (see Table 8.1), important differences still remain.

European soft power originates from the normative power of the EU, and it deals with how the EU member states are linked to the shared European identity (internally), and how this post-modern polity of regional integration could exert pulls on other countries/regions (externally) (Manners, 2001; Michalski, 2012). The Chinese origin of soft power could be traced back to Confucius, asserting that a country's influence and attractiveness is gained from how it governs its own state under "morality/virtue" (de, 德). It is this "morality/virtue" and the civilization achieved through self-governance that attracts others to follow. No "external" efforts need to be made on purpose, but a world of justice and virtue—the "Great Unity (tianxia datong, 天下大同)"[3]—can be reached. As stated in the *Analects*, "he who exercises government by means of his morality/virtue is like the north polar star, which keeps its place and all other starts turn towards" (*yi zheng wei de, pi ru bei chen, ju qi suo, er Zhong xing gong zhi*, 以政为德, 譬如北辰, 居其所, 而众星共之).[4] Following this Confucian origin that guided the

Middle Kingdom to achieve its ancient civilization before the European Indus-trial Revolution, Xi Jinping's new leadership focused intensively on the inter-nal construction of Chinese contemporary "morality/virtue" and nationalism to unite the Chinese people. From a Chinese perspective, the external aspect of soft power is only extended as a showcase of China being a modern socialist nation that "boasts a grand civilization and is open and attractive to the world" (Zhang, 2014).

Faced with a "national sense of apathy" (Wu, 2011), "an ambiguous moral sense" (Lee, 2011) and a crisis in Chinese cultural identity (Shen, Liu and Ni, 2011), Xi introduced a full set of Chinese contemporary moral appeals—"socialist core values"—to guide the Chinese people during the "social transition and ideological turnaround in economic thinking" (Aukia, 2014). With his commit-ment to "democracy," "freedom," "equality," "justice" and the "rule of law," Xi adopted Western political language in order to foster a sense of commonal-ity with the international community. However, the Chinese interpretations of these values differ significantly from the meanings understood in the West. "Socialist core values" operate on three levels: on the national level, it refers to prosperity (*fuqiang*, 富强), democracy (*minzhu*, 民主), civility (*wenming*, 文明) and harmony (*hexie*, 和谐); on the social level, it refers to freedom (*ziyou*, 自由), equality (*pingdeng*, 平等), justice (*gongzheng*, 公正) and the rule of law (*fazhi*, 法治); and on the individual level, it refers to patriotism (*aiguo*, 爱国), dedication (*jingye*, 敬业), integrity (*chengxin*, 诚信) and friendship (*youshan*, 友善) (Guo, 2014). The basic European respect for individual rights and freedom is not on the individual level in the Chinese value system, but instead on the social level. That means that freedom is not about one's individual freedom, but is rather a collective freedom for the group and society. Chinese moral values for individu-als concern the contributions an individual can make to the nation (patriotism), society (dedication) and other people (integrity and friendship).

Since assuming power in 2012, Xi pushed for a national education plan cover-ing all schools and requested the Chinese media to strengthen self-discipline and responsibility in spreading mainstream socialist values as the soul of soft power. Children were taught to memorize the 24 characters celebrating the core values, and these characters were also printed on stamps, painted on walls and adapted into songs and square-dancing steps across China (Zhao, 2016). Xi declared that, "Authorities should make full use of various opportunities to create circum-stances for the values' cultivation, and make them all-pervasive, just like the air" ("China focus," 2013). This full-range, top-down reinforcement on values about "freedom" and "democracy" are in marked contrast to the European beliefs regarding such values, and the different rhetoric and inferences of the values inhibited China's soft power in Europe. The internal-to-external inflexibility appeared in such a way that the harder the authorities sought to emphasize the campaign internally, the more difficult it became to improve its image with Europeans externally. What could have been a charm campaign for Chinese soft power then resulted in a "charm offensive" (Kurlantzick, 2008).

The Chinese soft power rollout in Europe

Soft power is considered a part of "comprehensive national power" in China (Keane, 2010). Components of Chinese soft power, according to Kurlantzick (2006), include not only popular culture and public diplomacy, but also more coercive economic and diplomatic levers like aid and investment and participation in multilateral organizations. Although the Chinese official discourse only refers to the cultural aspects of soft power, in practice China embraced a mix of diplomatic-economic efforts, political efforts and cultural efforts in projecting its soft power. Beijing deliberately framed this mix as a "soft effort" in order to sustain a healthy environment for deepening cooperation with European partners and presenting something attractive to the European public; nonetheless, it was perceived rather negatively in the European societies.

Diplomatic-economic efforts

One year after the establishment of the "Comprehensive Strategic Partnership" between the EU and China, the EU became China's biggest trading partner in 2004, while for the EU, China is the second most important trading partner, following only the United States since 2010. Highlighting the cooperation as "multi-dimensional, wide-ranging and multi-layered" (Shambaugh, 2013), the EU and China have created a bilateral dialogue and cooperation in more than 50 areas and have more than 200 cooperative projects in operation (Zhang, 2011), such as the China–EU Near Zero Emission Coal (NZEC) project in the area of cooperation for climate change. Following the Eurozone debt crisis, China's outbound investment to Europe sharply increased from fewer than 7 billion euros in 2008 to 35.1 billion euros in 2016 (Hanemann and Huotari, 2016). That is around a five times increase, targeting a more diverse mix of sectors. One of the most important factors that contributed to this increase was what the Chinese have called "Premier Diplomacy" after Premier Li Keqiang made two trips to Europe in 2014. Following these visits, many new contracts worth millions of euros were signed. Although a country's successful economy can be an important source of attraction (e.g., Nye, 2006), such practical focus of China's soft power on economic cooperation was instead mostly criticized as "all about the power of money" (Troyjo, 2015). Through these state visits to Europe by high-level officials, China allowed economic cooperation to play a vital role in engaging with European stakeholders. Nevertheless, the "power of money" did not translate into economic attraction as China wished. Instead of being seen as a friendly backup, China has been perceived more as an "economic competitor" and "systemic rival" according to the most recent policy paper published by the European Commission (2019).

While most of the Chinese capital flows to the western part of the continent (e.g., the United Kingdom, France, Germany, and Italy), another platform was created in 2012 for more direct cooperation with Central and Eastern European

(CEE) countries—the "16 + 1 framework." Adding Greece as the 17th member country in 2019 to this framework, China dispersed its "power of money" again, with negotiations and investment in the 17 CEE countries, focusing especially on transportation infrastructure projects. Furthermore, the ambitious Belt and Road Initiative, which came out in 2013 as a demonstration of the global vision of Xi Jinping's "Chinese Dream" (Jash, 2016), sought to reconnect China with Europe through Central and West Asia, both to achieve economic development and to promote the image of a powerful and benevolent China (Scobell et al, 2018). With 18 EU member states joining the Asian Infrastructure Investment Bank (AIIB) and the establishment of the EU Connectivity Platform in 2015, the interdependence between China and Europe for regional infrastructure projects, trade liberalization, financial integration and policy agreements all deepened.

The new framework of soft power initiatives indicated China's commitment to enabling economic integration and regional cooperation with its European partners. It is viewed positively in China as Beijing's contribution to EU integration through easing the gap and tensions between the core and peripheral areas (Shi, 2016). Europeans, however, remained skeptical about the intensified internal competition for the Chinese investments in Europe (Stanzel et al., 2016), as well as Beijing's strategy of using such interdependence to influence EU policymaking on issues such as lifting the EU arms embargo or granting China full market-economy status (Pavlićević, 2016). Indeed, China is situating itself as a networking power to connect the developed and developing part of the European continent, as it tries to balance its investment and connectivity with different stakeholders in Europe. China had high expectations about its relationship to the EU for a long time (Zhang, 2011), but the critical reaction from the EU in response to the Eurozone crisis failed to satisfy such expectations. The slow process of EU constitutional development, which, in a European understanding, demonstrates the strength of deliberative consolidation, was seen as the weakness of the EU's legitimate power in decision-making in the eyes of the Chinese government. Consequently, China began to shift its focus from working on a common EU approach to giving priority to bilateral cooperation with individual European nations, and also expanded its pan-European strategy to cover less developed areas that had been left out of the EU's primary focus. China's diplomatic-economic outreach in Europe has become more complex. Following the Brexit vote and the rise of right-wing parties, the escalating tensions in the region about a possible disintegration of the EU caused Beijing to be more aware of its strategic relationship with Brussels.

Political efforts

As D'Hooghe (2010: 7) pointed out, building political trust is "more prominent in China's public diplomacy in Europe than elsewhere in the world." This is especially important given that Europe is even more concerned about China's domestic (human rights) conditions than is the United States (Shambaugh,

Sandschneider and Hong, 2008). It is therefore not surprising to see the Human Rights Dialogue has been taking place between China and the EU since 2001. During the meetings that take place twice a year, the EU is able to express concerns about "what is happening in China regarding the rights of persons belonging to ethnic and religious minorities, deprivation of liberty, and criminal and administrative punishment." The strategic setting of these dialogues has effectively avoided collision with the EU's economic interests and political values when dealing with China. As part of the gap in political and moral values dividing Europe and China discussed above, the European concept of human rights also highlights individual civil and political rights and follows the principle of "non-interference," while the Chinese concept of human rights attaches great importance to collective rights, and China is "opposed to interfering in other countries' internal affairs on the pretext of human rights" (White paper, 1991). Given the significant gap in principles and perspectives, the Human Rights Dialogues have delivered very few results.

Xi Jinping's phrasing of "socialist core values" in line with certain "Western" terms (i.e., democracy, freedom) can be seen as another political effort made by Beijing. Although big gaps remain in understanding such values between the Chinese and the Western context, it is still a big step forward to demonstrate China's attempt to "coexist" with the West on these universal contemporary values. These political efforts did show Beijing's willingness to acknowledge European fundamental values; however, China's openness to negotiate and deal with such issues in real situations remains inconsistent, which feeds European suspicions from time to time.

What's more, the EU itself has been characterized as "the world's first truly postmodern international political form" (Ruggie, 1993). It enables each member state to partially "unbundle" territorial sovereignty and national identity in order to generate the prosperity of a single European market and replace "Europe of States" with "Europe of the Regions" (Anderson and Goodman, 1995). As an alternative to nationalism since the foundation of Westphalian state system from the 17th century, the EU's new regional model offers a new shift to redefine territorial politics in the face of a globalized world. However, China is still in its phase of constructing and reinforcing nationalism as a rising country for both territorial sovereignty and national identity. Therefore, when China stages its modernization as a single state with fast growing power (especially, under its one-party governance) in the European continent, where a new transnational form of democracy and supra-state collectivities are in the making, mutual acceptance is crucially conditioned by the different stages of political adaption.

Cultural efforts

China doesn't like its international image crafted by the global media sphere. From a Chinese perspective, the global dominance of Western transnational media results in "a systematically, and maliciously, distorted account of Chinese realities" (Sparks, 2010). Seeking to tell its own stories to the world, China had no choice but to globalize its own networks in order to obtain "the most access to multiple channels of communication and thus more influence over how issues are framed" (Nye, 2002). Under this specific goal of competing with well-established Western media organizations that mostly are situated in the United States and Europe, the Chinese "Big Four"—as China's former minister of foreign affairs Yang Jiechi called Xinhua News Agency, China Central Television (CCTV), China Radio International and *China Daily*—have all expanded their European services.

Xinhua established its headquarters in Brussels in 2004, and now has 34 branches all over Europe. The multimedia center of the Xinhua Europe Regional Bureau cooperates with the European News Exchanges providing special news to target European audiences ("Multi-media reports," 2012). A mobile app called Xinhua Europe was also launched in 2014, offering users access to "a state-of-the-art app offering fresh news, in-depth stories and images from Europe and China" ("Xinhua launches," 2014). CCTV began its early broadcasting of two channels (CCTV-4 and CCTV-9) in the United Kingdom, Germany and France in 2001, and now the English-language channel of CCTV-News (formerly CCTV-9) is available in 46 European countries, while CCTV-French and CCTV-Spanish are also available in Europe. In January 2017, CCTV was rebranded into China Global Television Networks (CGTN) for its international service and digital presence. This is a strategic move to soften the "surveillance" characteristic of CCTV from its literal meaning as "closed-circuit television" for security purposes and to advance its messages on multiple digital platforms. China Radio International signed agreements with European broadcasting companies to provide packages of programming to be locally produced and aired (i.e., the trilateral agreement with Propeller TV and Spectrum Radio in the UK for a digital radio station in London) and also moved to print media, cooperating with European partners on bilingual magazines (i.e., *Cinitalia* in Italy, *Bursztyn* in Poland, and *Opportunities China* in the UK). *China Daily* established its European Weekly edition in 2010, targeting European business executives who have already established or are interested in seeking opportunities with Chinese partners. With its specific focus on reporting business news, it reached a large circulation by overtaking *The Independent* (Rushton, 2013) and also won some awards in the UK (i.e., "International Newspaper" Award in 2014).

China has thus inaugurated an impressive array of legacy media outlets to expand its voice in Europe in recent years, although most Europeans do not know of them. Only after 2014, Chinese media began to also embrace Western social media by taking full advantage of an uncensored civil society, despite the questions that Bishop (2013) posed: "Can you really win hearts and minds when you are known as a country that blocks Facebook, Google, YouTube and Twitter?"

The answer is ambiguous. Before 2014, for example, no Chinese media outlet had more than 4 million followers on their Facebook page, but five years later, three of the "Big Four" have reached a fan community of over 65 million followers on Facebook: CGTN (84 million), *China Daily* (79 million), and Xinhua News (66 million), far surpassing well-known Western media outlets like BBC News (49 million) and CNN (31 million).[5] What's more, according to statistics from Socialbakers in September 2019, four of the top five fastest-growing media pages on Facebook are Chinese state media (CGTN, *Global Times*, Xinhua Culture and *People's Daily*), while CGTN is already ranked the number one media outlet on Facebook in terms of followers, with YouTube (83 million) ranked second.[6]

The Economist reported about the surge of Beijing's approach on Facebook ("China is using", 2019), and mapped out the geographic origins of those followers—mostly located in Southeast Asia, Latin America and especially Africa. On this map, the entire European continent was colored grey (except Romania and Albania), indicating that European Facebook users' engagement with Chinese state media remained low. This is true by looking at the very poor performance of *China Daily European Weekly* in contrast with *China Daily* on Facebook. Until September 2019, it has only 150 followers and likes.[7]

Such quantity of imbalanced growth certainly raises doubts of fraudulent activities around these "popular" Chinese media Facebook pages. In March 2019, Facebook officially filed a lawsuit against four Chinese companies for selling fake Facebook and Instagram accounts and related offenses (Grewal, 2019). This move by Facebook might push European web users even further away from the Chinese media pages. The internal-to-external inflexibility is evidenced here again, that as long as such digital platforms are blocked in China, Europeans, different from other global web users, will not find Chinese content distributed there enchanting.

The expansion of Confucius Institutes is another component of China's cultural soft power, as an attempt to promote Chinese language and Chinese culture, supporting local Chinese teaching internationally, and facilitating cultural exchanges (Guo, 2008). More Confucius Institutes have opened in Europe than in any other region,[8] but it is also the place where those institutes have received the most vocal criticism. In September 2013, Université Lumière Lyon II and Université Lumière Lyon III shut down their Confucius Institutes; in January 2015, Stockholm University, which built the first branch in Europe and the second one in the world, also closed its Confucius Institute. Despite how careful Beijing was in branding those institutes as non-profit and non-government organizations and encouraging those language centers not to act as overt purveyors of the Party's political viewpoints ("A message from Confucius," 2009), the financing structure as well as the close relationship of the institutes to the Ministry of Education and State Council Information Office still makes European partners wary. In the end, Confucius Institutes in Europe remain primarily centers for instruction in the Chinese language without offering much introduction to Chinese culture or understanding of contemporary China. When certain sensitive topics arise, according Hartig's case studies in Germany (2010), the teaching staff of the institutes "turn quiet or even silent."

Limits of China's soft power in Europe

In contrast to China's effort, the growing interaction with European stakeholders on multilevel cooperation, and the cultural expansion to ensure that Chinese voices are heard in Europe, did not produce much change in European perceptions about China. Indeed, the favorability of China in many European countries even dropped over the last decade.

Based on data collected by the Pew Research Center, we could observe that in the UK, France, Germany and Spain (see Figure 8.1), public perceptions of China declined in comparison to the "honeymoon" period (2003–2006) a decade ago. If we place the European attitudes toward China into a global comparison, we can see that as an entire region, Europe (mostly Western Europe) has close to the most unfavorable view about China (54%, 22% higher than the median of the world).

But interestingly enough, in another survey about people's attitudes toward whether China will or has already replaced the United States as a global superpower, an average of 57% of European citizens believed in China's superiority (8% higher than the median of the world). This means that the European public sees China's potential for growing into a world-leading force, but they are not in favor of this development. In other words, Europeans agree on the hard (military-economy) part of China's power developments, but not yet on the soft (economy-culture) part of China's power attractiveness. Thus, all the soft power efforts made in Europe seem not to have helped China achieve its specific objective—improving its image. What, then, are the main obstacles?

The ambiguous "seeds"

China wishes to promote its achievements and virtues in order to draw an attractive image through its own voice. But this "own voice" selects what China wants to relate rather than to address the concerns of the European audience. This ideal narrative that is in line with the Party script cannot satisfy the European audience, which prefers a multilayered and uncensored discussion that reflects a genuine image of the changing Chinese society. By introducing "media mindsets" as the fourth resource of soft power in connecting China with Europe, Zhang, Perrin and Huan (2019) discussed that the Chinese tendency to whitewash problems and form a clean and positive version of its image to avoid international critics is far from the Western European audience's habits and expectations of receiving multivoiced media messages that are designed to help citizens form different opinions and critical understandings of socially relevant topics. As long as Chinese media crafts stories according to this mindset, it would lack credibility for European hearts and minds, and eventually result in accentuated criticism and uncertainty.

The introduction of China's Belt and Road Initiative in Europe is another example. As Godehardt (2016) commented, Chinese leadership intends to "provide as little concrete information as possible" about the political labels behind the Belt and Road concept, and always focuses on the "common benefits and economic opportunities, but less on security threats and difficulties." Zhang (2019) reviewed the media coverage of the Belt and Road Initiative from mainstream Western European media and pointed out the continuous skepticism around news frames like "inclusiveness," "sustainability" and "trade/debt diplomacy." She also pointed out that the Chinese media stories about the Belt and Road Initiative failed to provide sufficient arguments in answering those doubts and shifting such frames. Thus, the initiative remained empty without cohesive classification, practical guidelines or regulatory frameworks that would better match better the expectations of European partners.

The EU rejected the granting of full market-economy status to China in 2016. What's more, instead of formulating a unified EU policy toward the Belt and Road Initiative, a new "EU–Asia Connectivity Strategy" was signed-off in 2018 as a rival to the Chinese initiative for the EU's engagement with Asia under a "European standard." This represented a clear sign that China's "capital" power did not translate into "soft" economic attraction, and China's state-regulated market still raised deep concerns from its biggest trading partner. The EU sees the importance of Asia, but it is clearly not ready to accept China taking the lead in the Eurasian integration process. Especially given the rise of protectionism, populism and anti-globalization in different European countries, China's economic prosperity might make it even more difficult to attract Europeans (especially to the right-wing parties and their supporters).

The visible "hands"

The Chinese government has been visible on all levels carrying out its soft power campaign. Critics of the Confucius Institutes in Europe focus on the fact that they are funded directly by the government, thus increasing the potential that the Chinese state might limit European academic freedom. The enormous support from the "state" to Chinese state media also arguably impaired the ability of these outlets to reach European audiences. For the Chinese, the hands of "authority" may give the media credibility and accountability, but in Europe (especially in North-Western Europe), media accountability is constructed on the basis of independence and deliberative public discourse where critical opinions can be discussed overtly for the good of society. The more assertive the role played by the "authority," the less credibility the media has with the audience. Knowing that the Chinese government propagates a less-than-free model of journalism and media practice (Farah and Mosher, 2010), it is unlikely that Europeans will accept messages crafted by such visible hands without resistance. The "soft" campaign, for both its domestic and international performance, seems to be understood as the projection of "hard" authoritarian power for European publics.

Lack of "media-soil" analysis

Hallin and Mancini (2004) divided the European media into three main systems and discussed the complexity of the European media landscape located within different cultural, social and political contexts. In a fragmented inter-regional market such as Europe, media outlets face difficulties when crossing borders. It is not easy to enter the European media networks due to their significant differences from one market to another, and the Chinese media products were not tailored to recognize such variances when crossing borders in Europe. Instead, they delivered the same content in different European language packages. In addition to regional differences, the European market is characterized by social diversity along various criteria such as age. Media content distributed on legacy (targeting older audiences) or new media platforms (targeting younger audiences) should be better customized, with considerations given to the national differences. Lacking a specific strategy to tailor media content to specific audiences, the Chinese content may be "valued to a lesser extent by foreign audiences that lack the cultural background and knowledge needed for full appreciation of the product" (Lee, 2006). In this statement, the diversity of the European audience and markets translates into a less standardized and predictable previous knowledge—which, again, shows the incompatibility of perspectives and approaches to instruments of China's soft power.

Unnatural engagement with "media dynamics"

In today's world, audiences can easily access information through multiple channels so that "it is no longer possible for political regimes to create alternative messages and thus preserve a level of nuance, local contextualizing and perhaps even outright deception when they had to respond to challenging messages" (Riley and Hollihan, 2012: 61). On the one hand, what the Chinese media has been doing is still creating alternative messages and sending symbolic counter-information that is very easily identified as a state-owned voice. On the other hand, the Chinese way of pushing forward such counter-information through social networks and online activities are too aggressive both in speed and in quantity. Therefore, even if the number of followers of Chinese state media surges on Facebook, whether it brings in real engaged readers for the possible improvement of China's image overseas or is merely a boosted business of inflated numbers from "click farms" to just satisfy Beijing remains a vexing question.

Moreover, the daily news consumption by European publics is still centered on European (and American) information sources, but the communication strategies Beijing applies to the local bureaus of these international media organizations in China hasn't significantly improved. Xi Jinping gave a speech after his appointment as the Party leader in 2012 to encourage "foreign friends from the press" to "make more efforts and contributions to deepen the mutual understanding between China and the world." But in 2014, the State Administration of Press, Publication, Radio, Film and Television published Administrative Measurements indicating that Chinese journalists should not violate the rules of passing on any critical information obtained in the course of their work to any foreign media groups. The more constraints and pressures the foreign media receive in China, the further the European audience may depart from the Chinese messages, because such activities, from a Western perspective, cannot but result in reinforcing the stereotype of "Chinese manipulation."

Conclusion

China and Europe clearly need each other, for both the EU's and the European countries' relations with China top their agenda of concerns, in particular with reference to economic cooperation. Together, China and the EU generate more than one third of the world's economic output (Amadeo, 2017), and a healthy Europe–China relationship matters greatly to the integration of the global economy, as well as the structural changes that are required urgently for the world's trading and financial systems. The presidency of Donald Trump in the United States brought more uncertainty to the traditionally strong transatlantic relationship as he backed away from the Transatlantic Trade and Investment Partnership (TTIP). And the nascent trade war between the United States and China is causing collateral damage to economies that are heavily dependent on trade, including the EU. China's Belt and Road Initiative might have the potential to open new windows for deeper regional cooperation, but the challenges to the rule-based Eurocentric model have not made cooperation easier within the clouding investment environment of hampered business confidence. Situating itself between the United States and China, Europe is arriving at its own crossroads, where both the danger of dis-integration of the EU and the danger of cutting itself off from the contemporary quest for a new international order must be faced (Kissinger, 2014).

The world is drawn to China. As the second largest economy benefiting from the globalization sparked by the West, and as the biggest socialist country offering an alternative model of growth and governance, China's contribution to global development is becoming more complex in an attempt to respond to different regional and global challenges. The rise of China—both in terms of its hard and soft power—and the reception of and reaction to such a rise worldwide unfolds at an especially important time. This chapter discussed China's dilemma in projecting greater soft power in Europe. The flourishing economic cooperation and China's rising capital flow into the continent did not increase China's attractiveness to Europe, and neither did the efforts made by the Chinese government through its soft power campaign. Doubts and skepticism about China still persist or even grow in Europe since the limits of China's efforts to promote its soft power have worsened the shadows hanging over European minds. A more pragmatic approach and a long-term socialization process is needed to profoundly improve mutual understanding and, eventually, to improve China's image as both a grand civilization and an open and attractive society in Europe.

First, China's image building in Europe should not be framed only according to the Chinese media mindset (Zhang, Perrin and Huan, 2019) as a precise selection of only the ideal elements of the nation that China wishes to showcase. Nations should share their virtues but also their mistakes, since nations sometimes earn more sympathy and credibility for their vulnerabilities than they win respect for their strengths. Being open and clear to discuss both domestic problems and China's new economic-political framework in Europe, being confident to show its resolution while also welcoming the criticisms that will help the nation along on its path to improvement, would actually be more attractive than hiding the problems or offering only ambiguous concepts. In Europe, where criticism is part of the power game and strong leaders tend to encourage criticism while weak ones suppress it, China's soft power projection needs a thorough conceptual change.

Second, the "all-pervasive" involvement of the Chinese government into the soft power campaign, both internally and externally, seriously constrained European impressions of China's move to an open and attractive society. In 2016, several privately held Chinese media companies acquired European companies (i.e., Tencent bought Supercell and Wanda bought Odeon and UCI). Huawei, being the second-largest smartphone vendor in Europe, signed 28 out of 50 commercial contracts for 5G with European operators (announced by its vice president Hu Houkun in June 2019). But whether these private-sector companies will be constrained by China's central government in their overseas performance, and how the new business models could open European media users' minds for Chinese content, platforms and technology, are still open questions.

Third, China should provide a variety of customized media products for different markets and audiences across Europe, especially well-designed, user-oriented online media products. Media organizations should expand to take full use of what the Internet platforms offer, and the Confucius Institutes, Chinese embassies/consulates, Chinese companies or other non-governmental organizations should all upgrade their web services and communication skills for direct interactive engagement with European publics. The huge gap in number of followers between *China Daily* and *China Daily European Weekly* on Facebook indicated not only the conspicuously low interest from European web users in Chinese content, but also the lack of interest and effort from Beijing to invest in purposefully attracting a European audience. Kalathil (2017) argued that China has been using its market power to influence Hollywood content in order to shape global public opinion. No evidence can be found yet to prove such Sino–Hollywood blockbusters would make a breakthrough into the European market, but coproduction (with Hollywood or European partners) might become a potential approach for the global reach of China's soft power in the long run.

Last but not least, and in fact arguably the most urgent goal, must be to change the tension between the Chinese authorities and the international media professionals based in China. Understanding that they are (and will always be) the main channels for European audiences to get information from China, it would be wiser to find a new cooperative mode to work together. As long as the current mechanism is focused on restriction, isolation and monitoring, in the end it will restrict the reach of China's soft power and isolate the Middle Kingdom from European hearts and minds.

Differences remain, and challenges lie ahead. But neither Europe nor China should allow the differences or challenges to prevent them from addressing their common interests—building a multipolar world (see Table 8.1), and working together toward common goals. In his visit to Europe in early 2017, President Xi Jinping spoke at the Davos Economic Forum. By openly showing China's commitment to trade and globalization, Xi responded to calls for protectionism and limits on free trade, and sent a strong signal to Europe that the world system is shifting from a unipolar world dominated by America to a multipolar system where China and Europe could share their common goals. Given the calls for American isolationism by President Trump, the vacuum of the world leadership calls for other great players to step in. China aims at taking a leadership role in reducing free-trade barriers and improving conditions in the global economy. How will the Europeans welcome China's efforts to spark global development? How will they react to the multipolar shift toward a new power balance in the world's economy and politics? China's soft power engagement in Europe will become more fruitful if European partners can thoroughly understand the good reasons to engage with China in shaping the future.

Notes

1 This chapter is made possible through the support from Professor Thomas Hollihan, my postdoctoral supervisor at the University of Southern California. His insights and comments greatly improved the work. I am also grateful to Professor Daniel Perrin from the Zurich University of Applied Sciences, for sharing his wisdom from a European expert perspective, which strengthened the manuscript. This chapter was accomplished during my early postdoctoral mobility project that is funded by the Swiss National Science Foundation.

2 The table is drawn by the author and is derived from the works of Nye (1990, 2002), Wang (2017), Zheng (2010), Manners (2001), and Mickalski (2012).

3 The society in Great Unity (*da tong*, 大同) was ruled by the public, where the people chose men of virtue and ability and valued trust and harmony. People not only loved their own parents and children, but also secured the living of the elderly until the end of their lives, let the adults be of use to the society and helped the young grow. Those who were widowed, orphaned, childless, handicapped and diseased were all taken care of. Men took their responsibilities seriously and women had their homes. People disliked seeing resources being wasted but did not seek to possess them; they wanted to exert their strength but did not do it for their own benefit. Therefore, selfish thoughts were dismissed, people refrained from theft and robbery and the outer doors remained open. http://ctext.org/liji/li-yun.

4 The *Analects* (*lun yu*, 论语, 475–221 BC) is a collection of sayings and ideas from Confucius and his contemporaries. It is considered the central text of Confucianism.
5 The number of followers is accurate as of September 1, 2019, on Facebook pages including: CGTN, www.facebook.com/ChinaGlobalTVNetwork/; *China Daily*, www.facebook.com/chinadaily; Xinhua News, www.facebook.com/XinhuaNewsAgency/?brand_redir=369959106408139; BBC News, www.facebook.com/bbcnews/; and CNN, www.facebook.com/cnn/.
6 Socialbakers is an artificial intelligence–powered social media marketing website that provides statistics for companies and brands. www.socialbakers.com/statistics/facebook/pages/total/media/.
7 The number of followers is accurate as of September 1, 2019, on *China Daily European Weekly*'s Facebook page: www.facebook.com/China-Daily-European-Weekly-196052993764057/.
8 Confucius Institute website, accessed by the author in March 2017: www.hanban.edu.cn/.

References

Amadeo, Kimberly. 2017. "What Is the World's Largest Economy?," *The Balance*, February 23. www.thebalance.com/world-s-largest-economy-3306044.

Anderson, James and James Goodman. 1995. "Regions, States and the European Union: Modernist Reaction or Postmodern Adaptation?," *Review of International Political Economy* 2(4), pp. 600–631.

Aukia, Jukka. 2014. "The Cultural Soft Power of China: A Tool for Dualistic National Security," *Journal of China and International Relations* 2(1), pp. 71–94.

Barr, Michael D. 2011. *Who's Afraid of China? The Challenge of Chinese Soft Power.* New York: Zed Books.

Bishop, Bill. 2013. "Can China Successfully Build Soft Power without a Global Internet Strategy?," *The Atlantic*. www.theatlantic.com/china/archive/2013/04/can-china-do-soft-power/274916/.

"China Focus: China Promotes Core Socialist Values," 2013. *Xinhua News Agency*, December 23. http://news.xinhuanet.com/english/china/2013-12/24/c_132990379.htm.

"China Is Using Facebook to Build a Huge Audience Around the world," 2019. *The Economist*, April 20. www.economist.com/graphic-detail/2019/04/20/china-is-using-facebook-to-build-a-huge-audience-around-the-world.

D'Hooghe, Ingrid. 2010. *The Limits of China's Soft Power in Europe: Beijing's Public Diplomacy Puzzle.* The Hague, Institute of International Relations Clingendael Diplomacy Papers no.25, Netherlands.

Edney, Kingsley. 2012. "Soft Power and the Chinese Propaganda System," *Journal of Contemporary China* 21(78), pp. 899–914.

European Commission. 2019. "EU-China Strategic Outlook," Joint Communication to the European Parliament, the European Council and the Council. https://ec.europa.eu/commission/sites/beta-political/files/communication-eu-china-a-strategic-outlook.pdf.

Farah, Douglas and Andrew Mosher. 2010. "Winds from the East: How the People's Republic of China Seeks to Influence the Media in Africa, Latin America, and Southeast Asia," *Centre for International Media Assistance*, September 8. www.cima.ned.org/wp-content/uploads/2015/02/CIMA-China-Report_1.pdf.

Godehardt, Nadine. 2016. "No End of History: A Chinese Alternative Concept of International Order?," *Stiftung Wissenschaft und Politik*. www.swp-berlin.org/fileadmin/contents/products/research_papers/2016RP02_gdh.pdf.

Grewal, Paul. 2019. "Cracking Down on the Sale of Fake Accounts, Likes and Followers," *Facebook Newsroom*. https://newsroom.fb.com/news/2019/03/sale-of-fake-accounts-likes-and-followers/.

Guo, Janning. 2014. "Explanation of Socialist Core Values" ["*Shehuizhuyi hexin jiazhiguan jiben neirong shiyi*社会主义核心价值观基本内容释义"]. http://theory.people.com.cn/GB/68294/384764/.

Guo, Xiaolin. 2008. "Repackaging Confucius: PRC Public Diplomacy and the Rise of Soft Power," *Asia Paper*, January, pp. 1–50.

Hallin, Daniel C. and Paolo Mancini. 2004. *Comparing Media Systems: Three Models of Media and Politics*. Cambridge: Cambridge University Press.

Hanemann, Thilo and Huotari, Mikko. 2017. "Record Flows and Growing Imbalance: Chinese Investment in Europe," *Rhodium Group*. http://rhg.com/wp-content/uploads/2017/01/RHG_Merics_COFDI_EU_2016.pdf.

Hartig, Falk. 2010. "Confusion about Confucius Institutes: Soft Power Push or Conspiracy? A Case Study of Confucius Institutes in Germany," paper presented at the 18th Biennial Conference of the Asian Studies Association of Australia, Adelaide.

"Hu Jintao's Report at 17th Party Congress 2007," 2007. *Xinhua News Agency*, October 24. http://news.xinhuanet.com/newscenter/2007-10/24/content_6938568_6.htm.

Jash, Amrita. 2016. "China's 'One Belt, One Road': A Roadmap to 'Chinese Dream'?," *IndraStra Global* 2.

Kalathil, Shanthi. 2017. "Beyond the Great Firewall: How China Became a Global Information Power," *Center for International Media Assistance*, March. www.cima.ned.org/resource/beyond-great-firewall-china-became-global-information-power/.

Keane, Michael. 2010. "Re-Imagining China's Future: Soft Power, Cultural Presence and the East Asian Media Market," in Daniel Ariad Black, Stephen J. Epstein and Alison Tokita (eds.), *Complicated Currents: Media Flows, Soft Power and East Asia*. Clayton, Victoria: Monash University ePress, pp. 14.1–14.13.

Kissinger, Henry. 2014. *World Order*. New York: Penguin Press.

Kurlantzick, Joshua. 2006. "China's Charm Offensive in Southeast Asia," *Current History* 105(692), pp. 270–276.

Kurlantzick, Joshua. 2008. *Charm Offensive: How China's Soft Power Is Transforming the World*. New Haven and London: Yale University Press.

Lee, C. 2011. "Chinese Traditional Ethics from the Perspective of Modern Culture and Values" ["*Zhongguo chuantong lunli wenhua ji qi jiazhi de xiandai toushi*, 中国传统伦理文化及其价值的现代透视"], *Academic Research*, Integrated edition [Xueshu wenti yanjiu zonghe ban, 学术问题研究综合版] 2, pp. 26–30.

Lee, Francis L.F. 2006. "Cultural Discount and Cross-Culture Predictability: Examining the Box Office Performance of American Movies in Hong Kong," *Journal of Media Economics* 19(4), pp. 259–278.

Li, Mingjiang. 2008. "China Debates Soft Power," *Chinese Journal of International Politics* 2(2), pp. 287–387.

Manners, Ian. 2001. "Normative Power Europe: The International Role of the EU," paper presented at the European Union between International and World Society Conference. http://aei.pitt.edu/7263/1/002188_1.PDF.

"A Message from Confucius: New Ways of Projecting Soft Power," 2009. *The Economist*, October 22. www.economist.com/node/14678507.

Michalski, Anna. 2012. "China and the EU: Conceptual Gaps in Soft Power," in Zhongqi Pan (ed.), *Conceptual Gaps in China-EU Relations: Global Governance, Human Rights and Strategic Partnerships*. Houndmills, Basingstoke: Palgrave Macmillan, pp. 65–82.

"Multi-Media Reports and Multi-Media Digital Platform of Xinhua European Head-quarters" ["*xinhuashe ouzhou zongfenshe duomeiti caibian he duomeiti shuzi jiagong pingtai*新华社欧洲总分社多媒体采编和多媒体数字加工平台"], 2010. Case Study Offered by Redflag-Linux Company, 29 December. www.redflag-linux.com/userfiles/case.

Nye, Joseph S., Jr. 1990. "Soft Power," *Foreign Policy* 80, pp. 153–171.

Nye, Joseph S., Jr. 2002. *The Paradox of American Power: Why the World's Only Superpower Can't Go It Alone*. New York: Oxford University Press.

Nye, Joseph S., Jr. 2005. "The Rise of China's Soft Power," *Wall Street Journal Asia*, December 29. www.wsj.com/articles/SB113580867242333272.

Nye, Joseph S., Jr. 2006. "Think Again: Soft Power," *Foreign Policy*, February 23. http://foreignpolicy.com/2006/02/23/think-again-soft-power/.

Nye, Joseph S., Jr. 2015. "The Limits of Chinese Soft Power," *Project Syndicate*, July 10. www.project-syndicate.org/commentary/china-civil-society-nationalism-soft-power-by-joseph-s-nye-2015-07.

Pavlićević, Dragan. 2016. "China in Central and Eastern Europe: 4 Myths," *The Diplomat*, June 16. http://thediplomat.com/2016/06/china-in-central-and-eastern-europe-4-myths/.

Riley, Patricia and Thomas A. Hollihan. 2012. "Strategic Communication: How Governments Frame Arguments in the Media," in Frans H. van Eemeren and Bart Garssen (eds.), *Exploring Argumentative Contexts*. Amsterdam and Philadelphia: John Benjamins Publishing Company, pp. 59–78.

Ruggie, John. 1993. "Territoriality and Beyond: Problematizing Modernity in International Relations," *International Organization* 47(1), pp. 139–174.

Rushton, Katherine. 2013. "European Version of China Daily Overtakes the Independent," *The Telegraph*, February 4. www.telegraph.co.uk/finance/newsbysector/mediatechnologyandtelecoms/media/9847516/European-version-of-China-Daily-overtakes-The-Independent.html.

Scobell, Andrew., Lin, Bonny., Schatz, Howard J., Johnson, Michael., Hanauer, Larry., Chase, Michael S., Cevallos, Astrid S., Rasmussen, Ivan W., Chan, Arthur., Strong, Aaron., Warner, Eric., and Ma, Logan. 2018. At the Dawn of Belt and Road, China in the Developing World. Rand Corporation Publication. https://www.rand.org/content/dam/rand/pubs/research_reports/RR2200/RR2273/RAND_RR2273.pdf

Shambaugh, David. 2013. *China Goes Global: The Partial Power*. New York: Oxford University Press.

Shambaugh, David, Eberhard Sandschneider and Zhou Hong. 2008. "From Honeymoon to Marriage: Prospects for the China-Europe Relationship," in David Shambaugh, Eberhard Sandschneider and Zhou Hong (eds.), *China-Europe Relations: Perceptions, Policies and Prospects*. London: Routledge, pp. 303–338.

Shen, Haigang., Liu, Qingshun., Ni, Yong. 2011. "The Analysis of Chinese Cultural Soft Power Based on Cultural Safety," in Konglai Zhu and Henry Zhang (eds.), *Soft Power Innovation and Development in Today's China*. Riverwood: Aussino Academic Publishing House.

Shi, Zhiqin. 2016. "China-EU Relations: Crisis and Opportunity," *The Diplomat*, March 15. http://thediplomat.com/2016/03/china-eu-relations-crisis-and-opportunity/.

Sparks, Colin. 2010. "Coverage of China in the UK National Press," *Chinese Journal of Communication* 3(3), pp. 347–365.

Stanzel, Angela, Agatha Kratz, Justyna Szczudlik and Dragan Pavlićević. 2016. *China's Investment in Influence: The Future of 16+1 Cooperation*. European Council on Foreign Relations. https://defence.pk/pdf/threads/chinas-investment-in-influence-the-future-of-16-1-cooperation.467475/.

Troyjo, M. 2015. "China's 'Soft Power' Is the Power of Money," *Financial Times*, June 15. www.ft.com/content/7ffc4d94-f87b-3c84-b8b7-4a37eb6508e6.

Wang, Yiwei. 2017. "Debate the Soft Power and Its Development in China" ["Lun ruan shili beilun ji qi zhongguo chao yue 论软实力悖论及其中国超越"], February 7. www. aisixiang.com/data/103047-2.html.

"White Paper: Human Rights in China," 1991. Information Office of the State Council of the People's Republic of China, November. www.china.org.cn/e-white/7/.

Wu, X. 2011. "Global Transmission of Cultural Identity" ["Quanqiu xing wenhua chuanbo zhong de wenhua shenfen, 全球性文化传播中的文化身份"], *Social Scientist* [*Shehui kexuejia,* 社会科学家] 8, pp. 111–114.

"Xi: China to Promote Culture Soft Power," 2014. *Xinhua News Agency*, January 1. www.china.org.cn/china/2014-01/01/content_31059390.htm.

"Xinhua launches APP at the Sixth Hanmburg Summit: China Meets Europe." 2014. Xinhua News Agency. October 13. http://www.xinhuanet.com/world/2014-10/13/c_127 093498_3.htm

Zhang, Li. 2011. *News Media and EU-China Relations*. New York: Palgrave Macmillan.

Zhang, Lihua. 2014. "China's Concern on Soft Power," *Carnegie-Tsinghua Center for Global Policy Interviews*, April 28. http://carnegietsinghua.org/2014/04/28/zh-pub-55460#2.

Zhang, Zhan. 2019. "Charm European Minds with New Silk Road," in *Common Prosperity: Global Views on Belt and Road Initiative*. Beijing: China Intercontinental Press.

Zhang, Zhan, Daniel Perrin and Changpeng Huan. 2019. "Soft Power in the Newsroom: Media Mindsets as Limiters of China's Media Strategies in Europe," in Gabriele Balbi, Fei Jiang and Giuseppe Richeri (eds.), *China and the Global Media Landscape: Mapping or Remapped*. Newcastle upon Tyne: UK: Cambridge Scholars Publishing.

Zhao, Kiki. 2016. "China's 'Core Socialist Values,' the Song-and-Dance Version," *The New York Times*, September 1. www.nytimes.com/2016/09/02/world/asia/china-dance-socialist-values.html.

Zheng, B. 2010. *China's Soft Power: Two Ways to Decide China's Fate* [*Zhongguo ruan shili: jueding zhongguo mingyun de liang zhong si lu*中国软实力:决定中国命运的两种思路]. Beijing: Central Compilation and Translation Press.

9

THE EVOLUTION OF CHINESE SOFT POWER IN THE AMERICAS

R. Evan Ellis[1]

The abrupt switch in diplomatic recognition by Panama, the Dominican Republic and El Salvador from Taiwan to the People's Republic of China (PRC) during 2017 and 2018 (Ellis, 2018a) following the end of the "diplomatic truce" that had restrained the PRC from actively pursuing diplomatic relations with states recognizing Taiwan highlights the growth and evolution of Chinese soft power in the Americas (Fleischman, 2018). Not only did each of the three quickly move to take advantage of the opportunity once the 2016 changes by the African states of Gambia and Sao Tome and Principe made it clear that the "truce" was over, but more strikingly, the Dominican Republic, El Salvador and Panama had traditionally been some of the closest partners of the United States in the Western Hemisphere, linked by bonds of investments and commercial flows, immigrant communities and history (including a significant US expatriate and business community in Panama, reflecting the legacy of almost a century of US control of the Panama Canal and the basing of military forces in the country). In each case, the governments switched relations to the PRC virtually without consultation with or notification of the United States and responded to US concerns over the lack of transparency regarding new Chinese activities in the country with polite but resolute defiance ("Panama Asks . . . ," 2018).

The embrace by the region of political and commercial engagement with the PRC, and its markedly cool tone toward the United States (Johnson, 2018) contrasts sharply with the situation in 2005 when, following Chinese President Hu Jintao's November 2004 trip to the region with attention-grabbing promises of massive PRC investment in Latin America, US policymakers testified before Congress that Chinese commerce and influence in the region was dwarfed by that of the United States, and not a factor for immediate concern ("China's Influence . . .," 2005). The leap in PRC engagement and associated influence (Piccone, 2016) has occurred in little more than a decade without any of the traditional cold-war artifacts of military threat, such as the establishment of exclusive alliances or basing agreements (Ellis, 2011a). It illustrates the degree to which the PRC position and that of the United States, has been transformed through a relative change in soft power, and the associated importance of understanding it as a critical factor in the strategic dynamics of the region.

The nature of PRC soft power in Latin America and the Caribbean is different from that of the United States (National Endowment of Democracy, 2017), although in many ways equal or greater in its magnitude and effects.

The term soft power was first popularized by scholar Joseph Nye in 1990, and refers to the ability of a state to induce others to behave in its interests, albeit not through coercion or even indirect threats (Nye, 1990), but because relevant authorities in those states believe that doing so is in their interests (Nye, 2004). Most discussions of soft power focus on the United States, as it relates to Latin America or other regions, and highlight the identification by the relevant elites with US objectives and values, particularly democracy and a market economy (Nye, 1990). The vehicle for this soft power is often (albeit not exclusively) through the influenced living or receiving some part of their education in the United States or otherwise internalizing key values.

Parallel to the US concept of soft power, the Chinese have traditionally held their culture in reverence, in part, for its ability to influence adversaries and others with which they had to deal. Indeed, in the Chinese recollection of their history, even successful invaders such as the Mongols ultimately became enamored with the greatness of Chinese civilization and were transformed by and assimilated into it (Poo, 2005).

Today, the PRC organization Hanban funds Confucius Institutes (Volodzko, 2015) and other projects to disseminate and promote Chinese culture (Isenberg, 2008), following the logic that such understanding will correspondingly spread the influence of China, and open doors to its political, business and other agendas ("Another U.S. deficit . . . ," 2011).

Ironically, despite evidence of the enormous amount of PRC soft power in Latin America and the Caribbean, many Chinese scholars (see, for example, Liu, 2016) and others believe that the country lacks influence there (among other parts of the globe) (Eades, 2014), because so few of its residents speak Mandarin Chinese, deeply understand or embrace the Chinese culture (Gao, 2017), or because the PRC seemingly lacks the power that the United States does to rally an international consensus around the values it represents (Nye, 2012).

Such an assessment is, however, too pessimistic, because it measures Chinese soft power in the region in a manner that overlooks its true bases for influence there. By contrast to US soft power, which (as noted before) is principally based on shared values, Chinese soft power in Latin America and the Caribbean is more rooted in the expectation of benefits from the PRC.

Much of the take-off in interest in China by political leaders and businessmen in the region was fueled by then Chinese President Hu Jintao's proclamation that the PRC trade with the region would expand to $100 billion and Chinese investment in the region would double in the decade to come ("Hu hails . . . ," 2004). President Xi Jinping similarly promised $250 billion in Chinese investment and $500 billion in trade with the region (Rajagopalan, 2015). In both cases, it was arguably the plausible expectations, more than actual levels of trade and investment, an analysis of its feasibility or potential implications, that drove interest in the region, and to an extent, action by its business and political leaders.

Such expectations are arguably amorphous and differ among those holding them, yet generally include hope for enrichment through access to the Chinese market, and business opportunities from working with a Chinese partner (which presumably has access to production capabilities and financing in China). These hopes arguably help persuade Latin American business leaders that the potential opportunities merit their investment of the significant time and money required to establish the company in the PRC, or at least develop contacts with Chinese business or other partners. They explain the monumental investments (some more successful than others) by internationally oriented Latin American companies such as Maseca (including Bimbo bakery products), JBS, Pollo Campero, Juan Valdez, Café Britt, Fogoncito and others to establish themselves in the Chinese market, including the hundreds of Latin American businessmen who pay thousands of dollars to attend trade fairs in China in the hope of finding an appropriate buyer for their goods, a producer from which they can import or other partner.

For Latin American and Caribbean students, the expectation of opportunities in or with China is a motivator to spend the years required to learn the (very difficult) Mandarin language and associated Chinese character set, as well as Chinese history and culture (Ellis, 2014a).

At the state-to-state level, PRC soft power reflects beliefs about the sustainability of Chinese economic growth and development, and to some degree, political and military influence vis-à-vis the United States and other actors, including the expectation that the PRC will be among the wealthiest and most powerful nations on the globe (Rines, 2016).

For state-level decision makers, in the commercial realm, expectations about the future of China lead to the accompanying belief that the PRC will be able to purchase significant amounts of the country's exports if only the partner can position its products adequately and solve other problems. China is similarly seen as a source of loans for private and state-led development projects, investments in commercial operations that will employ its people and produce tax revenues and, possibly, facilitate or engage in transactions that produce lucrative side benefits for the decision makers entering into them (from political credit, to commissions and other business opportunities for family and partners of the businessman).

In examining the behaviors of Latin American politicians toward China, expectations about future Chinese wealth and power and the opportunities it could provide the country helps to explain respectable Latin American leaders courting the PRC, including initiatives to establish diplomatic relations by Costa Rica's President Oscar Arias in 2007 (Casas-Zamora, 2009), Panama's President

Juan Carlos Varela in 2017, Danilo Medina of the Dominican Republic in 2017, and Salvador Sanchez Ceren of El Salvador in 2018.

For anti-US leftist regimes such as Cuba, Venezuela and Bolivia, and the previous government of Rafael Correa in Ecuador, and Christina Fernandez de Kirchner in Argentina, China's soft power has a political, as well as an economic component, with the PRC seen as an economic and political counterweight to dependence on Western financial institutions and political ties. Indeed, for such leaders, the success of the PRC demonstrates that development, wealth and power can be achieved without submission to Western proscriptions regarding open markets and pluralistic democracy (Barker, 2017), and gives them an ally for pursuing such a path.

Beyond such "populist socialist actors," even the conservative governments of more politically mainstream states such as Peru, Chile and even Colombia see the PRC as a market, source of investment, financing, political and sometimes military interactions that complements the pro-Western, pro-market orientation of the government and gives the country additional options. As a reflection of these views, of the nine "strategic partners" that the PRC has established in Latin America, only two (Venezuela and Bolivia) are leftist regimes, and two (Ecuador and Argentina) have continued their strategic partnerships with the PRC even after returning more politically moderate governments with associated access to Western institutions, investors and capital markets.

As suggested previously, the driver of Chinese soft power is how the country and its trajectory are perceived, although the reality of Chinese success may feed those perceptions. Indeed, the Chinese appear to be particularly adept in allowing partners to believe what they want, if such beliefs lead the partner to behave in ways that support Chinese strategic or business objectives.

In understanding the vehicle of Chinese soft power in Latin America, by contrast to US soft power, expectations of individual benefits, rather than abstract principles or value alignment, arguably play a greater role. As noted previously, decisions by businessmen to seek Chinese partners may be driven by hopes for lucrative deals. Reciprocally, decisions by scholars to tone down criticisms of the PRC (Stone Fish, 2018) may be driven by a desire not to lose access to Chinese colleagues, funded trips to the PRC or other privileges. Political decision makers concluding deals with the Chinese may take into account side benefits of those agreements, such as bonuses or business opportunities for family or friends.

Finally, the expansion of Chinese soft power arguably coexists with a persistent lack of understanding of, and substantial mistrust for the Chinese (Le Corre et al., 2015). In an October 2018 poll, only minorities in three key Latin American countries surveyed (Mexico, Brazil and Argentina) had favorable opinions toward the PRC (Devlin, 2018). Far more than when dealing with the United States, the calculus of political and corporate decision makers in Latin America includes an understanding that the PRC will aggressively, and sometimes unfairly, seek advantage in their dealings, including cutting corners on contracts, attempting to steal intellectual property and other bad behavior. The choice to engage with the Chinese almost invariably reflects a calculation by the decision maker (whether or not justified) that they can manage the risk while securing personal or collective benefit from the engagement.

The United States, for its part, has enabled the expansion of Chinese soft power in the region, initially through its relative indifference, and most recently, by alienating the region.

Prior to the US administration of Donald Trump, the relative lack of political emphasis on the region by the US government, and limited investment by US-based companies, allowed Chinese influence to expand despite the mistrust of the PRC. Most recently, rhetoric and actions from Washington, including degrading references to the countries of the region (Watkins and Phillip, 2018), and policies to end Temporary Protected Status (TPS) and deferred immigration actions (e.g., DACA) for immigrants from the region contribute to a perception of the United States as hostile toward the people of Latin America, and indifferent toward regional challenges (Holmes, 2018). Such negative perceptions of the United States, in turn, help to take a lack of trust toward China off the table as a factor mitigating the effect of Chinese soft power.

Evolution of PRC soft power

The balance of this chapter examines the ways in which Chinese soft power in Latin America and the Caribbean, and its application, has evolved over the last decade, with an emphasis on the expansion of the Chinese corporate presence, cultural activities and shifting patterns of Chinese government engagement in general.

Expanding effect of Chinese companies on the ground

The most significant driver in the growth of Chinese soft power in Latin America and the Caribbean is the expanding presence of PRC-based companies in the region, combined with their increasing effectiveness as local actors.

The initial growth of Chinese soft power in the region in the early 2000s was driven principally by the lure of the PRC as a potential market for the region's exports, and as a source for loans.[2] From the year prior to China's 2001 ascension into the World Trade Organization through 2017, PRC trade with Latin America and the Caribbean grew exponentially from $12.0 billion to $278 billion (Direction of Trade Statistics, 2018), catapulting the PRC from a relatively insignificant player, to the first or second trade partner for many Latin American countries, although most PRC imports from the region were relatively low value–added commodities (Jenkins, 2015). Similarly, from 2005 through 2017, China's two major policy banks (China Development Bank and China Export-Import Bank) loaned an estimated $150 billion to the region, far more than Western institutions such as the World Bank and International Monetary Fund (China-Latin America Finance Database, 2018). While such flows were a significant motivator for politicians and businessmen in the region to court the PRC (Ellis, 2011b, 2014a), or avoid offending it (Stone Fish, 2018), the expanding trade and loans contrasted with the relative absence of Chinese equity investment in the region, and the associated activities of PRC-based companies there.

The relative lack of investment by PRC-based firms in the region began to change in 2009 as a product of multiple factors, including the expansion of Chinese demand, the maturation of PRC-based companies, the growth of supporting legal and financial infrastructure and the Global Financial Crisis of 2008–2009, which created a financial liquidity crisis and associated opportunities for Chinese companies to acquire billions of dollars' worth of new assets in the region through mergers and acquisitions, buying from Western entities who needed the cash and competing with those which didn't have it (Ellis, 2014c). Multi-billion-dollar deals such the $3.1 billion acquisition of Bridas in May 2010, Occidental Petroleum (October 2010), the $3.1 billion purchase of the Peregrino field in Brazil in May 2010 and the $7.1 billion purchase of Statoil's holdings in Brazil by Repsol in the petroleum sector five months later were but a few major examples (Ellis, 2014c).

By 2017, Chinese firms had invested almost $114 billion in the region through mergers and acquisitions, greenfield projects and other activities (Dussel and Ortiz, 2017), giving them important new opportunities for leverage as employers, generators of tax revenues and partners to local governments. Brazil was the focus of almost half of that new investment, an estimated $55 billion in the decade ending in 2017 ("Chinese companies," 2018), including a broad range of sectors from petroleum and mining to agriculture, to medical goods, technology, and non-traditional finance, and expanding into construction and logistics with the collapse of Brazil's national champion in the sector, Odebrecht (Ellis, 2017).

The new PRC commercial presence was associated with many difficulties, including conflicts with workers ("Strike at Shougang . . . ," 2018) and local communities ("Protesta contra . . . ," 2015). Similarly, while PRC companies have often been less engaged than their Western counterparts in local communities and business circles (Ellis, 2013), that has changed in recent years, as they have gained more experience and confidence as local actors.

While there are important differences in the sophistication and level of engagement of the Chinese, based on the nature of their business, and even among different companies in the same sector, and with Chinese businesses doing better in areas such as telecommunications and autos where they have built a presence gradually with local partners (Ellis, 2014c), the sophistication of Chinese companies has generally increased, expanding their influence as local actors, magnifying the effect of the expanding dollar value of that presence. Such improvements have included PRC companies making better choices of local consultants and partners, management of contractors and the integration of Chinese managers and technical personnel with local workforces. They also include greater sophistication by companies in outreach to and integration with the local community, such as the successful negotiation by the mining firm China Aluminum Corporation (CHINALCO) to convince 5,000 residents of the mining community Morococha to relocate their entire town from its location on top of a copper-rich mountain that the company planned to strip mine (Poulden, 2013). It also includes sponsorship by the telecommunications firm Huawei of local soccer teams in Colombia ("Huawei . . . ," 2015), Brazil ("China's Huawei . . . ," 2014), Panama ("Huawei to sponsor . . . ," 2015) and elsewhere ("Making connections . . . ," 2015).

PRC-based companies also are increasingly effective not only in participating in formal bidding processes, but also in wooing Latin American decision makers to win contracts in competitive circumstances, particularly in streamlined acquisition processes, such as public–private partnerships, both an expression of their growing soft power, and something which expands it through the increasing effectiveness and weight of Chinese companies as a part of the local community.

The award by Colombia's government to China Harbour to construct a road under the 4th Generation Highway program is one example of such self-reinforcing soft power success (Ramirez, 2015). Chinese firms have also made gains in investment projects funded with their own equity capital, such as the $4.2 billion Baha Mar resort in the Caribbean, whose local partner Sarkis Izmirlian was forced out in complex bankruptcy proceedings in a Hong Kong court (Hartnell, 2018), and the $600 million North–South highway in Jamaica, where China Harbour used their own capital to fund the project, in exchange for a 99-year lease on 1,200 acres of real estate from the Jamaican government, on which the Chinese company will build luxury hotels (Laville, 2015).

Cultural power

While experience in China and affinity with the Chinese language and culture is not the most important driver of Chinese soft power in the region, as noted previously, it is nevertheless rooted in China's historical self-concept of how to transform potential rivals and others into collaborators. This is something in which the Chinese government invests considerable resources. The use of such cultural and people-to-people diplomacy is explicitly spelled out in the PRC November 2008 ("China's Policy Paper . . . ," 2008) and November 2016 ("Full text . . . ," 2016) white papers, which describe the nation's intentions toward Latin America and the Caribbean.

With respect to educational activities in the region, Hanban now has 39 Confucius Institutes, plus 18 Confucius Classrooms in Latin America and the Caribbean, for the teaching and promoting of Chinese language and culture through officially sanctioned instructors ("Confucius Institute . . . ," 2018). There has not been, however, much pushback against the Confucius Institutes in Latin America as there has been in some parts of the United States (Dodwell, 2018).

Perhaps more important, in the 2019–2021 China–CELAC plan for the region, the Chinese government has committed to almost 6,000 scholarships for students, journalists, academics and others to study in the PRC at the undergraduate and graduate levels, as well as paid trips to the region by 1,000 Latin American and Caribbean leaders ("China to offer . . . ," 2014), with 200 members of the region's leading political parties to be hosted in China between 2019 and 2021 ("CELAC and China . . . ," 2018), in a manner similar to what the Chinese are doing in Africa. Such exchanges are particularly important in shaping the region's orientation toward China over the long term. By rolling out the red carpet for funded trips for current and future Latin American leaders and influencers in the PRC, China garners the goodwill of the region's senior decision makers, as well as arguably opening up potential opportunities for Chinese intelligence services to compromise them for later influence or intelligence collection operations.

With respect to scholarships for Latin American and Caribbean students, because learning the Mandarin language and Chinese character set is a relatively difficult undertaking, engagement in this area represents a long-term bond that these young individuals are entering into with their Chinese patrons, and one which positions those individuals for future positions of responsibility with their governments and industry in dealing with China. This PRC investment is aimed at gaining the goodwill of key future leaders in the region, who will be able to speak with authority regarding the PRC and China's internal affairs. Indeed, many of the young technical staff supporting governments in Central America and the Caribbean which have recently recognized the PRC gained their experience (and associated gratitude) while studying in the PRC.

With respect to journalists, the gratitude and positive image of China and its government that the PRC is inculcating through its scholarships is likely to persuade a portion of those journalists to cover the PRC in a more positive, understanding way, or at least avoid expressing their concerns about China in an excessively harsh fashion, in the interest of not being ungrateful to their benefactors ("China 'Buying positive . . .'," 2018).

Yet beyond the persons in the region covering China in the news, the PRC is also influencing news coverage of China in the region in other subtle ways, such as providing free or discounted feeds from its news service to news outlets in the region which, by their nature emphasize positive stories and present them through positive images of China's leaders and the PRC itself ("China state broadcaster . . . ," 2016), as it has also done in other parts of the world.

PRC government engagement

Beyond the activities of its companies and the low-key work of its cultural diplomacy, Beijing's increasingly bold pursuit and advocacy of its interests in Latin America and elsewhere is a factor in both expanding and leveraging its soft power.

With the expansion of PRC wealth and power, and the confidence of China's new generation of leadership, the nation is far less deferential to the United States in pursuing its interests in Latin America and the Caribbean than it was just a decade ago. In addition to the active diplomacy of President Xi with four multicountry trips to the region since assuming the Chinese presidency in March

2013, the PRC has expanded its official engagement through both bilateral and multilateral vehicles.

Exercising soft power through multilateral engagement, China has designated nine countries in the region as "strategic partners" (Argentina, Brazil, Mexico, Venezuela, Chile, Ecuador, Bolivia, Peru and Uruguay), a status which generally comes with at least once-a-year meetings at the ministerial level to review the status of and advance economic programs (and sometimes political cooperation) (Xu, 2017). Reflecting the compelling power of expected benefits, not even Chile, with its strong institutions and generally conservative pro-West stance, had a serious public debate before binding itself to the Communist government of China through fundamentally the same "Comprehensive Strategic Partnership" vehicle for economic and political coordination that ties the PRC with the populist socialist regimes in Venezuela and Bolivia ("Spotlight . . . ," 2016).

At the multilateral level, the PRC has chosen to work through the CELAC forum (a body representing all nations of Latin America and the Caribbean, but lacking a permanent secretariat), as its vehicle of choice for advancing its roadmap for deepening its relationship with the region (Ellis, 2015). By contrast to the Organization of American States, at which the PRC has been an active participant-observer since 2004, CELAC's lack of a permanent secretariat has made it ideal for the PRC to present its concept for gifts to and projects with the region, in a fashion in which the region cannot effectively present a countering "collective position" regarding what it wants from China.

While the attraction of Chinese imports, loans and investments are important to explaining the region's attraction with China, the explicit coordination between the Chinese government, its companies and financial institutions is critical in understanding how the PRC systematically develops, consolidates and exploits that influence across the region. In particular, the Chinese government plays a critical role in transforming the diffuse array of potential deals and interests in working with the PRC across economic sectors and other areas (including the military, security and diplomatic engagement) into a series of Memorandums of Understanding (MOUs) and agreements which formalize and facilitate the achievement of those deals.[3] The previously noted entry of Chinese companies into the country which that infrastructure enables, in combination with coordinating activities by both the companies and the government, in turn expands the leverage of the Chinese government team.

For the Chinese government, participation in the Belt and Road Initiative (BRI), established by President Xi Jinping's government in 2013, and its explicit extension to Latin America in 2018, has been an important component of marketing engagement with the PRC on terms beneficial to Chinese economic and strategic interests, as well creating the structures for doing so. The BRI, growing out of the legacy of the wealth brought to China through its connection to the heart of Western civilization via the Silk Road, reflects the underlying, historically well-rooted concept of structuring trade between the China as the "Middle Kingdom" and the surrounding nations of what were once considered the barbarian periphery, to ensure a flow of value to the imperial center.[4]

In Latin America and the Caribbean, as an illustration of soft power, the attraction of the concept to so many governments of the region has contributed strongly to the desire to link themselves to China as the presumed source of wealth and development; indeed, seven states have signed up to participate in BRI, although the region is not technically connected to the PRC in the actual maps of the belt and road, and many of the new Latin American signatories such as Uruguay, Guyana, Suriname, and Trinidad and Tobago, are not even on the Pacific side of the continent. Given that Latin America and the Caribbean have long lamented the need for greater interconnectivity among states of the region to facilitate development, a handful of dissenting scholars have noted that the BRI seems less about connecting the region together for its own development, than tying it to China for the latter's resource needs. As one scholar put it, "the BRI is owned by China and is for China" ("The belt . . . ," 2018), yet Latin American and Caribbean states continue cueing up to be part of the project.

For the states joining, the enthusiasm to participate in BRI reflects the compelling nature of the promise to hook themselves economically and politically into a particular set of economic and infrastructural relationships with the PRC, whose opportunity costs in terms of other infrastructural and other relationships are not clear. Moreover, that enthusiasm seems unabated by indications that the cost of doing so is accepting certain conditions, giving PRC-based companies privileged consideration in operating the ports on their sovereign territory, building the roads and railroads, and operating the mines, oilfields and other commercial operations for transferring resources out of their nations to the PRC at the lowest possible value-added point.

Beyond the impulse of nations in the region to commit themselves to the neo-mercantilist BRI, as noted previously, China's soft power in the region is highlighted by the willingness of nations of the region to rapidly switch diplomatic relations to the PRC once Beijing decided to resume the diplomatic struggle with Taiwan. At the same time, the building of those new relationships, which have an economic component through the signing of MOUs and the entry of Chinese companies and financial entities, serves to consolidate and expand that power.

With respect to the dynamics of the "war for diplomatic recognition" of the nine states in the region still maintaining relations with Taiwan, the relatively strong US diplomatic reaction to the surprise change in recognition by El Salvador, coming in the wake of similar surprises from the Dominican Republic and Panama (Ellis, 2018b), appear to have given some of the countries of the region pause in establishing relations with the PRC, yet important questions remain about the intentions of most that continue to recognize Taiwan, particularly Haiti and the three small Caribbean states in the Lesser Antilles that still recognize Taiwan, and possibly Honduras (Ellis, 2018b).

The question of PRC hard power

The detailed discussion of PRC soft power in the preceding sections of this chapter does not imply that the PRC has a lack of relevant military and other hard power assets, but rather, that for both cultural reasons, and due to changes in the global environment, China finds it in its interest to rely more on its soft power to achieve its commercial and other strategic objectives in Latin America.

At present, PRC influence in Latin America and the Caribbean is arguably far greater than that of the Soviet Union at the height of its power during the Cold War, despite the latter's alliances with client states such as Cuba and Nicaragua and attempts to overthrow pro-US regimes, such as that in El Salvador, Guatemala and the Dominican Republic (among others) through proxy wars and political movements.

The difference between those actions by the Soviet Union, which received substantial attention from Washington, versus the present Chinese behavior, which has downplayed its military component, reflect differences in PRC strategic goals, as well as the greater level of global interdependence between the PRC, its principal geopolitical rival the United States and the rest of the world.

Because the PRC principally seeks to order global value added in a way that provides benefits, rather than impose a global political order, it is more interested in the region's compliance with flows that serve its interests, than regimes which formally serve and ally themselves with Beijing. In this framework, so long as the United States does not directly threaten China and its interests militarily, the PRC's dependence on the United States as a market, financial partner and source of technology gives it compelling strategic interests to avoid establishing military bases and exclusive alliance agreements in the region that would alarm the United States (even beyond the significant tension seen in the current trade dispute) (Godbole, 2018), and could oblige a response by other actors, without advancing specific Chinese interests.

Ironically, the greatest contribution of PRC military capabilities to its position in Latin America is the promotion of Chinese *soft* power in the region. Specifically, the growing size and capabilities of the People's Liberation Army (PLA), including long-range hypersonic missiles such as the DF-21D, capable of putting US carriers and other surface ships at risk (Shimm, 2018), may help to convince those Latin American states less than enthusiastic about US geopolitical dominance, that Washington, in the foreseeable future, may cease to be the world's unquestionably supreme military power, or at least, that the United States is unquestionably capable of prevailing in a conflict against the PRC in its own back yard. Such shifting calculations, in turn, may convince a critical handful of anti-US regimes that they can safely cooperate against the PRC, and possibly even against the United States, particularly in time of a global conflict, if that conflict does not appear to be going in America's favor.

While the Chinese military is a vehicle for soft power as well as hard power, not all Chinese non-military capabilities are soft power. If, as the National Endowment for Democracy (2017) suggests, the alternative to soft power is coercive power, then the PRC does clearly use its economic and other national instruments to coerce Latin American states into doing its will (even while often allowing them to save face while doing so). One very public example occurred in 2010, when the Chinese government cut soy oil purchases from Argentina, valued at $2 billion per year, presumably to punish the South American nation for applying protectionist measures against Chinese products. While less explicit than the US style of imposing "sanctions" on errant regimes such as Iran and Venezuela, the Chinese economic pressure eventually obliged Argentina's President Christina Fernandez de Kirchner to re-program a canceled trip to the PRC, and without ever admitting a quid pro quo, agreed to purchase more than $10 billion in Chinese products and services in exchange for the restoration of soy oil purchases (Ellis, 2014b).

Conclusion

China's substantial and growing soft power is fundamental to understand the appeal of the PRC, and accurately assess its prospects for success as it engages with the nations of Latin America and the Caribbean. The evolution of that power and China's application of it in Latin America, suggests the need for adjustments by those who seek to understand the dynamics of Chinese engagement in the region, as well as those seeking to devise appropriate strategies to insulate democratic and free market institutions in the region from some of its more corrosive effects.

For students of political science and international relations, the concept of soft power applied in this chapter suggests the importance of a broad definition centered not on the vehicles for that influence (such as culture), but on its character, with the influenced seeing alignment with the goals of the influencer as within his/her own interests, or arising out of an internalized system of values compatible with that of the influencer.

With respect to assessing the level of Chinese soft power in the Americas specifically, and the effect of that soft power on outcomes, it is important to recognize that PRC soft power is more reliant than its US counterpart (but not exclusively so) on an expectation of benefits, and somewhat less reliant on value alignment and cultural appeal.

Adequately measuring PRC influence also requires recognition that Chinese soft power in the region is a function of perception, and where the nation may be going in the future relative to the United States and other nations, rather than merely a function of actual levels of PRC benefits or engagement.

Finally, Chinese soft power in the region does not exist in isolation, or in competition with that of the United States, but in a multidimensional space with a myriad of other actors from the European Union, Great Britain and Canada, to India, Japan, Korea and Australia, to states in the Middle East and Africa, among others. While the PRC arguably occupies an inordinate amount of the region's attention, those developing strategies to protect the region's institutions and democracy in the face of commercial and other temptations from the PRC should consider the possible contributions of those other actors, not only as alternative commercial partners, but also as sources of norms, pressures and incentives.

Through all mechanisms by which it operates, it is also clear that Chinese soft power is having a transformative effect on Latin America and the Caribbean, its dynamics and institutions, and the strategic position of the United States within the region. That transformation will be critical, not only for those who live in, and study the region, but also to the United States, which not only finds itself in a global competition with the PRC of expanding intensity, but which is inseparably connected to Latin America by ties of geography, commerce and family.

Notes

1 The author is Latin America research professor with the U.S. Army War College Strategic Studies Institute. The views expressed in this work are strictly his own.
2 One of the best-known early analyses by Latin American scholars regarding the potential impact is Rodriguez, Blazquez and Santiso (2006).
3 As an example, the PRC and Panama signed a total of 47 MOUs in the brief 16-month period from establishing diplomatic relations in June 2017 to President Xi's December 2018 state visit to the country in areas from visas to extradition to port construction and the funding of electricity infrastructure projects (Li, 2018).
4 Indeed, President Xi Jinping's 2013 Belt and Road Initiative was first referred to as the "New Silk Road" (see "A new Silk Road?" 2018).

References

"Another U.S. Deficit: China and America: Public Diplomacy in the Age of the Internet," 2011. Minority Staff Report. Prepared for the Committee on Foreign Relations. United States Senate. 112th Congress. First Session. February 15. www.gpo. gov/fdsys/pkg/CPRT-112SPRT64768/html/CPRT-112SPRT64768.htm.

Barker, Thomas. 2018. "The Real Source of China's Soft Power," *The Diplomat*, November 18. https://thediplomat.com/2017/11/the-real-source-of-chinas-soft-power/.

"The Belt and Road Initiative," 2018. *Kaieteur News*, August 5. www.kaieteurnewsonline. com/2018/08/05/the-belt-and-road-initiative/.

"Bolivian Elected President Woos China," 2006. *MercoPress*, January 8. http://en.mercopress. com/2006/01/08/bolivian-elected-president-woos-china/.

Casas-Zamora, Kevin. 2009. "Notes on Costa Rica's Switch from Taipei to Beijing," *Brookings*, November 6. www.brookings.edu/on-the-record/notes-on-costa-ricas-switch-from-taipei-to-beijing/.

"CELAC and China Joint Plan of Action for Cooperation on Priority Areas (2019–2021)," 2018. Ministry of Foreign Affairs of Brazil, December 10. www.itamaraty. gov.br/images/2ForoCelacChina/Joint-Action-Plan-II-CELAC-China-Forum-FV-22-01-18.pdf.

"China 'Buying' Positive News Coverage from Foreign Journalists: Report," 2018. *Radio Free Asia*, November 27. www.rfa.org/english/news/china/china-buying-positive-news-coverage-11272018114512.html.

"China-Latin America Finance Database," 2011. *Interamerican Dialogue*. www.thedialogue. org/map_list/.

"China State Broadcaster Rebrands in International Push," 2016. *CNBC*, December 31. www.cnbc.com/2016/12/31/china-state-broadcaster-rebrands-in-international-push.html.

"China to Offer LatAm 6,000 Scholarships within Five Years," 2014. *Sina English*, July 18. http://english.sina.com/china/2014/0718/719642.html.

"China's Huawei Signs Santos Sponsorship Deal," 2014. *China Daily*, October 29. http://usa.chinadaily.com.cn/business/2014-10/29/content_18820058.htm.

"China's Influence in the Western Hemisphere," 2005. Hearing before the Subcommittee on the Western Hemisphere of the Committee on International Relations. House of Representatives. One Hundred Ninth Congress. First Session. April 6. www.webharvest.gov/congress109th/20061114104954/www.internationalrelations.house.gov/archives/109/20404.pdf.

"China's Policy Paper on Latin America and the Caribbean (Full Text)," 2008. Government of the People's Republic of China, November 5. www.gov.cn/english/official/2008-11/05/content_1140347.htm.

"Chinese Companies Invest US$55 Billion in Brazil over 10 Years," 2018. *MacauHub*, December 11. https://macauhub.com.mo/2018/12/11/pt-empresas-da-china-investem-55-mil-milhoes-de-dolares-em-10-anos-no-brasil/.

"Confucius Institute/Classroom," 2018. *Hanban*. http://english.hanban.org/node_10971.htm.

Devlin, Kat. 2018. "5 Charts on Global Views of China," *Pew Research Center*, October 9. www.pewresearch.org/fact-tank/2018/10/19/5-charts-on-global-views-of-china/.

"Direction of Trade Statistics," 2018. *International Monetary Fund*. http://data.imf.org/?sk=9D6028D4-F14A-464C-A2F2-59B2CD424B85&sId=1409151240976.

Dodwell, David. 2018. "US Politicians Linking Confucius Institutes with Espionage Is Taking Paranoia to the Extreme," *South China Morning Post*, September 18. www.scmp.com/business/article/2160362/us-politicians-linking-confucius-institutes-espionage-taking-paranoia.

Dussel Peters, Enrique and Samuel Ortiz Velásquez. 2017. "Monitor of China's OFDI in Latin America and the Caribbean (2001–2016)," *Red ALC-China*, June 5. www.redalc-china.org/monitor/images/pdfs/menuprincipal/DusselPeters_OrtizVelasquez_2017_MonitorOFDIchinaALC_English.pdf.

Eades, Mark C. 2014. "Soft Power, America vs. China: America Still Wins," *Foreign Policy Association*, January 22. https://foreignpolicyblogs.com/2014/01/22/soft-power-america-vs-china-america-still-wins-2/.

Ellis, R. Evan. 2011a. "China: Latin America Military Engagement," Carlisle Barracks, PA: U.S. Army War College Strategic Studies Institute, August. https://ssi.armywarcollege.edu/pubs/display.cfm?pubID=1077.

Ellis, R. Evan. 2011b. "Chinese Soft Power in Latin America: A Case Study," *Joint Forces Quarterly* 60(1st Quarter), pp. 85–91.

Ellis, R. Evan. 2013. "China, S.A. como empresa local en América Latina," *Temas de Reflexión* 7. www.eafit.edu.co/centrodepensamientoestrategico.

Ellis, R. Evan. 2014a. "A Hard Look at China's Soft Power in Latin America," in Andrew Scobell and Marylena Mantas (eds.), *China's Great Leap Outward: Hard and Soft Dimensions of a Rising Power*. New York: The Academy of Political Science, pp. 175–194.

Ellis, R. Evan. 2014b. "Chinese 'Face' and Soft Power in Argentina," *The Manzella Report*, January 1. www.manzellareport.com/index.php/world/792-chinese-face-and-soft-power-in-argentina.

Ellis, R. Evan. 2014c. *China on the Ground in Latin America: Challenges for the Chinese and Impacts on the Region*. New York: Palgrave-Macmillan.

Ellis, R. Evan. 2015. "The China-CELAC Summit: Opening a New Phase in China-Latin America-U.S. Relations?," *The Manzella Report*, January 13. www.manzellareport.

com/index.php/world/945-the-china-celac-summit-opening-a-new-phase-in-china-latin-america-u-s-relations.

Ellis, R. Evan. 2017. "Washington Should Take Note of Chinese Commercial Advances in Brazil," *Newsmax*, October 9. www.newsmax.com/EvanEllis/china-brazil-investment-washington-dc/2017/10/09/id/818644/.

Ellis, R. Evan. 2018a. "El Salvador Recognizes the PRC: Confrontation on the FMLN's Way 'Out the Door'," *Global Americans*, August 22. https://theglobalamericans. org/2018/08/el-salvador-recognizes-the-prc-confrontation-on-the-fmlns-way-out-the-door/.

Ellis, R. Evan. 2018b. "Taiwan's Struggle for Partners and Survival," *Global Americans*, December 7. https://theglobalamericans.org/2018/12/taiwans-struggle-for-partners-and-survival/.

Fleischman, Luis. 2018. "China's Soft Economic Power Grows in Latin America but U.S. Can Play a More Important Card," *Center for Security Policy*, September 7. www.center forsecuritypolicy.org/2018/09/07/chinas-soft-economic-power-grows-in-latin-america-but-u-s-can-play-a-more-important-card/.

"Full text of China's Policy Paper on Latin America and the Caribbean," 2016. *Xinhua*, November 24. http://en.people.cn/n3/2016/1124/c90000-9146474.html.

Gao, George. 2017. "Why Is China So . . . Uncool?," *Foreign Policy*, March 18. https:// foreignpolicy.com/2017/03/08/why-is-china-so-uncool-soft-power-beijing-censorship-generation-gap/.

Godbole, Shruti. 2018. "Implications of the US-China Trade Dispute," *Brookings*, September 4. www.brookings.edu/blog/up-front/2018/09/04/implications-of-the-us-china-trade-dispute/.

Hartnell, Neil. 2018. "Cca Slams 'Implausible' $2.25bn Sarkis Lawsuit," *Tribune242*, May 1. www.tribune242.com/news/2018/may/01/cca-slams-implausible-225bn-sarkis-lawsuit/.

Holmes, Nate. 2018. "Trump's First Year: Everyone Hates Us Now," *Esquire*, January 18. www.esquire.com/news-politics/a15367684/trump-world-leadership-gallup-poll/.

"Huawei, nuevo patrocinador del Santa Fe," 2015. *Portafolio*, December 4. www.portafolio. co/negocios/empresas/huawei-nuevo-patrocinador-santa-fe-28302.

"Huawei to Sponsor Football National Teams of Panama," 2015. *Xinhua*, March 25. www.xinhuanet.com/english/photo/2015-03/25/c_134096198.htm.

"Hu Hails Friendship with All Latin America," 2004. *China Daily*, November 14. www. chinadaily.com.cn/english/doc/2004-11/14/content_391329.htm.

Isenberg, David. 2008. "A Hard Look at China's Soft Power," *CATO Institute*, May 15. www.cato.org/publications/commentary/hard-look-chinas-soft-power.

Jenkins, Rhys. 2015. "Is Chinese Competition Causing Deindustrialization in Brazil?," *Latin American Perspectives* 42(6), pp. 42–63.

Johnson, Courtney. 2018. "Fewer People in Latin America See the U.S. Favorably Under Trump," *Pew Research Center*, April 12. www.pewglobal.org/2018/04/12/fewer-people-in-latin-america-see-the-u-s-favorably-under-trump/.

Laville, Sandra 2015. "Beijing Highway: $600m Road Just the Start of China's Investments in Caribbean," *The Guardian*, December 24. www.theguardian.com/world/2015/ dec/24/beijing-highway-600m-road-just-the-start-of-chinas-investments-in-caribbean.

Le Corre, Philippe, Yun Sun, Amadou Sy and Harold Trinkunas. 2015. "Other Perceptions of China: Views from Africa, Latin America, and Europe," *Brookings*, May 27. www. brookings.edu/blog/order-from-chaos/2015/05/27/other-perceptions-of-china-views-from-africa-latin-america-and-europe/.

Li, Weida. 2018. "China and Panama Sign String of Deals during Xi's First State Visit," *Global Times*, December 4. https://gbtimes.com/china-and-panama-sign-string-of-deals-during-xis-first-state-visit.

Liu, Charles. 2016. "China Ranks Last in Soft Power, Despite Spending Billions to Buy It," *The Nanfang*, May 12. https://thenanfang.com/despite-billions-spent-china-ranks-dead-last-world-soft-power/.

"Making Connections: Why Huawei Is Investing Big Money in Soccer," 2015. *Soccerex*, June 22. www.soccerex.com/insight/articles/2015/making-connections-why-huawei-is-investing-big-money-in-soccer.

National Endowment for Democracy. 2017. *Sharp Power: Rising Authoritarian Influence*. Washington, DC. www.ned.org/wp-content/uploads/2017/12/Sharp-Power-Rising-Authoritarian-Influence-Full-Report.pdf.

"A New Silk Road?," 2018. *The New Yorker*, January 8. www.newyorker.com/magazine/2018/01/08/a-new-silk-road.

Nye, Joseph S., Jr. 1990. "Soft Power," *Foreign Policy*, 80, pp. 153–171.

Nye, Joseph S., Jr. 2004. *The Means to Success in World Politics*. New York: Public Affairs.

Nye, Joseph S., Jr. 2012. "Why China Is Weak on Soft Power," *The New York Times*, January 17. www.nytimes.com/2012/01/18/opinion/why-china-is-weak-on-soft-power.html.

"Panama Asks US to 'Respect' Taiwan Snub," 2018. *The Straits Times*, September 10. www.straitstimes.com/world/americas/panama-asks-us-to-respect-taiwan-snub.

Piccone, Ted. 2016. "The Geopolitics of China's Rise in Latin America," *Brookings*, November. www.brookings.edu/wp-content/uploads/2016/11/the-geopolitics-of-chinas-rise-in-latin-america_ted-piccone.pdf.

Poo, Mu-chou Poo. 2005. *Enemies of Civilization: Attitudes toward Foreigners in Ancient Mesopotamia, Egypt, and China*. New York: SUNY Press.

Poulden, Gervase. 2013. "Morococha: The Peruvian Town the Chinese Relocated," *China Dialogue*, April 15. www.chinadialogue.net/article/show/single/en/5898-Morococha-the-Peruvian-town-the-Chinese-relocated.

"Protesta contra la explotación minera frente a embajada de China," 2015. *Ecuavisa*, July 14. www.ecuavisa.com/articulo/noticias/politica/113731-protesta-contra-explotacion-minera-frente-embajada-china.

Rajagopalan, Megha. 2015. "China's Xi Woos Latin America with $250 Billion Investments," *Reuters*, January 7. www.reuters.com/article/us-china-latam/chinas-xi-woos-latin-america-with-250-billion-investments-idUSKBN0KH06Q20150108.

Ramirez, Noah. 2015. "ANI Awards 4G Highway Concession to Chinese-Colombian Consortium," *BNAmericas*, September 23. www.bnamericas.com/en/news/infrastructure/ani-awards-4g-highway-concession-to-chinese-colombian-consortium1.

Rines, Samuel. 2016. "These 5 Countries Will Dominate the Global Economy in 2030," *The National Interest*, June 25. https://nationalinterest.org/feature/these-5-countries-will-dominate-the-global-economy-2030-16724.

Rodriguez, Javier, Jorge Blazquez and Javier Santiso. 2006. "Angel or Devil: China's Trade Impact on Latin American Emerging Markets," *CEPAL Review* 90, pp. 15–41.

Shimm, Elizabeth. 2018. "China Says That It Has Perfected 'Aircraft Carrier Missile'," *UPI*, October 17. www.upi.com/Top_News/World-News/2018/10/17/Chinese-firm-says-it-has-perfected-aircraft-carrier-killer-missile/4131539793409/.

"Spotlight: China, Chile Lift Ties to Comprehensive Strategic Partnership," 2016. *Xinhua*, November 23. www.xinhuanet.com/english/2016-11/23/c_135853001.htm.

Stone Fish, Isaac. 2018. "Why Are America's Elite Universities Censoring Themselves on China?," *The New Republic*, September 4. https://newrepublic.com/article/150476/american-elite-universities-selfcensorship-china.

"Strike at Shougang's Iron Ore Mine in Peru Halts Exports-Manager," 2018. *Reuters*, October 22. www.reuters.com/article/peru-shougangiron-ore-strike-idUSL2N1X20X1.

Volodzko, David. 2015. "China's Confucius Institutes and the Soft War," *The Diplomat*, July 18. https://thediplomat.com/2015/07/chinas-confucius-institutes-and-the-soft-war/.

Watkins, Eli and Abby Phillip. 2018. "Trump Decries Immigrants from 'Shithole Countries' Coming to US," *CNN*, January 12. www.cnn.com/2018/01/11/politics/immigrants-shithole-countries-trump/index.html.

Xu, Yanran. 2017. *China's Strategic Partnerships in Latin America*. Lanham, MD: Lexington Books.

10

THE SINO–AFRICAN RELATIONSHIP

An intense and long embrace

Antonio Fiori and Stanley Rosen[1]

A recent cover story in *The Economist* highlighted what the author called "The New Scramble for Africa," and noted that the continent "will increasingly be a place where international rivalries play out" (Economist, 2019a). In comparing the investment of effort from different nations in Africa, China stood out and, indeed, China's success in Africa has already had the demonstration effect of stimulating the interest of other aspirants. For example, between 2010 and 2016, more than 320 embassies or consulates were opened in Africa, although China still leads the pack with 52. In terms of trading partners with sub-Saharan Africa, the European Union still leads with $156 billion in total merchandise trade, followed by China with $120 billion. However, while the EU showed an increase in trade of 41% from 2006–2018, China's increase was 226%. Over that same period trade between Africa and the United States *declined* by 45%, down to $36 billion, falling behind India into fourth place (Economist, 2019a). Continuing the contrast in engagement with Africa between the world's two superpowers, in the decade up to 2018, China's top officials made 79 visits to Africa; President Trump has never been there and has been overheard making disparaging comments about the continent. The 2018 Forum on China–Africa Co-operation (FOCAC) in Beijing, the origins of which are mentioned below, attracted more African leaders than the annual meeting of the UN General Assembly.

Perhaps more so than virtually anywhere else, at least in soft power terms, Africa has become a key battleground between China and the United States. In a recent speech at the Heritage Foundation, US National Security Adviser John Bolton laid out the new American strategy for Africa and contrasted it with China's policies, which he asserted "uses bribes, opaque agreements, and the strategic use of debt to hold states in Africa captive to Beijing's wishes and demands," further noting that China's "investment ventures are riddled with corruption, and do not meet the same environmental or ethical standards as US developmental programs." As with the One Belt, One Road strategic initiative, the United States views China's aims in Africa as part of their "ultimate goal of advancing Chinese global dominance" (National Security Council, 2018). However, what was most striking about Bolton's comments was his focus on US, not African, priorities, clearly stating that "every decision we make, every policy we pursue, and every dollar of aid we spend will further US priorities in the region." Thus, he highlighted countering the terrorist threat and eliminating "indiscriminate assistance across the entire continent," particularly noting that the United States would "no longer support unproductive, unsuccessful, and unaccountable U.N. peacekeeping missions." Not coincidentally, as will be discussed below, China is the biggest contributor to peacekeeping of the five permanent members of the Security Council, with as many as 80% of their troops stationed in Africa, contributing to China's positive image on the continent.

It is helpful to contrast Bolton's "America First" focus with China's self-assessment of its African initiatives. One intriguing way to do that is to examine how Africa appears in Chinese popular culture which is marketed primarily, but not exclusively, for China's domestic market. Most striking in this regard is the film *Wolf Warrior 2*, which in 2017 made over $850 million at the box office in China, far more than any other film ever marketed there. The film deals with China's efforts to evacuate its citizens from a war zone plagued by a deadly virus in an unnamed African nation, and shows China's efforts to improve public health in that country. In a scene which is clearly intended to generate domestic public support for Chinese investment in Africa, a Chinese convoy, seeking to evacuate not only Chinese but also endangered African citizens, has to pass through a battle zone contested by both sides in a civil war. Once the rival armies see the Chinese flag, they stop fighting, yelling out approvingly, "It's the Chinese, let them through," and the convoy is allowed to pass. By contrast, the Americans and other foreigners have already departed without offering any help, and the Chinese have to defeat a Western mercenary army, headed by an American, before they can succeed. This reflects the Chinese message, again in contrast to Bolton's presentation of the new American strategy that offers help only to those countries which are serving American interests, that China takes no sides in Africa, and will support policies that will benefit all Africans.

Because they "take no sides" and support whichever government is in office, no matter how dictatorial, China has often been accused of ignoring the *people* of Africa, so it is instructive to examine China's image in public opinion polls. Gallup has noted that all the major global powers earn their highest ratings in Africa, and in their most recent survey, the median approval rating of Chinese leadership was 53%, one percentage point higher than the United States, compared to Chinese approval ratings of 34% in Asia, 30% in the Americas and 28% in Europe (Reinhart and Ritter, 2019). The most recent Afrobarometer poll of 36 countries found that 63% of Africans had a "somewhat" or "very" positive view of Chinese influence, 56% saw China's development assistance as doing a "somewhat" or "very" good job of meeting their country's needs and 24% cited China as the most popular model for national development (behind the 30% who chose the United States). Respondents pointed to infrastructure/development, business investments and the cost of its products as the most important reasons for the positive results, while political and social considerations were not important factors affecting China's image (Afrobarometer, 2016). A recent survey from the Pew Research Center also found views of China across Africa "generally positive," with a 62% favorability rating in 2018, although only four states were polled that year; however, over the last decade the average favorability rating was 66% (Devlin, 2018). It is important to note that there are 54 nations in Africa, so positive perceptions of China vary. For example, despite considerable Chinese investment in Egypt and Algeria, in recent years both countries had favorability ratings of China below 40%, and Ghana, which held the highest views of China in the world in 2015 at 80% favorability, had dropped to 49% in 2017. Among the factors cited for the decline of China's image in some countries, the flooding of low-quality Chinese goods on domestic markets and the lack of employment opportunities created by Chinese investment have stood out.

Noting these generally positive survey results, the following sections will document China's initiatives in Africa in a variety of fields, in effect suggesting an explanation for China's favorable image, while also noting the critiques that have questioned China's motivations for these initiatives.

The development of China's interest towards Africa

The Sino–African relationship, which has developed through different stages, remained almost negligible during the first few years in the wake of the establishment of the PRC in 1949. Mao Zedong was too busy in stabilizing the country's borders with neighboring countries and too occupied with reorganizing the society to take into consideration the relationship with Africa. It was only with the Asian–African Conference, convened in Bandung in April 1955 and representing an important forum to condemn colonial oppression and every form of underdevelopment, as well as to enhance economic and cultural cooperation, that the two parties began to cooperate. Chinese Premier Zhou Enlai gave a speech at the conference on the "Five Principles of Peaceful Coexistence," introduced with India the year before, and focused on the mutual respect for sovereignty and territorial integrity; mutual non-aggression; non-interference in each other's internal affairs; equality and mutual benefit; and peaceful coexistence. The pragmatism of such an approach was particularly useful for China, allowing them to offer immediate recognition to newly independent nations on the basis of these principles, regardless of their political orientation or their ideologies. China's enhanced efforts were also stimulated by the attention to Africa demonstrated by the United States and, above all, the split with the Soviet Union in 1960 after a bitter ideological confrontation between Moscow and Beijing, which forced African movements to take sides, contributing to their further division (Yahuda, 1979).

The necessity to work hard to develop the so-called Bandung spirit, to strengthen China's policies in Africa and to promote the PRC's anti-Soviet policies brought Zhou Enlai to visit the continent, from December 1963 to February 1964, putting forward the "Eight Principles Governing China's Economic and Technological Assistance to Foreign Countries," which were designed to compete simultaneously with the "imperialists" (the United States) and the "revisionists" (the Soviet Union) for Africa's support, and the "Five Principles Governing Relations with African and Arab Countries." The first set of principles clarified the Chinese intention to assist African countries by providing economic and technical aid free of any conditions, with the economic support offered free (or almost free) from any interest rates, with long repayment periods and accompanied by technological transfer (Chinese Government, 1964). Moreover, the Five Principles reaffirmed the struggle against colonialism and for non-alignment, self-determination, non-aggression and respect for sovereignty. It was against this backdrop that China decided to offer its support to various liberation movements in Angola, Mozambique and Rhodesia-Zimbabwe, concurrent with the growing influence of the Soviet Union on the African continent.

China provided substantial foreign aid to Africa, in the form of interest free loans, combined with the construction of several infrastructural projects, including the 1,860-kilometer Tazara Railway bridging Tanzania with Zambia, whose construction took five years, from 1970 to 1975, and was driven, at least in part, by China's need to facilitate its access to copper. This aid was important to African governments during difficult times, as Western donors were both reluctant to become economically committed to such projects and averse to working in such remote areas. Chinese foreign aid played a role in the establishment of diplomatic relations with a number of African countries, and subsequent African support was instrumental in enabling Beijing to assume the "China" seat at the United Nations, in October 1971, replacing Taipei. The support from 28 African countries—accounting for 34% of the General Assembly votes—was recognized by Mao, who admitted: "It is our African brothers that carried us into the United Nations" (Li, 2012).

By the early 1980s, with the advent of Deng Xiaoping and the implementation of the reform and opening up policy, Africa lost much of its importance in Chinese eyes and was to some extent marginalized as Beijing's focus shifted to its own modernization; while China had no intention to abandon the African continent, economics had supplanted politics as the driving factor in the relationship. This was confirmed by the trip Chinese Premier Zhao Ziyang made from December 20, 1982 to January 17, 1983 to the African continent, where he introduced the new "Four Principles on Sino–African Economic and Technical Cooperation," stressing that, in contrast to the earlier set of principles which regulated the relationship in the 1960s and 1970s, the nature of engagement had to become the mutual promotion of the two economies.

The 1990s, however, represented an important moment for the upswing of Sino–African relations. In the aftermath of the military crackdown in Tiananmen Square in June 1989, China became a pariah state, increasingly isolated internationally and sanctioned economically, clearly demonstrating to the Chinese leadership their value differences with the West. In order to oppose what Beijing felt was an injustice, China turned its attention again to Third World countries, including the African states which had expressed their support to the Chinese government for its success in handling its internal problems. Therefore, soon after Tiananmen, Sino–African relations flourished, and Foreign Minister Qian Qichen visited 14 African countries between 1989 and 1992 in order to seek political support, followed by other leaders. This led to President Jiang Zemin's national visit in 1997, during which he sowed the seeds for the establishment of an organization based on friendship and cooperation between the two actors, which would later become FOCAC.

Economics in command

Much of the soft power displayed by China in its engagement with African countries is "economic." Overall Sino–African trade has expanded tremendously in the last two decades. Starting from a base of $10 billion in 2000, it had reached a volume of $220 billion in 2014, growing on average, since 2001, by more than 31% a year, so that it now surpasses the United States in trade and investment and has challenged the primacy of the European Union (Sutter, 2016, pp. 306–310; Grimm and Hackenesch, 2017). Beijing has become the largest export destination for several African countries, including the Democratic Republic of Congo, Zambia and Angola, among others. If China is currently buying mainly crude oil, copper and iron, confirming that its main interest is in Africa's natural resources, the quality of its exports has improved greatly, passing from primary agricultural products, as in the 1950s, to mechanical, electrical and high-tech items. Africa is considered as a huge potential market for Chinese products not only by Beijing's government, but also by private Chinese entrepreneurs (Wang and Zou, 2014); there are reportedly 10,000 Chinese businesses on the African continent (Economist, 2019a).

Beyond contributing to the anxiety of Western powers (Hirono and Suzuki, 2014), the expansion of China's economic presence in Africa has been accompanied by major political objectives, the most important of which has been gaining support for its "One-China Principle" and marginalizing Taiwan. According to some commentators, although the growth in trade relations between China and Africa, as well as China's investments, seem to be economically beneficial to Africa, they nevertheless further the "underdevelopment" of the continent, especially in terms of the limited involvement of African workers in infrastructural development (Zhao, 2014), or the inclination of the Chinese government to subsidize Chinese companies, depriving African nations of benefits that might otherwise accrue in terms of employment, technology transfer and the acquisition of working skills (Sutter, 2016). In turn, a number of African scholars and journalists, echoing the traditional Western critique that China is increasingly investing in Africa in order to gain access to natural resources, thereby exacerbating the continent's export dependency, and to cultivate the export market for Chinese products, have started to criticize Beijing for its neo-colonialist attitude and exploitative policies (Mbaye, 2011; Quinn and Heinrich, 2011). Thus, while many African leaders have embraced China, societal forces have protested China's trade and resource-related activities, pushing other politicians to voice their grievances. For example, the vocal objections of South Africa's trade unions to China's cheap imports was a major contributing factor in President Thabo Mbeki's decision to restrict China's textile exports (Cooke, 2009), and to his public assertion that Africa would be "condemned to underdevelopment" if China develops a "colonial relationship" with the continent such as that which used to exist between Africa and the West (Mohan and Power, 2008). These protests, which sometimes have turned violent against the Chinese community in some countries, have convinced China that the voices of societal groups cannot be ignored in the pursuit of its economic objectives. In response, Beijing has pursued policies that present a less mercantile side to the African public by committing to investments in numerous other fields, including education and the construction of schools and hospitals. The results have been positive, despite some skepticism that the implementation of these initiatives has limited their benefits to the general public (Fijalkowski, 2011; Kurlantzick, 2009). Thus, as noted above, surveys have suggested that the popular perception of Chinese efforts in Africa is favorable (Afrobarometer, 2016; Devlin, 2018; Reinhart, 2019).

Aid with Chinese characteristics

Chinese aid can be described as political and strategic rather than humanitarian, intended to enhance China's soft power charm offensive. Moreover, much of China's official financing is inherently more commercial than developmental, and not categorizable as "foreign aid" as defined by Western donors. It is, however, an important resource for many developing countries, albeit critics note its lack of transparency (Xu and Carey, 2015).

Han and Zhang (2018) have described the development of China's foreign aid to Africa as unfolding in three distinct phases: solidarity (1955–1978), reform (1978–2000) and comprehensive development (from 2000 to the present). The first stage was characterized by free assistance, guided by the Five Principles of Peaceful Coexistence and, later, by the Eight Principles on Economic Aid. The support was primarily intended for liberation movements; nonetheless, in that period 36 African countries enjoyed 58% of Beijing's total amount of foreign aid (Li and Liu, 1996, p. 14). The second period—coinciding with the advent of the reform and opening up policy—implied a shift in focus toward "mutual benefit" and a more active economic cooperation. By 1990, Beijing had restructured its foreign aid programs as interest-free government loans were replaced by guaranteed discount loans from Chinese banks, and aid grants were superseded by joint ventures and other forms of cooperation (Sheldon, 2001). The greatest success, however, was represented by the implementation of the so-called aid to profit method, implemented by Chinese state-owned corporations, which discovered the immense opportunities the "hopeless continent" could provide in terms of resource acquisition and trade opportunities. The consequence was that Chinese companies' mobilization was hidden under the banner of aid. The latest stage was a testimony to the economic success China had reached, as well as its rise in the international arena. From 2000, with the adoption of its proclaimed "win-win" strategy, Sino–African relations strengthened, with FOCAC playing a leading role.

While Brautigam (2009) notes that China's aid and development assistance can be seen in different sectors, more conventional aid usually takes the form of soft loans and debt relief, rather than direct grants; China rarely gives cash aid in any significant amount. Interest-free loans are used for public infrastructure and industrial and agricultural production, while concessional loans are employed mainly for supporting production projects and large-scale infrastructure construction (Kitano, 2016, p. 5). In the case of aid, as in many other cases, China's participation is shaped by its political and strategic interests, the most important of which has traditionally been to convince African leaders to take shelter under Beijing's umbrella rather than rely on Western institutions, and, later, to consolidate these relations with resource-rich nations. This model was successful in Africa because it differs sharply from the Western approach, which, originally, flowed through the International Monetary Fund (IMF) and the World Bank and was tied to the implementation of Structural Adjustment Programs (SAPs). This was the model that has become famous as the "Washington Consensus," according to which the debt crisis was the result of excessive government spending. The result was the proliferation of economic and political conditionality attached to economic assistance provided by Western donors. Beijing's aid, on the other hand, is free of conditionalities and the promotion of values like good governance, human rights, transparency and legality to be implanted in the counterpart country. The only requirement for nations who want to enter the "Chinese team" is the severance of ties with Taipei. As Senegalese President Wade noted approvingly in 2008, "China's approach to our needs is simply better adapted than the slow and sometimes patronizing postcolonial approach of European investors, donor organizations and nongovernmental organizations" (Wade, 2008). In short, they can accept aid without being accused of squandering it by not investing appropriately, such as building schools and hospitals. China has no problem in supporting the construction of infrastructural projects—such as sports facilities—which can hardly be considered as development projects. In this way, however, Chinese support the acquisition of domestic legitimacy by the African recipient government which, most likely, will repay Beijing by signing more agreements. However, this massive influx of finance aimed to sustain infrastructural investments creates, according to some observers, an instrument of "debt-trap diplomacy" that fosters economic leverage over recipients (Su, 2017; Bewley, 2018). As we shall see below, this critique, emphasized in American warnings to African nations and raised more generally in describing China's massive Belt and Road Initiative, has become a major fault line in assessing China's motivations in its policies for developing countries (Brautigam, 2019; Economist, 2019b).

The Chinese model, defined as the "Beijing Consensus," is a key element in China's economic soft power configuration, and represents a major challenge to Western institutions like the World Bank and the IMF. Very often, Chinese financing has been associated with securing natural resources, a procedure configured as the "Angola model," according to which China provides low-interest loans to countries which rely on commodities like oil. In exchange for Chinese financial aid, as in the telecommunications sector, Beijing requires that Africans favor a Chinese service provider. Politically, China's "non-interference" in the domestic affairs of other countries and its open support of undemocratic "rogue states," thereby perpetuating their survival, combined with what some observers have described as predatory financing with "no strings attached," has led to accusations that Chinese policies have prevented the implementation of good governance practices and anti-corruption reforms. The Angolan experience is a case in point, since the government was able to resist IMF pressure for oil revenue transparency because it was able to access an interest-free loan from the Chinese EXIM Bank (Lombard, 2006). Other observers, however, counter that China has become a paradigm for modern development finance, its financing model and its swift project implementation is exactly what developing countries need in order to ignite their economies.

Educational initiatives to promote soft power

Whereas in the past African students used to opt for higher education institutions in the United States or former colonial rulers, notably France or the United Kingdom, this attitude has recently started to change, and China has become a significant educational pole of attraction. This is one of the initiatives China has taken to improve its image, and counter the growing suspicion that their only real interest in the continent is economic.

China is also seeking to create a workforce capable of using Chinese high-tech industrial products in Africa. With Chinese companies engaged in major infrastructural development and with the success of IT companies such as Huawei, the need for skilled African professionals is strong. Moreover, as future leaders or members of the middle class, African students can be a crucial link between China and Africa, representing a worthwhile investment in the long-term future of the relationship, while promoting the internationalization of Chinese institutions (Liu, 2017; King, 2013).

This story of success in the field of education has been nurtured through a wide-ranging system of scholarships and incentives paid by the Chinese government.

At the time of Mao's death, in 1976, Beijing provided 144 scholarships to African students; by 2015 that number had climbed to 8,470 (Li, 2018). Even more striking, at the time of the first FOCAC in 2000 there were fewer than 1,400 Africans studying in China; 15 years later this number had ballooned to around 50,000, a 35-fold increase (Li, 2018). As these numbers indicate, the vast majority of Africans who decide to study in China are self-financed, attracted by low tuition fees and easy access to visas, unlike the long procedures required by many Western countries. During the 2018 FOCAC summit, Beijing promised to provide 50,000 scholarships for African students over the next three years, along with other benefits, such as inviting 2,000 Africans to China for cultural exchanges. Beijing's proactive policies in the overseas education sector appear even more attractive when contrasted with the declining opportunities in more traditional destinations. Although France still maintains the lead among francophone Africans, China has become, as of 2017, the leading destination for English-speaking African students (Nantulya, August 30, 2018) and represents a valuable alternative in terms of cost and preferential treatment. While educational cooperation contributes to the promotion of mutual relations, a number of concerns remain. Apart from problems of cultural adaptation, Africans studying in China often complain about the low quality of education, language barriers and consequent "segregation," as well as being the target of racism (Burgess, 2016). These difficulties, in Hauben's words, "obstructs the promotion of Chinese values, thus obliterating the soft power potential of Sino-African educational exchanges" (2013, p. 331). It is worth noting, however, that Africans who study in China, unlike those who study elsewhere, tend to go back to their native countries upon completion, thus contributing to national development and avoiding a brain drain effect, as well as generating warm feelings toward China (Sautman, 2006). In addition, some of those who go back to Africa were put, or will be put, in positions of power and influence, suggesting that their experience in China will make them well prepared to deal with Chinese businesspeople and officials, perhaps favoring the country which has invested in their education (Li, 2018; Allison, 2013).

A flagship instrument for China's educational engagement with Africa has been represented by the Confucius Institutes, which have rapidly spread across the region, constituting another important instrument of attraction for African students. Since December 2005, when the first one was inaugurated in Nairobi, 48 Confucius Institutes and 27 Confucius Classrooms located in 33 African countries have been established, mainly to develop Chinese language courses and provide information and services relating to Chinese culture. China has already surpassed both the United States and the United Kingdom in the number of cultural institutions in Africa, although it is still lagging behind France and its Alliance Française facilities. As in other countries, however, these efforts to gain soft power have been controversial, with Confucius Institutes, as Hartig's chapter in this volume suggests, sometimes facing harsh criticism for being

"Trojan horses" set up for political reasons (Paradise, 2009), and contributing to the marginalization of African culture, languages and identity.

The role of media to tell China's story

Even though Chinese media was already active in Africa in the late 1950s when ideological support was given to liberation movements on Chinese radio stations broadcasting to Africa (Madrid-Morales and Wasserman, 2017; Üngör, 2009), its recent expansion has become an integral part of the "going out" policy and an attempt to counteract China's perceived "demonized" international image presented by Western media (Li, 1996), and is linked to Beijing's broader economic activities and to its changing foreign policy orientation. In 2008 the central government invested RMB 45 billion in order to pave the way for the "Big Four" Chinese media actors, Xinhua News Agency, China Radio International (CRI), Chinese Central Television (CCTV) and *China Daily* to expand their overseas operations. Action plans in 2012 and 2015 have followed the same path. As highlighted by Madrid-Morales and Wasserman (2017), this expansion has also meant a gradual diversification, allowing Chinese corporations and state agencies to be involved in five key areas: *content production*, provided by Xinhua, to many African media houses; *content distribution*, mainly Chinese soap operas that have become quite popular in many countries on the continent; *infrastructure development*, largely supported by big companies like Huawei; *professional training*, mainly offered by Chinese universities; and *direct investment*, such as the 20% acquisition of South Africa's Independent Media by a group of Chinese investors.

China's state-led media have all established deep footprints on the African continent following a strategy characterized by a series of interconnected initiatives. Xinhua's long presence in Africa—in the 1950s and 1960s it provided support for the news agencies of African liberation movements in various forms—has expanded. In 2006 its Africa Regional Bureau in Nairobi took over the production and distribution of French-language reports from the Paris Bureau while, two years later, the China African News Service was officially launched. In 2011 Xinhua started its CNC World, the English-language TV channel and, responding to the massive growth of mobile devices in Africa, implemented an Internet application called "I Love Africa" as a source of news in sub-Saharan Africa, reaching millions of subscribers. Xinhua currently has more than 30 bureaus in Africa, with hundreds of local employees, and cooperates with the local state news agencies on content sharing. In addition, it offers its reports to all local media at little or no charge, acquiring an indisputable advantage over its competitors in the West (Grassi, 2014). In 2006, another actor with a long history of connections with Africa, CRI, launched its first overseas station with its FM channels in three East African cities—broadcasting in English, Mandarin and Swahili—and its AM channels covering Kenya (Wu, 2012). In January 2012, the state-run CCTV established CCTV Africa (now known as China Global

Television Network, CGTN), settling in Nairobi and becoming the largest non-African TV initiative on the continent. Counting on a large crew of employees, mostly Africans recruited from competitors, its objective was to compete with giants like CNN by reporting primarily on developments in Africa. At the end of 2012, the state-controlled English-language newspaper *China Daily* launched *Africa Weekly*, from its offices in South Africa and Kenya. Last but not least, Star-Times, a privately owned company founded in Beijing in 1988 and originally focused on broadcasting services, became a major international player only after it started its operations in Africa in 2002 (Rønning, 2016). StarTimes has activities that range from building broadcasting networks to distributing signals and training personnel hired locally. Being identified by the Chinese Ministry of Culture as a "cultural exports key enterprise," as well as being the only private Chinese company to obtain the authorization from the Ministry of Commerce to participate in foreign projects in the radio and TV industry, has enabled StarTimes to become a major actor in the media sector, receiving funds from EXIM Bank.

This seemingly unstoppable expansion of state-sponsored media organizations from an authoritarian country into Africa has raised concerns among some critics, who fear it might prevent the consolidation of fragile or imperfect democracies. China premises its media expansion into Africa on providing "positive reporting" or "constructive journalism," aimed at influencing perceptions of Beijing by "advancing new ways of looking at Africa" (Gagliardone and Geall, 2014), a completely different focus in contrast to the role of independent watchdog media plays in liberal democracies. According to Beijing, this means showing the positive side of Africa's development and providing solutions to governance challenges, instead of being hypercritical, as Western media tend to be. Some analysts (Marsh, 2017; Wan, 2017), however, have tried to demonstrate that this label of constructive journalism is mere rhetoric devoid of any substance, given the fact that stories deemed harmful to Chinese economic or political interests are filtered directly in Beijing, while "lighter" themes are left to the control of African editors. Thus, analysts often question the level of autonomy and independence African journalists retain when they have to cover aspects that are considered "inconvenient" by Beijing, such as human rights violations, elections, civil society participation or criticism of African dictators, like Mugabe or Al-Bashir (York, 2013).

Given its substantial investment, how successful has China been in extending its influence via media in Africa? Have they been able to convert economic capital into symbolic and cultural capital (Rønning, 2016)? Has China's promotion of itself met with a positive reception among African audiences? The available empirical research suggests a mixed picture, which is not surprising given the variation across 54 African nations. While public opinion polls suggest a more positive picture, one major effort that examined this question in various parts of the continent concluded that, whether conceived in terms of an expanding market, counter-hegemonic discursive struggles or soft power, despite some successes, Chinese media by and large had thus far been unsuccessful (Wasserman, 2016).

China's increasing footprint in telecommunications

As in other infrastructural sectors, China has emerged as one of the most pivotal actors in ensuring connectivity in the digital realm, thanks to its two Chinese information and communications technology giants—Huawei (privately owned) and Zhongxing Telecommunications Equipment Corporation (ZTE) (state owned)—who have come to dominate the African market, and continue to extend their footprint. Both companies look at Africa as a lucrative target, to the point that Huawei, which already generates 15% of its global sales on the continent, has opened dozens of local branches and offices, hiring more than 5,000 employees, over half of whom are claimed to be locals (Tsui, 2016). The secret behind this impressive success lies in the support provided by EXIM Bank or China Development Bank (CDB); in substance, state-owned Chinese banks provide loans on the condition that African governments buy equipment and services only from Chinese companies. This modality, unknown to major international competitors like Ericsson or Nokia, has been observed several times; in 2008, for example, EXIM Bank offered a soft loan to Tanzania to improve its telecommunications industry. According to that contract, the China International Telecommunication Construction Corporation (CITCC) was required to carry out the project with Huawei (Dreher et al., 2017). Another strategy lies in export credits offered directly to Chinese companies, which use them to implement a project envisioned by a national government (Gagliardone, 2014). Moreover, the strong Chinese interest toward the African telecommunications sector indicates a recalibration in its investment pattern, from an exclusive engagement in extractive industries to an increasing inclusion of services such as finance, banking and telecommunications, and manufacturing (Cissé, 2012).

When establishing operations in Africa, Chinese companies generally opt for joint ventures with local network operators in order to gain a better knowledge of a specific market in which they will operate, gaining access to information that will enable them to tailor products and services to local realities faster and with lower possible risk. Because of their importance in shaping China's image, when Chinese leaders visit Africa they make sure to include Huawei and ZTE executives (Cooke, 2012), allowing them to have preferential access to local governmental élites and build high-level relationships that can be important in gaining influence and winning contracts.

Chinese companies, however, have also been the targets of intense criticism, citing their lack of transparency, their insistence on "vendor-guaranteed" loans, where state-owned Chinese banks provide loans on the condition that African governments buy equipment and services only from Chinese companies, and the adoption of corrupt practices (Malakata, 2012), to which both Huawei and ZTE respond by stressing the importance of their corporate social responsibility portfolios. The gravest allegation, however, concerns spying operations, like inserting a backdoor on the servers of the African Union's Chinese-built head-quarters that allowed them to transfer data to servers in Shanghai. Beijing has consistently dismissed these accusations (Maasho, 2018).

UN peacekeeping as a Chinese success story

UN peacekeeping activities have become an important aspect of Beijing's foreign policy, especially because they are strongly intertwined with soft power. China, in fact, is currently not only among the world's 12 largest contributors of troops, but also the biggest contributor of peacekeepers among the five permanent members of the UN Security Council (Zürcher, 2019). The African continent, in fact, represents the most significant destination for Chinese peacekeeping contingents, with its ten UN missions in Africa, most notably in Mali, Central African Republic, Sudan, Democratic Republic of Congo and Darfur, constituting around 80% of the 2,500 troops China deploys abroad (Zürcher, 2019). China not only contributes personnel, but also medical expertise, transportation equipment, and engineering and logistical specialists for UN operations (Ayenagbo et al., 2012).

China's deep involvement in peacekeeping activities serves multiple purposes. First, Chinese troops are strategically deployed in resource-rich countries, like the Democratic Republic of Congo (mining concessions), Sudan (oil interests), South Sudan and Liberia (timber), or in countries where its greatest economic and military interests are at stake (Nantulya, 2019). Liberia started receiving Chinese investments in 2003, along with engineers and medical personnel for UN peacekeeping operations, immediately after having broken with Taipei. It was for this reason that the Liberian president, Ellen Johnson Sirleaf, declared that the country would "never forget the friendship of Chinese peace-keeping soldiers" (*People's Daily*, February 1, 2007). Given that other countries, including the United States, provide financial assistance but no troops, Sirleaf's declaration confirms the effectiveness of Beijing's soft power by means of its involvement in peacekeeping operations. A second reason is China's rising status on the global stage. With many countries wary of its strategic intentions, Beijing wants to demonstrate to the international community that it is seriously committed to contributing to the establishment of international peace and security by providing a constructive role for the People's Liberation Army. Third, Chinese security forces gain substantial benefits in terms of experience, professionalism and modernization by training alongside contingents from other nations. Finally, it is worth noting that China sells more weapons in sub-Saharan Africa than any other nation, accounting for 27% of the region's arms imports from 2013–2017, compared with 16% from 2008–2012 (Economist, 2019a).

Public health as public diplomacy

China has also been active in providing assistance in the area of public health. The practice of dispatching Chinese medical teams (CMTs) to Africa took shape in the early 1960s, when Beijing responded to the Algerian appeal to the international community for medical assistance in the wake of the liberation of the country and the withdrawal of French medical staff. The intervention of these medical teams proved efficacious in providing quality medical care in resource-poor settings and promoted the idea that Chinese health diplomacy could foster the sustainable development of African states' healthcare infrastructure (Youde, 2010).

China's commitment has generated about 255 projects in health, population and water and sanitation sectors in Africa with an investment of more than $3 billion (Lin et al., 2016) between 2000 and 2012. The most common form of China's health assistance is the dispatch of CMTs. In 2014, 43 of these teams were at work in 42 different African countries, treating over 5 million patients, with an estimated annual operational cost of between $29 and $60 million (Tambo et al., 2016). Apart from deploying personnel, China intervenes by building clinics for the local population, introducing Chinese traditional medical treatment (particularly acupuncture), donating pharmaceuticals, and providing equipment and training to African health workers. Between 2006 and 2013, China financed 345 healthcare projects, at a cost of $764 million (Guillon and Mathonnat, 2017). It is perhaps not surprising that the blockbuster film *Wolf Warrior 2*, mentioned above, highlighted Chinese efforts in public health in Africa as a key theme.

Beijing has also responded to specific medical emergencies on the continent. For example, between 2013 and 2016, when more than 11,000 people died from the Ebola virus, China not only dispatched more than 1,000 medical professionals to West Africa, but also provided $120 million in aid (Shan, 2016; Cheng, 2015). The contribution to the fight against malaria is also particularly important, and China has implemented various measures, including the distribution of Cotecxin, the effective antimalarial drug produced in China (Huang, 2011). Reflecting the continuing debate over Chinese motivations, however, some observers have seen such Chinese largesse more as a "low-cost" strategy to introduce Chinese-made medication to the African market (Shinn, 2006).

China's efforts are aimed at both the general population, who directly benefit from the infrastructure built and the services provided, and at African leaders, who can gain legitimation from their fellow citizens by cooperating with China in the healthcare sector. From the Chinese point of view health assistance represents another means to strengthen its diplomatic relations with Africa, and presumably help Beijing to gain favorable trading terms and access to necessary resources (Thompson, 2005; Youde, 2010), even though the Chinese government has consistently claimed that its health diplomacy is not linked to any material benefits they expect to derive. The evidence of this "altruistic" attitude should be seen, according to Beijing, in the fact that health aid to sub-Saharan Africa is not limited to resource-rich countries. Nonetheless, as Li (2011) suggests, China's medical cooperation has indeed often corresponded to Beijing's diplomatic strategy, as in the case of Senegal, where CMTs began to arrive in 1975 but were withdrawn from 1996 to 2007, a period when relations were severed.

Conclusion

As Africa becomes a focal point for international rivalries, particularly between the United States and China, it is important to consider the comparative advantages of the two antagonists in terms of soft power generation. China has long made Africa a priority for both political—its 54 nations make up more than 25% of the UN General Assembly and it always has 3 of the 15 non-permanent seats on the Security Council—and economic reasons, with other nations belatedly following China's lead in recognizing the importance of the continent. At the same time, under the Trump administration, the United States has moved in the opposite direction, cutting funding for development and diplomatic programs, announcing a 10% reduction in troops in Africa and generally treating the continent with at best benign neglect. For example, it took 18 months to fill the top Africa job at the State Department (Economist, 2019a). Nevertheless, alarmed at China's worldwide ambitions for the Belt and Road and other initiatives, Washington has asserted that in contrast to China's self-serving policies, it is the United States that can best help African nations move toward self-reliance. Bolton's December 2018 speech portrayed the struggle between China and the United States as a zero-sum game, noting that China was "deliberately and aggressively targeting their investments in the region to gain a competitive advantage over the United States" (National Security Council, 2018), comments that are reminiscent of the "Great Game" between Britain and Russia over Central Asia in the 19th century. In effect, American policy seeks to compel African nations to make a choice between China and the United States.

Early returns suggest that most nations will strongly resist making such a choice, and that by its consistent engagement across a variety of policy arenas China has become indispensable to these countries. As the former president of Nigeria suggested, in responding to Bolton's speech, China deserves credit for transforming the image of the continent from "a problem to be solved to a commercial prospect," and that "the history of superpower rivalry in Africa is messy, destructive and occasionally bloody," and should never be allowed to happen again; indeed, the very title of his op-ed indicates that such a policy is not conducive to promoting America's soft power in Africa, and that "the US is asking African countries to choose sides at a time when many don't have this luxury" (Obasanjo and Mills, 2018). As Obasanjo cautions, while the United States cannot compete with China in delivering low-cost infrastructure in exchange for resources and contracts, or provide workers willing to labor in remote African environments for low wages, American soft power in Africa is based on the values they represent, particularly since two-thirds of Africans routinely prefer democracy to any other form of government. The best way to compete with China would be to make use of this comparative advantage by helping to improve governance oversight, supporting greater transparency and vigilance over elections and funding scholarships for African students. Some of the other African responses to Bolton's speech have been far less polite (Maru, 2019) and suggest that promoting a confrontational, Manichean struggle between good and evil is likely to be counterproductive for the United States; in short, China is not going away, they have been welcomed in Africa and will be there for the long term.

Note

1 The chapter is the outcome of a joint effort by the two co-authors. In practice, though, SR wrote the introduction and conclusion, while AF wrote all the remaining sections.

References

Afrobarometer. 2016. "China's Growing Presence in Africa Wins Largely Positive Popular Reviews," Dispatch No. 122, October 24. http://afrobarometer.org/publications/ad122-chinas-growing-presence-africa-wins-largely-positive-popular-reviews.

Allison, Simon. 2013. "Fixing China's Image in Africa, One Student at a Time," *The Guardian*, July 5. www.theguardian.com/world/2013/jul/31/china-africa-students-scholarship-programme.

Ayenagbo, Kossi, Tommie Njobvu, James V. Sossou and Biossey K. Tozoun. 2012. "China's Peacekeeping Operations in Africa: From Unwilling Participation to Responsible Contribution," *African Journal of Political Science and International Relations* 6(2), pp. 22–32.

Bewley, Dakota. 2018. "China's Debt-Trap Diplomacy in Africa," *Nato Association of Canada (NAOC)*, October 4. http://natoassociation.ca/chinas-debt-trap-diplomacy-in-africa/.

Brautigam, Deborah. 2009. *Dragon's Gift: The Real Story of China in Africa*. Oxford: Oxford University Press.

Brautigam, Deborah. 2019. "Is China the World's Loan Shark?," *The New York Times*, April 26. www.nytimes.com/2019/04/26/opinion/china-belt-road-initiative.html.

Burgess, Lisa María. 2016, "Conversation with African Students in China," *Transition* 119, pp. 80–91.

Cheng, Feng. 2015. "China and UHC in Africa," *Devex*, April 21. www.devex.com/news/china-and-uhc-in-africa-85909.

Chinese Government. 1964. "The Chinese Government's Eight Principles for Economic Aid and Technical Assistance to Other Countries," January 15, in History and Public Policy Program Digital Archive, Zhonghua renmin gongheguo waijiaobu and Zhonggong zhongyang wenxian yanjiushi (eds.), 1990. *Zhou Enlai waijiao wenxuan [Selected Diplomatic Papers of Zhou Enlai]*. Beijing: Zhongyang wenxian chubanshe. http://digitalarchive.wilsoncenter.org/document/121560.

Cooke, Fang Lee. 2012. "The Globalization of Chinese Telecom Corporations: Strategy, Challenges and Human Resources Implications for the MNCs and Host Countries," *The International Journal of Human Resources Management* 23(9), pp. 1832–1852.

Cissé, Daouda. 2012. "Chinese Telecom Companies Foray Into Africa," *African East-Asian Affairs*. Stellenbosch, 69, pp. 16-23.

Cooke, Jennifer G. 2009. "China's Soft Power in Africa," in Carola McGiffert (ed.), *Chinese Soft Power and Its Implications for the United States*. Washington, DC: Center for Strategic and International Studies, pp. 27–44.

Devlin, Kat. 2018. "5 Charts on Global Views of China," Pew Research Center, Oct. 19.

Dreher Axel, Andreas Fuchs, Bradley Parks, Austin M. Strange and Michael J. Tierney. 2017. *Aid, China, and Growth: Evidence from a New Global Development Finance Dataset*, AidData, Working Paper no. 46. http://docs.aiddata.org/ad4/pdfs/WPS46_Aid_China_and_Growth.pdf.

The Economist. 2019a. "The New Scramble for Africa," March 9, pp. 19–22.

The Economist. 2019b. "Seeds of Suspicion," April 27, pp. 38–39.

Fijałkowski, Łukasz. 2011. "China's 'Soft Power' in Africa?," *Journal of Contemporary African Studies* 29(2), pp. 223–232.

Gagliardone, Iginio. 2014. "Media Development with Chinese Characteristics," *Global Media Journal* 4(2).

Gagliardone, Iginio and Sam Geall. 2014. "China in Africa's Media and Telecommunications: Cooperation, Connectivity and Control," Oslo: Norwegian Peacebuilding Resource Center (NOREF), Expert Analysis.

Grassi, Sergio. 2014. *Changing the Narrative: China's Media Offensive in Africa.* Berlin: Friedrich Ebert Stiftung.

Grimm, Sven and Christine Hackenesch. 2017. "China in Africa: What Challenges for a Reforming European Union Development Policy? Illustrations from Country Cases," *Development Policy Review* 35(4), pp. 549–566.

Guillon, Marlène and Jacky Mathonnat. 2017. "Is There a Strategy in China's Health Official Development Assistance to African Countries?," *Études et Documents,* 20, CERDI. https://halshs.archives-ouvertes.fr/halshs-01519715v2/document.

Han, Yi and Quanyi Zhang. 2018. "Understand China's Foreign Aid to Africa From a Historical and Chinese Ethical Perspectives Since 1955," *Pageo,* February 8. http://www.geopolitika.hu/en/2018/02/08/understand-chinas-foreign-aid-to-africa-from-a-historical-and-chinese-ethical-perspectives-since-1955/.

Haugen, Heidi Østbø. 2013. "China's Recruitment of African University Students: Policy Efficacy and Unintended Outcomes," *Globalisation, Societies and Education* 11(3), pp. 315–344.

Hirono, Miwa and Shogo Suzuki. 2014. "Why Do We Need 'Myth-Busting' in the Study of Sino-African Relations?," *Journal of Contemporary China* 23(87), pp. 443–461.

Huang, Yanzhong. 2011. "Domestic Factors and China's Health Aid Programs in Africa," in *China's Emerging Global Health and Foreign Aid Engagement in Africa,* Center for Strategic & International Studies, pp. 17–24. https://csis-prod.s3.amazonaws.com/s3fs-public/legacy_files/files/publication/111122_Freeman_ChinaEmerging-GlobalHealth_Web.pdf.

King, Kenneth. 2013. *China's Aid and Soft Power in Africa: The Case of Education and Training.* Suffolk: James Currey.

Kitano, Naohiro. 2016. *Estimating China's Foreign Aid II: 2014 Update.* JICA Research Institute Working Paper JICA Research Institute, Tokyo.

Kurlantzick, Joshua. 2009. "China's Soft Power in Africa," in Minjiang Li (ed.), *Soft Power: China's Emerging Strategy in International Politics.* Lanham, MD: Lexington Books, pp. 165–183.

Li, Anshan. 2011. "Chinese Medical Cooperation in Africa. With Special Emphasis on the Medical Teams and Anti-Malaria Campaign," discussion paper, Nordiska Afrikainstitutet, Uppsala. http://nai.diva-portal.org/smash/get/diva2:399727/FULLTEXT02.pdf.

Li, Anshan. 2018. "African Students in China: Research, Reality, and Reflection," *African Studies Quarterly* 17(4), pp. 5–44.

Li, Qi. 2012. "The 'Secrets' Behind the Success of China-Africa Relations," *China Daily,* July 20. www.chinadaily.com.cn/opinion/2012-07/20/content_15603361.htm.

Li, Xiguang and Liu, Kang. 1996. *Yaomohua Zhongguo de bei hou* 妖魔化中国的背后 *(Behind the demonization of China).* China Social Science Press.

Lin, Shuang, Liangmin Gao, Melissa Reyes, Feng Cheng, Joan Kaufman and Wafaa M. El Sadr. 2016. "China's Health Assistance to Africa: Opportunism or Altruism?," *Globalization and Health* 12(83).

Liu, H. 2017. "A Study on the Evolution and Effect of China's Scholarship Policy towards African Students," in A. Li and H. Liu (eds.), *Annual Review of African Studies in China 2015*. Beijing: Social Sciences Academic Press, pp. 141–192.

Lombard, Louisa. 2006. "Africa's China Card," *Foreign Policy*, April 11. https://foreign-policy.com/2006/04/11/africas-china-card/.

Maasho, Aaron. 2018. "China Denies Report It Hacked African Union Headquarters," *Reuters*, January 29. www.reuters.com/article/us-africanunion-summit-china/china-denies-report-it-hacked-african-union-headquarters-idUSKBN1FI2I5.

Madrid-Morales, Dani and Herman Wasserman. 2017, "Chinese Media Engagement in South Africa: What Is Its Impact on Local Journalism?," *Journalism Studies* 19(8), pp. 1218–1235.

Malakata, Michael. 2012. "Algerian Ban on ZTE, Huawei Highlights Corruption Controversy," *IDG News Service*, June 12. http://news.idg.no/cw/art.cfm?id=D7DAD3FD-F26D-177C-2EF38733406952D7.

Marsh, Vivien. 2017. "Africa Through Chinese Eyes: New Frames or the Same Old Lens? African News in English from China Central Television, Compared with the BBC," in Mel Bunce, Suzanne Franks and Chris Paterson (eds.), *Africa's Media Image in the 21st Century: From the 'Heart of Darkness' to 'Africa Rising'*. Abingdon and New York: Routledge, pp. 177–189.

Maru, Mehari Taddele. 2019. "Why Africa Loves China," *Al-Jazeera*, January 5. www.aljazeera.com/indepth/opinion/africa-loves-china-190103121552367.html.

Mbaye, Sanou. 2011. "Africa Will Not Put Up with a Colonialist China," *The Guardian*, February 7. www.theguardian.com/commentisfree/2011/feb/07/china-exploitation-africa-industry.

Mohan, Giles and Marcus Power. 2008. "New African Choices? The Politics of Chinese Engagement," *Review of African Political Economy* 35(115), pp. 23–42.

Nantulya, Paul. 2018. "Grand Strategy and China's Soft PowerPush in Africa," *Africa Center for Strategic Studies*, August 30, https://africacenter.org/spotlight/grand-strategy-and-chinas-soft-power-push-in-africa/.

National Security Council. 2018. "Remarks by National Security Adviser Ambassador John R. Bolton on the Trump Administration's New Africa Strategy," December 18. www.whitehouse.gov/briefings-statements/remarks-national-security-advisor-ambassador-john-r-bolton-trump-administrations-new-africa-strategy/.

Obasanjo, Olusegun and Greg Mills. 2018. "The US Should Focus on Soft Power and China Cooperation in Africa: Not Rivalry," *Quartz*, December 19. https://qz.com/africa/1501023/president-obasanjo-says-trumps-africa-strategy-cant-rival-china/.

Paradise, James F. 2009. "China and International Harmony: The Role of Confucius Institutes in Bolstering Beijing's Soft Power," *Asian Survey* 49(4), pp. 647–669.

Quinn, Andrew and Mark Heinrich. 2011. "Clinton Warns against "New Colonialism" in Africa," *Reuters*, June 11. www.reuters.com/article/us-clinton-africa/clinton-warns-against-new-colonialism-in-africa-idUSTRE75A0RI20110611.

Reinhart, R.J. and Zacc Ritter. 2019. "China's Leadership Gains Global Admirers," *Gallup*, March 4.

Rønning, Helge. 2016. "How Much Soft Power Does China Have in Africa?," in Xiaoling Zhang, Herman Wasserman and Winston Mano (eds.), *China's Media and Soft Power in Africa*. New York: Palgrave Macmillan, pp. 65–78.

Sautman, Barry V. 2006. "Friends and Interests: China's Distinctive Links with Africa," Hong Kong University of Science & Technology Center on China's Transnational Relation, Hong Kong, Working Paper no. 12.

Shan, Juan. 2016. "China's Role in Africa Grows in Ebola's Wake," *ChinaDaily*, October 27. www.chinadaily.com.cn/world/2016-10/27/content_27185505.htm.

Sheldon, Garth. 2001. "China and Africa: Building an Economic Partnership," *South African Journal of International Affairs* 8(2), pp. 111–119.

Shinn, David H. 2006. "Africa, China and Health Care," *Inside AISA* 3/4, pp. 14–16.

Sutter, Robert G. 2016. *Chinese Foreign Relations: Power and Policy since the Cold War*. Lanham, MD: Rowman and Littlefield.

Su Xiaochen. 2017. "Why Chinese Infrastructure Loans in Africa Represent a Brand-New Type of Neocolonialism," *The Diplomat*, June 9. https://thediplomat.com/2017/06/why-chinese-infrastructural-loans-in-africa-represent-a-brand-new-type-of-neocolonialism/.

Tambo, Ernest, Chidiebere E. Ugwu, Yayi Guan, Ding Wei, Xiao Ning and Zhou Xiao-Nong. 2016. "China-Africa Health Development Initiatives: Benefits and Implications for Shaping Innovative and Evidence-Informed National Health Policies and Programs in Sub-Saharan African Countries," *International Journal of MCH and AIDS* 5(2), pp. 119–133.

Thompson, Drew. 2005. "China's Soft Power in Africa: From the 'Beijing Consensus' to Health Diplomacy," *China Brief* 5(21), pp. 1–4.

Tsui, Benjamin. 2016. "Do Huawei's Training Programs and Centers Transfer Skills To Africa?," *Policy Brief*, Washington, D.C. China Africa Research Initiative (CARI).

Üngör, Çagdas. 2009. *Reaching the Distant Comrade Chinese Communist Propaganda Abroad (1949–1976)*, PhD thesis. State University of New York, Binghamton.

Wade, Abdoulaye. 2008. "Time for the West to Practise What It Preaches," *Financial Times*, January 24. www.ft.com/content/5d347f88-c897-11dc-94a6-0000779fd2ac.

Wan, James. 2017. "Perceptions of Chinese Media's Africa Coverage," in Mel Bunce, Suzanne Franks and Chris Paterson (eds.), *Africa's Media Image in the 21st Century: From the 'Heart of Darkness' to 'Africa Rising'*. Abingdon and New York: Routledge.

Wang, Jianwei and Jing Zou. 2014. "China Goes to Africa: A Strategic Move," *Journal of Contemporary China* 23(90), pp. 1113–1132.

Wasserman, Herman. 2016. "Chinese Soft Power in Africa: Findings, Perspectives and More Questions," in Xiaoling Zhang, Herman Wasserman and Winston Mano (eds.), *China's Media and Soft Power in Africa: Promotion and Perceptions*. Houndmills, Basingstoke: Palgrave Macmillan, pp. 195–203.

Wu, Yu-Shan. 2012. "The Rise of China's State-Led Media Dynasty in Africa," Occasional Paper no. 117, China Africa Project, South African Institute of International Affairs, Johannesburg.

Xu, Jiajun and Richard Carey. 2015. *China's International Development Finance: Past, present and future*. WIDER Working Paper 2015/130, UNU-WIDER, Helsinki.

Yahuda, Michael B. 1979. *China's Role in World Affairs*. London: Croom Helm.

York, Geoffrey. 2013. "Why China Is Making a Big Play to Control Africa's Media," *Globe and Mail*, September 11. www.theglobeandmail.com/news/world/media-agenda-china-buys-newsrooms-influence-in-africa/article14269323/.

Youde, Jeremy. 2010. "China's Health Diplomacy in Africa," *China: An International Journal* 8(1), pp. 151–163.

Zhao, Suisheng. 2014. "A Neo-Colonialist Predator or Development Partner? China's Engagement and Rebalance in Africa," *Journal of Contemporary China* 23(90), pp. 1033–1052.

Zürcher, Christoph. 2019. *30 Years of Chinese Peacekeeping*. Centre for International Policy Studies (CIPS), Ottawa, University of Ottawa.

11
CHINESE SOFT POWER IN JAPAN AND SOUTH KOREA

Gilbert Rozman

China has tremendous economic power and rapidly expanding military power, but it has had difficulty boosting its soft power. For neighbors long in China's shadow, soft power can include shared historical and cultural traditions, an image of an emerging regional community and the promise of some sort of common "Asian values." Given the prevalence of US and Western culture and English, efforts directed at expanding soft power also involve challenging the US cultural hegemony along with spreading one's own narrative on the past and on recent policies (Shambaugh, 2015), by popularizing Confucius Institutes and encouraging the study of Chinese and the PRC outlook on the history of China and of the earlier East Asian region under China. In the 1980s Japan placed priority on expanding soft power, invoking shared culture, but it did not challenge the international community, unlike China's frontal assault on the US-led world order. In the 2010s Xi Jinping's "China Dream" has become the symbol of a narrative about how China envisions itself at the center of a new, alluring, Sino-centric order.

Basically, there are two types of approaches to spreading a country's soft power. One is the *leadership model*, setting one's country on a path of exceptionality and holding it up as worthy of awe and reverence. The other is the *community model*, enticing others as a model partner in a wider endeavor. There can be a mixture of the two or some alternation between them, projecting superiority as a paragon of admiration and garnering respect as the champion of a common cause. As in the 1980s case of Japan, but more so, China has transitioned rapidly from earlier avid pursuit of multilateralism to undisguised insistence on its own regional leadership.

Soft power comes from a combination of admiration, trust and high expectations. In the case of Japanese and South Korean perceptions of China's soft power, there was potential for admiration of shared premodern culture and of growing trust based on new interactions, but, most important, were expectations about relations still on the horizon. These expectations depended not only on projections of Chinese behavior, but also on anticipation of how one's own country would benefit from it. I call this approach, centering on how another country is perceived in light of thinking about what is essential to one's own country's pride, the *analysis of national identity gaps* (Rozman, 2013).

Chinese soft power in Japan reached a peak in the mid-1980s, was still rather high in the mid-1990s, but fell in the late 1990s, mid-2000s and early 2010s. In South Korea it reached a peak in the early 2000s and revived in 2013–2015, but blows to it in 2004–2005, 2008–2010 and 2016 were successively more severe. Here, I compare perceptions of China in the two, each sharing a Confucian heritage but allied with the United States, concluding that as China's hard power grows, soft power matters less to it.

A framework for analysis of national identity gaps

Study of national identities has become commonplace since the 1980s, but the way they impact bilateral relations has largely been examined from the point of one or the other country. Those who examine South Korean anxieties about China, as in the Koguryo controversy over China's usurpation of the history of a founding state of the Korean people, that came to the fore in 2004, explain how the Koreans saw their national identity challenged (Rozman, 2011). Many who follow Chinese anger toward Japan discuss how this fits into the identity being constructed from above by communist leaders, especially in the 1990s as a replacement for the traditional communist narrative in disrepute (Wan, 2013). Much is said about an upsurge in revisionist historical thinking in Tokyo, especially under Abe Shinzo, and its deleterious impact on its relations with Seoul (Rozman, 2016). In 2019 the costs of not addressing such historical gaps were evident when Seoul so alienated Tokyo that relations were brought to a nadir. Adding the notion of national identity gaps, I seek to cover both sides of a bilateral relationship and to systematize the linkage between manifestations of identity on the domestic scene and the impact of national identities on international relations.

The starting point for a systematic approach is to differentiate multiple dimensions of national identity, making it possible to estimate how each is evolving and how the other nation in a dyad matters for one's own national identity. Doing this for Sino–Japanese and Sino–South Korean relations allows a comparison of soft power, too. As before, I differentiate six dimensions of national identity: (1) *ideology*, which has a strong and growing place in Chinese national identity, but also is visible in Japan's revisionist thought and South Korea's progressive thought, and, less so, in opposing currents in each of these countries; (2) *history* (*temporal* dimension), seen often in commentaries on bilateral identity disputes; (3) a *sectoral* dimension—combining political, economic and civilizational identity, of which the last is most pertinent; (4) a *vertical* dimension, which refers to state–society relations, including the impact of criticisms of Communist Party restrictions on civil society, NGOs, and human rights; (5) a *horizontal* dimension, concerned with shared thinking on international society, regionalism and the role of the United States in the world order; and (6) an *intensity* dimension, or how strongly attitudes are held (Rozman, 2012). As identities evolve—seen in official discourse, media narratives and public opinion—this approach clarifies soft power.

When we juxtapose perspectives on each of these dimensions in a pair of countries we shift to consideration of national identity gaps, revealing whether the divide between the way the two sides are looking at a dimension of identity and evaluating the other side in that context is growing or declining. A narrowing gap means more acceptance of the other; that is, finding its soft power less problematic. Japan matters greatly for China's national identity, and China also matters a lot for Japan's and South Korea's identities, and its significance has been growing in the most recent decades.

The comparisons center on three points in time: (1) when identity gaps were least as China's soft power peaked, (2) when gaps were growing as its soft power fell and (3) in the late 2010s when the gaps were the widest since normalization but narrowing somewhat at the end. Japan preceded South Korea in declining perceptions of Chinese soft power. China has long enjoyed more soft power in South Korea than in Japan. For each point in time, one can assess soft power—a composite of identity gaps on multiple dimensions—in comparison to the previous period and to China's other neighbor allied with the United States. Soft power has ebbed since the early 2000s, and it had fallen earlier in Japan, but it was *later* falling in South Korea fast.

China had apparently lost interest in soft power, first in Japan and more recently in South Korea. This happened in stages with an interval of 5 to 10 years found between the shifts toward these two countries. In 1987 the first-stage shift occurred to Japan, and around 1997 a similar shift occurred toward South Korea. In 1994 the second-stage shift occurred toward Japan, followed in 2004 toward South Korea. The third-stage shift came in two rounds: toward Japan in 2005 and, more fully, in 2011; toward South Korea in 2008 and, with full force, in 2016. These dates are approximate, supported by shifts that are traced in the sections that follow. Specifying the three stages, what affected the timing and what accounts for China's hardening position builds a foundation for drawing conclusions about why the Chinese priority for soft power was decreasing and for drawing comparisons that suggest why Japan and South Korea still diverge. China's image in South Korea and Japan improved from 2017, perhaps because of hedging due to Donald Trump's impact; it did not revert to earlier levels.

In the second half of 2017 Xi Jinping improved relations with Abe Shinzo, as Japan was more forthcoming on Xi's Belt and Road Initiative, and with the new leader of South Korea, Moon Jae-in, who offered assurances on some military activities opposed by China. Both Abe and Moon sought improved ties: to gain cooperation in pressing North Korea to change course, to bolster popularity at home and economic ties and to hedge against unpredictable or even threatening moves by Donald Trump, such as a preemptive military strike on North Korea or the end to US trade deficits. Yet, Xi, too, saw an opportunity to take advantage of the need for China's help and of the Trump effect. To the extent the Japanese and South Korean publics see a zero-sum relationship between Washington and Beijing, Trump's unpopularity could boost China's soft power, but there was little sign that China had a strategy to seize on this. Its domestic crackdown and claims of historical justice did not serve this objective, even if Xi Jinping was now claiming the mantle of globalization dropped by Trump.

Bilateral national identity gaps when Chinese soft power was at a peak

China's soft power peaked in Japan in the late 1980s, slipped in 1989, but remained rather high in the first half of the 1990s. Its soft power rose from a low level in South Korea in the late 1980s, kept climbing in the first half of the 1990s, and then peaked in the early 2000s. Indicative of substantial soft power was a tendency for Japanese and South Koreans to minimize gaps with China in ideology, historical memory, their political and economic systems, the character of state–society relations and plans to achieve regionalism. There was a tendency to give China the benefit of the doubt, dismissing evidence to the contrary. While events in China mattered, no less salient were expectations for one's own country and how China figured into them.

Japanese officials and public opinion were enamored of China by the late 1970s and grew increasingly so to the mid-1980s. Normalization of diplomatic relations in 1972 preceded Sino–South Korean normalization by two decades; economic ties boomed from the end of the 1970s, a decade before the Sino–South Korean boom began; and the feeling that the Chinese were looking to Japan more than the United States as a model rose in the early 1980s, also a decade before Koreans gained the impression their country was becoming a model. Despite some widening of the gap in 1989, it was rather low during the early 1990s. Explanations center more on Japan's identity than on China's since the gap narrowed while Mao's Cultural Revolution was ongoing and remained far lower than in Sino-US relations after the 1989 brutality. Explanations for rising South Korean approval for China also offer testimony more to Korean identity than to changes in Chinese identity since the events in 1989 did not lower optimism, nor did rising Sino–US tensions, as China tightened some domestic controls and grew more assertive. A positive image of China met an identity need in nations that had chafed at the limitations of their status and pride during the polarized era of the Cold War.

The rise in Chinese soft power can be attributed to three principal factors. First, the bulk of media coverage of ongoing events in China was optimistic, expecting better times to come: market openings, political reforms, international cooperation and, above all, improved bilateral relations. Accelerated improvement in bilateral ties overshadowed the impact of June 4th. Second, public opinion was persuaded that China's rise was taking place in a favorable regional and international context, and it that it would lead to that context growing even more so; economic and security expectations were high, international communism was collapsing and trade barriers were rapidly falling, but there was confidence, too, in "Asian values" forged outside of China. China's rise was widely interpreted as beneficial in the struggle against the domination of US identity, the pursuit of Asianism in some form and obsession with reconstructing historical memories and the quest for legitimacy for a unique model of state–society relations and civilization. Japanese anticipated that China would fall in line with the "flying geese" and confirm Japan's leadership in Asia; South Koreans foresaw China endorsing its victory against North Korea and enabling reunification.

In the late 1980s Japan and South Korea were each experiencing a spike in national identity. The news from China was filtered through that prism. The two main forces were the rush of optimism from Japan's "economic miracle" and "bubble economy" and South Korea's "democratization" and "economic miracle" on the one hand, and the far-reaching impact of Mikhail Gorbachev's "new thinking" on the other. Even if China could not be expected to follow the same path as the Soviet Union, its reforms along some of the same lines and its susceptibility to economic blandishments from a neighbor poised to transplant manufacturing and capital raised high hopes. There appeared to be a perfect fit, which would enable each in its own way to realize its deepest identity aspirations. Facing growing US pressure over protectionism, both states eyed China for balance and for assistance in building a civilizational buffer. *civilizational buffer*

The Hu Yaobang–Nakasone bond raised Japanese hopes that China would not play the "history card," while boosting youth exchanges with optimism about the future. After Hu was purged in 1987 amid criticism of being too cozy with Japan and after troubling 1989 images, satisfaction with Japan's success in reestablishing summit relations before others in 1991 and then with the emperor's visit to China in 1992 gave new impetus to China's soft power. Negative feedback was minimized because of high hopes for improving relations helping to realize Japan's own identity aims.

Jiang Zemin's visit to Seoul in 1996 suggested that China was tilting its way, not insisting on equidistance with Pyongyang. It appeared that economics was taking command. Jiang sought joint historical criticism of Japan, to which Kim Young-sam consented, as the Chinese sought joint opposition to Japan's new military posture in guidelines taking shape with the United States (Snyder, 2009, pp. 88–89). In agreeing to China's soft power on the history issue, South Koreans revealed a longing for Chinese cooperation versus North Korea and a susceptibility to playing the "Japan card." China's low profile, following Deng Xiaoping's dictum of 1992, lulled South Koreans into complacency, ignoring the fact that China's policy toward Pyongyang opposed reunification on terms Seoul envisioned and aimed to exacerbate rifts in Japan–South Korea ties (Huan, 1991).

South Korean confidence as North Korea suffered a debilitating famine and became an international pariah led to the assumption that "unification of Korea is inevitable. At the moment, chances for economically weak North Korea to unify on its terms are extremely minimal" (Lee, 1994, p. 109). The halo of Beijing choosing Seoul while states were abandoning Pyongyang hung heavily over South Korean thinking, echoed in positive thinking about Beijing not just as an economic partner but also as a partner whose soft power would be given the benefit of the doubt in feelings of friendship.

Why did China have such importance in balancing national identity? It had served as the focus of national identity thinking historically. It is the neighborhood behemoth, casting a deep shadow by its presence and by its distance in identity from the West. China was seen as vulnerable to leverage in order to achieve one's own national identity aspirations: Asianism for Tokyo after decades of awkward fidgeting as part of the West, and reunification for Seoul after decades stuck in hostility without any sense of normality. Gorbachev opened the door to dreams long suppressed. Deng Xiaoping offered hope, too, and even his about-face in June 1989 fueled such dreams. The wider gulf between China and the United States seemed to offer room for Japan to play a bridging role and for South Korea to serve as a model for an alternative path to development; both anticipated that China's new priority for Asian neighbors rather than the two superpowers would put their country in the forefront.

As the international environment was changing from 1986, new Japanese reasoning about the great powers revealed unexpected distancing from the United States, hopes for capitalizing in a big way on the transformation of the Soviet Union and shifting expectations for Sino–Japanese relations (Rozman, 1992). The legacy of "friendship" for China—often seeing it through rose-colored glasses—carried through a shift in rhetoric coming from China toward warnings about the danger of Japan seeking to become a political and military great power. Friendly feelings toward China slipped from high levels, but still predominated. Because its future was indeterminate and it served Japanese ambitions, it loomed like an opportunity. Guilt toward China, assuaged by massive economic assistance to elicit appreciation, contributed to sympathy. Anti-Americanism was transferred to pro-Chinese attitudes, while anti-Soviet attitudes (rising to the late 1980s) had an impact, too. Expectations for regional leadership boosted hopes for China, as Chinese briefly toned down criticisms of Japan in the early 1990s. It was not just Japan that would rise; Japan was poised to lead an Asian renaissance (Tsunoyama, 1995). Economic complementarity would be boosted by shared culture (Furuyama, 1994).

China was appealing for at least three reasons. Japanese confidence in the "flying geese model" of production networks operating under their country's management extended to the latest and biggest "goose," which, as others, would recognize the benefits of adhering to normalization agreements reached earlier (1972, 1978) and leaving historical resentments on the sidelines in official relations. Japan's ODA, the transfer of Japanese companies to China through high FDI, and a sense that the West was trailing Japan in economic integration with China, boosted anticipation. If more attention had been paid to Chinese sources, especially internal ones that could be found with some effort, optimism would have been restrained (*Riben wenti ziliao*).

Japan's optimism rested on a view of Asian history minimizing the impact of communism in China and Japan's expansionist legacy in favor of traditional culture conducive to consensus on "Asian values." Japan's hopes for "Asianism" preceded the gravity of its own decline at a time of resentment against "*gaiatsu*," as if the US enemy replacing the Soviet Union was Japan rather than China. Japan and South Korea also exaggerated the pressure coming from the United States in light of accusations of protectionism, responding to US identity gaps by minimizing gaps with China. The early 1990s saw idealism about a "*kanji* cultural sphere" (Mizoguchi et al., 1992). Chinese soft power was seen as malleable. Problematic aspects were dismissed as a fading legacy of communism, anger over the past as declining with generational change.

Jae Ho Chung closely examined the transformation of relations between Seoul and Beijing, including in the first half of the 1990s. In addition to booming trade, South Korean investments and mutual visitors, Chung points to the salience of feelings about China's value in reducing the perceived threat from Japan. The Japanese blamed South Koreans for naive feelings of closeness to China, but they overlooked the way Japanese statements about history alienated Koreans and led in that direction. These years were also marked by a lack of concern about a Chinese military buildup and a prevailing sense after 1992 that Sino–North Korean relations were on the decline (Chung, 2007).

Bilateral national identity gaps as Chinese soft power was waning

China's patriotic education campaign targeting Japan in the mid-1990s and disregard of Korean opinion in a historical reassessment of the Koguryo dynasty, which came into the open in 2004, served internal national identity objectives at the expense of soft power. They tarnished the images of these countries, blaming them in order to sharpen consciousness of a distinctive Chinese identity. Japanese were calling more than ever before for an East Asian regional community, which China's leaders feared Japan sought to lead. South Koreans were anticipating unification on their terms with an isolated, famine-stricken North Korea. The Koguryo theme cast doubt on the legitimacy of a unified Korea encompassing the northern part of the peninsula. Japan's spike in identity in the late 1980s and regional identity claims in the 1990s gave Chinese reason to denigrate it, drawing on familiar war stories with warnings of their growing relevance. South Korea's spike in identity—the poster boy of Asian dynamism before recovering from the Asian financial crisis with a Sunshine Policy to steer reunification and regionalism—led China to undermine its legitimacy in regard to North Korea.

Worsening mutual images impacted China's soft power in Japan, as Jiang Zemin's ill-fated visit in 1998 widened the identity gap. An effort was made in China to reverse this impact—in 1999 "smile diplomacy," which in 2003 turned into "new thinking"—but this was in vain given leadership priorities and the aroused emotions of the Chinese public. Then came the 2003–2005 open arousal of greater distrust. Japanese often drew the wrong lessons from lulls in

Shift in Chinese perception of Japan

Why China wanted to boost soft power by Japan

criticism, pining for positive messages about Japan as a modernization model (the 1980s), an economic benefactor (the 1980s–1990s), a bridge in new great power relations (1990s) and a force for shared regionalism (the 1990s-2000s). In stages, however, Chinese viewed Japan more negatively as pushing for regional political power, akin to the prewar era; posing a cultural threat with its values; opposing China's rise as a threat; and succumbing to historical distortions to revive pre-1945 militarism. Building identity at Japan's expense reverberated in Japanese distrust of China's soft power. With uncertainty over the Asian financial crisis and greater alarm about US assertiveness, China stressed the importance of bilateral friendship or mentioned gratitude for Japanese ODA, but the Internet had already emerged as a fountain of anger over such weakness (Rozman, 2002). "New thinking" came too late and with little top-down support, as the last gasp of soft power versus Japan.

From the Chinese perspective, boosting soft power with Japan had many benefits. It provided some balance against the United States, as China recognized that the decline in the remaining superpower was not happening as fast as anticipated. It deterred Japan from a more active turn to the alliance while increasing the chances for regionalism, which China sold to Japan as a "win-win." There were economic benefits. International relations experts in China anticipated greater benefits if the "history card" were set aside with a more positive assessment of postwar Japan and Japan's big contribution to the ongoing rise of China. Japan's political power need not be of much concern either, as its turn to Asia had the potential to open a big rift with the United States. Michael Green attributes Japan's persistence in expressing optimism toward China to the appeal of a special relationship willing to minimize human rights concerns, to keep silent over Taiwan, and to anticipate an Asian identity, which China in 1999, fearing worsening Sino–US relations, had encouraged with a softer approach (Green, 2001, pp. 106–109).

With Bush's unilateralism intensifying in 2002–2003, interest in using Japan had risen. Yet public negativity was too aroused, Koizumi's visits to the Yasukuni Shrine and close ties to Bush were too disturbing, and China's distorted narrative on Japan's history and current affairs was too useful for legitimacy to sustain "new thinking" (Cohen, 2005).

The Koguryo dispute shook Korean confidence in China, but the pull of positive thinking could not be denied. President Roh Moo-hyun even suggested that Seoul could become a balancer in Sino–US relations, as he raised hopes for reunification with China in a supportive role. Yet, the seeds of distrust planted when Koguryo hit the headlines grew in 2008 when China turned against Lee Myung-bak over his foreign policy and spurred a sharp rise in writings blaming civilizational differences.

Chinese publications on South Korea grew more critical, widening the identity gap. Sinocentrism crept into the story more and renewed support for North Korea hinted at socialism as a factor. On the temporal dimension views of successive periods in history grew more negative. Reacting to improved South

Korea–Japan relations, China sided with progressive opponents of Lee Myung-bak (prior to Lee's visit to Dokdo in August 2012), who said he was not vigilant in dealing with the collaboration issue and the legacy of Japan's occupation (Rozman, 2012a). In civilizational clashes on the Internet, the Chinese charged that South Koreans claimed Chinese civilizational achievements as their own.

Wang Xiaoling examined how South Koreans view China and Chinese view South Korea as attitudes were turning more negative from 2008, asking, "Do Chinese hate South Korea?" (Wang, 2009). Saying that a majority do not, she pointed to criticisms of "stealing China's cultural legacy" as in the Koguryo dispute and the advance showing by a Korean TV station of the Opening Ceremony of the Beijing Olympics. Acknowledging limited public interest in China in the "Korean wave," she stressed, unpersuasively, that "hate Korea feelings" had not been aroused at all by the Chinese government.

Efforts by Chinese academics to gain a better understanding of images of China in Japan and South Korea offered guidance on how China can improve its soft power. Distinguished from the sensationalist writing on Japan and even notably in 2008–2012 on South Korea aimed at mobilizing public outrage, they straddle a fine line between scholarship on a high plain and partisanship serving leadership objectives.

A book by Wu Guangwei offers a broad historical sweep of images in Japan, covering China at different points in time, stressing from the late 1990s the "China threat" image. The main focus is on negative images, explained as serving the goals of justifying military development in Japan, enabling it to escape from its postwar system, following the United States in its containment policy, distracting the Japanese public after years of stagnation and striving to block China from growing stronger (Wu, 2010. pp. 151–154). There is no attempt to treat China's responsibility or reflect on Japan's efforts to find common ground. The era of *neibu* publications delving more deeply into foreign policy themes peaked in the late 1980s, but it never allowed for a far-reaching assessment of policy mistakes and succumbed to tighter controls.

Another Chinese book is forthright in detailing negative images in South Korea of China, drawing on textbooks, survey data, a focus group study, and interviews with experts. It makes a powerful case for improving soft power, which Zhang Yunling's introduction urges, emphasizing the need to look squarely at how others view China and to strive hard, despite the difficulty, to forge a friendly, respected image. The book is largely in line with his appeal, but its explanations for Korean attitudes are one-sided, with no criticism of China's behavior. The authors stress the big impact of media on the public, but they explain that fierce market competition leads to extreme coverage, as in the way the Koguryo history dispute was handled, and they describe the South Korean public as naturally very emotional and easily aroused, as well as rather ignorant about the outside world. Its textbooks convey Cold War logic, taking the Western viewpoint and treating China as the communist "other" in an ideological approach on Tibet and Taiwan, as well as excessive coverage of periods such as the Great Leap Forward and the Cultural Revolution. Analyzing surveys, the authors conclude that South Koreans feel superior to China, but they are envious and do not want China's development to succeed. Respondents also blame Chinese for looking down on "little" South Korea. Convinced of South Korea's superiority, they are unwilling to accept China's rise and, except for business forces, are not optimistic about its impact. Viewing themselves as victims, they transfer blame for their own faults to the "other." The book recognizes a huge gap between Chinese self-perceptions and South Korean views of China and gives explanations rooted in history, culture and psychology, mainly subjective in nature. It argues that time will be required for psychologically accepting China's rise. Coverage of bilateral relations as a factor is brief without any attention to the forces that have mattered (Dong, 2011, pp. 41, 82, 190).

To strengthen Chinese soft power in South Korea, the book calls for more economic development, so South Koreans will no longer continue to underestimate China's world rank and focus on disadvantages rather than on opportunities in economic relations. Yet, the principal problem, as reported, is images of great inequality, environmental damage and less complementarity between economies as China becomes more competitive. To meet these concerns China would have to do more than become an economic colossus to overcome its image problem. A second piece of advice to China is to provide more positive signals about Sino–South Korean relations since China is less trusted than the United States, Japan and even Russia. The following lists in descending order what focus groups said about the causes of perceived problems in relations: the Sino–North Korean alliance (82% of respondents said China does not support reunification); divergence over history, especially Koguryo; and the contrast in social systems, indicated by those who are troubled by China's socialist system.

A third problem covered at length but absent in advice on what is to be done is the cultural gap, as seen in the adjectives selected by South Koreans to describe Chinese, and in the mutual distrust aroused by what Chinese see as Korean claims to have improved on Confucianism or to have invented cultural festivals that Chinese regard as their own. Chinese are seen as dirty, arrogant, insensitive to the feelings of others, and devious or calculating. No mention is made of how arrogantly China's leaders treat South Korean leaders or how little recognition they give to the diversity of Confucianism. In his introduction, Zhang Yunling warns that China cannot just stress the positive and improve its image. It must have the self-confidence to look squarely at how others view it and recognize that it can be seen as scary, a monster swallowing the world. The book, however, does not develop the warnings raised by Zhang.

Bilateral national identity gaps as Chinese soft power fell sharply

In 2010–2012 China upped its demonization of Japan. In 2016, it chose to demonize South Korea. In each case, there were specific causes—a rammed boat incident, the pretext of Japanese nationalization of the Senkaku Islands, the decision to deploy the THAAD missiles—but they served a larger purpose for Chinese national identity.

The seemingly irreversible drop in Japanese views of Chinese soft power and South Korean views of Chinese soft power came amidst conflicts over security. Yet, the Chinese response to matters deemed for self-defense shocked the public in Japan and South Korea. All dimensions of national identity were invoked by the Chinese: warning of an ideological gap; blaming all eras in the other state's history; elevating the dispute into a civilizational divide; taking offense at comments on state–society relations with consequences for foreign policy; insisting that their neighbor is abetting unjust, US hegemonic designs; and also intensifying the existing identity gap. For Japan, there has been little reprieve from this onslaught, leading to little hope to repair ties, although the second half of 2017 began some amelioration. For South Korea, the downturn is too recent to know if some reprieve is ahead: progressives are inclined to give China the benefit of the doubt, given identity gaps with Japan and the United States and desperate hopes for help with North Korea. Japan sees no way to work with China toward regionalism in Asia and is left organizing states against China to salvage some Asianism, while South Korea clings to ideas about cooperating to achieve its reunification objectives, unwilling to contemplate what would be lost if the identity gap worsens. Given the alarm over North Korea's burgeoning threat and the possibility of Trump taking military action as well as the uncertainty about Trump's Asia policies, both Abe and Moon saw a need to reach out to Xi Jinping, who also saw an opportunity in late 2017 and may have decided that, as he centralized more power and Trump left a vacuum, he could try his hand at boosting soft power backed by economic power. Yet, this did not signal a reversal of the trends that had drawn concern.

Both Japan and South Korea were shocked by China's disregard of soft power appealing to their country, but the consequences were different. Fearing a full-fledged assault on their national interests and identity, many in Japan came to see a "China threat." In the case of Koreans, they tended to blame their own government or, in the case of the Koguryo challenge, overzealous local Chinese officials. Driving the debate on Korean identity, progressives have tamped down alarm over China.

Charging that Abe Shinzo is remilitarizing Japan and breaking the status quo in the regional order that has long existed, the Chinese justify China's assertive behavior as a defensive response to Japan's new course. Since the late 1980s the Chinese have warned that Japan has unhealthy ambitions to become a political and military great power, forging a link between Japan's past militarism and its current intentions (Rozman, 2013). The shift in 2004 from "smile diplomacy" and then "new thinking" showing understanding of Japan and appreciation for its post-1945 choices, to charges that Koizumi's visits to the Yasukuni Shrine were linked to containment of China and fabrication of a "China threat," accompanied an effort to pressure Japan into Sinocentric regionalism in Northeast and

Southeast Asia. In 2009–2010 demonization of all dimensions of Japan's national identity preceded aggressive policies around its borders, with only minor restraint in 2011 before resuming. There were softer interpretations of Japan's nature and intentions, as in the 2006–2008 thaw in relations, but they did not last. Since 2012 the drumbeat of criticism on identity themes has barely paused. The argument that Abe is driving Japan not only to revised memories about history but also to a militarized foreign policy threatening to the rise of China has become a mainstay in *Huanqiu shibao*, as well as on the Internet. Articles about Japan in many journals of an academic as well as popular nature echo these sentiments and amplify in this way alarm about the historical and cultural background of Japan's evolution.

A voice of "new thinking," Ma Licheng wrote in 2015 about talk of reviving it, saying that without Sino–Japanese reconciliation stability in East Asia is not possible (Ma, 2015). He said that instead of each country only presenting its own case and arousing people to behave emotionally, which intensifies the dispute, helps Japan's right wing to win, and thus makes China feel threatened, it would be beneficial for China to convey an image of supporting peace and respecting international law. Ma supports remembering two histories: the war calamities and the reconciliation and cooperation as Japan's postwar mainstream—government and society—chose the path of peace and war responsibility, with the government apologizing 25 times for the war from 1972 to 2008, as found in Chinese reports. Ma looks back to the more benign statements of Chinese leaders in 2007–2008 for forward-looking ties. However, the Chinese are in no mood to entertain such recommendations, and Ma's voice is stifled on social media as "pro-Japan." The loss of soft power appears to matter little.

Unlike Japan, where the far right has persistently sought to shift national identity in defiance of postwar opinion, South Korea has seen alternating calls for identity to move in one direction or the other. If a strong consensus on identity matters versus Japan, China is treated more as an identity afterthought in inverse relationship to identity swings toward the United States or tied to prospects for ties to North Korea. Yet, the mood soured in 2016 as China punished the nation for deploying THAAD.

Coverage of South Korea is more ambivalent, leaving the door open to finding a way to overcome public suspicions. There is also a reluctance to acknowledge realist attitudes, as if North Korea's behavior or China's military rise and assertiveness are of little or no influence. Yet, criticism of national identity themes comes with an element of possibility that they can be overcome. Japan is no longer in play. South Korea is.

In January 2014, Chinese officials doubled down on the theme that Abe is reviving militarism. The issue is less erroneous understandings of history and more the rise of Japan as a military power bent on treating China as a threat and joining with the United States in a containment strategy. If Chinese analysts treated Japan as well as China as a realist state, then they would establish a foundation for diplomacy aimed at narrowing differences. By glorifying Chinese national identity at the same time as they demonize Japan's national identity, they are arousing the public and making new attempts at diplomacy more difficult. Discussion in Japan of the "China threat" has, arguably, been more muted than that of Japanese "militarism" in China, and is generally couched in terms of the need for dialogue to narrow differences. Given the Chinese literature on Japan, there is little sign of a similar inclination unless political change is more drastic in Japan than observers expect. Demonization is here to stay.

Chinese soft power has been much more successful in South Korea than in Japan, as seen in 2013–2015 when Xi Jinping cultivated the image of a "honeymoon" with Park Geun-hye. For progressives this followed from the priority on reunification as well as autonomy versus the United States, but even for conservatives supportive of Park it was a response to wishful thinking that China's impact was mostly positive, that Sino–US relations were competitive but not confrontational, that China is not the problem but part of the solution on security and economic matters and that Japan is more likely to initiate a security conflict than China. At the root of the problem is a divide between Japanese (mainly conservatives) who regard China as the biggest threat to their aspirations for a "normal Japan" and South Koreans (progressives most of all) who regard China as more positive than negative in realizing their hopes for a "normal Korea." The two sides have perceived China through different prisms. Yet, offensive Chinese moves since 2004 have kept dimming any Korean optimism.

The Genron NPO Poll 2016 sheds light on Chinese soft power in both Japan and South Korea (Genron, 2016). As for soft power linked to expectations that China's influence in Asia will grow over the next decade, the percentage who expect this to occur fell from the previous year from 60.3% to 51.9% in Japan and from 80.0% to 71.2% in South Korea. The levels are still high, but a sense of inevitability is falling. Another change was a sharp drop in both China (24.7% to 18.0%) and South Korea (45.6% to 24.2%) in expectations that South Korea's influence in Asia will increase. China's media has portrayed South Korea in a negative light, as South Koreans note that poor relations with China (and Japan and North Korea) and domestic problems make it vulnerable. Chinese who see South Korea as a reliable partner fell from 56.3% to 34.9%; 25% more in 2016 see it as unreliable. Koreans are still more hopeful about working with China as well as the United States to achieve a peaceful regional order (27.8% vs. 14.0% percent in Japan). Japanese worry about China's intrusions into nearby seas and coercive actions against the international community rose 20% from 2015. These opinion polls in the summer of 2016 show deteriorating trust in China, while from late 2017 there were some signs of reversal in these trends.

Conclusion

Chinese social science has little interest in realist or liberal theory. It sticks closely to constructivist theory, obsessed with national identity manifestations in political thought as expressed by leaders and the national media. These writings accept a top-down view of how identity changes and public opinion is reshaped. More-over, their simplistic framework posits a sharp dichotomy between what others would call pacifist Japan and what the Chinese see as militarist Japan. Finding Abe a useful symbol of the linkage between right-wing extremism and real-ist internationalism, they dispense with the latter as if it is only a byproduct of nostalgia for pre-1945 national identity. Abe serves the narrative far better than Hatoyama did in 2009. For anyone still hoping for common ground on strate-gic issues, finding a pathway to put historical matters aside or reach an interim agreement on certain symbols, such a Chinese understanding of Japan makes it clear that a realist Japan is unacceptable.

China had a golden opportunity to capitalize on Japanese and Korean pro-gressives' aspirations for balancing dependency on the United States, pursuing regionalism in Asia and affirming some version of "Asian values." There was talk in the early 2000s that in welcoming an "East Asian community" China would prioritize soft power with "new thinking" appreciative of Japan and cultural receptivity to newly popular Korean dramas at a time many Koreans trusted China. Yet, in allowing the Koguryo issue to fester in 2004 and stifling the "new thinking" toward Japan before arousing massive demonstrations against it in 2005, China cast soft power aside. Again, in a wave of demonization of Japan and also of South Korea during the "culture wars" of 2008–2010, China paid no heed to soft power. Finally, under Xi Jinping China has put even more effort into vilifying its neighbors allied to the United States, doubling down on castigating Japan and, in 2016, reversing course after the "honeymoon" with Park Geun-hye for three years. The door has been kept ajar for South Korea in hopes that a progressive president would change course, but it is closed for Japan.

South Korean responses to China's efforts to find common cause against Japan for historical transgressions and a growing drift to the right at times showcased shared values and served China's soft power—as in the early response to Abe in 2013—but when Xi Jinping carried this too far in the eyes of many Koreans in a speech at Seoul National University in July 2014 there was a backlash. The overlap of thinking about Japan was acknowledged in a joint statement by leaders in November 1995 (Snyder, 2009, p. 186), and has generally served to keep the gap narrower with China, but by early 2017 views of Japan had become more favorable than those of China at a time of strained ties. Discarding soft power as it wielded enhanced economic and military power, China has alienated Japanese and South Koreans alike under the spell of a narrow version of Sinocentrism and a polarized national identity opposed to Western identity, not only in the United States but in Asian countries contaminated by "universal values."

China's soft power in Japan has sunk to an unprecedented low since the 1972 normalization of relations, while its soft power in South Korea had revived some through 2015 before dropping sharply in 2016. The decline in both cases can be attributed to a conscious decision in China that other objectives take priority. To suggest altering the image in Japan by revived "new thinking" or in South Korea by capitalizing on the "honeymoon" image encouraged by Park Geun-hye, is to invite censorship and demonization insistent on the opposite outlook. Geopolitics may appear to take precedence, but charges that either of these countries posed a threat to China, however persuasive to Chinese audiences, are concocted with scant evidence. The Chinese public accepted that Japan has shifted to "militarization" and poses the greatest threat to start a conflict in the Asia-Pacific region (greater than North Korea by 6:1) (The Asian, 2016, p. 22). Later, it was persuaded that Seoul's decision to allow the deployment of THAAD means it has joined the United States in containing China.

The Trump impact on national identity gaps is worth a treatise of its own. Suffice it to say that China found new reason to improve relations with Japan, but the focus was economic and political rather than any buildup of soft power. With Hong Kong demonstrations giving the Japanese a telling example of how China was aloof to winning the trust of others, better ties did little to forge trust in China's model or its strategic intentions. In the case of South Korea, both Beijing and Seoul were too preoccupied with maneuvering with Pyongyang to pay much heed to narrowing their identity gap. Xi Jinping in 2019 visited Kim Jong-un but not Moon Jae-in and continued to pressure South Korea over THAAD and US alliance ties. Even with US soft power falling, China did little to boost its own soft power in East Asia. *missed opportunity*
Since neither Tokyo nor Seoul sought conflict with Beijing—both prioritizing North Korea's threat—the explanation has to be sought apart from geopolitics. China has in mind a different notion of soft power than is customary. It is Sinocentric, demands deference and respect for China's political and cultural preferences, and excludes an orientation deemed "Western." Viewing respect for China and the United States in zero-sum terms, Chinese leaders decided that friendly attitudes from Tokyo and Seoul are insufficient. There did not seem to be any point wasting energy on boosting soft power except to the extent domestic opposition there can overcome elite attitudes. Whether Xi Jinping, entering his second term as the party leader in a strong position, is beginning to reconsider how to use soft power, it is too early to determine and too late to reverse Japanese and South Korean attitudes.

[handwritten margin note: Chinese sense of soft power (unconventional)]

References

The Asian Research Network. 2016. *Survey on America's Role in the Asia-Pacific, June 2016.* Sydney: United States Studies Centre, University of Sydney.

Chung, Jae Ho. 2007. *Between Ally and Partner: Korea-China Relations and the United States.* New York: Columbia University Press.

Cohen, Danielle F.S. 2005. *Retracing the Triangle: China's Strategic Perceptions of Japan in the Post-Cold War Era*, Maryland Series in Contemporary Asian Studies, no. 2. College Park, Maryland.

Dong Xiangrong, Wang Xiaoleng and Li Yongchun. 2011. *Hanguoren Xinmuzhong de Zhongguo Xingxiang.* Beijing: Renmin chubanshe.

Furumaya Tadao. 1994. *Ajia shi no saihakken: rekishizo no koyu o motomete.* Tokyo: Yushindo.

The Genron NPO. 2016. *The Genron NPO Poll 2016: The Future of Northeast Asia and Public Opinions.* Genron: Tokyo.

Green, Michael J. 2001. *Japan's Reluctant Realism: Foreign Policy Challenges in an Era of Uncertain Power.* New York: Palgrave.

Huan, Guocang. 1991. "China's Policy towards Northeast Asia: Dynamics and Prospects," *The Korean Journal of Defense Analysis* 3(2), pp. 178–181.

Lee, Hung Yong. 1994. "China and the Two Koreas: New Emerging Triangle," in Young Whan Kihl (ed.), *Korea and the World: Beyond the Cold War.* Boulder, CO: Westview Press.

Ma Licheng. 2015. His Article Appeared in China in July and in Japanese in *Chuokoron*, August, pp. 86–111.

Mizoguchi Yusan et al. (eds.). 1992. *Kanji bunkaken no rekishi to mirai.* Tokyo: Taishukan shoten, p. 213.

Ribenwenti ziliao, which was meant for internal use in the 1980s.

Rozman, Gilbert. 1992. *Japan's Response to the Gorbachev Era, 1985–1991: A Rising Superpower Views a Declining One.* Princeton, NJ: Princeton University Press.

Rozman, Gilbert. 2002. "China's Changing Images of Japan, 1989–2001: The Struggle to Balance Partnership and Rivalry," *International Relations of the Asia-Pacific* 2, pp. 95–129.

Rozman, Gilbert (ed.). 2011. *U.S. Leadership, History, and Bilateral Relations in Northeast Asia.* Cambridge: Cambridge University Press.

Rozman, Gilbert (ed.). 2012. *East Asian National Identities: Common Roots and Chinese Exceptionalism.* Washington, DC and Stanford, CA: Woodrow Wilson Center Press and Stanford University Press.

Rozman, Gilbert. 2012a. "History as an Arena of Sino-Korean Conflict and the Role of the United States," *Asian Perspective* 36, pp. 263–285.

Rozman, Gilbert (ed.). 2013. *National Identities and Bilateral Relations: Widening Gaps in East Asia and Chinese Demonization of the United States.* Washington, DC and Stanford, CA: Woodrow Wilson Center Press and Stanford University Press.

Rozman, Gilbert. 2016. "Changes in the Japan-South Korea National Identity Gap," in Gilbert Rozman (ed.), *Joint U.S.-Korea Academic Studies: Rethinking Asia in Transition.* Washington, DC: Korea Economic Institute of America, pp. 128–141.

Shambaugh, David. 2015. "China's Soft Power Push: The Search for Respect," *Foreign Affairs*, July/August.

Snyder, Scott. 2009. *China's Rise and the Two Koreas: Politics, Economics, Security.* Boulder, CO: Lynne Rienner.

Tsunoyama, Sakae. 1995. *Ajia no renesansu.* Tokyo: PHP.

Wan, Ming. 2013. *Sino-Japanese Relations: Interaction, Logic, and Transformation.* Washington, DC and Stanford, CA: Woodrow Wilson Center Press and Stanford University Press.

Wang, Xiaoling. 2009. *Zhongguoren xinmuzhongde Hanguo xingxiang.* Beijing: Minzu chubanshe.

Wu, Guangwei. 2010. *Riben de Zhongguo xingxiang.* Beijing: Renmin chubanshe.

12

CHINA'S SOFT POWER OVER TAIWAN

Dalton Lin and Yun-han Chu

Between 2008 and 2016, in stark contrast to previous years, China downplayed the forcible options in its toolbox for unifying Taiwan. Even though it by no means forwent the possibility of achieving the goal by force, Beijing did emphasize winning the hearts and minds of the Taiwanese people. In other words, China tried to co-opt rather than coerce Taiwan into its unification agenda. Moreover, the exchanges were often sweetened by extra concessions made by the Mainland, in the hope that such "peace dividends" would earn the Taiwanese public's willing embrace of unification.

However, China's experiment with the soft (i.e., non-coercive) elements of its power seemed to lose traction in the end. The efforts to set a favorable agenda toward greater cross-Taiwan Strait integration, through a flurry of bilateral agreements in the period between 2008 and 2016, apparently backfired. As the term of President Ma Ying-jeou, who was more sympathetic to the Mainland than most Taiwanese politicians were, approached its end, China's endeavors to bring the island closer were met with a rising local identity that was exclusively Taiwanese, a large-scale youth-led protest against a service trade pact with China that has since stalled cross-strait integration, and a return to office of the pro-independence Democratic Progressive Party (DPP).

Why did China's offers of stability and prosperity in this period fail to attract the Taiwanese people? The question has theoretical and practical implications. Explaining conditions that contribute to the ebb and flow of Taiwan's receptiveness to China's embrace helps advance our understanding of the sources and limits of soft power in international politics. More important, drawing lessons from this past soft power experiment helps clarify options for both Beijing and Taipei in their future efforts to maintain cross-strait stability and answer the disturbing question: could China again turn to hard power to deal with the island?

In this chapter, we focus on China's paramount soft power resource over Taiwan—its economic strength—and propose an argument to explain the variation

economic strength has soft & hard power implications

in China's economic soft power attraction. Admittedly, economic strength situates in the gray area between hard and soft power. However, economic strength's mechanics of hard power—coercion—are distinct from its mechanics of soft power—influence. Due to Taiwan's asymmetric economic dependence on China, the Mainland could use the threat of interrupting the relationship as a coercive lever. However, as Jonathan Kirshner argues, this is not the only story, and Beijing likely recognizes such exercise of economic power to be self-defeating of its broader objectives of winning hearts and minds in Taiwan (Kirshner, 2008, 242).

What Beijing tries to accomplish through its economic soft power attraction takes place in the mundane—the political influence accruing to the bigger trade partner that Albert Hirschman points out in his seminal work *National Power and the Structure of Foreign Trade*. As Taiwan trades more with China in the process of deeper economic integration, the constellation of interests in the Taiwanese society might reshuffle. When more and more economic sectors in Taiwan rely on China for their prosperity, a growing part of the Taiwanese society will develop vested interests in a friendly relationship with China (Hirschman, 1980/1945; Abdelal and Kirshner, 1999–2000). This can accrue political influence to Beijing as societal interests in Taiwan aggregate through domestic political processes and reshape how the island perceives its collective interests—it will place increasing value on amicable relations with China and even see its interests as converging with those of the Mainland. *economic long game ↑*

In other words, through the normal business exchanges, Taiwan's domestic political coalitions and, in turn, the island's perceptions of national interests might be remolded, not by pressure but by economic incentives (Hirschman, 1980/1945; Kirshner, 2008). Though such political influence derives from the pull of China's economic gravity instead of the attractiveness of values and culture that Joseph Nye emphasizes, it still operates through the logic of soft, not hard, power: getting others to want what you want instead of forcing them to do what you want them to do (Kirshner, 2008, pp. 242–243; Abdelal and Kirshner, 1999–2000, pp. 120–121).[1] Nye in fact does not rule out this type of soft power when he claims that co-optive power includes the "ability to manipulate the agenda of political choices in a manner that makes others fail to express some preferences because they seem to be too unrealistic" (Nye, 2004, p. 7).

not quite Nye's concept

We argue China's soft power work toward Taiwan through economic attraction seemed to have failed during Ma's presidency because it has put the cart before the horse. The logic of soft power starts from building up the attraction of the wielding country's soft power resources, and the attraction then leads to soft power response from the receiving country as it willingly heeds the wielding country's preferences.[2] China's ultimate hope is that its soft power attraction will lead to Taiwan's soft power response, that is, embracing an agenda of unification. However, Beijing so far has been demanding the island demonstrate this desired soft power response, that is, committing to unification one way or another, *before* the Mainland's soft power attraction actually remolds Taiwan's interests and produces the desired behavior. Furthermore, Beijing has been imposing its desired

pressure w/ China's presumptive strategy

outcome upon the island by obstructing Taiwan's economic integration with countries other than China—denying Taiwan the capacity to act autonomously in the world to substantiate Beijing's claim that Taiwan is part of China. The demand and obstruction puts the logic of soft power upside-down. They make demonstrating favorable soft power response an ostensible (and sometimes genuine) political precondition for Taiwan's access to China's soft power resources. They also make the desire for cross-strait integration seemingly a preference imposed by Beijing. This blurs the line between attraction and coercion and puts China's sympathizers in an awful position—anyone who advocates for closer relations with China is suspected of kowtowing to Beijing and selling out the island. It thus becomes difficult to encourage soft power response in Taiwan. As a result, despite the fact that China's economic soft power is potentially mighty, the soft power response it has produced so far remains meager.

In other words, we argue economic soft power must fundamentally come from free exchanges and others' voluntary, instead of forced, dependence on a country. Following this theoretical proposition, we expect the perceived rigidity and urgency of China's political precondition and the observed impediments from the Mainland to Taiwan's economic integration with others to have negative impacts on China's soft power attraction in Taiwan. Rhetorically, the timeline and format of China's unification agenda conveyed through Chinese leaders' statements affect the Taiwanese public's perception of its stringency. Behaviorally, how much China maintains its obstruction to Taiwan's economic integration with trade partners other than the Mainland, in the name of its "One China" principle, also reminds the Taiwanese people of the tightness of Beijing's political straitjacket. When Taiwan's high trade reliance on China is put into the context of grim prospects for economic integration with others due to Beijing's impediments, China's economic pull to the island becomes forced dependence imposed by the Mainland. Such forced dependence together with the perceived political precondition breeds no affection but skepticism toward Beijing's intention behind its economic offers and undermines Chinese soft power.

We use Taiwanese people's attitudes toward economic integration with China as a proxy for the underlying appeal of the Mainland's economic soft power. The premise is that the more people view Beijing's interests as compatible with their own, the more likely they would regard China's economic prosperity with affection instead of apprehension, and more likely they would favor economic integration with China.

We argue that during President Ma's first term, the hope that trade pacts with China would open the door to economic integration with other trade partners alleviated the Taiwanese public's worries about forced dependence on the Mainland and convinced people to embrace cross-strait integration. In addition, Beijing's explicit efforts to loosen the form and the urgency of its unification agenda created an environment more conducive to Taiwan's soft power response. However, seeing little progress on diversifying economic relations outside the Mainland in Ma's second term, Taiwanese people perceived the island's condition as remaining in forced high dependence on China. Furthermore, Chinese leadership's rhetoric hinted new urgency in the agenda of unification, raising anxieties about the Mainland's economic embrace in some parts of the Taiwanese society. Such perception of forced dependence on the Mainland and heightened awareness of China's political precondition led to pushback against cross-strait economic integration and undermined Taiwan's soft power response.

In a nutshell, Joseph Nye carefully distinguishes soft power resources from soft power responses[3] and warns that having a soft power resource is only a necessary but not sufficient condition for producing soft power and changing behavior (i.e., producing soft power responses) (Nye, 2004, pp. 11–12). China's soft power work toward Taiwan is a good case in point that vindicates Nye's caveat. In what follows, we therefore first identify China's potential soft power resources that might produce Taiwan's behavior of attraction, and then discuss when and why the soft power resources lead to the desired outcomes or not.

The chapter proceeds as follows. The first section discusses China's potential soft power resources over Taiwan and justifies our focus on economic soft power. The second section uses the results of the Asian Barometer Surveys and polls conducted by Taiwan's Mainland Affairs Council (MAC) to illustrate the general strength of Mainland China's economic soft power attraction and the ebb and flow of such attraction perceived by the Taiwanese public during Ma's presidency. The third section fleshes out our theoretical mechanisms. We conduct a comparative analysis of the attractiveness of China's soft power during President Ma's first and second term to test our propositions in the fourth section. The final section concludes by looking at implications for stability across the Taiwan Strait.

China's soft power resources over Taiwan

Given that academic discussion of soft power has been covered in the Introduction, this chapter focuses on measuring China's soft power in the practical cross-Taiwan Strait relations. To operationalize Nye's concepts of soft power resources, we refer to the Soft Power 30 index composed by the consultancy firm, Portland, as a benchmark. The Soft Power 30 index measures a country's soft power by its cultural, economic prowess, digital and diplomatic outreach, and political and educational appeal. The index's records have underlined that contemporary China's attractiveness to the world primarily comes from its economic potency, apart from its cultural attraction.

More than any cases in the rest of the world, China's soft power lure to Taiwan needs to mostly come from its economic strength rather than culture or other resources. The island not only shares the same Chinese culture with Mainland China but arguably preserves the culture more consistently—Taiwan was spared from the destruction of traditional elements in the culture and society that China suffered during the Cultural Revolution. Other than economic and cultural attraction, China's soft power allure to Taiwan is anemic in other

[handwritten annotation: psychological distance across strait]

categories identified by the Soft Power 30 index. From Taiwan's perspective, China's diplomatic outreach represents a zero-sum competition, instead of cooperative engagement, in the international community. Through its territorial claim over the island, China's illiberal political system poses a threat to Taiwan's democratic society and contributes to what former President Ma Ying-jeou called the "psychological distance" across the Taiwan Strait (Gracie, 2015). Also, China's schools are hardly Taiwanese youth's top destinations for higher education per se.[4]

Surveys by Taiwan's *United Daily News* on young Taiwanese people's attitudes toward China vindicate the above evaluation. In 2016, 82.8% of respondents regarded China as economically advanced, up from 53.6% in 2000. As a result, 40% of Taiwanese youth were willing to work in China in 2016, an increase of 5 percentage points from the year 2000. These results of relatively high portions of positive attitudes and upward moving trends revealed China's soft power attraction to Taiwanese youth based on its economic strength. However, in 2016, only 11.5% of respondents were willing to immigrate to China (a drop of almost 7 percentage points from 2000) and only 18.7% were inclined to study there. The reason for the contrasting outcomes may be summarized by a question in the survey: when asked whether they thought the Chinese on the mainland were civilized, only 15.8% of Taiwanese youth responded positively in 2016. In 2000, the ratio was in fact higher at 23.9%. In other words, apart from economic potency, China's soft power resources broadly lacked attractiveness in Taiwan (UDN Survey Center, 2016).

Taiwan's soft power attraction to China

[handwritten annotation: soft power can create a favourable environment to produce a policy (China jumping the gun)]

As Nye points out, and analogous to the mechanics of Hirschmanesque influence,[5] soft power resources often work indirectly by shaping a favorable policy environment in another country that makes it easy or even natural to adopt policies preferred by the country wielding soft power (Nye, 2004, p. 99). To paraphrase Nye, friendly foreign leaders may have more leeway if their publics and parliaments have a positive image of the soft power–wielding country and its policies (Nye, 2004, p. 105). It follows naturally that whether a particular asset is a soft power resource that produces attraction can be measured by asking people's opinions on the appeal of the resource and the attraction of the wielding country's policy goals through opinion polls (Nye, 2004, p. 6).

However, if we measure China's economic soft power over Taiwan by how much China's charm offensive has made the Taiwanese people re-embrace a Chinese identity or the idea of unification—two indicators that are closely related to China's ultimate goals—China's soft power experiment during Ma Ying-jeou's presidency had little positive effect. Surveys by Taiwan's MAC showed that between March 2008 and August 2016 Taiwanese people who supported "immediate unification" or "the status quo for now and unification in the future" had together stayed at around 10% of the population. That means China's soft power work had failed to co-opt more Taiwanese people onto its agenda (Mainland Affairs Council, 2016). In addition, polls conducted by the Election Study Center of Taiwan's National Chengchi University showed that respondents who had an exclusive Taiwanese identity had grown from 48.4% in 2008 to 59.3% in 2016. Meanwhile, those who identified themselves exclusively as Chinese or inclusively as both Taiwanese and Chinese had together decreased from 47.1% to 36.6% (Election Study Center, 2016). In other words, China's soft power work did not forge an identity in Taiwan that might be conducive to the goal of unification.

That said, forging identity or promoting political integration sets a high bar for soft power responses and should not be considered as the only yardstick with which to measure China's soft power. Intuitively, the prospect of jumping on Mainland China's economic bandwagon toward more prosperity should impact people's views on cross-strait economic integration. To move from having a positive attitude toward economic integration to creating (or re-creating) a common identity and/or an inclination toward political integration, however, is a prolonged process—it took European Union member states several decades from the early 1950s to build up a European identity. Therefore, using Taiwanese people's identity to measure the effectiveness of China's recent economic soft power work constitutes several conceptual leaps and may in fact hinder a nuanced understanding of China's soft power over Taiwan.

Given that China's economic strength grew exponentially after the country joined the World Trade Organization in 2001 and that Ma's election brought a receptive leader into power in Taiwan in 2008, the PRC was able to fully experiment with its economic soft power toward the island only recently between 2008 and 2016. We thus should realistically measure China's soft power attraction by Taiwanese people's perception of China's economic prowess in this period. In the same vein, we should measure Taiwan's soft power responses by the people's attitudes toward cross-strait economic integration, instead of political integration or identity. Therefore, we use the Taiwanese public's opinions on various facets of China's economic strength and cross-strait economic integration as proxies for the underlying appeal of the Mainland. The premise is that the more people view Beijing's interests as compatible with their own, the more likely they would view the economic power of China and economic integration with the Mainland favorably.

The focus on the Taiwanese people's attitudes toward economic integration also has an empirical basis. According to the Asian Barometer Surveys (ABS), in 2010 (the ABS Third Wave), 67% of Taiwanese people considered China as the most influential country in Asia, and 82% of them thought China would be the most influential country in Asia in ten years. In 2014 (ABS Fourth Wave), these ratios stayed roughly the same at 63% and 80%, respectively. More strikingly, 67% of the Taiwanese respondents in 2010 and 63% in 2014 regarded China's impact on the region to be positive. Even though Taiwanese people were acutely aware of the stark contrast between China's illiberal political system and their democracy,[6] that did not prevent them from having a favorable view of China's regional influence.

Our discussion above and quantitative analysis of the ABS data in the literature make it clear that it is predominantly China's role as an economic locomotive that drives the Taiwanese people's positive perception of Beijing's regional impact. Correlation analyses based on the ABS Third Wave data found that, in East Asia, people with greater perceived democratic distance between their country and China were more likely to view China's influence negatively. Meanwhile, people with a more sanguine assessment of their domestic (both household and country-wide) economic conditions were more likely to view China's influence positively. The latter opinions underlined the high-level interdependence between China's prosperity and individual neighboring countries' economic prospects widely perceived by the people in East Asia (Chu, Kang and Huang, 2014, pp. 409–413). Therefore, the favorable perception of China's regional influence held by the majority of the Taiwanese people, in spite of the Mainland's illiberal political system and irredentist claim over the island, highlights China's soft power attraction for Taiwan generated by its economic strength.

Figure 12.1 zeroes in on the Taiwanese public's attitudes toward cross-strait economic relations. Between 2008 and 2016, the Ma Ying-jeou administration's approach to cross-strait exchanges was "economics first, politics later," which was accepted by Beijing.[7] The 23 cross-strait agreements signed during this period thus focused primarily on economic issues, including the cross-strait Economic Cooperation Framework Agreement (ECFA) and the agreements on transportation, finance, investment, tax, trade in services, etc. Therefore, the opinions surveyed in this period primarily reflected Taiwanese people's attitudes toward institutionalized economic exchanges and economic integration with the Mainland.

Figure 12.1 shows that when cross-strait exchanges stalled, as under Ma's predecessor Chen Shui-bian before May 2008 and under Ma's successor Tsai Ing-wen after May 2016, Taiwanese people became noticeably impatient about the pace of cross-strait exchanges—significantly more respondents thought the speed of cross-strait exchanges was too slow than those who thought it was too fast.[8] During the period of stable and constant progress of cross-strait economic exchanges between 2008 and 2016, people's attitudes showed another interesting pattern. The Taiwanese public tended to feel an increasing need to put the brakes on cross-strait economic integration in the lead-up to the conclusion of major economic agreements. In contrast, during the hiatus after the signing of a major agreement and before the emergence of new negotiations on the next one, people switched attitudes and hoped to maintain the current pace of progress.

The uneven attitudes toward cross-strait economic integration provide empirical leverages to investigate our propositions on Taiwan's soft power attraction to China. Such variation in attitudes was particularly noticeable around the time of the crucial cases of the ECFA and the Cross-Strait Service Trade Agreement (CSSTA). In mid-2009 after Taiwan explicitly proposed to negotiate a cross-strait trade agreement, gradually more and more people felt the need to slow down

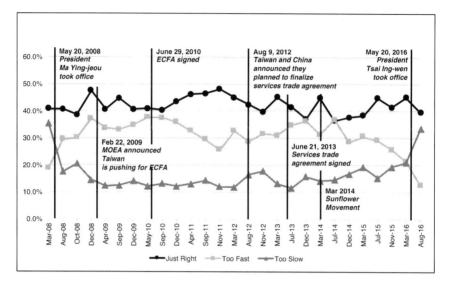

FIGURE 12.1 People's views on the speed of cross-strait exchanges

cross-strait integration, and the proportion peaked around the time the ECFA was signed in June 2010. After that, the ratio of respondents who felt cross-strait exchanges were proceeding too fast dropped, until August 2012 when Taiwan and China announced their plan to finalize the CSSTA. Between August 2012 and the signing of the CSSTA in June 2013, the proportion of people wanting to slow down cross-strait economic integration gradually increased. Then again, after the signing of the CSSTA in June 2013, the larger trend was a decreasing proportion of people who thought cross-strait exchanges were too fast, though two significant deviations in survey results occurred in December 2013 and July 2014. We will explain the two deviations later, but the second deviation resulted from a poll that still captured the aftershocks of the youth-led Sunflower Movement in March 2014.[9] After the Sunflower Movement, cross-strait economic integration basically stagnated, and the proportion of people who thought the speed of cross-strait exchanges was too fast dropped. Interestingly, the share of respondents who wanted to speed up the exchanges gradually increased.

From the generally positive perception of China's impact in the region to the fact that, whenever cross-strait exchanges stalled, the Taiwanese public hoped to see progress, we can observe China's (economic) soft power attraction for Taiwan. However, whenever cross-strait economic integration indeed proceeded ahead, Taiwanese people's anxieties observably arose and worked counterproductively to China's wish of producing soft power responses in Taiwan. The anxiety eventually compounded with other sources of discontent with the Ma administration to lead to the Sunflower Movement and grind the progress of cross-strait economic integration to a halt. The Sunflower Movement sounded the death knell for China's soft power experiment under Ma Ying-jeou's tenure.

The apparent outcomes of the experiment were reactions in Taiwan totally contrary to the soft power responses China would like to produce. So, what went wrong with China's soft power work toward Taiwan?

Political preconditions, forced dependence and Taiwan's anxieties about China's embrace

China's economic attraction so far has not been able to bring about Taiwan's soft power response that Beijing desires because China's soft power work toward Taiwan has been on a self-defeating path. The logic of soft power starts from building up the attraction of the initiator's soft power resources, which then leads to soft power responses of the target in the manner that it willingly heeds to the initiator's preferences out of reshaped and converging interests or a sense of affection (Kirshner, 2008; Nye, 2004). However, China's soft power operations toward Taiwan have turned the whole logic upside down.

A historical survey of China's soft power work over Taiwan makes it clear that China has ostensibly put up a political precondition for its soft power options. China's soft power attempts toward Taiwan can be traced back to as early as the "Message to Compatriots in Taiwan" (the Message, hereafter), issued on January 1, 1979, when Deng Xiaoping held the reign. His successors, Jiang Zemin and Hu Jintao, followed suit and had their Eight-Point Proposal in 1995 and Six Proposals in 2008, respectively, to guide China's peaceful unification agenda in the following eras.[10]

From the Message to Hu's Six Proposals, some noticeable trends in China's soft power work toward Taiwan emerged. First, China struggled to maintain Taiwan's sense of belonging to the Chinese nation. The Message was full of emotional calls to Chinese national feelings, but Jiang Zemin and Hu Jintao, working against a backdrop of an emerging Taiwanese identity, had to resort to more explicit cost-benefit calculation on the Taiwanese side. Second, and related to the above trend, as China moved from an economic backwater to an economic powerhouse and as Taiwan's Chinese consciousness became more and more remote, economic attraction featured more and more prominently in China's soft power work. Third and more important, against the backdrops of Taiwan's democratization and the emergence of indigenous voices of Taiwan independence as viable political forces, the "One China" principle has become a prominent precondition for the PRC to maintain a soft power course toward the island. Jiang's Eight-Point Proposal began by stating that insisting on the One China principle was the precondition of realizing *peaceful* unification. Hu's Six Proposals also first and foremost emphasized that the position that Taiwan and the Mainland belong to the same one China was a critical precondition of the PRC's soft power work. As Chinese leaders love to assert, the One China principle is the *basis* of peaceful development of cross-strait relations.

In other words, accepting Beijing's One China principle one way or another is the apparent prerequisite for China's soft power options to come into play.

Therefore, despite in reality China did not always, and certainly not across-the-board, interrupt cross-strait economic relations even when a pro-independence government ruled the island, China has nominally demanded Taiwan demonstrate the desired soft power response, that is, committing to Beijing's agenda of unification (or the notion of one China), *before* the PRC's soft power resources build up their attraction. This precondition blurs the line between attraction and coercion because when accepting China's demands seemingly preconditions access to soft power resources, anything that might build up affection looks like carrots of enticement that can be forfeited to punish disobedience. The demand also makes anyone who advocates for friendly attitudes toward China look like a fifth column working for China's interests. It thus becomes challenging to encourage soft power response in Taiwan. In a nutshell, as Nye cautions in his seminal work that having soft power resources is not a sufficient condition for producing soft power response and that context is the key, China's political precondition has poisoned the context of China's soft power attraction for Taiwan (Nye, 2004, pp. 11–12).

Our argument of the counterproductive effects of China's upside-down soft power operation implies that it matters whether China rhetorically and behaviorally put up this One China political precondition at all and in what format the political precondition was described and enforced. We should expect to see when China is less rigid about its political precondition, its economic attraction is more pronounced. On the contrary, when China intentionally or unintentionally highlights its political objectives as preconditions, its economic strength creates anxieties and resistance that are counterproductive to soft power attractiveness.

Accordingly, in rhetoric, how China states the urgency and priority of its political aims in relation to cross-strait economic exchanges, and in what form of the One China principle that Beijing asserts, would make a difference. The soft power response that China looks for is Taiwan's embrace of national unification. If we view this political objective from a spectrum of formats, its softest end is a very vague form of a Chinese nation where Taiwan has great latitude to decide its relations with this Chinese nation. On the hardest end, it is unification on the PRC's terms where Taiwan has no options but to be deprived of any autonomy and become a local administration of the PRC. China's "One Country, Two Systems" formula for unification, and the pre-2000 One China principle this formula connotes, which stated "there is only one China in the world; the PRC is the only legitimate government representing China; and China's territory and sovereignty cannot be separated," is close to the hardest end. After 2000, Beijing revised its One China principle to be "there is only one China in the world; both Taiwan and the Mainland belong to this one China; and China's territory and sovereignty cannot be separated." This is a softer form compared to the previous one because becoming a part of the PRC is no longer the only form one China can take. The KMT's preferred term "1992 Consensus," which states that there is only one China, and the two sides each interpret this one China as they see fit, is softer still. From the KMT's perspective, the 1992 Consensus implies that two governments now exist under the rubric of China, where the Republic of China on Taiwan should enjoy the same full entitlements as the PRC on the Mainland does, at least until the unification of the nation. The harder the format Beijing conveys, the more rigid its political precondition is perceived in Taiwan.

In behavior, whether China relieves its constraint on Taiwan's integration with the rest of the world, measured by the island's ability to negotiate free trade agreements (FTAs) with third-party countries without China's obstruction, will also impact Taiwanese people's perception of the rigidity of China's political precondition. Economic integration typically encourages participating countries to trade more with each other and leads the smaller economy to have higher trade concentration, or dependence, on the larger one due to their huge difference in economic sizes. Such dependence is natural and less threatening when the smaller economy is free to pursue economic integration with the rest of the world to balance the asymmetric dependence. For that reason, the attraction of economic integration with China needs to be put into the context of Taiwan's overall level of economic integration in the world. When China blocks Taiwan's pursuance of FTAs with other countries under the name of its One China principle, economic integration with China turns into forced dependence on China. Consequently, the co-optive power of economic integration can be easily perceived as coercive power orchestrated through forced dependence and thus court pushback.

Explaining China's soft power (or lack thereof) over Taiwan

To empirically validate our arguments, we look into various opinion polls conducted by Taiwan's MAC. During its first term, the Ma Ying-jeou administration's primary selling point of cross-strait economic integration was that a trade agreement with China would open the door to trade agreements with other countries. The majority of the Taiwanese public at that time bought the argument, which helped temporarily alleviate concerns about China's political precondition. According to a MAC poll in April 2009, 60.3% of Taiwanese people agreed that signing the ECFA with China would help Taiwan's efforts in reaching FTAs with other countries (while 24.8% disagreed). In the same survey, when asked right after this question (probably intentionally to cue the answer) whether it was necessary to sign the ECFA, 70.0% of respondents answered positively, while only 23.5% responded negatively (Mainland Affairs Council, 2009). The same question on the linkage between the ECFA and Taiwan's chances on other FTAs was asked again in a MAC poll in July 2010 (right after the ECFA was signed), and 62.6%, an even higher percentage of respondents than that of the previous survey, bought the idea that ECFA would help Taiwan negotiate other FTAs (while 25.9% did not) (Mainland Affairs Council, 2010b). A related question was asked in another MAC poll in April 2010, and 57.4% of Taiwanese respondents agreed that cross-strait economic and trade exchanges and negotiations would help Taiwan's economic development in Asia and in the world (while 27.8% disagreed) (Mainland Affairs Council, 2010a). In other words, the prospect of more economic integration with the world subdued perceived political constraints imposed by the Mainland and enabled the majority in Taiwan to embrace cross-strait integration during Ma's first term.

It is also noteworthy that during this period, in rhetoric, China was relatively muted in asserting its political precondition of cross-strait exchanges. Right after Ma's successful election in March 2008, Hu Jintao told US President George W. Bush in a telephone conversation that "it is China's consistent stand that the Chinese mainland and Taiwan should restore consultation and talks on the basis of the '1992 Consensus.'" The phone conversation was then publicized by China's official Xinhua News Agency in its English reports, indicating that the press release was vetted by the authorities (Xinhua, 2008a). As discussed earlier, the 1992 Consensus was a much softer form of Beijing's One China principle. More significantly, Xinhua explicated the Consensus as that "both sides recognize there is only one China, but agree to differ on its definition," a stand that the KMT emphasized but the CCP hitherto never endorsed.[11] Mentioning the differentiated definitions was probably a signal too subtle, but endorsing the 1992 Consensus was a gesture too significant to be ignored by the Taiwanese public, and it showed Mainland China's intention in general to downplay its political precondition at that time. In addition, the PRC refrained from mentioning the "One Country, Two Systems" formula for unification after Ma took office, alleviating the Taiwanese public's perceived rigidity and urgency of China's political goals. Beijing's subdued rhetoric on unification, together with the prospect of broader economic integration with the world mentioned above, helped create an environment conducive to the Ma administration's push for cross-strait integration. The Taiwanese public's embrace of Ma's agenda, particularly the ECFA, manifested Taiwan's soft power response.

However, halfway through Ma's second term, Taiwan had only made marginal progress on economic integration with countries other than China. The argument that integration with the Mainland was a gateway to integration with the world began to lose its luster. In December 2013, during the lead-up to the (failed) ratification of the CSSTA, a MAC poll found that only 51.6% of Taiwanese respondents thought signing the agreement would help Taiwan reach economic and trade agreements with other countries (while 28.6% thought otherwise). In comparison with the time when the Ma administration was promoting the ECFA in April 2009, this represented a drop of almost 9 percentage points in the support of the agenda of using integration with China to open the door to integration with the rest of the world, and the difference is statistically significant ($p < 0.001$).[12] It is also noteworthy that the drop was substantial despite strong positive cues embedded in the survey question. The question reads as follows: "In June this year, after signing the cross-strait service trade agreement, Taiwan signed similar economic and trade cooperative agreements with New Zealand (July) and Singapore (November). Do you think signing the

CSSTA is conducive to Taiwan's signing economic and trade cooperative agreements with other countries or not?" Arguably, such a lead-in sentence should strongly sway people's responses positively, but the survey results still showed lukewarm support for the idea. Correspondingly, the support for the CSSTA was only 45.7%, while the opposition was not far behind at 40.4% (Mainland Affairs Council, 2013).

Counterfactually, were China to allow Taiwan a freer hand in negotiating economic integration with other countries, would the situation have been different? In a MAC poll in July 2014, 59.8% of the respondents agreed that if Taiwan could successfully negotiate economic and trade cooperation with other countries and participate in regional economic integration, people's confidence in cross-strait economic and trade liberation would increase (while 22.2% disagreed). In December 2014, the same survey question again got affirmative responses from the majority (61.3% of respondents agreed while 20.2% disagreed). In other words, people were mindful of Taiwan's forced dependence on China. The disappointing progress and dim prospect for economic integration with major trade partners other than China became evident in Ma's second term and brought back the specter of Beijing's political straitjacket. As our proposition expects, China's economic embrace created suspicion in this situation and discouraged Taiwan's soft power response that China desired.

Meanwhile, China's rhetoric was not reassuring either. On the sidelines of the Asia-Pacific Economic Cooperation (APEC) summit in October 2013, Chinese President Xi Jinping told Vincent Siew, Ma's envoy to the meeting, that the cross-strait political divide must step by step reach a final resolution and could not be passed on from generation to generation. Xi further asserted that the two sides should begin equal consultations on political issues under the framework of one China (Xinhua, 2013). Xi's statements raised eyebrows in Taiwan and heightened a sense of Beijing's renewed urgency to push for its political agenda.[13] The resulting anxiety in Taiwan led to a jump in people's desire to slow down cross-strait integration, which was captured in a December 2013 opinion poll. The sentiment explained the deviation mentioned in the earlier section in the general trend of wanting to continue cross-strait economic exchanges. Also at the APEC summit, Taiwan and Mainland China's top officials in charge of cross-strait affairs, the chiefs of Taiwan's MAC and China's Taiwan Affairs Office (TAO), respectively, made their historic first meeting. That was followed by the MAC minister's first ever visit to Mainland China in February 2014. For people who were wary of China's political straitjacket, Xi's statement at APEC and the meetings between MAC and TAO were alarmingly hasty pushes toward political negotiations.[14] Together with Ma's several remarks during this period such as proclaiming that cross-strait relations were not "international" relations in his National Day speech on October 10, 2013, which seemingly succumbed to China's political precondition, part of the Taiwanese society was galvanized to utter opposition to further integration with China.[15] These people grabbed

the opportunity of the KMT's clumsy handling of the ratification of the CSSTA and combined efforts with other forces dissatisfied with the Ma administration for other reasons to instigate the Sunflower Movement in March 2014. As one interviewee said, the CSSTA was not the primary concern of the Sunflower Movement. Rather, it was a surge of anxiety about China's political precondition behind its economic embrace that set the movement in motion. The Sunflower Movement ground the ratification of the CSSTA to a halt and, more important, brought China's active soft power experiment during Ma's presidency to an end.

To sum up, China's lack of soft power over Taiwan resulted from its operation that put the political objective cart before the economic soft power horse. To allow its economic attraction to fully develop into a soft power resource and attract the Taiwanese public to embrace its agenda of cross-strait economic integration and hopefully unification, China needed to downplay its political precondition. Beijing also needed to refrain from using its One China principle to obstruct Taiwan's deeper economic cooperation with other trade partners.

However, China faced a dilemma in its charm offensive aimed at Taiwan. China worried that were the Taiwanese government's external legitimacy to be strengthened by greater economic integration with other countries, the island would be in a better position to resist the Mainland's political agenda. Given the CCP's reliance on nationalist credentials for legitimacy, the ruling regime in Beijing could not afford to be flexible on its political precondition. Therefore, China refused to give Taiwan a free hand to negotiate FTAs with the rest of the world and frequently demanded political leaders in Taiwan recommit to Beijing's political prerequisite. Such conduct was counterproductive because it highlighted the preferences and constraints that China imposed on the island. It also fed the Taiwanese public's suspicion of and resistance to China's agenda, undermining China's soft power over Taiwan that might result from its economic attractiveness.

The dilemma certainly reflected China's lack of confidence in its soft power attraction for Taiwan, but more important, it reflected the limit of soft power— because it was "soft," the outcome was much less certain than the exercise of hard power. Given the heavy doses of nationalism that the PRC had been feeding its population through patriotic education (Dickson, 2004), the salience of the Taiwan issue in the CCP's conception of nationalism (Shirk, 2007, pp. 181–211), and the reliance of the CCP on nationalism for its legitimacy (Garver, 2015, pp. 349–351, 476–482), Beijing could not leave Taiwan's unification with the motherland simply to chance. China's hesitance to count solely on soft power for its work on Taiwan was thus understandable.

Conclusion

In this chapter, we argue that China's soft power attraction for Taiwan generated by its economic strength is potentially mighty, but the soft power response that China's attraction has produced in Taiwan remains meager. We

[handwritten margin notes: "why Beijing's soft power have efforts have not been successful in Taiwan"]

attribute the lackluster outcome of China's soft power work in Taiwan to Beijing's self-defeating operation of its economic soft power. China demands the island show the preferred soft power response, that is, committing to a form of one China acceptable to Beijing, before its soft power resources build up attraction. This turns the soft power logic on its head and blurs the line between attraction and coercion. When accepting China's demands seemingly preconditions access to soft power resources, anyone sympathetic to China is suspected of selling out Taiwan, and this discourages instead of encourages soft power response. Unfortunately, as long as the CCP regime on Mainland China relies on nationalist credentials for its legitimacy, and as long as Taiwan is an inextricable element of the CCP's nationalist narrative, it is difficult for Mainland China to let soft power fully develop in its relations with Taiwan. *[handwritten: "role of nationalism"]* Looking over the longer run, for the Chinese leadership, Taiwan's eventual political integration with the PRC is not an option but a core interest that must be secured. That means, since the CCP cannot achieve this goal through exercising soft power as long as it is unwilling to leave to chance an issue so critical to its regime legitimacy, a return to hard power to handle cross-strait relations is probably inevitable.

[handwritten: "return to hard power inevitable?"]

Notes

1 This is also different from the so-called sharp power, which refers to China's use of lucrative benefits to influence international views to the favor of China and suppress expression of opinions that go against China's interests. See Walker and Ludwig (2017).

2 In his seminal work, Joseph Nye calls a receiving state's favorable response to the wielding country's soft power attraction "soft power behavior." We use the term "soft power response" in place of Nye's "soft power behavior" to make the meaning a bit more straightforward.

3 Just to remind readers again, in Nye's original text, he uses the term "soft power behavior," but we use "soft power response" to make what we mean more straightforward.

4 Recent surveys in late 2017 and early 2018 showed that Taiwanese youth have become increasingly willing to study in China, but the incentives came primarily from practical economic considerations, such as job prospects in China and Beijing's offers of preferential measures. In other words, the attraction resulted fundamentally from China's economic strength, not quality of education per se. See UDN Survey Center (2017), Lin (2018) and Peng (2018). The *People's Daily*, in its overseas version, also attributed this surging interest to China's preferential measures for Taiwanese rolled out at the end of February 2018. See Li and Niu (2018).

5 The term "Hirschmanesque influence" is adopted from Abdelal and Kirshner (1999–2000).

6 Taiwanese people's perceived democratic distance between their country and China, which was calculated by taking the difference between where one places Taiwan on a ten-point scale of democratic development (where 1 represents "completely undemocratic" and 10 "completely democratic") and where one puts China on the same scale, was among the greatest in East Asia. Data from Yun-han Chu, "How East Asians View a Rising China," presentation at Harvard University, September 2015, and Chu, Kang and Huang (2014, p. 411).

7 The authors' interview with a KMT party official working on this issue area during the period.

8 The latest MAC survey outcomes in January 2017 maintained the pattern: 34.7% of the respondents considered the pace of cross-strait exchanges too slow, while only 12.8%

considered them too fast. The survey also showed the narrowest gap since March 2008 between those who thought the pace was just about right and those who thought it was too slow (37.6% to 34.7%). For the first time, the difference was within the margin of error (2.99%), further vindicating our argument that when cross-strait exchanges stalled, the Taiwanese public became impatient about the pace. See www.mac.gov.tw/public/Attachment/71191756591.pdf (accessed on February 15, 2017).

9 The Sunflower Movement was instigated in the first place by protests against the attempted ratification of the CSSTA. The MAC conducted its March 2014 poll between March 7 and 10, when the Sunflower Movement had not yet fully blown up.

10 To view the English version of the document "Message to Compatriots in Taiwan," see http://german.china.org.cn/english/taiwan/7943.htm (accessed on November 11, 2019). To view the English version of Jiang Zemin's Eight-Point Proposal, see Jiang (1995). To view the English version of Hu Jintao's Six Proposals, see Hu (2008).

11 In a typical tactic of distinguishing domestic audience from international audience, Xinhua's Chinese report on the same phone conversation did not explicate that the two sides agree to differ on the definition of one China. See http://news.xinhuanet.com/tw/2008-03/26/content_7865604.htm

12 The p-value is based on a two-tailed z-test of proportions comparing the approval percentages.

13 Observers in China, Taiwan and the United States in general considered Xi's statement as renewed pressure on Taiwan to engage in talks on political issues. See for example Enav (2013), Areddy and Hsu (2013) and Ng (2013).

14 Authors' interview with a senior DPP official.

15 Authors' interviews, and see Chen and Hsu (2013) for contemporary analyses on the rising disapproval of China's political objective (i.e., unification), or in other words, behavior contrary to China's desired outcomes of its soft power work, in several survey results.

References

Abdelal, Rawi and Jonathan Kirshner. 1999–2000. "Strategy, Economic Relations, and the Definition of National Interests," *Security Studies* 9(1/2), pp. 119–156.

Areddy, James T. and Jenny W. Hsu. 2013. "China Seeks 'Equal Consultations' with Taiwan," *Wall Street Journal*, October 7. www.wsj.com/articles/SB100014240527023 03442004579120901720455792.

Chen, Hui-ping and Stacy Hsu. 2013. "Ma's Pro-China Tilt Breeding Anxiety: Political Analysts," *Taipei Times*, November 2. www.taipeitimes.com/News/taiwan/archi ves/2013/11/02/2003575969.

Chu, Yun-han, Liu Kang and Min-hua Huang. 2014. "How East Asians View the Rise of China," *Journal of Contemporary China* 24(93), pp. 398–420.

Dickson, Bruce J. 2004. "Dilemmas of Party Adaptation: The CCP's Strategies for Survival," in Peter Hays Gries and Stanley Rosen (eds.), *State and Society in 21st-Century China: Crisis, Contention, and Legitimation*. New York and London: RoutledgeCurzon.

Election Study Center. 2016. "Taiwanese/Chinese Identification Trend Distribution in Taiwan (1992/06~2016/06)," *Election Study Center, National Chengchi University*, August 24. http://esc.nccu.edu.tw/app/news.php?Sn=166#.

Enav, Peter. 2013. "Ma Under Pressure as Xi Calls for Cross-Strait Political Solution," *China Post*, October 8. www.chinapost.com.tw/taiwan/china-taiwan-relations/2013/ 10/08/390724/Ma-under.htm.

Garver, John W. 2015. *China's Quest: The History of the Foreign Relations of the People's Republic of China*. New York: Oxford University Press.

Gracie, Carrie. 2015. "Taiwan President Rues Lack of Progress with China," *BBC*, July 27. www.bbc.com/news/world-asia-china-33649127.

Hirschman, Albert O. 1980/1945. *National Power and the Structure of Foreign Trade*. Berkeley and Los Angeles, CA: University of California Press.

Hu, Jintao. 2008. "Let Us Join Hands to Promote the Peaceful Development of Cross-Straits Relations and Strive with a United Resolve for the Great Rejuvenation of the Chinese Nation," *Taiwan Affairs Office of the State Council, PRC*, December 31. www.gwytb.gov.cn/en/Special/Hu/201103/t20110322_1794707.htm.

Jiang, Zemin. 1995. "Jiang Zemin'g Eight-point Proposal," *Taiwan Affairs Office of the State Council, PRC*, January 30. www.gwytb.gov.cn/en/Special/Jiang/201103/t20110316_1789198.htm.

Kirshner, Jonathan. 2008. "The Consequences of China's Economic Rise for Sino-U.S. Relations," in Robert S. Ross and Feng Zhu (eds.), *China's Ascent: Power, Security, and the Future of International Politics*. Ithaca, NY: Cornell University Press, pp. 238–259.

Li, Pengyu and Ning Niu. 2018. "Weishenmo dalu gaoxiao zai taiwan 'yiye baore'" ["Why Mainland Colleges Become 'Super Popular Overnight'"], *Haiwai Net*, April 4. http://opinion.haiwainet.cn/n/2018/0404/c456465-31292318.html.

Lin, Rangjun. 2018. "Critical Survey on the Tsai Ing-wen Administration: Independence Reaches 10-Year New Low While Unification Reaches 10-Year New High," *Global Views Monthly*, February 12. www.gvm.com.tw/article.html?id=42863.

Mainland Affairs Council. 2009. "Survey on People's Opinions on 'Cross-Strait Economic Cooepration Framework Agreement (ECFA) and Chinese Investment in Taiwan'," *Mainland Affairs Council, the Republic of China*, April 11. www.mac.gov.tw/public/Attachment/96210255328.pdf.

Mainland Affairs Council. 2010a. *Regular Survey on 'People's Opinions on the Current Cross-Strait Relations'*, May 2. www.mac.gov.tw/public/Attachment/05715144143.pdf.

Mainland Affairs Council. 2010b. "Survey on 'People's Opinions on the Fifth "Jiang-Chen Meeting"'," *Mainland Affairs Council, the Republic of China*, July 4. www.mac.gov.tw/public/Attachment/07621323436.pdf.

Mainland Affairs Council. 2013. "Regular Survey on 'People's Opinions on the Current Cross-Strait Relations'," *Mainland Affairs Council, the Republic of China*, December 9. www.mac.gov.tw/public/Attachment/3122711421259.pdf.

Mainland Affairs Council. 2016. "The Opinions of People in the Taiwan Region of the Republic of China on Cross-Strait Relations," *Mainland Affairs Council, the Republic of China*, August 3. www.mac.gov.tw/public/Attachment/6891644393.pdf.

Ng, Teddy. 2013. "Xi Jinping Says Efforts Must Be Made to Close the China-Taiwan Political Divide," *South China Morning Post*, October 6. www.scmp.com/news/china/article/1325761/xi-jinping-says-political-solution-taiwan-cant-wait-forever.

Nye, Joseph S., Jr. 2004. *Soft Power: The Means to Success in World Politics*. New York, NY: Public Affairs.

Peng, Xingzhu. 2018. "31 Preferential Treatments Unnerve Taiwan: The Ruling Party Faces One Looming Issue and Three Warning Signs," *Global Views Monthly*, March 14. www.gvm.com.tw/article.html?id=43280.

Shirk, Susan L. 2007. *China: Fragile Superpower*. New York: Oxford University Press.

UDN Survey Center. 2016. "Mainland from Taiwanese Youth's Viewpoints," *United Daily News*, November 20. http://p.udn.com.tw/upf/newmedia/2016_data/20161118_china_1/index.html.

UDN Survey Center. 2017. "Annual Survey on Cross-Strait Relations," *United Daily News*, November 20. https://udn.com/news/story/7331/2828323?from=udn-relatednews_ch2.

Walker, Christopher and Jessica Ludwig. 2017. "The Meaning of Sharp Power," *Foreign Affairs*, November 16. www.foreignaffairs.com/articles/china/2017-11-16/meaning-sharp-power.

Xinhua. 2008a. "Chinese, U.S. Presidents Hold Telephone Talks on Taiwan, Tibet," *Xinhua Net*, March 27. http://news.xinhuanet.com/english/2008-03/27/content_7865209.htm.

Xinhua. 2013. "Xi zongshuji huijian Xiaowangchang yixing" ["General Secretary Xi Meets with Vincent Siew's Delegation"], *Xinhua Net*, October 6. http://news.xinhuanet.com/world/2013-10/06/c_117603401.htm.

13

FAMILIARITY BREEDS CONTEMPT

China's growing "soft power deficit" in Hong Kong

David Zweig

Hong Kong–Mainland relations as a special case of soft power

In all other cases in this book, soft power refers to the acceptance of the social, political, cultural and/or moral values of one state by officials or citizens of a second state who, as a result of the former state's soft power, accede to its foreign policy preferences without coercion or the use of force.

In this chapter we are assessing the ability of China's Central Government (CG) to persuade the Hong Kong government (HKG), members of Hong Kong's legislature (Legco), and, most important, Hong Kong citizens residing in a region of China whose norms and laws differ significantly from the dominant rules and values in the national system, to accept the CG's policies for Hong Kong and to privilege the CG's interests in Hong Kong without Beijing resorting to coercion. Apropos to Nye's argument for the international system (1990), the use of force, or the exercise of coercive power in the Hong Kong–Mainland relationship, would be extremely deleterious to the relationship for decades to come. Persuading Hong Kong people to accede to the policies of the Mainland and accept the People's Republic of China (PRC) as their sovereign state, is the essence of Deng Xiaoping's "one country, two systems" strategy of allowing two separate economic, political and legal systems to coexist in China (one in Hong Kong and one on the Mainland) for a minimum of 50 years (until 2047).

Under "one country, two systems," Hong Kong employs the "rule of law" under an independent judiciary; it has its own legislature (Legco), where over 50% of legislators are directly elected by popular vote within geographic districts; the Chinese Communist Party (CCP) has no official standing in Hong Kong; and, Hong Kong maintains a capitalist system, as compared to the socialist system on the mainland. Under Hong Kong's "high degree of autonomy" and

"Hong Kong people governing Hong Kong," local people, not mandarins from the Mainland, govern Hong Kong directly and are expected to make the key decisions on their own.

Moreover, because "one country, two systems" was codified in the British–Chinese Joint Declaration on Hong Kong, is registered as an international treaty at the United Nations, and because the world is watching whether China keeps its commitment to maintain a hands off policy for 50 years, Beijing is under enormous pressure to limit its interference in Hong Kong's society and polity. Thus, unlike in the rest of China, Chinese officials, as of the writing of this chapter, have not used force when Hong Kong citizens take to the streets in massive, even violent, protests—actions that in the Mainland would trigger mass arrests.

As Hong Kong is a Special Administrative Region (SAR) of the PRC, the CG is far better positioned to generate popular support from Hong Kong's polity and society for its policies in a way that one sovereign state trying to influence another sovereign state simply cannot. The CG appoints the chief executive (CE) of Hong Kong, who dominates Hong Kong's "executive-led" system. The CG can legally create and organize various pro-government groups, actively support open political parties that favor its interests and even employ an official organization in Hong Kong called the Central Liaison Office (CLO) to employ a "United Front" strategy to promote its viewpoints, interests and soft power within the territory (Loo, Lo and Hung, 2019).

However, a massive "soft power deficit" has emerged in Beijing's relationship with Legco and with society. Legco houses a strong contingent of forces opposed to most of the CG's policies which has regularly voted down policies and resorted to filibusters to complicate the passage and funding of legislation favored by Beijing. More important this soft power deficit is due to the general disaffection for, and mistrust of, the CG among large sections of the Hong Kong population, particularly 18 to 30 year olds, but generally people under 40, concerning numerous issues such as freedom of speech and assembly; an independent judiciary; "national security"; the extent of pro-CCP content in the school curriculum; the pace of democratization, including the selection of candidates for the post of CE and the introduction of "universal suffrage" (one person-one vote) for the CE and Legco elections; and the ability of the CG to keep its word and grant Hong Kong a "high degree of autonomy" without interfering in Hong Kong's affairs.

Three problems highlight the difficulty for the CG to enhance its soft power. First, Hong Kong society has a pluralistic and democratic culture. Moreover, citizens who participate in its vibrant civil society largely identify as "Hong Kongers," and not as "Chinese," so they resist efforts by the CG and its agent in Hong Kong, the CLO, to establish hegemony over Hong Kong society (Ma, 2007, p. 199).

Second, the CLO, the leadership in Beijing and the officials in the Mainland who comment on Hong Kong policy are handicapped in their efforts to enhance the CG's soft power because the natural mechanism to do so, the United Front strategy, born of almost a century of communist experience in penetrating Chinese societies, treats opponents as enemies, placing Beijing and a significant part of Hong Kong society at loggerheads, with few measures available to reconcile their differences (Lam and Lam, 2013, pp. 301–325).

Third, other than trying to build its soft power by staying out of Hong Kong's affairs entirely, efforts at engagement with Hong Kongers, through cultural policy, changing the public perception of the Mainland in the minds of Hong Kongers through education or by offering progress on democracy, even if somewhat limited, are all seen as activities that contravene the "two systems" principle, under which Hong Kongers hoped that the CG would let them run their own system, while allowing them greater democracy.

Building soft power in Hong Kong: the United Front

Beijing mobilizes societal support for its norms in Hong Kong through various mechanisms, the most important being its traditional United Front strategy. Under the United Front, the CCP tries to mobilize non-communist allies or friends within society who support its dominance (often by encouraging them to join new organizations that local underground communists create), win over neutral members of society who do not oppose their rule, and isolate, contain, if not defeat, forces opposed to its hegemony over society (Lam and Lam, 2013, p. 318).

The United Front strategy was implemented in Hong Kong before 1997 by the Hong Kong and Macau Work Committee within the Xinhua News Agency and, after 1997, has been coordinated by the CLO headquartered in Sheung Wan, in Western Hong Kong Island. According to the 2014 *State Council White Paper on Hong Kong* (The Information Office of the State Council, 2019), the CLO is an organ of the CG whose duties involve communication with the Office of the Commissioner of the Ministry of Foreign Affairs and the PLA Garrison, both of which are located in Hong Kong, promoting various exchanges and cooperation between Hong Kong and the mainland, facilitating communication with leading people in Hong Kong society and managing affairs involving Taiwan.

However, the CLO works under the CCP in Beijing. The CLO's Coordination Department and its Social Group Liaison Department report directly to the United Front Work Department, an organization under the Secretariat of the CCP's Central Committee in Beijing (The Information Office of the State Council, 2019). According to Torode, Pomfret and Lim (2014), the CLO uses its broad networks, spanning grassroots associations, businessmen and politicians, to help the HKG push through policies needing approval from a somewhat pro-Beijing legislature. These have included partial democratic reforms in Hong Kong and the multi-billion-dollar high-speed rail link to China. The CLO also tries to improve the local press's portrayal of China.

Yet numerous forces undermine Beijing's ability to use a United Front strategy to enhance its soft power in Hong Kong. Members of the Democratic Party, one of the leading opposition parties, worry that very close ties between their party and the PRC will undermine their party's position at the ballot box (Ho, 2014), as well as the determination of young democrats to fight for universal suffrage (Lo, 2010, p. 208). The Mainland still limits the role of the members of the pro-democracy parties, known as the Pan-Democrats, in the 47 consultative bodies affiliated with the HKG, filling the posts mostly with Beijing loyalists (Lo, 2010, p. 215), and in 2015, it strengthened its control over Legco by having its allies take the positions of chair and vice-chair of the most important committees, rejecting the past custom of sharing the posts with democratic members (Bush, 2016, p. 141). Beijing still sees the various forces in Hong Kong through Maoist lenses, comprising "friends and enemies," limiting Beijing's ability "to coopt the vociferous civil society groups in Hong Kong" (Lo, 2010, p. 221).

Under its "politics of cooptation" (Lo, 2010, p. 215), it grants certain Hong Kong people positions in the national Chinese People's Political Consultative Conference (CPPCC) or in provincial or municipal CPPCCs on the Mainland. According to Loh (2010, p. 32), membership in these organizations obligates individuals to support CCP leadership in Hong Kong. But while the CG hopes that members of such organizations will enhance Beijing's soft power in Hong Kong, many Hong Kongers do not believe that these people represent Hong Kong's interests to the CG (Loh, 2010, p. 33). Instead, they are only a transmission belt for explaining the CG's views on issues to Hong Kongers.

The CG and the HKG try to build soft power and enhance patriotism through propaganda (Loh, 2010, pp. 36–38), such as sending Chinese heroes to Hong Kong, through cultural performances, by criticizing foreign interference and by trying to introduce a more nationalistic education curriculum. But national education is also an important policy which must gain the support of legislators and which needs the silent acquiescence of many educators and students in Hong Kong; so whether the HKG and the CG can legislate it is an important measure of Beijing's soft power, and to date, the effort to introduce "national education" has undermined the CG's efforts to enhance soft power by triggering concerns of ideological interference.

Misjudged efforts to build soft power: Beijing's white paper on "one country, two systems"

The CG's "White Paper on Hong Kong," issued in June 2014 (The Information Office of the State Council, 2019), tried to increase China's popularity by reminding the SAR's citizens of the major contributions the CG had made to Hong Kong's economic development since 1997 as well as to demonstrate its "comprehensive authority" over the territory.

The contributions listed in the section entitled "Efforts Made by the Central Government to Ensure the Prosperity and Development of the HKSAR" included assistance given during the 1997 Asian Financial Crisis, when the Hong Kong Stock Market came under attack; the Comprehensive Economic

Partnership Arrangement or CEPA (June 2003), which gave Hong Kong professionals enhanced access to the Mainland economy before the rest of the world under China's WTO agreement; and the "Individual Visitors Scheme," which has allowed millions of Mainlanders to visit Hong Kong and according to Sung et al. (2014) generated $27.2 billion in 2012, which was 1.4% of Hong Kong's GDP.

While these policies did help Hong Kong, the white paper emphasized how Beijing had assisted Hong Kong's economy after the 2003 Sudden Acute Respiratory Syndrome (SARS) epidemic, without mentioning that SARS had entered Hong Kong via Guangdong Province and that Mainland officials had not warned the HKG that such a dangerous disease was incubating across the border. Hong Kongers laughed cynically at such a disingenuous perspective. The document also reminded Hong Kongers of the assistance afforded to the SAR by the CG after the 2008 Global Financial Crisis. The underlying message, therefore, was that the CG delivered economic prosperity to Hong Kong, which Hong Kongers themselves undermine by excessive politicization of policy decisions.

However, the document also cautioned Hong Kongers that the "one country, two systems" structure existed at the goodwill of the CG, striking at the dominant perception (or perhaps misperception) in Hong Kong that Beijing was legally bound by the Joint Declaration to maintain Hong Kong's "high degree of autonomy" and "two systems" for 50 years, and that Britain, as a cosignatory to the Joint Declaration, had an obligation (and the right) to press Hong Kong's case with China and that China would respond. Instead, the document argued that Hong Kong's "high degree of autonomy" was granted only at the bequest of the CG and the Mainland's parliament, and that Beijing, which had "comprehensive jurisdiction" over Hong Kong, could limit Hong Kong's autonomy as it saw fit.

The white paper challenged the "rule of law" and moved Hong Kong closer to "one country" rather than "two systems." It argued that Hong Kong judges are public employees who owe their first loyalty to the state, not to the rule of law, legitimizing the Chinese state's interference in local judicial decisions. Mainland legal scholars saw this aspect of the white paper as an unfortunate point that was misunderstood. But this viewpoint triggered strong protests by a large number of lawyers who insisted on protecting the independence of Hong Kong's judiciary, which is one of the key aspects of the "two systems" (Lau, Chiu and Yap, 2014) without which Hong Kong would lose much of its comparative advantage over cities, such as Shanghai, which cannot pull in Western firms that prefer Hong Kong's rule of law. In this way, the white paper undermined China's soft power in Hong Kong, particularly among lawyers and other professionals.

Promoting patriotism: sending Hong Kong students to the Mainland

For much of the past decade, Mainland officials and the HKG have argued that greater patriotism and understanding of China would lessen resistance

[handwritten marginalia: ✝ Umbrella movement ?]

[handwritten marginalia left side: effect of studying on the mainland on the HK students]

[handwritten marginalia left side: difference in freedoms]

to the CG's policies toward Hong Kong. So, in 2013–2015, the HKG sent 126,200 students to the mainland at the cost of $26.7 million (Zhao, 2015). This perspective became particularly strong after the Umbrella Movement in fall 2014 (Lam, 2015). However, some Hong Kong parents saw these efforts as "brainwashing," and some Hong Kong schools eschewed any trips labeled with terms such as "understanding our motherland" or that referred to "national education."

Does studying on the Mainland affect Hong Kong students? In 2009, with funding from the Central Policy Unit of the HKG, I and a team of researchers interviewed Hong Kong students studying in Hong Kong and on the Mainland to assess whether studying in China affected the identity and attitudes of the latter group.[1] Interestingly, many students studying in the Mainland had a parent living or working on the Mainland, so they probably began with a more positive view of China than most Hong Kong students.

Our students understood the limits on individual rights in China (Table 13.1), as 86.7% of Hong Kongers studying on the Mainland believed that individual rights on the Mainland were either "much worse" (49.1%) or "slightly worse" (37.6%) than in Hong Kong. Also, 68.5% of college students in Hong Kong felt that individual rights in China were "much worse than in Hong Kong," while 20.4% thought individual rights were "slightly worse." Thus, while Table 13.1 shows that those Hong Kong students who study on the Mainland appear to be less hostile than students in Hong Kong toward the Mainland, more than 85% of Hong Kong students saw a deep chasm between freedom in Hong Kong and the Mainland, regardless of where they studied.

In our face-to-face interviews, students expressed their views on the lack of freedom in the Mainland:

> In Hong Kong you'll feel it's more democratic. In the Mainland the media is all controlled by the government. Besides, internet is strictly blocked here. In Hong Kong, there is no website you can't visit. You can also see whatever movie you want without any omissions. The Mainland is comparatively reclusive.[2]

TABLE 13.1 Students' views on individual rights and freedom in the Mainland (%), 2009

Location of HK students	Slightly better than HK★	Same as HK	Slightly worse than HK	Much worse than HK	Total
Mainland	0.9	12.4	37.6	49.1	100
Hong Kong	2.5	8.6	20.4	68.5	100

Source: Survey by Zweig's team in Hong Kong, Beijing, Guangzhou and Shenzhen, summer 2009.

Note: ★ Only one person selected "Mainland is much better than HK." $p > .05$.

A second student suggested that time on the Mainland may undermine Beijing's soft power:

> Some of the students from HK have some antipathy towards the Mainland. They feel life in the Mainland is somewhat depressed with not much freedom. Like during the "Green Dam" incident [internet censorship software], our impression of the Mainland deteriorated.[3]

Limits on Beijing's soft power in Hong Kong: the question of identity

The more Hong Kong people identify as ethnic Chinese and as citizens of the PRC the more likely they are to accept Beijing's legitimate authority to guide Hong Kong. Unfortunately for China, Hong Kongers' "Chinese" identity has decreased since 1997.

Hong Kong people have multiple identities. But a survey by Hong Kong University Public Opinion Program (HKUPOP) in December 2016 showed that well over 60% of people in Hong Kong saw themselves as "Hong Kongers" (35%) or "Hong Kongers in China" (30%), while only 37% of them saw themselves as "Chinese in Hong Kong" (19%) or "Chinese" (18%), making "Hong Konger" the largest single identity in the territory. Moreover, in June 2017 the same research center found that only 3.1% of Hong Kongers under 30 felt that they were "Chinese," a 20-year low (HKU Poll, 2017).

According to the Hong Kong Transition Project, Hong Kongers in 2013 related much more to the outside world than they did to their Chinese identity, and they strongly wanted to maintain that identity (DeGolyer, 2014). This is not surprising, since 27% of Hong Kongers under the age of 50 have lived overseas for a minimum of one year. Thus, when asked to select among three identities which they consider as most important to promote and protect—(1) China's identity as ruled by the CCP, (2) China's historical and cultural identity or (3) Hong Kong's identity as a pluralistic and international society—only 4% selected the first, 31% selected the second and 65% selected the final option. Such an orientation should reinforce support for Western norms of democracy, democratic freedoms and human rights, which inherently undermine the soft power of an authoritarian state. Moreover, over 80% of those under 40 selected the third option.

In addition, between June 2007 and December 2015, Hong Kongers' identity as citizens of the PRC declined significantly (Table 13.2).

While the strength of identity averaged 7.3 in June 2007, it had dropped to 5.95 in June 2014, on the eve of the Umbrella Movement and just after the State Council's white paper on Hong Kong. Thereafter, it continued to decline.

Looking forward, do Hong Kongers anticipate that after 2047 Hong Kong should integrate more deeply into the Chinese polity and adopt the norms of the Mainland? As of 2016, the answer was an emphatic "no." Well over two-thirds

TABLE 13.2 Strength of identity as a citizen of the People's Republic of China, 2007–2015

Date of Survey	Sample	Rating	Standard Error	No. of Respondents
Jan–Jun 2007	1,026	7.28	0.07	998
Jan–Jun 2008	1,012	6.84	0.10	932
Jan–Jun 2009	1,002	6.99	0.11	511
Jan–Jun 2010	1,004	6.38	0.12	515
Jan–Jun 2011	1,028	6.41	0.12	480
Jan–Jun 2012	1,001	6.12	0.13	501
Jan–Jun 2013	1,055	6.11	0.12	633
Jan–Jun 2014	1,026	5.95	0.12	653
Jul–Dec 2014	1,016	5.66	0.12	641
Jan–Jun 2015	1,003	5.87	0.13	625
Jul–Dec 2015	1,011	5.75	0.13	612

Source: www.hkupop.hku.hk/english/popexpress/ethnic/.

Note: The question read: "On a scale of 0–10, please rate the strength of your identity as a citizen of the People's Republic of China, with 10 indicating extremely strong, 0 indicating extremely weak, and 5 indicating half-half."

(69.6%) said that the "one country, two systems" principle should be extended after 2047, another 17.4% said Hong Kong should become independent after that date, and among those aged 15 to 24, nearly 40% demanded independence after 2047 (Cheung and Fung, 2016).[4]

Dissatisfaction with the Chinese government

Hong Kong citizens, since 1997, have usually blamed local political and economic difficulties on the HKG. This view dominated, even though the CG controlled the election of the CE and should have been ultimately responsible for his or her actions. However, if Hong Kongers believe that Beijing is managing China well, they could be more willing to accept its policies for Hong Kong, especially on normative issues. Second, they could have separate views on Beijing's management of Hong Kong, feeling confident that despite concerns about how the CG was running China, they could believe that the "one country, two systems" policy was working and the CG was not interfering too much in Hong Kong affairs.

Data from the Hong Kong Transition Project (Figure 13.1) show that on the eve of the reversion of sovereignty (ROS) from Britain to China in 1997, Hong Kongers were quite critical of how the CG was managing China; then, after the ROS, Hong Kongers' views on this dimension became more positive until 2009, when dissatisfaction shot up precipitously.[5] Similarly, from 1993 until the ROS, Hong Kongers were quite dissatisfied with how Beijing was managing Hong Kong affairs (Figure 13.2), but after the ROS, Hong Kongers became much more positive about the CG's policies toward the HKSAR. Yet in 2009, negativity toward the CG's governance of both China and Hong Kong rose simultaneously, as the level of dissatisfaction surpassed the level of satisfaction on both issues.

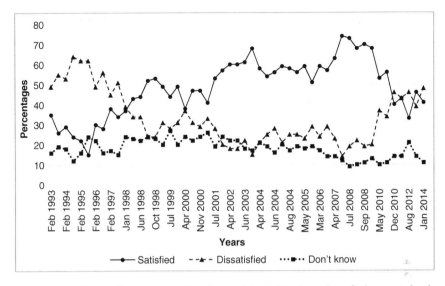

FIGURE 13.1 Hong Kongers' satisfaction with Beijing's rule of the mainland, 1993–2014

Source: DeGolyer (2014).

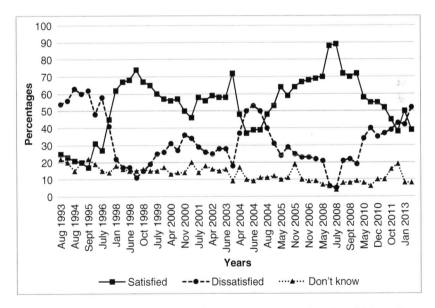

FIGURE 13.2 Level of satisfaction with PRC government's rule of Hong Kong, 1993–2013

Source: DeGolyer (2014).

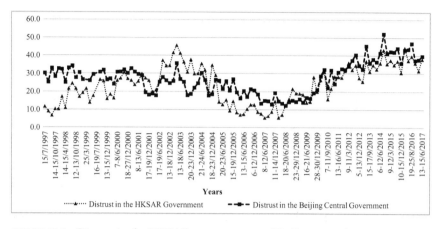

FIGURE 13.3 Distrust in the HKSAR government and Beijing central government (%)

Source: Public Opinion Programme, University of Hong Kong (HKUPOP), www.hkupop.hku.
hk/english/popexpress/trust/trusthkgov/overall_dis/chart_poll/datatables.html.

DeGolyer, who ran the Hong Kong Transition Project for over 20 years, emphasized this correlation, and its likely impact on political reform (DeGolyer, 2014):

> The strongest correlation of all is between satisfaction with the perfor-
> mance of the PRC government's rule of China and satisfaction with the
> PRC government's handling of SAR affairs. Few dissatisfied with one are
> satisfied with the other. . . . They are closely tied, in respondent's minds, to
> each other. This is particularly important for constitutional reform as any
> proposal coming from Chief Executive Leung will be seen as a proposal
> approved by Beijing officials.

Thus, as we moved toward 2014, the year of the Umbrella Movement, the CG's ability to influence key policies on National Education and Constitutional Reform floundered.

Moreover, Hong Kongers greatly mistrust Beijing, and, similar to the previous two figures, a significant shift began after 2008, when support overall for China peaked due to the Beijing Olympics (Figure 13.3). By 2013, distrust had well surpassed the levels of 2003, at the height of the crisis over Article 23 and the National Security legislation.

Soft power and competing perceptions of national security

The first significant popular action (or reaction) that highlighted Beijing's lack of soft power in Hong Kong after 1997 was the failure of the HKG to introduce a National Security Law, which is mandated in the Basic Law, Hong Kong's mini-constitution. In 2003, the economic climate for introducing a policy that constricted the freedoms of Hong Kong people was less than propitious. Hong Kong was still suffering the effects of the Asian Financial Crisis (1997–1998), which had suppressed housing prices in which many members of Hong Kong's middle class had invested their savings, and which led to significant unemployment. Also, in spring 2003, Hong Kong suffered a massive health epidemic, SARS, to which the HKG's response was slow and somewhat ineffective. By fall 2003, the people's confidence in the HKG had reached a nadir of 16% from a high of 73% in February 1997 (Bush, 2016, p. 15).

Also, the HKG was extremely clumsy, in that it tried to force this change in civil rights and freedoms down the throats of Hong Kongers. Despite a period of consultation which reflected quite negatively on the law, the HKG appeared to be committed to introducing a policy based on Beijing's unwarranted perception that outside forces were actively trying to subvert China's sovereignty over Hong Kong. Thus on July 1, 2003, 500,000 to 700,000 people used the sixth anniversary of the ROS to pour out their social grievances and political concerns by marching through the streets of the city. The following July 1, an estimated 350,000 marched again. As a result, the law was never introduced (and still remains off the books as of this writing), while the CE, Tung Chee-hwa, and his secretary of security, Regina Ip, who led the push for the policy, were forced to resign.

The bottom line is simple: Chinese government officials are convinced that Western powers will use the opportunity afforded by democratization to mobilize civil society to undermine China's sovereignty over Hong Kong and, therefore, its national security. But as Hong Kong people do not share Beijing's concerns about the delicate state of national security and sovereignty in Hong Kong, they cannot accept policies that address China's unwarranted concerns about national security if those steps involve restricting their own freedoms.

National education policy: a strategy and an outcome

Miffed that Hong Kongers do not feel more Chinese 20 years after becoming part of the nation, the CG believes that if Hong Kong young people received a more positive picture of China's historic reemergence as a great power they would identify more with the Chinese nation and the CG's concerns with national security and sovereignty. Former CE, Tung Chee-hwa, has long emphasized that Hong Kong youth need to understand Chinese history better, because doing so would allow them to participate more willingly in the economic opportunities emerging on the Mainland (Cheung, 2017, p. 3).

To remedy this lacuna in national identity, the HKG proposed a "National Education" program, whereby civics courses in Hong Kong's high schools would present a more patriotic view of the Chinese system. But no single act of defiance better demonstrates the CG's deficit of soft power in Hong Kong than the protests of 2012, which forced the Hong Kong government to withdraw another proposal.

Young Hong Kongers, in particularly high school students, refused to learn the CCP's narrative on China's history, seeing it as propaganda, if not outright "brainwashing." Posters displayed at the protest site in 2012, when hundreds sat-in outside Legco and some engaged in a hunger strike, similar to the protestors in Tiananmen Square in 1989, complained about the efforts of the Mainland to brainwash (*xi nao*) young people.[6] Much of the resistance was triggered by one-sided, pro-CCP and anti-capitalist, education materials proposed by a left-ist Hong Kong academic. While his teaching materials had yet to be accepted, students preferred a Western, and they believed more objective, narrative unencumbered by Marxism. However, Western narratives of contemporary China undermine the CCP's and CG's soft power in Hong Kong, as they focus on the negative side of life on the Mainland and its lack of freedoms, as well as the gap between the right to assemble, free speech and a free press, and the values engrained in Hong Kong's identity, versus the identity proffered by the Mainland, which suppresses civil society, thereby reinforcing the importance of maintaining "two systems."

Ironically, although Hong Kong is part of China, neither the CG nor the HKG can introduce a more pro-Mainland curriculum which could enhance the CG's "soft power." In 2015, Fanny Law, a former deputy secretary of education in the HKG, who was forced to resign from the government in 2002 for interfering in academic freedom in Hong Kong, proposed that all incoming schoolteachers spend a month on the Mainland to enhance their knowledge of China and improve their ability to teach "national education" (Lau and Zhao, 2015). But Law's proposal was rejected by two prominent, pro-government politicians, Ho Hon-kuen, a member of the CE's Executive Council, and by Bernard Chan, a Hong Kong deputy to the National People's Congress in Beijing. Chan believed that

> the local quality of education was more sophisticated [in Hong Kong] than on the mainland, which was why so many mainlanders furthered their education in the city, so it's important for schools to make their own choices. . . . In Hong Kong, most people do not accept having things foisted on them. Hongkongers prefer to have an option.

Ironically, while in charge of education from 1998 to 2006, Law had overseen the removal of Chinese history as a compulsory subject in senior secondary schools making her responsible for children in Hong Kong growing up "ignorant about Chinese history."

Still, Carrie Lam, the new CE, has mentioned that she feels pressure to enhance the sense of Chineseness among Hong Kong's youth, and during his three-day visit to Hong Kong in late June, early July 2017, the CCP's general secretary and Chinese president, Xi Jinping, "highlighted the need to enhance education and awareness on the history and culture of the Chinese nation" (Lau, 2017).

Kidnapping the booksellers: a dramatic undermining of soft power

The most troublesome event of the past several years to undermine China's soft power in Hong Kong was the kidnapping and arrest of five booksellers from Causeway Bay Books, several of whom were transported into China (Lian, 2016). One was kidnapped in Thailand; two were arrested while crossing the border into China; and, most problematically, one was kidnapped in Hong Kong and then mysteriously reappeared on the Mainland with no record of his having left the territory. Two held foreign passports, but their overseas citizenship was ignored by the authorities. Suddenly over one million Hong Kongers, who hold foreign passports as insurance against running afoul of the CG, were worried about their safety as the pendulum was again swinging from "two systems" toward "one country."

The confession of one of the booksellers on Chinese television harkened back to Stalinist trials of the 1930s and was shocking (Forsythe, 2016). While the reason for these clear violations of the "one country, two systems" agreement remains unclear, the CG has to date made no effort to explain this extrajudicial behavior.

The booksellers created much of their own problem by shipping books into China, rather than simply selling them to Mainlanders visiting Hong Kong; to that extent, they engaged in illegal activities on the Mainland. So, the arrest of two of the booksellers in Guangdong Province after they crossed the border is less problematic. But the fact that unnamed officers from the Ministry of Public Security in the Mainland crossed the border into Hong Kong and Thailand and brought a citizen of a foreign country back to the Mainland dealt a major blow to China's position in Hong Kong, as it showed that public security bureaus in China do not recognize the existence of a "second" system which functions under the "rule of law." Second, forcing the booksellers to confess their guilt on Mainland television reinforced the hostility many Hong Kongers feel toward the "communist system" to the north.

The failure of political reform, 2014–2015

Another indicator of the deficit of soft power has been the CG's inability to introduce its own truncated version of political reform into Hong Kong. While some may believe that the CG never wanted to implement "universal suffrage," Beijing feels pressure to demonstrate its commitment to the Basic Law, which stipulates such an electoral format (*Basic Law*, 1989).[7] Thus, in 2007, then CE, Donald Tsang, who had committed during the 2005 campaign for the post of CE to resolve the issue of political reform on his watch, asked the NPC-SC, which is ultimately responsible for constitutional reform in Hong Kong, to declare a date for introducing universal suffrage. Under pressure, the NPC-SC accepted universal suffrage for the CE election, but not until 2017, delaying the reform for another 10 years; moreover, it did not stipulate the exact format of the nomination process, only that candidates would have to pass through a Nomination Committee, which would be dominated by the pro-Beijing forces.[8]

Then, on August 31, 2014, after five months of "consultation," the NPC-SC established a severely restricted nomination procedure. That decision stipulated that any candidate for CE would have to garner the support of 50% of the members of the Nomination Committee if they were to be allowed to run in the CE election. This proposal, which certified that no Pan-Democrat would be able to vie for the post of CE, was juxtaposed to an extreme position that had emerged from the Pan-Democratic camp in May–June 2014, which called for popular or "civic nomination" and rejected the use of a Nomination Committee entirely, even though the Basic Law stipulated it. By ignoring the Basic Law, the Pan-Democrats totally rejected Beijing's format for political reform.

Moreover, a survey commissioned by the *Ming Pao* newspaper in May 2014 found support for the Nomination Committee among the overall population (51% support, 28% opposed), among people 30 or older, and among those without a college education (55% to 26%). But due to its lack of influence in Hong Kong, the CG could not garner sufficient support for its reform package among college educated people under the age of 30 who opposed the plan, 48 percent to 39 percent (Ming Pao, 2014).

The CG's August 31, 2014, decision, and its courting of the business tycoons of Hong Kong, all coming on the tail of the failed white paper on "one country, two systems," reinforced the CG's inability to attract Hong Kong's middle class to its side on political reform. The day before college students began their class boycott to protest the August 31 decision, Xi Jinping met a delegation of approximately 30 top Hong Kong businessmen in Beijing, and the photo of that meeting appeared on newspapers across the territory. The juxtaposition of the announcement of the class boycott and a meeting by the leader of China with mostly anti-democratic capitalists says a great deal about the CG's ability to misplay its hand. After all, the massive 2003 protest march of 500,000 and the forced resignation of the Hong Kong capitalist Tung Chee-hwa from his post as CE had shown the immense distance between Hong Kong's middle class and the business tycoons; yet the meeting in Beijing illustrated that the CG still thought that the wealthy classes in Hong Kong could help with its cause.

After the Umbrella Movement of 2014 disbanded without garnering any political concessions on the issue of the CE election and the August 31 proposal, no Pan-Democratic party in Hong Kong could support the HKG's political reform package which the Hong Kong and Beijing governments had refused to adjust. Had they supported it, they would have been pilloried by their supporters. But, the CG had been forewarned that by establishing a threshold of more than 25% of the votes from the Nomination Committee for participation in the CE election they were inviting social unrest (Zweig, 2014). Despite strenuous efforts by the CLO to pry a few democratic legislators away from the opposition camp, and co-opt them into supporting the August 31 formula, the Pan-Democrats in Legco remained united in their rejection of this constrained form of political reform and in June 2015 voted down the reform package tabled in Legco, foolishly believing that the CG would offer the city better terms (Zweig, 2014). The CG, for its side, proved unwilling to promise Legco that its 50% threshold would be softened in subsequent elections, reinforcing Pan-Democratic resistance. Thus, despite a huge effort to promote a political reform package, that if passed would have demonstrated the CG's soft power, Hong Kong's democracy did not progress and the CG's reputation suffered a serious setback.

Localism, independence and the total rejection of the Mainland's soft power

After the failure of the Umbrella Movement, "localism" strengthened among young Hong Kongers. This movement's goal was to maintain, if not intensify, the barriers between Hong Kong and the Mainland. Importantly, while "nativism" around the world is predominantly supported by older citizens, who feel threatened by the inflow of foreigners, localism in Hong Kong has taken root largely among the younger sectors of the society (Rebel, 2017), who are well educated or politically aware, and do not necessarily take their cues from political parties or exercise their will through elections; instead they are prone to civil disobedience.

The growth of "nativism" and the rejection of closer links to the Mainland manifested politically in the September 2016 Legco elections. In that vote, 15–17% of the Hong Kong electorate voted for six localist candidates who directly opposed the CG and China, and refused to swear allegiance to, or recognize the legitimacy of, Beijing or the Hong Kong SAR when they took their oath of office. Moreover, much of their support came from middle-class residents of private residential estates, rather than more working-class neighborhoods, suggesting that Hong Kong's middle class grants the CG little soft power (Fung et al., 2016). In fact, as of 2017, 40% of people aged 15 to 24, and 24% of people aged 25 to 39, wanted the CG to become a foreign government after 2047 (Bland, 2017, p. 103), preferring to establish an independent Hong Kong state.

The extradition bill and the failure of the CG's Hong Kong policy

Rather than use the relative tranquility in Hong Kong after the defeat of the Occupy Central Movement to enhance the HKG and Beijing's popularity in the territory, in the following five years, the HKG tightened up the political system, and, in concert with Beijing, engaged in policies that fed precisely into the concerns of Hong Kongers, particularly younger people under 30.

Based on a ruling by the Standing Committee of the NPC, the six localists who were elected were ejected from Legco for not taking the oath of office in a serious enough manner, ending the Pan-Democrats ability to block unpopular legislation. Several candidates for public office who had advocated "self-determination" for Hong Kong after 2047 were denied the right to run, the pro-independence Hong Kong National Party was banned in September 2018 and any discussion of independence was deemed treasonous. In April 2019, nine people who encouraged Occupy Central were found guilty of creating a public nuisance, a rarely used crime under British colonial law, and several of them, including two professors, were sentenced to jail for 16 months. Also pending was a National Anthem Law under which people who misbehave during the playing of China's "March of the Volunteers" could be fined $6,500 and sentenced to three years in prison.

Still, the event that triggered another crisis was the decision of the CE, Mrs. Carrie Lam, who had been elected in March 2017 by a pro-Beijing Electoral Committee, to rush through a revision of the Fugitive Offenders Ordinance and the Mutual Legal Assistance Ordinance in one fell swoop. The first would allow Hong Kong to extradite citizens of a government with whom Hong Kong did not have a treaty, such as the Mainland, without any due process in Hong Kong where the accused could present their own case. The second meant that when such requests were made, if the paperwork was in order, the "criminal's" assets could be frozen. Lam claimed that her decision was motivated by sympathy for the parents of a Taiwanese woman murdered by her Hong Kong boyfriend who had fled back to Hong Kong, which had no extradition treaty with Taiwan. At this point in time, there is no proof that Lam was pressured by the CG to introduce this policy, and while one must assume that the CLO and perhaps even the HKMAO in Beijing approved of this effort, Lam probably saw this as a chance to ingratiate herself with President Xi Jinping, as the new laws would help Beijing to get its hands on a reported 300 Mainland financial criminals who were safely ensconced in Hong Kong. It would also increase her support in Beijing for a second term as CE.

As these revisions would lower the barrier between Beijing's and Hong Kong's legal systems, which were supposed to remain separate under "one country, two systems," most Hong Kongers strongly opposed the policy and felt deeply threatened by it. The local chambers of commerce, the legal community, professionals, academics, foreign consulates and foreign firms, were all in an uproar. From January through late May, supporters and opponents of the bill jockeyed for support. But as the scale of opposition intensified, so did Mrs. Lam's stubbornness. From Lam's perspective, opponents were ill-informed, and would realize that after the bill was passed and no massive sweep of dissidents occurred, the bill was no threat to Hong Kong's "rule of law" and independent judiciary.

But surveys taken at that time show the level of opposition to the policy, the lack of trust in Mrs. Lam and the continuing mistrust of the CG. One survey was carried out by Hong Kong University's POP on June 4, 2019, just five days before the protest march of June 9, when an estimated one million Hong Kong residents took to the streets, insisting that Mrs. Lam withdraw the bill (POP, 2019). The survey asked whether people supported a policy that would allow

Hong Kongers to be sent to the Mainland to face trial. On a five-point scale, with 5 as totally opposed and 1 as extremely supportive, 60% selected 5, showing that they were "extremely opposed" to this policy, while only 11% strongly supported it. Moreover, if respect for the "influencing" territory's institutions, such as its legal system, is an important part of the development of soft power within the polity that is the target of influence, the PRC clearly faced a huge deficit in this aspect of soft power at precisely the time that Mrs. Lam chose to try to lower those barriers. According to the same survey, 45% of Hong Kongers were "absolutely" convinced that the Mainland lacked "fair legal procedures," while another 14% selected a 4 on the five-point scale. Thus in total, 59% of Hong Kongers did not see judicial procedures on the Mainland as "fair" (*gong ping*). Similarly, 67% of Hong Kongers surveyed said that if the extradition process were established, they would have no confidence in the "one country, two system" policy. Clearly, Hong Kongers were unwilling to privilege the CG's concern about national security and sovereignty if it meant decreasing their own freedoms or legal rights.

An effective measure of soft power would be the level of trust in the influencing government, with the absence of trust increasing the difficulty of getting the target government and/or its population from supporting its policies voluntarily. A survey taken July 24–26, 2019, asked 1,002 randomly selected Hong Kong respondents what they saw as the source of disaffection among young Hong Kongers (POP, 2019). Results showed that 81% of Hong Kongers saw the lack of confidence in the CG as the major reason for youth disaffection, and 91% of youth aged 14 to 29 saw a lack of confidence in the CG as the most important source of youthful disaffection. As of that date, 75% of Hong Kongers saw the lack of confidence in "one country, two systems" as the major source of the youthful disaffection, with 86% of 14 to 29 year olds feeling that way. Thus Beijing did not have the authority to win support for the extradition law among Hong Kong citizens.

Finally, we should assess the extent to which Beijing considered its need for soft power as a reason that, as of the date of the writing of this chapter, the CG had not called in the PLA garrison in Hong Kong to bring order during the many weeks of violent protests. Most observers felt that it was concerns about the views of foreign businesses, and perhaps foreign governments, as well as the desire to demonstrate successful policy management and the continued role of "one country, two systems" as a possible solution for Taiwan, that reinforced Beijing's cautious approach. But from the perspective of this chapter's theme, doing so would destroy any semblance of cooperation between the CG and a significant proportion of the people of Hong Kong, further undermining if not destroying Beijing's soft power in the territory.

Conclusion

The CG has tried to enhance its soft power in Hong Kong since well before the ROS in 1997. Employing numerous stratagems, mostly reflective of the CCP's

United Front strategy, it has tried to mobilize its supporters, neutralize the non-committed segments of society and isolate opponents to its rule over Hong Kong. But the first 22 years of Chinese rule show that although the CG can get the HKG to do its bidding by introducing policies that increase economic integration between HK and the Mainland and limiting political freedom in HK, the CG has failed to increase its popularity, prestige or stature within HK society; as a result, every effort to tighten political control has been met with strong resistance, capping off in the summer of 2019 with the anti-extradition movement, which suggests a total failure of the CG's strategy of using the "one country, two systems" policy to integrate HK peacefully into China's system.

Over the years, the CG focused primarily on economics to consolidate popular support in Hong Kong. The white paper of June 2014 highlighted this perspective. But that effort was frustrated from the start by the depth of the populace's "Hong Kong identity" and the overall absence of a "Chinese identity," which undermined the CG's soft power.

China's soft power is also constrained by the differing perspectives among many Hong Kongers and the CG over the "one country, two systems" policy. If we view "one country, two systems" as a continuum, Beijing would like Hong Kong to be situated closer to the "one country" end of that continuum, where Hong Kong citizens would demonstrate a stronger "Chinese" identity, ebullient nationalistic pride in the Mainland's accomplishments under its post-1978 "reform and opening" policy, deeper sympathy for Beijing's concerns about sovereignty and national security, fuller appreciation for the contributions of the CG to Hong Kong's economic well-being since 1997, more entrenched opposition to foreign values and external influences and greater love for the symbols of the Chinese state, such as the national flag, national anthem and national emblem. The CG also assumes that the closer Hong Kong is to the "one country" edge of the continuum, the easier it will be to govern this troublesome region without resorting to physical coercion.

Hong Kongers, on the other hand, were hoping that the territory's "system" would become more liberal and democratic, or at least remain at the same point on the "one country, two systems" continuum, and that the "one country," China, would look more and more like Hong Kong, rather than the Maoist system of the pre-reform era. Thus, since 1997, Hong Kongers have resisted each and every effort by Beijing to implant components of China's "system" into the territory and move HK closer toward "one country." Particularly as the regime under Xi Jinping, who came to power in 2012, is quite draconian, many Hong Kongers' concerns about the intrusion of the CG have grown significantly. The "localist" movement showed that familiarity breeds contempt, as efforts to enhance political, ideological or legal controls since 2012 have led many Hong Kongers to advocate withdrawing Hong Kong from China after 2047. Moreover, events in 2019 blew the lid off the assumption that any peaceful reunification under the CG's terms was possible.

Notwithstanding the above analysis, some may question if Beijing takes the enhancement of its soft power as a key component of its Hong Kong strategy.

Given the CG's priorities for Hong Kong, including economic, social and political stability, non-interference by Hong Kong's democratic forces in Mainland politics, keeping Hong Kong as an outlet for Mainland overseas investment and as a source of funds for its state-owned enterprises and deeper integration into the economy of the Pearl River Delta—a strategy known as the Greater Bay Area—the sacrifice of some soft power may be an acceptable price to pay to achieve what the CG sees as higher ranked values.

Still, although Beijing prevented young post-Occupy politicians from gaining seats in Legco after 2016 (Chung and Cheung, 2018), and shut down serious discussion of independence after 2047, those victories loomed pyrrhic in light of the continuing expansion of the localist, anti-China movement and the massive explosion of anti-Mainland sentiment in the anti-extradition struggle. In light of data showing the disaffection of Hong Kongers below age 30 toward Hong Kong's integration with the Mainland, Beijing would have been well advised to engage these younger Hong Kongers and try vigorously to expand its soft power within that segment of society, rather try to tighten control. Only in that way could the CG increase its influence over the hearts and minds of the people of Hong Kong.

Notes

1 Students came from 13 universities in Beijing and Guangdong Province, and 3 universities in Hong Kong. We included top universities, such as Tsinghua and Peking universities in Beijing and Zhongshan University in Guangzhou, as well as middle-ranking universities, such as Jinan University in Guangzhou. Of the 219 Hong Kong students interviewed in the Mainland, 98 were in Beijing, 86 in Guangzhou and 35 in Shenzhen. We also created a control group of 159 students in HK. All data were collected through face-to-face interviews.
2 Student No. 001 from Chinese University of Finance and Economics.
3 Student No. 003 from Peking University.
4 1,100 residents were surveyed in the summer of 2016.
5 Several factors might have driven the negative sentiment. First, was a post-Olympics return to the more prevalent concerns and therefore a return to pre-Olympic scores. Second, 2009 saw major protests in Xinjiang and a subsequent crackdown by Chinese security forces.
6 The author's personal observations and conversations with protestors at that time.
7 The Basic Law explicitly stipulates that the chief executive and all members of Legco must be elected by universal suffrage, making universal suffrage a legal objective.
8 The 31st Session of the Standing Committee of the Tenth NPC decided on December 29, 2007 "that the election of the fifth chief executive of the HKSAR in 2017 may be implemented by the method of universal suffrage; that after the chief executive is selected by universal suffrage, the election of the Legislative Council of the HKSAR may be implemented by the method of electing all the members by universal suffrage."

References

Basic Law. 1989. *Basic Law of the Hong Kong Special Administrative Region of The People's Republic of China (Draft)*. Peking: Drafting Committee for the Basic Law.
Bland, Ben. 2017. *Generation HK: Seeking Identity in China's Shadow*. Australia: Penguin.

Bush, Richard C. 2016. *Hong Kong in the Shadow of China: Living with the Leviathan*. Washington, DC: Brookings Institution Press.

Cheung, Gary and Owen Fung. 2016. "Why Beijing's Headache over Calls for Hong Kong's Independence Has Only Just Begun," *South China Morning Post*, August 26. www.scmp.com/week-asia/politics/article/2009538/why-beijings-headache-over-calls-hong-kongs-independence-has-only?utm_source=edm&utm_medium=edm&utm_content=20160827&utm_campaign=scmp_today.

Cheung, Tony. 2017. "Tung Urges Youth to Understand the Mainland Better," *The South China Morning Post*, June 25.

Chung, Kimmy and Tony Cheung. 2018. "Political Storm in Hong Kong as Activist Agnes Chow Banned from By-Election over Party's Call for City's 'Self-Determination'," *South China Morning Post*, January 27. www.scmp.com/news/hong-kong/politics/article/2130714/hong-kong-activist-agnes-chow-banned-legco-election.

DeGolyer, Michael. 2014. *Constitutional Reform: Confrontation Looms as Hong Kong Consults*, April. Available at slideplayer.com/slide/4664290/

Forsythe, Michael. 2016. "Missing Man Back in China, Confessing to Fatal Crime," *New York Times*, January 17. www.nytimes.com/2016/01/18/world/asia/missing-man-back-in-china-confessing-to-fatal-crime.html?action=click&contentCollection=Opinion&module=RelatedCoverage&region=Marginalia&pgtype=article.

Fung, Owen, Shirley Zhao, Emily Tsang and Kinling Lo. 2016. "Middle-Class Voters Turned Out in Big Numbers for Localists in Hong Kong Legislative Council Polls, Analysis Shows," *The South China Morning Post*, September 6. www.scmp.com/news/hong-kong/politics/article/2016218/middle-class-voters-turned-out-big-numbers-localists-hong.

HKU Poll. 2017. "HKU Poll: Only 3.1% of Young Hongkongers Identify as Chinese, Marking 20 Year Low," www.hongkongfp.com/2017/06/21/hku-poll-3-1-young-hongkongers-identify-chinese-marking-20-year-low/.

Ho, Albert. 2014. Author's Interview with Albert Ho, Then Leader of the Democratic Party, Spring, Hong Kong.

Hong Kong Residents. 2016. 1,100 Residents Were Surveyed in the Summer of 2016. www.scmp.com/week-asia/politics/article/2009538/why-beijings-headache-over-calls-hong-kongs-independence-has-only?utm_source=edm&utm_medium=edm&utm_content=20160827&utm_campaign=scmp_today.

Information Office of the State Council. 2019. "The Practice of the 'One Country, Two Systems' Policy in the Hong Kong Special Administrative Region," www.scmp.com/news/hong-kong/article/1529167/full-text-practice-one-country-two-systems-policy-hong-kong-special.

Lam, Lana. 2015. "University of Hong Kong Plan to Enforce Student Visits to Mainland China Sends Ripples across Campus," April 18. www.scmp.com/news/hong-kong/education-community/article/1769303/hku-make-mainland-china-experience-compulsory.

Lam, Wai-man and Kay Lam Chi-yan. 2013. "China's United Front Work in Civil Society: The Case of Hong Kong," *International Journal of China Studies* 4(3), pp. 301–325.

Lau, Stuart. 2017. "Xi Marks the 'Red Line'," *Sunday Morning Post* (Hong Kong), July 2, p. 1.

Lau, Stuart, Austin Chiu and Brian Yap. 2014. "Hong Kong Lawyers March to Defend Judiciary in Wake of Beijing's White Paper," *SCMP*, June 27. www.scmp.com/news/hong-kong/article/1541814/hong-kong-lawyers-stage-silent-march-oppose-beijings-white-paper.

Lau, Stuart and Shirley Zhao. 2015. "National Education for New Hong Kong Teachers Gets Thumbs Down All Round," *South China Morning Post*, March 15. www.scmp.com/news/hong-kong/article/1737965/idea-national-education-hong-kong-teachers-gets-thumbs-down-all-round.

Lian, Yi-Zheng. 2016. "Hong Kong's Missing Booksellers," *New York Times*, January 20. www.nytimes.com/2016/01/21/opinion/hong-kongs-missing-booksellers.html?_r=0.

Lin, Gene. 2016. "CUHK Survey Finds Nearly 40% of Young Hongkongers Want Independence after 2047," *Hong Kong Free Press*, July 25.

Lo, Sonny Shiu-Hing. 2010. *Competing Chinese Political Visions: Hong Kong vs. Beijing on Democracy.* London: Praeger.

Loh, Christine. 2010. *Underground Front: The Chinese Communist Party in Hong Kong.* Hong Kong: Hong Kong University Press.

Loo, Jeff Hai-Chi, Shui Hing Lo and Steven Chung-Fun Hung. 2019. *China's New United Front Work in Hong Kong: Penetrative Politics and Its Implications.* Singapore: Palgrave MacMillan.

Ma, Ngok. 2007. *Political Development in Hong Kong: State, Political Society and Civil Society.* Hong Kong University Press.

Ming Pao. 2014. Ming Pao, May 1. www.hkupop.hku.hk/chinese/report/mpCEnOCCw4/crosstab.pdf.

Nye, Joseph S., Jr. 1990. "Soft Power," *Foreign Policy* 80, pp. 153–171.

POP. 2019. www.hkupop.hku.hk/english/report/singming_extradition_bill/.

Rebel, Anna-Maria. 2017. "Political Inquiry Into Anti-Mainland Sentiments in Hong Kong: Examining the Nexus between Age Cohorts and Localism," Capstone Thesis, May 19. Division of Social Science, The Hong Kong University of Science and Technology.

Sung, Yun-Wing, Alex, C. Y. Ng, Yuhao, Wu and Alex, W. H. Yiu. 2014. "Economic Benefits of the Independent Visitor Scheme for Hong Kong: How Large Are They?," Occasional Paper No. 34, Shanghai-Hong Kong Development Institute, The Chinese University of Hong Kong. @cuhk.edu.hk/shkdi/pub/op34.pdf.

Torode, Greg, James Pomfret and Benjamin Kang Lim. 2014. "Special Report: The Battle for Hong Kong's Soul," *Reuters*, June 30. www.reuters.com/article/us-hongkong-china-specialreport-idUSKBN0F62XU20140701.

Zhao, Shirley. 2015. "Teachers and Parents Take a Critical Approach to Mainland School Exchange Trips amid Claims of a 'Hidden Agenda'," *South China Morning Post*, February 10. www.scmp.com/news/hong-kong/article/1708798/teachers-and-parents-take-critical-approach-mainland-school-exchange.

Zweig, David. 2014. "Negotiating Hong Kong's Democratization," Report for the Center on Social Development, Guangdong Provincial Government, Guangzhou, May 8.

14

HOW EAST ASIANS VIEW A RISING CHINA

Yun-han Chu, Min-hua Huang and Jie Lu[1]

Over the past two decades, China's increasing economic power, military strength and political influence has been widely acknowledged in the world, particularly in the region of East Asia. Overtaking the United States as the world's largest economy in real terms in 2014, a rising China poses serious challenges to US hegemony in virtually every aspect (Christensen, 2015). In response, the Obama administration's strategic pivot to Asia clearly indicated America's key interest in consolidating its dominance in Asia, strengthening its alliance system with East Asia, and upgrading its engagement with and possible containment of China's rise. The Trump administration's first National Security Strategy (NSS) mentioned China 23 times and concentrated on identifying the mounting threats posed by China and pledged that the United States would push back against them.

Meanwhile, significant changes in China's foreign policies, shifting from Deng Xiaoping's principle of "concealing our ability and biding our time" to Xi Jinping's more ambitious and assertive approach, have shown that Beijing now vigorously seeks to play a leadership role in the region, enhance its influence over the global agenda and prepare for a possible strategic showdown with the United States and/or Japan. Nonetheless, the change of China's foreign policy was not a sudden event, but rather an incremental process which started from the 2008 Global Financial Crisis (caused by the US subprime mortgage crisis) and further accelerated since 2012 when Xi Jinping rose to power as the top leader. China's strong economy and its robust performance during the Global Financial Crisis gave Chinese policymakers a clear vision that the power gap between China and the United States has rapidly narrowed. Some observers have predicted that if the trend continues that the replacement of the United States by China as the world's dominant economic power will materialize in the foreseeable future (Subramanian, 2011). A school of thought, led by prominent Chinese scholars such as Yan Xuetong at Tsinghua University, also quickly emerged and called for China to be prepared to become a responsible great power and argued that its power competition with the United States is inevitable (Yan, 2011).

China's East Asian neighbors, in view of the high stakes involved in their inescapable geographic, economic or political connections with China, are keenly aware of the activeness, vigorousness and assertiveness associated with such foreign policy changes. The question of how East Asians view a rising China, therefore, does not just make eye-catching headlines in news media but also has serious implications for international relations in East Asia and even the world today.

Most media coverage and academic work has focused on how China and the United States have deployed economic, political and even military tools for their competition in East Asia. Clearly, flexing their respective muscles plays a critical role in sending clear signals to each other in their strategic interactions by demonstrating their capability and commitment. Showing off "hard power" also generates valuable information for their East Asian audiences, who continuously update their assessments and reflect on their strategic options and responses. Nevertheless, as Joseph Nye has famously argued, there is more than one way to influence others' behavior and achieve one's goals. China and the United States also are keen on "softer power" competition in East Asia, by winning the hearts and minds of East Asians and, hopefully, getting East Asians "to want the outcomes that you want" (Nye, 2004, p. 5). *also engaged in soft power competition in Asia*

Over the last decade, Chinese policy elites have increasingly recognized that soft power and national image management are essential aspects of China's foreign policy agenda. To pursue the peaceful rise/peaceful development policy in Chinese grand strategy, Chinese leaders have sought to integrate Chinese hard power and soft power to create a soft rise for China (Wang, 2008, p. 257). China's charm offensive places emphasis on presenting itself as a responsible rising power with a sincere and benign intention of contributing to a new regional and global order with its vision of "harmonious world" and "the shared destiny of human beings." It has launched a public diplomacy campaign on a worldwide scale through establishing hundreds of Confucius Institutes around the world, running 24-hour CCTV news channels in major languages and offering scholarships for tens of thousands of international students.

However, despite its recent effort to prop up its soft power, most Western observers remain doubtful that Beijing can convince the world that China is a benign and benevolent power and attract others to Chinese culture, its way of life and vision for the global community (Kurlantzick, 2009; Nye, 2010). They believe that China's authoritarian political system could always be its liability and that its mercantilist economic strategy still tarnishes it reputation (Shambaugh, 2015, p. 99).

Southeast Asia could be an important test site for China's charm offensive. On the one hand, China has resolved to deepen the economic partnership with the Association of Southeast Asian Nations (ASEAN) by signing the first major free trade agreement. China has become either the most important source of import or the top export market for a great majority of ASEAN countries. Furthermore,

[handwritten: SE Asia is test for Chinas charm offensive]

Southeast Asia is poised to benefit from the massive inflow of China's soft loans and foreign direct investments under the auspices of the Belt and Road Initiative (Leverett and Wu, 2017). At the same time, China has been keen in expanding its cultural ties with ASEAN countries as there exist very few ideological barriers. By 2016 China had established 31 Confucius Institutes in Southeast Asia and more than 500 scholarships for citizens of ASEAN countries to study in China each year. On the other hand, the tug-of-war over political and economic influence between a receding American hegemony and an ascending China has been felt strongly among the ASEAN countries, in particular, the heat of the escalating tension in the South China Sea. The anxiety has grown out of the worry that they might be pressured to take a side. *[handwritten: ASEAN doesn't want to take a side]*

[handwritten: findings] And yet there have been few systematic investigations using public opinion data to evaluate how its neighbors view a rising China. In this chapter, we utilize the latest two rounds of the Asian Barometer Survey (ABS) to investigate how Asian citizens evaluate the rise of China.[2] Our survey shows that although China's economic pull is so strong, its distinctive post-socialist political system no longer stands in the way of earning more respect among its democratic neighbors. Our data also clearly show that Southeast Asian publics are not prepared to take sides in the US–China strategic competition because they believe that the benefit and cost of US influence and Chinese influence are not mutually replaceable, nor incompatible. We begin our analysis with an overview of the important developments in terms of the changing configuration of the strategic competition between China and the United States in the region during this critical juncture.

China's emerging global and regional strategy under Xi's leadership

Since 2012, Beijing has shown a clear break from its longstanding low-key foreign policy. Today, China does not just promulgate its peaceful intentions as an ascending power and its willingness to contribute to the region's stability and prosperity, but also launches new initiatives of economic partnership and mechanisms of regional integration and multilateral cooperation, hence actively fostering new international order at both the global and regional level. Such distinctive change was widely perceived as the result of China's changing leadership from Hu Jintao to Xi Jinping, who has carried out a wide-ranging anti-corruption campaign at home and become the most powerful Chinese leader since Deng Xiaoping. Formally Xi still shares power with six other members of the Standing Committee of the Politburo of the Communist Party of China (CPC) through a scheme of collective leadership. He nevertheless has centralized decision-making power over all important policy domains in his own hands and his confidence about the bigger role Beijing could and should play in world affairs also reflects his strong leadership.

[handwritten: centralization of power under Xi]

The policy turn of China's global and regional strategy under Xi Jinping can be summarized by the following narrative: we are witnessing a more resourceful, more assertive, more ambitious and more aggressive China under his steward- ship. To begin with, nowadays there are many more policy instruments as well as the greater economic leverage at China's disposal due to its rapid economic development. According to the International Monetary Fund, China's gross domestic product (GDP) adjusted for purchasing power parity (PPP) reached $17.6 trillion in 2014, surpassing the United States' $17.4 trillion. The outflow of China's foreign direct investment (FDI) also grew dramatically, topping $120 billion in 2015 and making China a net capital exporter. Furthermore, China continues to be a major engine for global economy growth even as its economic growth rate has slowed down. In 2016, China contributed an estimated 39% of the annual growth in the world's economy (Roach, 2016). China is already the top trading partner for most ASEAN countries. Under Xi Jinping, China is embracing Southeast Asia with a renewed trade and investment push. Chi- nese investment is transforming its smaller Southeast Asian neighbors like never before, especially for the region's frontier-market economies, such as Laos, Cam- bodia and Myanmar (Roman, 2016).

Another notable change in China's international strategy lies in its greater willingness to assert its demands, vision and policy objectives. China under Xi is eager to promote the "Chinese Dream" of national rejuvenation to the world and to claim China's global economic leadership among the developing countries of the world. Most notably, China under Xi has made more explicit demands on other countries to respect its core interests, in particular its ter- ritorial integrity, including its sovereign claims over the East and South China Sea, as well as its long-standing positions on Tibet and Taiwan. Beijing has also become more assertive in playing an agenda-setting role with a much broader regional and global scope, for instance by proposing a "New Model of Great Power Relations" for Sino–US relations, peddling the initiative of Asia-Pacific Free Trade Area through the APEC Summit and driving the agenda of the 2016 G20 Summit with its promotion of the "Hangzhou Consensus," which was intended to reorient the G20's mission away from putting out fires to one of spearheading measures that will encourage development and stability around the globe on a long-term basis.

In a wide range of issues areas, China has undertaken ambitious new initia- tives, something unthinkable just a few years ago. The launch of the One Belt One Road initiative in 2013 has become the hallmark of Xi's global strategy with the ambition to reshape the region's geopolitical and geoeconomic land- scape (Leverett and Wu, 2017). Many important strategic moves emanate from the One Belt One Road grand strategy. They include enlarging and upgrading the Shanghai Cooperation Organization through recruiting both India and Pak- istan as new members and the launching of the Asian Infrastructure Investment Bank (AIIB) to channel financial resources into ambitious infrastructure projects abroad. All these strategic moves entail China's ambitious goals to rewrite the rules of economic engagement and the parameters of globalization.

However, its rapid military buildup may also trigger negative views of China's rise. In particular, China has become visibly less self-restrained in flexing its muscles. The commission of its first aircraft carrier, Liaoning, into the Chinese Navy in 2012 signified Beijing's commitment to strengthen its power projection capability far beyond its coastal waters. China has also undertaken a more confrontational approach in handling the territorial disputes in the East and South China Sea. For example, China conducts frequent military exercises in the area, sends out China Coast Guard vessels to patrol in the disputed waters, and continuously enlarges the construction of manmade reefs in the name of providing public services for international society. The PLA is also pushing for a grandiose upgrade program for acquiring a range of cutting-edge weapon systems, from anti-satellite missiles and stealth bombers to hypersonic glide vehicles. All the above evidence indicates that China is resolved to counterbalance the Obama administration's rebalance to Asia and compete with the United States head-on in military deployment.

All the above discussions indicate that the United States under the Obama administration made some progress to thwart the trend of a declining US presence and influence in the region, but probably not enough to counterbalance China's growing influence in the military, political and economic spheres in East Asia. The changing configuration in the region's strategic landscape would no doubt shape Asian people's views toward China versus the United States, to which we now turn.

How are China and the United States perceived by East Asians?

Soft power is an important concept for explaining why a great power can achieve its political influence more effectively through appeal and attraction rather than inducements or coercion. From the sender's perspective, Chinese leaders have long understood the importance of how China is perceived by other countries and have attempted to cultivate it for some time. Since 2004, China has invested tremendous resources to conduct a public diplomacy campaign, even before China's rise was widely perceived as a hard fact. However, it is important to look at the picture from the receivers' side, since as Nye correctly pointed out, soft power depends on willing interpreters and receivers. If the targeted receivers are not aware of the sender's messages, the soft power simply does not exist.

Many observers believe that while Asian people are increasingly cognizant of China's growing political and economic power, they are not necessarily persuaded by its stated foreign policy objectives and strategic intention, and much less attracted by its political system. To verify this received view, we need scientifically reliable public opinion data across Asian countries. Although a number of cross-national survey projects, such as Pew Global Attitudes Survey and BBC

Global Scan, are in place they only cover a few Asian countries. The Asian Barometer Survey (ABS) fills an important void in our understanding of the phenomenon of China's rise and its implications for policymakers. The Fourth Wave of the ABS was administered in 14 East Asian countries and territories based on country-wide probability sampling and face-to-face interviews. In its most recent two waves, the ABS has incorporated a battery containing several questions related to the rise of China. The results from this battery can help us understand how citizens in the region view China in the context of its growing economic influence and international stature.[3]

The first question regarding the rise of China is to ask the respondents "Which country has the most influence in Asia now?" The answer set provides the following five choices: "China," "Japan," "India," "United States" and "Others." As Figure 14.1 shows, in countries which are territorially adjacent (such as Myanmar) or culturally proximate to China (such as South Korea and Singapore) more than 50% of people think China has the most influence in Asia for both Waves 3 and 4 of the survey. In about half of Southeast Asian countries (namely the Philippines, Indonesia, Cambodia and Malaysia), citizens continue to believe that the United States has more influence in the region. However, more and more Southeast Asians have recognized China as the most influential. Between our two waves of the survey, this perception grew by a magnitude of at least 2% (in Cambodia) and as much as 14% (in Indonesia), while in most countries the influence of the United States was perceived to be in decline. There was a particularly dramatic change in Thailand, where the percentage perceiving that the United

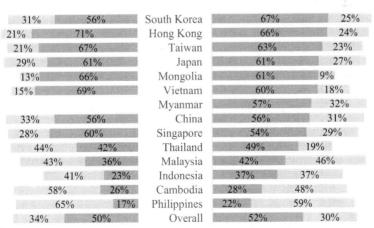

	←ABS 3			ABS 4→	
South Korea	31%	56%		67%	25%
Hong Kong	21%	71%		66%	24%
Taiwan	21%	67%		63%	23%
Japan	29%	61%		61%	27%
Mongolia	13%	66%		61%	9%
Vietnam	15%	69%		60%	18%
Myanmar				57%	32%
China	33%	56%		56%	31%
Singapore	28%	60%		54%	29%
Thailand	44%	42%		49%	19%
Malaysia	43%	36%		42%	46%
Indonesia	41%	23%		37%	37%
Cambodia	58%	26%		28%	48%
Philippines	65%	17%		22%	59%
Overall	34%	50%		52%	30%

■ Wave 3 China ■ Wave 3 US   ■ Wave 4 China ■ Wave 4 US

FIGURE 14.1 Which country has the most influence in Asia now?

Source: Data from ABS 3 (2010–2012) and ABS 4 (2014–2016).

Chinas neighbors recognize its rise

States has the most influence in the region declined from 49% to 19% in the context of the worsening US–Thailand relationship following the 2014 coup and the strengthening of Sino–Thai economic ties. Our data suggest that Obama's pivot to Asia policy did little to reverse the perception of the United States' declining influence. However, one can also argue that the decline could have been steeper without the strategic rebalancing on Obama's watch.

but do they welcome it?

So far our data have shown that the rise of China has been recognized by the great majority of East Asians. But the more important question is: do East Asians welcome China's growing influence? ABS Wave 4 includes two sets of questions that ask respondents to evaluate Chinese and American influence in terms of whether it does more good than harm, or more harm than good, with reference to the region and to their own countries, respectively. If the reference point is the region (see Figure 14.2), we find that American influence was generally perceived as more positive (average 73%), with the country breakdowns ranging from 92% (Philippines) to 45% (Indonesia). On the other hand, evaluation of China's influence was not as favorable (average 56%) and highly polarized: predominantly negative in Japan (11%), Vietnam (20%), Myanmar (28%), and Mongolia (32%), predominantly positive in Cambodia (67%), Korea (75%), Singapore (71%), Thailand (86%), Hong Kong (79%), Malaysia (75%), and Indonesia (67%), and very much divided in the Philippines (41%) and Taiwan (55%). This suggests that most Asians view the presence and influence of the United States in the region as largely benign, but views of China's influence are very divergent. While many clearly regard China as an opportunity and welcome it, some perceive it as a threat and regard its rise with apprehension. If the reference point is changed to each respondent's country (see Figure 14.3), we find similar results: unanimously positive for the United States (above 60% in all countries, average 79%) and very much polarized for China (varying from 20% to 94%, average 58%).

perception of US presence as benign

In the ABS Wave 3, the same evaluative questions were also asked about China's influence, and it is interesting to examine the magnitude of change in popular perception toward the impact of China on the region. As Figure 14.4 illustrates, in most countries there was little change in popular views of China's influence, with the exceptions of significant declines of favorable evaluations in the Philippines (73% to 41%) and Vietnam (56% to 20%), and significant increases in Thailand (68% to 86%) and South Korea (53% to 75%). The decline in the first two countries is most likely associated with the escalation of territorial disputes with China in the South China Sea, while the increase in the latter two countries might be associated with the pro-China policy direction of the Thai military government and President Park's administration. In the latter case, we have to bear in mind that the recent controversy between China and South Korea over THAAD deployment might lead to a decline in positive evaluations of China's influence. Overall, Asians' views of China's influence over the region are rather divergent and depend very much on the contextual dynamics within each country.

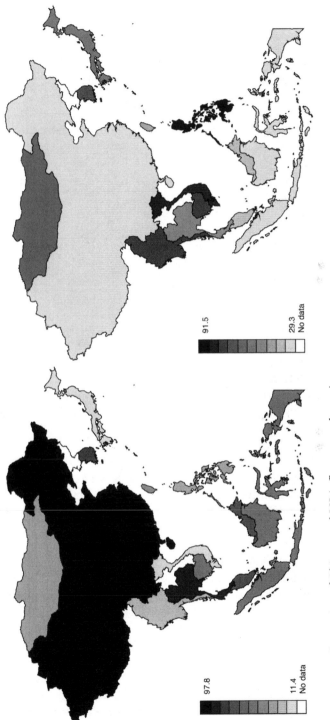

FIGURE 14.2 Perception of Chinese and US influence on the region

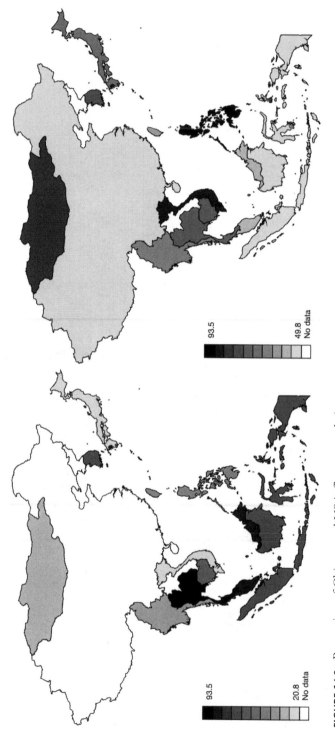

FIGURE 14.3 Perception of Chinese and US influence on their own country

93.5

49.8
No data

93.5

20.8
No data

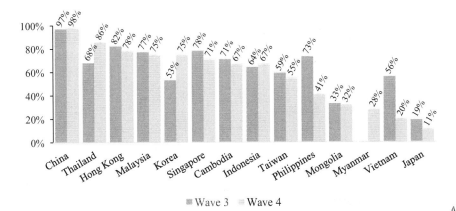

Wave 3   Wave 4

FIGURE 14.4 Positive perception about the impact of China on the region

Source: Data from ABS 3 (2010–2012) and ABS 4 (2014–2016).

The two important findings so far are the following: first, the rise of China has been recognized by the great majority of East Asians and that China's growing influence in the region is more intensely felt by countries that are geographically or culturally proximate to China. Second, there is great divergence among East Asians regarding whether they welcome China's expanding influence. In the most general sense, Asian people acquire their view toward China on the basis of the perceived risk and benefit brought by a rising China. For countries that are geographically non-adjacent and without territorial disputes with China, the consideration is predominantly about the pros and cons of expanding economic ties with China. For countries that are geographically adjacent and/or geopolitically adversarial, the consideration might be more complicated and more emphasis is placed on security and the geopolitical consequences of China's ascendance. Still for others, such as Taiwan and Korea, the myriad factors that should be taken into consideration entail multidimensional calculations under the constraints of competing objectives and acute trade-offs. We need to carefully interpret the meaning of these data with due consideration of each country's historical past and contemporary contextual dynamics.

Ambivalent attitudes toward US–China strategic competition

The conventional wisdom in foreign policy circles tends to be that pro-US and pro-China attitudes are mutually exclusive. But this might not be the case in the Asia-Pacific region, even for those citizens whose countries are facing a potential security threat from a rising China because for most East Asians the role of China and the United States are not mutually replaceable.

In the following, we correlate the measures of favorable perceptions of China and the United States in selective country samples and report the results in Table 14.1. As can be seen, only Hong Kong and China show significant negative

TABLE 14.1 Selected country correlations of favorable perception of China and the United States

Country	Correlation
Hong Kong	−.236★★
China	−.102★★
Vietnam	−.017
Philippines	.009
Mongolia	.021
Cambodia	.023
Taiwan	.033
Myanmar	.125★★
Japan	.146★★
Korea	.224★★
Singapore	.284★★
Indonesia	.308★★
Malaysia	.314★★
Thailand	.408★★

Note: Correlation coefficients between respondents' view of the nature of US influence and that of China, ABS Wave 4.

correlations between the two measures, which is perfectly understandable given their roles as one of the contesting parties. For the following five countries—Vietnam, Philippines, Mongolia, Cambodia and Taiwan—the correlations are not significant, which suggests that most people do not make a sharp contrast between the United States and China. For the remaining countries, including Myanmar, Japan and Korea, the correlations are all significantly positive. It suggests that many people take a benign view of both the United States and China at the same time while other people might take a skeptical view toward both. In a nutshell, for many Asians both the United States' influence and China's influence could be desirable (as well as compatible) at the same time. Assuming that the nature of strategic competition between the two great powers in the Asia-Pacific region is a zero–sum game might misrepresent what most countries in the region think.

In most Asian countries, people welcome the strong presence of both simply because the United States cannot replace China as the locomotive of economic growth while China can hardly replace the United States as the ultimate guarantor of their country's security. For more sophisticated Asian minds, Sino–US competition could be beneficial and the balance of two great powers in the Asia-Pacific region might be in their best interest. At the same time, in some countries the popular backlash against globalization might lead to anger at both. So it is also not difficult to understand why certain Asian people take a skeptical view of both the United States and China. For people who are harmed by economic opening, financial instability, and foreign competition, the United States is viewed as the primary architect of this neo-liberal economic order while China is the direct source of foreign competition.

What shapes East Asians' perceptions of China and the United States?

Asian peoples' perceptions of the nature of China's rise and its impact on the region are determined by a multitude of factors, including contextual factors and the respondents' socio-economic status as well as political inclination. In the following, we focus on two contextual factors with important policy implications. The first contextual factor is the perceived democratic distance, which is a measure of the difference between the self-rated level of democracy in one's own country and in China (generally the lowest) or in the United States (generally the highest).[4] As shown in Figure 14.5, perceived democratic distance and positive perception of China's influence are unrelated in 12 of the country samples (Hong Kong and China not included), while there is a strong positive correlation ($r = .57$, $p = .06$) between perceived democratic distance from the United States and positive perception of US influence. This finding indicates that many Asians still look to the United States as a model of democracy, and that this view of American democracy is an important factor that affects whether the influence of the United States is seen in positive or negative terms. In contrast, perceived democratic distance makes no difference to whether the influence of authoritarian China is viewed in positive or negative terms ($r = .00$, $p = .99$). This suggests that China's one-party authoritarian system is no longer an obstacle to winning recognition and respect among East Asians.

Another important contextual factor is associated with the perception of economic opportunity versus threat from China's fast-growing economy. We measure this factor by taking the aggregated mean of supportive attitudes toward economic openness. As Figure 14.6 makes evident, support for economic openness is associated with positive evaluations toward US influence ($r = .16$, $p = .62$), but negative evaluations toward China's influence in the region ($r = -.42$, $p = .18$), although neither finding passes the significance test. This indicates that, along with democratic distance, economic rationality might be another consistent contextual factor in swaying people's perceptions of the favorability of the impact of China and the United States in the region. Specifically, if the outlier case of Japan is dropped, the negative correlation in the perceptions in the China case converge back to a neutral effect as we saw in Figure 14.3 regarding the democratic distance ($r = -.04$, $p = .90$), while the positive correlation in the perception of the US case becomes slightly stronger ($r = .22$, $p = .52$). This indicates that the appeal of China's economy may be a mixed factor in shifting people's cognitive preference when assessing the impact of the two great powers. However, it is clear that those who support economic openness do not necessarily view China and the United States as strategic rivals in the Asia-Pacific region.

The competition over soft power

To effectively capture the essence of soft power, the ABS survey measures the attractiveness of various countries as development models. Our respondents were

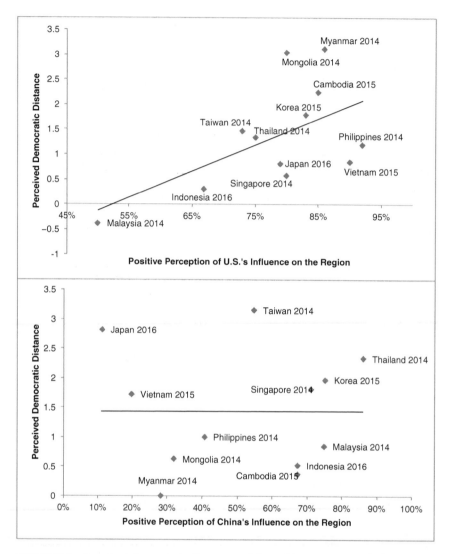

FIGURE 14.5 Perceived democratic distance and favorable perception of Chinese and US influence

presented with the following question: "Which country should be a model for our country's future development?" Options included "the United States," "China," "India," "Japan," "Singapore," "Others" (with detailed answers recorded) and "We should follow our own model." The basic logic is that if East Asians volunteer to endorse any society as the model for their respective societies' future development (without mentioning any of these societies' military, economic and political leverage over their own), it should be reasonable to argue that the society they endorsed has quite effectively won their hearts and minds

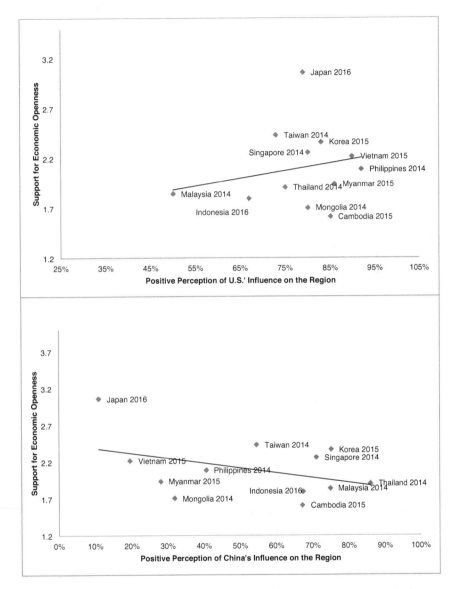

FIGURE 14.6 Support for economic openness and favorable perception of Chinese and US influence

Notes: Support for economic openness is the mean of q152 and q153, excluding 7, 8, 9 in Wave 3.

q168, q169 used in Wave 4, excluding 7, 8, 9. Individual country weights used.

Mean because Indonesia only asked q168 in Wave 4.

For Wave 3, positive image of the United States is based on those who chose the United States as the most influential country in the region.

through attraction rather than coercion or payments. Table 14.2 summarizes the findings from the two waves of ABS surveys (2010–2016).

To make the information more accessible for our readers, we organized the findings based on the consistency in the results of the two waves of surveys and separated the 13 societies into two groups.[5] Basically, we identified the mode (which is the answer category chosen by the largest percentage of respondents) of popular endorsement in each society for each wave and then compared the differences between the modes. If the mode of popular endorsement in a society did not change between the two waves of the survey, this society is labeled as a "consistent follower"; otherwise, it is labeled as a "switcher." As shown in Table 14.2, in nine East Asian societies there is a consistent mode in their people's preferred models for future development; while in four societies there are some changes in the modes of their popular preferences.

TABLE 14.2 Preferred models for future development in East Asian societies

		China	United States	Our Own	Japan	Singapore
Consistent followers						
Philippines	2010	7%	**68%**	0%	17%	6%
	2014	6%	**66%**	1%	17%	8%
Cambodia	2012	20%	**42%**	5%	22%	6%
	2015	15%	**47%**	3%	12%	3%
South Korea	2011	8%	**39%**	10%	23%	16%
	2015	10%	**47%**	11%	10%	18%
Indonesia	2011	14%	26%	8%	**35%**	13%
	2016	16%	17%	13%	**34%**	16%
Taiwan	2010	5%	15%	22%	**31%**	23%
	2014	6%	14%	13%	**31%**	20%
Japan	2011	2%	19%	**52%**	–	10%
	2016	1%	21%	**45%**	–	10%
Singapore	2010	13%	24%	**38%**	17%	–
	2015	17%	22%	**36%**	16%	–
Myanmar		–	–	–	–	–
	2015	1%	10%	**27%**	23%	18%
Hong Kong	2012	7%	13%	25%	8%	**43%**
	2016	23%	15%	23%	11%	**24%**
Switchers						
Thailand	2010	16%	16%	**46%**	12%	8%
	2014	23%	18%	8%	**27%**	13%
Vietnam	2010	22%	9%	**42%**	16%	10%
	2015	2%	29%	6%	**38%**	19%
Malaysia	2011	14%	8%	**34%**	31%	11%
	2014	21%	11%	17%	**31%**	17%
Mongolia	2010	10%	25%	**29%**	18%	8%
	2015	8%	**22%**	16%	21%	11%

Source: ABS Survey Waves 3 and 4.

Among the consistent followers, the largest percentage of people in the Philippines, Cambodia and South Korea identified the United States as their preferred model for future development in both waves of the survey. The endorsement rate was the highest in the Philippines (around 67%) and relatively low in Cambodia (around 44%) and South Korea (around 43%). Japan was consistently endorsed by the largest percentage of people in Indonesia and Taiwan as their preferred model for future development and this enthusiasm did not change much between the two waves of the survey: around 34% in Indonesia and 31% in Taiwan. Meanwhile, for the largest percentage of people in Japan, Singapore and Myanmar, none of the foreign societies claimed the largest group of followers.[6] Instead, "Our own model" won the hearts and minds of the largest percentage of Japanese, Singaporeans and Myanmar people (around 49% in Japan, 37% in Singapore and 27% in Myanmar). The largest group of Hong Kong residents embraced Singapore as a promising model for their future development in both waves of the survey, although the percentage dropped significantly from 43% in 2012 to 24% in 2016. Among the switchers, the largest percentage of people in Thailand, Vietnam, Malaysia and Mongolia preferred "Our own model" in 2010 and 2011 (around 46% in Thailand, 42% in Vietnam, 34% in Malaysia and 29% in Mongolia), but the endorsement rate dropped significantly in all four societies four or five years later (around 8%, 6%, 17% and 16%, respectively). In 2014 and 2015, the mode of popular preferences in Thailand, Vietnam and Malaysia switched and Japan was widely embraced by these people as the model for their future development (around 27% in Thailand, 38% in Vietnam, and 31% in Malaysia respectively). Meanwhile, the largest percentage of Mongolians endorsed the United States as their preferred model for future development in 2016 (around 22%, just one percentage point higher than that for Japan).

Clearly, the United States and Japan are the two major country models that a large number of East Asians find attractive and are willing to embrace as the model for their respective societies' future development. As we pooled the two waves of survey data together and used country-year as the unit of analysis, the pattern is quite obvious: among the 25 country-year cases, (1) the United States is the mode of popular endorsement in 7 cases, (2) Japan is the mode in 9 cases (including Japan itself), (3) "Our own model" is the mode in 5 cases and (4) Singapore is the mode in 4 cases (including Singapore itself). It is worth noting that in two cases—Hong Kong 2016 and Thailand 2014—China is quite close to the most popular model. Overall, in none of the 13 East Asian societies polled in the two waves of the surveys was China the most popular preferred model for future development. Clearly the United States has the upper hand in this soft power competition against China in East Asia. Even Japan and Singapore have done a better job than China in winning the admiration of East Asians.

However, one should interpret the significance of the above findings with due consideration of the varying level of economic development. China, the United States, Japan and Singapore are not competing on a level playing field. After all, it is very natural for Asian people to endorse the United States, Japan or

Singapore as a model for future development because the three are widely recognized as countries enjoying a high standard of living. It is unrealistic to expect that people living in countries with very high per capita income will endorse the Chinese model as China is still a middle-income developing country. The more meaningful question to ask is twofold: first, whether the Chinese model can attract a significant number of followers in countries that are still economically lagging behind; second, whether the Chinese model has gained strength versus the American model over time in these countries.

To pick up these interesting nuances and dynamics, we zoomed in on how East Asians viewed China versus the United States as competing models for their future development. Basically, we examined changes in the gap between popular endorsement of the United States and China between the two waves of the ABS survey. The results are presented in Table 14.3.

Similar to the approach used for presentation in Table 14.2, we categorized the thirteen East Asian societies into two groups: (1) East Asian societies showing consistently higher popular endorsement of the United States over China (or the other way around) between the two waves of surveys and (2) those with the higher popular endorsement switching from the United States to China (or the other way around) between the two waves of the survey. The former were labeled societies with "consistent preferences" while the latter were labeled societies with "switching preferences."

Overall, among the 13 East Asian societies, 11 have shown consistent popular preferences as their people assessed the United States and China as distinct models for their respective societies' future development. More specifically, in the Philippines, South Korea, Cambodia, Japan and Mongolia, a much larger percentage of people repeatedly endorsed the United States than endorsed China as the preferred model for future development. The difference in popular endorsement ranges between 14 percentage points (in Mongolia) and 61 percentage points (in the Philippines). In these societies the United States outperforms China consistently and by a large margin in soft power competition.

Although the United States still beats China in soft power competition in Myanmar, Indonesia, Singapore and Taiwan, the popular endorsement gap is much smaller. Furthermore, this endorsement gap shrank dramatically between the two waves of the survey. In 2010 and 2011, the endorsement rate of the United States in Indonesia, Singapore and Taiwan outnumbered that of China by around ten percentage points. Years later, the difference dropped significantly, particularly in Indonesia (to around 1 percentage point) and Singapore (to around 5 percentage points). In these societies, although the United States still enjoys more popularity than China, its advantage clearly has been checked and weakened.

It is also interesting to see that in Malaysia and Thailand China did equally well as or even better than the United States in winning their people's hearts and minds between 2010 and 2014. There was an increase in the percentage of Malaysians and Thai people preferring China over the United States as the model for future development between the two waves of the survey, increasing from

TABLE 14.3 Preferences over the Chinese versus the US models in East Asian societies

	China > United States	United States > China
Consistent preferences		
Philippines 2010		• (61%)
2014		• (60%)
South Korea 2011		• (31%)
2015		• (37%)
Cambodia 2012		• (22%)
2015		• (32%)
Japan 2011		• (17%)
2016		• (20%)
Mongolia 2010		• (15%)
2015		• (14%)
Myanmar		–
2015		• (9%)
Indonesia 2011		• (12%)
2016		• (1%)
Singapore 2010		• (11%)
2015		• (5%)
Taiwan 2010		• (10%)
2014		• (8%)
Malaysia 2011	○ (6%)	
2014	○ (10%)	
Thailand 2010	○ (0%)	
2014	○ (5%)	
Switching preferences		
Hong Kong 2012		• (6%)
2016	○ (8%)	
Vietnam 2010	○ (13%)	
2015		• (20%)

Source: ABS Survey Waves 3 and 4.

Note: Percentage differences in parentheses.

6% to 10% in Malaysia and from 0% to 5% in Thailand. Although China still
was not endorsed by the largest percentage of people as their preferred model for
future development in the two societies (Japan was the mode of popular endorsement in 2014 in both cases), its charm offensive has paid off to some extent. In
Malaysia and Thailand the Chinese model has gained popularity probably for
following two reasons. First, China has significantly deepened its economic ties
with both countries and emerged as a major source of foreign investment and
as well as a major financial underwriter of their infrastructure projects. Second,
both countries have experienced democratic backsliding and clearly embarked
on a path of authoritarian consolidation and thus leaned closer to China in terms
of ideological distance.[7]

When it comes to East Asian societies with switching preferences, the stories are quite complex as both China and the United States have made gains and losses (without a clear-cut pattern). Hong Kong presents a rather interesting case. Between the two waves of the survey, Hong Kong witnessed a switch from a higher endorsement of the United States (a difference of 6%) as the preferred model for future development in 2012 to a higher endorsement of China as the preferred model (a difference of 8%) in 2016.[8]

Despite rising political activism among its youth in promoting direct popular election for the chief executive and some rising tension between Hong Kong residents and mainland Chinese tourists, public opinion data suggest that the Chinese model has gained popularity, jumping from only winning 7% of the respondents to 23% largely at the expense of the Singaporean model whose popularity dropped from 43% to 24% between 2011 and 2016. The fact that not many Hong Kong people embraced the American model is probably due to a very practical reason: the overarching framework of "One-Country, Two-Systems" precludes the possibility of adopting the US democratic model. The Chinese model has gained popularity perhaps due to the fact that China is expected to overtake the United States as the biggest economy in the world in the near future and across the border Shenzhen has been a showcase of technological innovation and industrial upgrading, something Hong Kong is lacking.

In contrast, the Vietnamese almost reversed their endorsement of China over the United States as their preferred model for future development between the two waves of the survey. In 2010, China defeated the United States by a margin of 13 percentage points but in 2015 the United States outperformed China by a margin of 20percentage points. Although the largest percentage of Vietnamese people endorsed neither the United States nor China as their preferred model for future development, clearly territorial disputes between China and Vietnam have played a key role in dragging China down in the soft power competition against the United States.

Similar to the message delivered by Table 14.2, the evidence presented in Table 14.3 suggests that the United States, at least for the time being, enjoys the upper hand in Sino–US soft power competition in East Asia by securing a higher endorsement rate than China in 19 out of the 25 country-year cases. Nevertheless, this is not a static equilibrium but a dynamic and ongoing process with both sides continuously making efforts and strategically adjusting policies for the soft power competition. One interesting dynamic is worth noting: China is narrowing its gap with the United States in Indonesia, Singapore and Taiwan, and consolidating gains or even furthering its advantage in Indonesia and Thailand, while the United States is reinforcing and expanding its advantage in the Philippines, South Korea, Cambodia, Japan and Mongolia. In the battlegrounds of Hong Kong and Vietnam, both sides made some gains while suffering some setbacks.

By way of conclusion: policy implications

With the marked shift of the center of regional economic gravity from Japan to China and an abdication of economic leadership by the United States under Donald Trump, East Asia is destined to become one of the few regions in the world where a non-democratic regional power dominates the agenda of regional economic cooperation and perhaps the only region in the world where newly democratized countries become economically integrated with and dependent on non-democratic countries. As China's economic pull is so strong, its distinctive post-socialist political system no longer stands in the way of forming closer economic ties with its democratic neighbors. A similar trend is taking place in the steady deepening of economic ties between China and the newly democratized Central and Eastern European countries. This also implies that the overall regional political environment will become more hospitable for many authoritarian and hybrid regimes, such as Thailand, Cambodia and Malaysia.

While the ideological cleavage is withering away, the conflict over economic openness might stand in the way because in virtually every East Asian society the benefits and risks of economic integration with China have been unevenly distributed. If China aspires to become a more respectable architect of regional integration and champion of free trade, it will have to create a regional environment more conducive to inclusive growth. Otherwise, growing economic polarization will take its toll on domestic support for a pro-China coalition in most of its trading partners. Chinese leaders also need to be aware of the sensitivity of ethnic cleavages in Malaysia and Indonesia, where the ethnic Chinese minority have been struggling with their fragile political cohabitation with the Muslim majority.

Our data suggests that following Donald Trump's swearing in as the President of the United States, his country will still enjoy a reservoir of goodwill in most of East Asia, even though his campaign rhetoric might have already reduced somewhat the generally positive view of US influence in the region. The Trump administration's anti-Muslim propensity is likely to do the worst damage to the American image in the places where the United States can least afford it: Malaysia and Indonesia.

His administration should not take the reservoir of goodwill for granted and ought to be alarmed by the fact that perceptions of US influence relative to that of China are not in his country's favor. In our Wave 4 (2014–2016) surveys, the Philippines was the only country where a majority of those questioned believed that America had the most regional influence at that time. Regarding other treaty allies, only 27% of the Japanese surveyed and 25% of Koreans thought that the United States had the greatest influence. In this regard, his decision to withdraw from the Trans-Pacific Partnership (TPP) will only strengthen this impression of American decline and withdrawal from the region.

US influence will still be more favorably perceived as long as Asians continue to identify America as their democratic model. However, this long-standing advantage for American soft power could be undermined by US foreign policy under Trump, which runs the risk of squandering both America's policy credibility and its image as an icon of liberal democracy in the eyes of Asian people. Over the long run, however, the United States can still improve its image in East Asia if it is able to improve its currently dysfunctional democratic system and if it can serve as an economic alternative to China.

Our data also clearly show that East Asians are not prepared to take sides in the US–China strategic competition because they believe that the benefit and cost of US influence and Chinese influence are not mutually replaceable nor incompatible. In fact a balance of two great powers in the Asia-Pacific region might serve their interest best. If the United States under Donald Trump decides to step up the containment game against China, he should not expect too much support from Asian countries except Japan. All these countries are dependent on China economically and recognize that China will always be their neighbor, and therefore none would agree to be part of an effort to contain China. For better or for worse, their citizens have already taken the view that China either is already the most influential power or soon will be.

Notes

1 This chapter is based on the articles "Enter the Dragon: How East Asians View a Rising China" and "Xi's Foreign-Policy Turn and Asian Perceptions of a Rising China" which appeared in *Global Asia* in September 2015 and June 2017, with the addition of new and updated analysis and discussion. For other articles by the authors on this topic, see Huang and Chu (2015) and Chu, Liu and Huang (2015).

2 The Asian Barometer Survey is a research network dedicated to democratic studies through survey methodology. The network comprises 14 country teams. Its regional headquarters is co-hosted by the Institute of Political Science, Academia Sinica and the Center for East Asia Democratic Studies at National Taiwan University. For the methodological details of the ABS, please refer to the project's website: www.asianbarometer.org.

3 The ABS Wave 3 was administered between the autumn of 2010 and the spring of 2012 and the fieldwork of the ABS Wave 4 was implemented between the autumn of 2014 and spring of 2016.

4 The perceived distance between China and one's own country is calculated for each respondent by taking the difference between where one places one's own country on a ten-point scale of level of democratic development (where 1 represents "completely undemocratic" and 10 "completely democratic") and where one places China on the same scale.

5 The situation in China is quite unique, given our focus on the Sino–US soft power competition in East Asia. A serious problem of social and political desirability bias is expected among the Chinese respondents when probed for their preferred model for China's future development. Therefore, we dropped the China case in the following analysis.

6 There was just one wave of the survey completed in Myanmar in 2015.

7 Our survey data also revealed that in Thailand and Malaysia the perceived democratic distance between China and their own country has closed up somewhat between the two waves.

8 Actually, in 2016, Hong Kong residents were evenly divided in their endorsement of China (around 23%), "Our own model" (around 23%) and Singapore (around 24%) as their preferred model for future development.

References

Christensen, Thomas J. 2015. *The China Challenge: Shaping the Choices of a Rising Power*. New York, NY: W. W. Norton and Company.

Chu, Yun-han, Liu Kang and Min-hua Huang. 2015. "How East Asians View the Rise of China," *Journal of Contemporary China* 24(93), pp. 398–420.

Huang, Min-hua and Yun-han Chu. 2015. "The Sway of Geopolitics, Economic Interdependence and Cultural Identity: Why Are Some Asians More Favorable toward China's Rise Than Others?," *Journal of Contemporary China* 24(93), pp. 421–441.

Kurlantzick, Joshua. 2009. *Charm Offensive: How China's Soft Power Is Transforming the World*. New Haven, CT: Yale University Press.

Leverett, Flynt and Wu Bingbing. 2017. "The New Silk Road and China's Evolving Grand Strategy," *The China Journal* 77, pp. 110–132.

Nye, Joseph S., Jr. 2004. *Soft Power: The Means to Success in World Politics*. New York, NY: Public Affairs.

Nye, Joseph S., Jr. 2010. "American and Chinese Power after the Financial Crisis," *Washington Quarterly* 33(4), pp. 143–153.

Roach, Stephen S. 2016. "Global Growth: Still Made in China," *Project Syndicate*, August 29. www.project-syndicate.org/commentary/china-still-global-growth-engine-by-stephen-s-roach-2016-08?barrier=accessreg.

Roman, David. 2016. "China Is Transforming Southeast Asia Faster Than Ever," *Bloomberg*, December 6. www.bloomberg.com/news/articles/2016-12-05/china-transforms-frontier-neighbors-with-cash-for-rails-to-power.

Shambaugh, David. 2015. "China's Soft Power Push: The Search for Respect," *Foreign Affairs* 94(4), pp. 99–107.

Subramanian, Arvind. 2011. *Eclipse: Living in the Shadow of China's Economic Dominance*. Washington, DC: Peterson Institute for International Economics.

Yan, Xuetong. 2011. "How China Can Defeat America," *New York Times*, November 11.

Wang, Yiwei. 2008. "Public Diplomacy and the Rise of Chinese Soft Power," *Annals of American Academy of Political and Social Science* 1, pp. 257–273.

INDEX

Note: Page numbers in *italics* indicate a figure and page numbers in **bold** indicate a table on the corresponding page.